INFORMATION-FINDING AND THE RESEARCH PROCESS

INFORMATION-FINDING AND THE RESEARCH PROCESS

A Guide to Sources and Methods for Public Administration and the Policy Sciences

Antony E. Simpson

Greenwood Press
Westport, Connecticut • London

Library of Congress Cataloging-in-Publication Data

Simpson, Antony E.
Information-finding and the research process : a guide to sources and methods for public administration and the policy sciences / Antony E. Simpson.
p. cm.
Includes index.
ISBN 0-313-25251-3
1. Public administration—Bibliography. 2. Bibliography—Bibliography—Public administration. 3. Public administration—United States—Bibliography. 4. Bibliography—Bibliography—Policy sciences. 5. Policy sciences—Bibliography. I. Title.
Z7164.A2S53 1993
[JF1351]
016.35—dc20 92-21358

British Library Cataloguing in Publication Data is available.

Library of Congress Catalog Card Number: 92-21358
ISBN: 0-313-25251-3

First published in 1993

Greenwood Press, 88 Post Road West, Westport, CT 06881
An imprint of Greenwood Publishing Group, Inc.

Printed in the United States of America

The paper used in this book complies with the Permanent Paper Standard issued by the National Information Standards Organization (Z39.48-1984).

10 9 8 7 6 5 4 3 2 1

TABLE OF CONTENTS

FIGURES

PREFACE

The purpose of this book is to address the full range of information needs of academic researchers in the social and policy sciences with particular attention to public administration. Traditional guides to finding information view the creation of topical bibliographies as a self-contained activity divorced from the process of primary research. Construction of bibliographies is obviously an important step in a broader research strategy, but one that is entirely influenced by earlier decisions on the nature and scope of the research topic. The traditional perspective is misguided. It assumes a linear model of research design that determines exactly what literature is needed at a very early stage in the process and obtains it through standard bibliographic techniques. Instead, literature searching should be intimately connected to all stages of the research project. The precise form of a research topic should be flexible through much of the life of the project and should be altered to reflect a growing understanding of its scope and potential. The literature search helps refine the parameters of the research topic.

Information-finding has important dimensions that go beyond simply defining a comprehensive bibliography on a narrow topic, using printed sources. Those who plan original research must set up a theoretical model to direct the research approach. This requires many types of resources, different means of identification of resources, and selectivity in their use.

The researcher must consider also the nature of the data that will support the investigation and the methodology best suited for his or her analysis. A carefully refined research model is of little value if it is applied to a data set that is inadequate or otherwise inappropriate for its examination. Carefully planned searches for interesting primary data and methodological techniques should be incorporated into the overall information-finding strategy. The prime objective of this research guide is to show how the library search strategy can be developed to meet these various important research needs. The discussions that follow are designed both for those teaching research design and for scholars conducting various kinds of research projects.

Chapter 1 shows that in the social and policy sciences the search for either primary or secondary research sources can rarely be limited to one specialty or even discipline. This is especially true in the field of public administration since it is interconnected to many other areas of study. Thus a researcher in public administration must first become familiar with the bibliographic and other research tools in a number of related disciplines.

The thrust of this book is research in public administration, but it also discusses important sources in other disciplines on a selective basis. For example, the sources in the field of psychology in chapter 3 include only those likely to be of value to the public administration researcher concerned with related psychological issues. If greater exploration of the literature of psychology (or any other social or behavioral science) is needed, the means to this can be found through the discipline-oriented bibliographic guides discussed in section 4 of chapter 4.

Some areas of direct relevance to public administration are not given much attention here. Government is a subject not addressed explicitly; its documentation is largely technical, and its theoretical orientation is generally drawn from the discipline of political science. Few almanacs, factbooks, or guides to governmental structure are noted here unless reference to them serves some larger purpose. If sources of this nature are needed, they can readily be identified through the general guides to the bibliography of the social sciences discussed at the beginning of chapter 3. Law is a field largely ignored in this discussion, even though legal issues have come to dominate many areas of research and practice in public management. The reason is that legal research involves specialized skills well covered elsewhere. The substance of legal research is such that it must be addressed in detail or not at all.

This guide covers sources and methods of approach essential to research dealing with the mainstream of public administration. The wise researcher will use this book as a general guide and as a starting point for delving into various disciplines in greater depth.

Those using this book will be quickly made aware of the tremendous inroads being made by the computer on many aspects of the research process. Students and researchers with a penchant for the quantitative have, of course, long been aware of the importance of computerized statistical packages and data sets. These developments are duly given attention here. Beyond this, researchers should be aware that many standard bibliographic tools are becoming accessible in machine-readable form. Many of the indexing and abstracting services, current bibliographies, statistical compendia, and other sources noted here are now (or shortly will be) available in electronic form. This technological movement is proceeding with bewildering speed and no conventionally-published text can be relied upon to do it justice for more than a short moment in time.

Discussion in the text provides the means of keeping abreast of at least the principal developments of relevance to a particular substantive or methodological focus. This is, however, not just a matter of becoming aware of the purely bibliographic and quantitative advantages of the new technology. The movement is also speedily coming to affect those whose interests in original research are qualitative. Collections of non-numeric primary data are increasingly becoming accessible (in some cases available) through electronic means. This trend is especially important for those concerned with the law, the popular press, and other contemporary expressions of governmental and public concerns. One objective of this book is therefore to make the reader aware of the significance and potential of new developments for a variety of research interests and to do so through discussion of a range of sources. Again, when this is done, care is taken to direct the reader to the means of gaining an ongoing perspective on the expanding wealth of computerized sources now available.

Revolutionary though these technological developments are, their significance must be seen in proper context. Electronic means of access, whether to secondary bibliography or primary sources, are only of value when the research objective has been properly identified. They are valuable in the implementation of a research strategy; they do not help in its conceptualization or definition. Project definition is perhaps the most difficult, as well as the most important, of the researcher's many tasks and is emphasized throughout this book, but especially in chapters 1 and 2. The guiding principle behind this work is that the many and sophisticated sources of access to materials, valuable though they are, are but handmaidens to the overall research process. Technological expertise can never improve a research project that is not informed by thought and knowledge.

INFORMATION-FINDING AND THE RESEARCH PROCESS

1

INFORMATION-FINDING AND PUBLIC ADMINISTRATION AS A FIELD OF STUDY

This reference guide presents to readers (and particularly to those concerned with preparing a doctoral dissertation or other original research project) efficient and effective methods for conducting library research in the social and policy sciences in general, but especially in the field of public administration.

Anyone undertaking a sustained library research project (whether for a term paper, a scholarly article, a dissertation, or a book), must develop a strategy for selecting material from the vast quantity of available information. This has long been true, but the problem of how to cope with an accelerating volume of new data has recently become more pressing. The problem is now acute in many disciplines, particularly in the pure and applied sciences, where the effects of the "information explosion" are being most strongly felt. It is also a considerable obstacle to scholarly communication in fields such as public administration, which are eclectic in their origins and have come to be even more sprawling in their links to other disciplines.

In the last decade the problem of information selection has gone beyond one of coping simply with the explosion of publications. One must now grapple also with new forms of information due to the proliferation of microforms, machine-readable data, and alternatives to conventional forms of publication stimulated by the availability of fax machines, computer bulletin boards, and other modes of electronic transmission.

One indication of the extent to which public administration has been affected by such developments is shown by the expansion of journals in the field since 1975. Then the standard international directory of journals included just over 300 titles in "Public Administration." The 1992/93 edition includes about 1,500 in this category (Ulrich 1975, pp. 1277–85; 1992, 2:4052-96).

Discussion of the well-documented "information explosion" addresses the worldwide proliferation of books, articles, and other secondary sources generally. Scholars and practitioners in public administration point also to the expansion of government-generated information. The volume of current material produced on magnetic tape or in other computer-readable form, as well as in conventional print, has skyrocketed, and the thorough investigation of a current issue concerning a public agency requires the investigator to wade through a massive volume of raw data. (The unkind have suggested that the production of unmanageable and indigestible amounts of data has become one routine bureaucratic response to unwelcome, but unavoidable, attention.) Readers of this book must deal carefully with this diarrhetic production of data to set out a research idea and a real-life setting within which to explore it. Greater availability of raw data permits a greater choice of setting, but this greater choice works only for those who see a universe of possibilities, sift through them purposefully, and devise a game plan for focused research.

Information-finding techniques for primary and secondary sources must be directed and systematic. These techniques must be used to isolate the best and most appropriate sources, define research objectives, and identify everything relevant to the topic. Yet the majority of scholars in the social sciences do not gather their data in this way. Dissertation students tend to choose their sources of original data, and sometimes their topics, on the basis of advice from colleagues and mentors. These choices may work out well, even if they are not based on a full survey of available sources. The danger is that the ultimate selection may not be adequate and probably will not be the best if it is based on partial knowledge. Understandably, most researchers like to use one kind of primary source, but this limits the range of research possibilities dramatically.

There is great variety in the forms of primary data and in bibliographic tools that can point to them. Survey analysis is but one option among many. Agency or other institutional records can be supplemented by commentaries upon the agency prepared for secondary purposes (for example, in the form of newspaper articles), oral histories or other memoirs of its former employees, ethnographic observations on its functioning, and court cases or other legal materials addressing its origin or operation. Primary sources can be materials that are published, in manuscript, or in machine-readable form. They may be compiled by an agency, a researcher, or someone else. Knowledge of different possibilities makes the researcher aware of what can be done and what has been done using different kinds of primary sources. An appreciation of such things will surely make the final choice a better-informed one.

Choices of research settings and primary data sets are often determined by student academic environments and the particular interests of mentors or departments. They are rarely sought in formal or expansive ways. This circumstance attracts little attention. Studies of information-finding patterns are far more concerned with documenting the ways in which scholars search the secondary literature and how established practice seems casual, inefficient, and slighting of formal technique. This focus addresses literature-searching exclusively and fails to extend the principle to the coequal scholarly task of identifying a research setting in which to examine theoretical ideas. This point is of some concern, as this book is devoted to the formal techniques for finding information, whether this is primary or secondary and is published, unpublished, or published in some unconventional form. Equal attention is given to searches for primary and secondary sources, and this approach reflects the nature of the research process as this exists in reality.

There is no conflict between finding information in informal ways, through personal contacts and unstructured use of library collections, and in formal and structured techniques. They are both useful. But the advantages of formal methods should be apparent in the discussions that follow. They are, however, intended to supplement rather than to replace less formal, but more entrenched, approaches to information-finding. Given what has been said about the tremendous and ongoing production of information, why should any serious person be content with less than systematic methods of information retrieval? The answer is that the informal methods are systematic in their own way.

Academics in a field, students and scholars, develop extensive networks of contacts fostered by scholarly associations and conferences. These networks include people who, although they may rarely meet, do correspond and comment upon each other's papers. They make up exclusive groups working in narrow and self-defined areas of limited interest to the outside world. They share information and know-how about resources; they help each other get published and boost each other academically and professionally; they broadcast new developments; and they tell each other about job opportunities. Each of these groups makes up an "invisible college" that supplies the most up-to-date information available. Usually members of this informal institution are favored with excellent knowledge obtained from conventional sources. This will be updated by reading current issues of journals deemed important and, perhaps, glancing through recent issues of a couple of appropriate indexes or abstracting services.

Every scholar can profit from belonging to an "invisible college." In academic specialties that are limited and self contained this avenue may provide all that anyone needs in the way of sources of information. Unfortunately, this is not usually true in a field such as public administration. This field has always been so disparate that developments within a subspecialty may be known to only one small group of researchers. Developments in each specialization affect others. Researchers who are not aware of what is going on in the discipline as a whole and in related disciplines risk losing track of research that affects their areas of particular interest.

For instance, suppose that I am interested in the modernization of the U.S. courts in the 19th century (this example will be picked up and expanded at various points in this book). My "invisible college" would include legal and social historians, sociologists, and political scientists who use legal sources from this period for their varied studies. Yet modernization did not occur just in mid-19th-century America or early 19th-century England; it is occurring now, with diverse social and legal implications, in countries throughout the Third World. If I stick with personal contacts, I shall gain no knowledge of what different social scientists are developing in the way of new approaches to understanding modernization today and around the world. My "invisible college" would limit me to the perspectives of those interested in the use of narrow approaches and historical sources.

The need for formal information-finding techniques is greater, the broader one's parent discipline. In a field like public administration where the connections with other disciplines are so strong and reliance upon their theoretical perspectives so profound, the need for structured information-finding methods is paramount. Support for this point is provided by a consideration of the historical development of public administration and of its present status in the world of the social and policy sciences as an eclectic and broadly based field of study.

Public administration has long been dominated by political science perspectives. Origins of modern approaches to it are ascribed to various points in 19th-century thought. Many consider Max Weber's classic analysis of the bureaucracy as an ideal type a watershed in this regard, although this discussion was not published in English until after World War II. The bureaucracy has been seen as the dominant organizational structure in all modern large organizations, whether public or private. At the time it was conceptualized by Weber, however, it was viewed primarily as a tool for analyzing organizations in the public sector. Weber's influence is therefore seen in his construction of a precise model intended primarily for the analysis of state institutions.

Woodrow Wilson's view of the relationship between policy development and its implementation in public agencies marks the beginning of academic discussion of administrative problems peculiar to government. His 1887 article, which sparked a debate that helped mold public administration as a field, advocated a complete separation between policy-making, as the function of the legislature, and policy implementation, as the responsibility of the executive agencies. Debate over what he meant by this strict dichotomy continues to the present (for example, see Martin 1988). Policy-making attributes seem to be inherent in the implementation of the will of a legislature. There is a qualitative difference between *management* and *government*. Scholars have used this difference as a stepping-stone to examine the form and extent of administrative policy development and its relation to bureaucratic structure, the needs of the agency's clients, and the balance of political power between legislative and executive government. Because developing themes within the subject owe so much to these origins, it is not surprising that much of the academic activity in public administration has always been dominated by political science and by those educated in this discipline.

However, public administration has always been subject also to strong influences from other fields. During the first half of this century there was considerable discussion of the application of management models to public agencies to combine administrative efficiency with effective goal achievement. These models, which originated in the private sector, are exemplified by "scientific management" or "Taylorism" and its concern for monitoring individual tasks within the enterprise and placing them under intense supervision. Efficiency is the primary goal of "scientific management." Those who have applied such models to the public sector have necessarily emphasized the similarities between the public agency and the private corporation. In doing so, they have effectively oversimplified the functions of government and therefore greatly limited the subject matter of the discipline that studies it. If private and public organizations are largely the same, analysis of the latter can presumably be undertaken quite adequately with the perspectives of the former.

This reliance upon the precepts and models of business administration is quite apparent in early public administration texts. One of the first textbooks ever written in this field attempts a definition of its subject matter through a series of direct comparisons between the public administration and the management of large, private corporations. Different goals are minimized. Both types of organization are discussed primarily in terms of the criterion of efficiency, which produces, in the one case, maximum profits, and in the other, "the rendering of proper services to the public served . . . at the minimum of cost consistent with the maintenance of proper standards" (Willoughby 1927, p. 5). There is little in this account to suggest that the definition of the latter goal may be problematic when it is presented in terms comprehensible within an entrepreneurial framework.

The influence of scientific management grew from the beginning of the 20th century. The acceptance of its philosophy as the basis for the management of federal agencies was stimulated by the Taft Commission on Economy and Efficiency of 1911, which argued for the widespread application of business principles to government. The most influential statement of this perspective was presented by Gulick and Urwick in 1937 in a report commissioned by the federal government. This emphasized the technical and universal aspects of administration, perhaps at the cost of proper recognition of the unique nature of the "products" delivered by agencies in the public sector. Their report synthesized earlier thinking and produced a statement of the principles of administration collectively known by the acronym POSDCORB (planning, organizing, staffing, directing, coordinating, reporting, budgeting). For many public managers the implementation of POSDCORB through the application of the principles of scientific management remains the key to the practice of administration today.

Management models and the reliance on the field of business administration for theoretical guidance persist. The commonality of public and private managerial problems was given formal recognition in the academic world by the establishment of the Yale School of Organization and Management (SOM) in 1976, the first, and so far the only, Ivy League institution to offer a graduate program in management intended for both sectors within the economy. (It must be said that the coexistence of two competing philosophies has not always been a happy one at this institution. In recent years the Yale SOM has come to emphasize perspectives of the private sector at the expense of the public. However, this is probably more a reflection of the school's interest in the job prospects of the current generation of students than of any principled rejection of its original philosophy.)

Business administration may exert even further influence on the theory of public management. As government bureaucracies become leaner, issues of privatization and the contracting out of public services become increasingly important. These issues help forge closer links between styles and theories of management in the two sectors.

There are less clearly articulated reasons for the continuing influence of variants of scientific management on thinking in public administration. One attraction of movements like Taylorism has been their assumption that human behavior is rational and that generalizations about its administration can be specified within a series of laws or lawlike generalizations. This implied wish, coupled with consumer desires to see principles of "efficiency" applied to government, will keep the management influence on public administration strong for the foreseeable future.

Apparently public administration is unable to transcend its many earlier theoretical and historical associations with other disciplines. The field continues to rely extensively on the findings, models, and theories of other disciplines. This is why anyone engaged in public administration research should always examine sources of potential value outside of the field.

On the other hand, scholarly approaches to public administration in the 1980s exhibited more internal cohesion. At least one recent study has shown that the core of knowledge common to the field is now reflected the literature devoted largely to the public enterprise (McCurdy 1986, pp. 1–9). In the early 1970s most works cited by scholars in public administration were produced outside of the field. In the mid-1980s about half were studies limited to the public sector. By this standard, the field has begun to develop its own body of literature defining the arenas of its most important debates. However, it is also true that the reliance of public administration on the theory and findings of other disciplines will continue to expand. Students of bureaucracy, for example, will continue to do most of their reading in studies generated by sociologists. Those interested in organizational development (a burgeoning area of study) will become familiar with the findings of psychologists. One of the more interesting approaches of recent years addresses the common phenomenon of Third World countries constrained by the demands of Western bureaucratic structures they have inherited. This important study in comparative public administration presents an ecological theory of administrative development that addresses processes of local adaptation (Riggs 1964). Without an understanding of theories and findings in anthropology and political science, the author of this study, as he would certainly concede, would have been unable to develop his thesis.

One of several areas in which public administration may make some reasonable claim to pioneering status is the area of organizational ethics, which is currently attracting a great deal of attention in American society. One could argue that much of this attention is no more than lip service and that the study of ethical issues will never come to take pride of place in, for example, the curriculum of a graduate school of business. In one sense this is reasonable, although it is also a little disturbing if true. The principal long-term objective of a business enterprise is to make profits for its stockholders, and any additional goals it may have will be secondary to this.

Public agencies are in a very different situation. Because of the nature of the services they provide and their own roles in determining the nature and scope of these services, public agencies cannot avoid addressing ethical considerations. These are of paramount importance in perennial issues such as the responsibility of the agency to its clients and to its legal obligations, its reconciliation of the democratic ideal and the bureaucratic ideal, and the need to juggle expanding functions and shrinking resources. Appreciation of this has always been implicit in academic approaches to the study of public administration. The centrality of ethics was reaffirmed explicitly in a much-quoted 1962 article that clearly stated the relative importance of ethical and other value-laden concerns as the essence of the difference between the study of private- and public-sector organizational structure (Golembiewski 1962). Concern for ethics is strengthened anew by more rigorous notions of public accountability. An indicator of the continued strength of this concern is the fact that a recent issue of the *Public Administration Review* (March/April 1992) included a collection of essays addressing Golembiewski's classic article. These generally asserted the ongoing primacy of his position. For mainstream scholars an ethical concern remains a definitive characteristic of the field (Burke 1989, Denhardt 1989, Rohr 1978). If this concern is translated into theoretical development, there will be a greater interaction between public administration and the discipline of philosophy in the future.

Management models do not always address administration as a pure system of rewards and incentives aimed at the rational satisfaction of the economic man.

The period between the two world wars saw the development of an appreciation of the psychological factors affecting the smooth functioning of the organization. This appreciation had its effect on management theory in all sectors. Recognition of the power of the Hawthorne effect (see Roethlisberger & Dickson 1939) had a widespread influence in propagating the understanding that factors other than tangible incentives were of major importance in encouraging employee cooperation. Managers saw that psychological research has much to offer in indicating the effects of work environment and organizational structure on the operation of an organization. The importance of the branch of this discipline known as industrial psychology is now well established.

Recently other areas of psychology have come to be of great interest to administrators and other policymakers, especially those in the public sector. A number of recent court decisions collectively require that tests of employee aptitudes and competency be related directly to job requirements. They also require that these tests exert demands uninfluenced by cultural or other bias. As psychology is a discipline now clearly linked to management, the sources of its literature must be part of scholarly research in many areas of public administration. Since organizations have become increasingly concerned with the noneconomic aspects of the work setting and their importance for increasing worker responsibility and productivity, the discipline of psychology is coming to play a greater role in management research. If this is true in the private sector, it is more so in the public, where the nature of the service or product rendered is less quantifiable and the nature of decisions made by line workers usually more discretionary. Such understanding is the basis of the "organization development" school that, since the early 1970s, has sought ways to integrate the personal goals of functionaries with those of the bureaucracies to which they belong.

A further concern that is developing, although not yet in the mainstream of research in the field, recognizes the importance of comparative analysis. American public administration has often been accused of insularity, and not without justification. The lack of studies providing international or cross-cultural perspective has been viewed as inhibiting the theoretical development of the field. Work of this nature has been done in the past and is now being done, although the drying-up of grant monies for research overseas can hardly contribute to its expansion. There is little doubt that such research has enormous potential. Great differences between cultures obviously exist, but a common characteristic seems to be the prevalence of bureaucracies. Comparative study of how this universal triumph operates in countries as disparate as France and Burkina Faso will surely add to the rather slender corpus that is theory in public administration. One slight problem is that research in areas such as this is being done, but not by those who consider themselves members of any invisible college that reflects public administration. Traditionally, scholars in anthropology and political science and, to a lesser extent, those in sociology, economics, and fragmented fields such as urban affairs have done this kind of work. Researchers in comparative studies must necessarily gain a familiarity with the bibliographic sources serving these disciplines.

A different, and perhaps more immediate, influence on public administration comes from the field of economics. Finance and economic planning are important specialties within the public sector. As national economic planning has become less centralized, local planning has become part of the normal business of government. Econometrics and economic forecasting have similarly become elements of both local and national agendas. As specialists in these areas come almost entirely from the circumscribed field of economics, those who would engage in them must deal overwhelmingly with data generated from within this discipline.

In the late 1960s the field was faced with a crisis regarding the face of the so-called "new public administration." This short-lived phenomenon seemed then to call into question every facet of thought in the area. This perspective called for a client-centered and client-sensitive approach to the delivery of public services and interpreted public service as a vehicle for client advocacy. There have been many eloquent statements of the hopes of the "new" public administration (see Marini 1971; Frederickson 1989 and the sources cited in it). There have also been those who have praised this perspective for its vision in hoping to make social equity part of the agenda of public institutions. Others have castigated it for the naivete of its conceptions of bureaucracy (see, for example, Thompson 1975). From the perspective of 1993 the principal surviving accomplishment of the new public administration has been to turn attention back to the old object of concern: bureaucratic structure. The nature of bureaucracy has again become the focus of attention of scholars in public administration.

Many current issues affecting government institutions relate to the nature of the bureaucratic institution. Traditional concerns for ethics must recognize the characteristics and limitations of traditional bureaucratic structure (Rohr 1978). Most research on bureaucracy is not done in the context of public agencies. Public administration must, once again, rely upon research findings from outside of its boundaries.

Of continuing and particular importance to the field is the amount of attention directed at the old problem raised by Woodrow Wilson: the difficulties of distinguishing between the creation of policy and its implementation. No one would now deny the importance of agencies in creating policy, if only by virtue of their function of translating broad principles of law to minute and individual settings. This phenomenon has engendered its own area of study, implementation theory (for a review of this, see Palumbo & Calista 1987). Regardless of public administrators' efforts to dominate this field, even to the point of giving a new name to it, political scientists continue to make their own substantial contributions to it.

Such issues quite reasonably remain the substance of what is now done in the name of public administration. There are other important themes that should be named. Legal issues affect almost every aspect of public administration, especially those related to personnel matters. This has become more true as the body of law addressing affirmative action and related areas has become more complex. Knowledge of the law is important for understanding the basis of many dilemmas associated with the practice of public management. The translation of legislation into public policy requires legal interpretations regarding the wording of a statute and the intent of the legislature that enacted it. It is, of course, one of the functions of the courts to provide binding interpretations of this nature. Courts have recently become much more aggressive in regulating administrative policy in this way. The agency that is working toward consistent policy must have the legal expertise to implement the wishes of the legislature in a fashion that will be upheld by the courts. Thus legal facility is now central to both the practice and the theory of management in the public sector. The old question of how far agencies should go in creating policy clearly involves issues that are legal in nature. Given the modern trend of greater accountability of public agencies, both to government as a whole and to the particular clientele served, the importance of the law to the field of public administration is not likely to diminish. Such developments have motivated a recent call for greater recognition of the centrality of law to the field and the strong recommendation for the inclusion of this subject in the basic graduate curriculum: "[L]aw as a course requirement in schools of public administration is more than a nicety; it is a necessity" (O'Leary 1989, p. 115).

Legal and political history have influenced research and thinking in public administration largely because the development of the public sector has been so much a product of this history. The influence of social and economic history, on the other hand, lies more in its potential than in its substance. A great deal of excellent research has been done, for example, on the relationship between the rise of the middle classes and the rise of the modern bureaucratic state. However, little of this research has emerged from within public administration. The influence of history is an accepted one, but it has not generated much research interest within the field. Many research projects in public administration do, however, reflect assumptions and positions that are basically historical. It would perhaps benefit research in the field if such assumptions were explored through the findings and the methods of conventional historical study.

In common with other institutions in modern Western society, public agencies and those who study them have been obliged to address the massive amount of relevant data generated and new technological means of controlling and manipulating them. As has been noted in this discussion, the public sector has been especially affected by this proliferation of information. Many have observed that information in its various forms is not something that will ever again be in short supply (although good information always will be): "Resource economics is a science for the allocation of scarcities—but information is a nondepletive resource; it expands when it is used; it may even be said to be in chronic surplus" (Cleveland 1982, p. 516). Information management has become a recognized specialty within public administration and one that, although very technical in its exercise, has implications for policy and theory that extend the breadth of the field.

Other recent emphases reflect the general trends of making public institutions more accountable to their various constituencies and more cost-effective in these days of tighter government budgets. Productivity and program evaluation are two specialties that have grown apace in the last two decades. Both have developed their own methods and measurement techniques and have their own journals, handbooks, and other bibliographic sources. Application of sophisticated approaches has been made possible by the ability of researchers, courtesy of the new technology, to collect and analyze large quantities of data. In this sense, many new approaches to public bureaucracies are in effect technology-driven and are intimately connected to the management of information.

Nonetheless, the strongest academic influence on public administration continues to be the discipline of political science, which still provides much of the theory and many of the perspectives. Most who now teach and do research in public administration are products of departments of political science. Teaching and research in public administration are likely to remain largely in the hands of those trained in political science. This grasp will be only slightly weakened by the entrance of specialists trained as economists, statisticians, or researchers in other disciplines that relate most closely to ongoing developments in the field.

There are clearly many approaches to research in public administration—if, indeed, this field can reasonably lay claim to the status of a discipline. Many would argue that its status is yet, and perhaps always will be, that of an amalgam of the approaches pioneered within other disciplines. In this view, public administration should be jedged by the extent to which it upholds the integrity of its watchful parents. Delineation of subspecialties within the field goes nowhere toward resolution of this identity crisis. Criminal justice, for example, may be a policy-oriented concern with strong links to public administration. However, it has links at least as close to criminology and even to social work. Those working in it must cope with the familiar dilemma of applying the schema of one field, but with a close eye to the approaches of several others.

This potted summary has clear implications for the seeker of information in areas related to public administration. In information-finding terms, definitions of public administration have little value. Researchers within it are not concerned with a general field. They engage topics. The topic may take the exploration for secondary and even primary sources in many directions. These may lead into various disciplines that constitute the social, behavioral, and policy sciences. If they do, then the literature sources of these disciplines must be mastered. It is not a value judgment about public administration that is being presented here. The point is rather that those who do research within it must appreciate the practical necessity of surveying the literature of several related areas. Failure to do so will bring adverse consequences.

The research situation is even more complicated than this. The secondary literature of interest to the researcher of public administration is not always published commercially. Many important case studies and other materials are published by organizations that do not always make great efforts to disseminate them. Such organizations can include universities, research institutes, professional and trade associations, consulting firms, recipients of research grants, and, of course, government agencies. Scholars in public administration often face a daunting task in working up a good topical bibliography. They must usually delve into the bibliography of one or more related disciplines. At the same time, they must endeavor to locate the sources identifying relevant nontrade publications of the ephemeral or fugitive kind.

This reference guide cannot be all things to all who work under the umbrella of public administration. However, it is hoped that this book will prove valuable in providing pointers in areas not usually addressed and in doing so will help put readers with various specialties on the right path. One purpose of this chapter has been to document the position that whether or not public administration qualifies as a discipline in its own right, it relies heavily on the methods and findings of virtually every other discipline within the social sciences. Thus the researcher must be prepared to master the bibliographic sources of a variety of related fields. Such is life, and, unfortunately, no one can make things any easier in this regard.

Current research suggests that this research requirement will be even more important in the future. Studies indicate that barriers between disciplines are eroding rapidly (Graham 1989). Researchers in the future will rely much more on interdisciplinary approaches than those in the past. Public administration will be strongly affected by this trend. Research in this field continues to be mostly of a practical or problem-oriented nature (Stallings & Ferris 1988; Watson & Montjoy 1991). Those seeking interesting current theoretical perspectives must continue to look toward other disciplines. This is not necessarily a negative trend. There is no doubt that scholars in public administration are very sensitive to criticisms that their approaches are too applied in focus and/or are lacking in original theoretical perspective. It is probably a healthy sign that those within the field are continually ready to raise these issues to one another. Since the publication of a benchmark article (McCurdy & Cleary 1984), there has been a constant stream of articles in the journal literature of public administration addressing the direction and content of research in the field. Many have been quite self-critical. One of the most recent articles reviews much of the earlier related literature and confirms the familiar view that research approaches in this area are diverse and of varying scholarly quality (Box 1992).

One can argue that an area that is so self-conscious and recognizes its disciplinary debts while tolerating a broad range of research objectives cannot be accused of inflexibility. It is at the very least welcoming in providing its adherents with a number of alternative methodologies and research goals. In this sense public administration profits from being something other than an integrated discipline. Given the interdisciplinary nature of much of the exciting research elsewhere in the social and behavioral sciences, this characteristic may yet prove to be a substantial asset.

One position taken in this book is that formal means of information-finding possess no virtue or excellence in themselves. They are purely a means to an end and should be judged according to their effectiveness. For reasons given, it is clear that knowledge of formal methods is especially important to those groping in unfamiliar theoretical territory. This book does not entirely vaunt the formal over the informal. There are many situations in which the "invisible college" works well and yields the most superior results. People who know a field very well can always find shortcuts to finding information. These are quite valid, provided, of course, that one does indeed know the field and can appreciate its nature and possible spillover into other disciplines. No antagonism exists between the librarian's rigorous identification and searching of bibliographic sources and the scholar's reliance upon a personal network and directed library browsing. The intelligent and well-informed researcher will appreciate the situations in which each of these approaches should be emphasized and those in which they should be combined.

A final point. This book is intended to orient readers to theory and to direct them to appropriate sources. There are many works that are guides to workaday problems and that address the technical needs of practitioners and not the techniques and strategies of researchers. The object of this book is not to address these works (sources for finding them, however, are, discussed). Nonetheless, a few practitioner-oriented works are mentioned here—especially in fields like finance, which seem to have as their compelling force the production of results and not opportunities for intellectual inquiry. My justification is that public administration, whatever it is, has always, for better or worse, been an enterprise geared to the practice of government.

REFERENCES

Box, Richard C. (1992). An Examination of the Debate over Research in Public Administration. *Public Administration Review, 52*, 62–69.

Burke, John P. (1989). Reconciling Public Administration and Democracy: The Role of the Responsible Administrator. *Public Administration Review, 49*, 180-85.

Cleveland, Harlan. (1982). Education for the Macrotransition We Are In. In Lane, F. S. (Ed.) *Current Issues in Public Administration* (2nd ed.) (pp. 513–20). New York: St. Martin's.

Denhardt, Kathryn G. (1989). The Management of Ideals: A Political Perspective on Ethics. *Public Administration Review, 49*, 187–93.

Frederickson, H. George. (1989). Minnowbrook II: Changing Epochs of Public Administration. *Public Administration Review, 49*, 95–100.

Golembiewski, Robert T. (1962). Organization as a Moral Problem. *Public Administration Review, 22*, 51–58.

Graham, Peter S. (1989). Research Patterns and Research Libraries: What Should Change? *College and Research Libraries, 50*, 433–40.

Gulick, Luther H. & Urwick, Lyndall F. (Eds.). (1937). *Papers in the Science of Administration.* New York: Institute of Public Administration.

McCurdy, Howard E. (1986). *Public Administration: A Bibliographic Guide to the Literature.* New York: Dekker.

McCurdy, Howard E. & Cleary, Robert E. (1984.) Why Can't We Resolve the Research Issue in Public Administration? *Public Administration Review, 44*, January/February, 49-55.

Marini, Frank. (Ed.). (1971). *Toward a New Public Administration: The Minnowbrook Perspective.* Scranton, PA: Chandler.

Martin, Daniel W. (1988). The Fading Legacy of Woodrow Wilson. *Public Administration Review, 48*, 631–36.

O'Leary, Rosemary. (1989). Response to John Rohr. *Public Administration Review, 49*, 115.

Palumbo, Dennis, & Calista, Dennis. (Eds.). (1987). Implementation: What We Have Learned and Still Need to Know. *Policy Studies Review, 7*, 91-246.

Riggs, Fred W. (1964). *Administration in Developing Countries: The Theory of Prismatic Society.* Boston: Houghton Mifflin.

Roethlisberger, Fritz J., & Dickson, William J. (1939). *Management and the Worker.* Cambridge, MA: Harvard University Press.

Rohr, John A. (1978). *Ethics for Bureaucrats: An Essay on Law and Values.* New York: Dekker.

Stallings, Robert A., & Ferris, James M. (1988). Public Administration Research: Work in *PAR*, 1940–1984. *Public Administration Review, 48*, 580-87.

Thompson, Victor A. (1975). *Without Sympathy or Enthusiasm.* University, AL: University of Alabama Press.

Ulrich's International Periodicals Directory, 1975–1976. (1975). (16th ed.). New York: Bowker. 2 vols.

Ulrich's International Periodicals Directory, 1992–1993. (1992). (31st ed.). New York: Bowker. 3 vols.

Watson, Douglas J., & Montjoy, Robert S. (1991). Research on Local Government in *Public Administration Review*. *Public Administration Review, 51*, 166–70.

Weber, Max. (1946). Bureaucracy. In Gerth, H. H., & Mills, C. Wright (Eds.), *From Max Weber: Essays in Sociology* (pp. 196–244). New York: Oxford University Press.

Willoughby, William F. (1927). *Principles of Public Administration*. Washington, DC: Brookings Institution.

Wilson, T. Woodrow. (1887). The Study of Administration. *Political Science Quarterly, 2*, 197–222.

2

THE RESEARCH PROBLEM AND SEARCH STRATEGY

This chapter places the techniques of bibliographic research within a conceptual framework intended to achieve maximum results with the least expenditure of time and effort. For someone preparing a term paper, this goal is usually a selected bibliography of the outstanding works in the general area addressed, together with a thorough, even comprehensive, bibliography on some narrow aspect of this topic. For those engaged in research for a dissertation or other project involving research of an original nature, the goal will be more complex and must go beyond the identification and assessment of published findings in the investigator's chosen area of endeavor.

The researcher must develop a form of *search strategy*. This is, in essence, a framework for determining, at each stage of the information-finding process, the kind of data being sought and the forms of published material in which these data are likely to be found. The search strategy should help investigators define exactly what they need and break the process for meeting these needs down into a series of discrete and manageable tasks.

After the topic of interest has been properly stated and defined, each step in the strategy will be geared to searching the bibliographic resources most likely to provide the needed information. The search techniques applied must be systematic, efficient, and, above all, well thought-out and tailored to the particular situation under study. If the strategy is a good one and has been properly implemented, the investigator can be confident that searches of the literature have been thorough and that the materials so identified are an appropriate expression of what the world of published information has to offer on the topic. The key decisions made in formulating the search strategy are in no sense mechanistic or routine. Sometimes the implementation of the strategy will prove pedestrian, even wearisome, but its development should not. The search strategy is the *game plan* of the research project, and its soundness and value are direct indicators of the quality of the research project and the level of understanding held by thc researcher.

Effective information-finding is essentially a *feedback* process. One cannot reasonably separate the process of finding information from the process of absorbing it. The search strategy is not a laundry list of indexes and other bibliographic tools to be searched passively, nor are the results set aside to be collated at some later time. At each stage in the endeavor the student must read and evaluate material that has been identified thus far and attempt to integrate it into the framework of the project. Commonly, the objectives of the project must be reevaluated in the light of the investigator's better understanding of the implications of the project. Each stage in the strategy is determined by the researcher's current understanding of the project as this is influenced by the information yielded in the stage that went before.

This continual reassessment and, if necessary, redefinition of the research project is a very usual characteristic of the research process. It arises quite simply because the investigator knows more about the project at each successive stage of it and is naturally in a better position to decide exactly what is interesting about it from a social sciences perspective and what aspects of it show the most potential for further examination. As with anything else in life, greater knowledge gives one a more developed critical sense and a better idea of how to relate the subject at hand to broader administrative, political, and scholarly issues.

Choice of a topic for a term paper or dissertation should depend on a level of knowledge informed by some level of interest and a certain amount of background reading in the general area of concern. Unfortunately, a preliminary assessment of what the topic involves may not be supported by the evidence as it emerges through the literature search. It is obvious that a researcher who picks a topic carefully and on the basis of his or her prior knowledge will obviously limit the extent to which it must later be modified. Thoughtful selection of the initial topic accordingly represents the crucial stage in the search strategy. But even the best-planned projects must be critically and continually reassessed at every stage in the research process. The reason, again, is that the more one knows, the greater is one's understanding of the truly interesting issues involved and the greater is the opportunity for the imagination to make linkages between the narrow object of study and the universe within which it is embedded. All parts of the project, from the development of the idea through the identification and examination of previous research to the analysis of the data, are part of the same intellectual process.

It can be argued that a student working on a term paper that has been assigned or otherwise approved has limited flexibility in modifying the substance of the research. This is certainly true up to a point, although those who teach courses at the graduate level are usually receptive to reasonable and well-informed modifications of student projects. However, even if they are not sympathetic in this sense, most undertakings of any ambition in the social and policy sciences are amenable to different approaches. Someone conducting a literature search in preparation for a case study of bureaucratic dysfunction, for example, might find that critical reading offers different approaches, depending on the nature and circumstances of the bureaucracy in question. Punitive and ineffective management styles could be associated with poorly designed alternative systems of accountability. They could also be strongly influenced by the political context of the bureaucracy and by its desire to defend itself because of its inability to meet unrealistic administrative goals. Whatever the case, the student will find a number of theoretical frameworks to guide a study of it. These will be identified in one of the early stages of the search strategy, which in this sense can help provide a choice of theoretical approach to the problem, as well as documentation of the particular object of attention.

A further characteristic of the search strategy is the particular and restricted nature of its products. The product of the search strategy is a bibliography. Bibliographies are, however, generally considered in two groups: *comprehensive* bibliographies, which attempt to include everything it is possible to identify on the topic addressed, and *selective* bibliographies, which are limited in specified ways. Conscientious investigators invariably seek to construct a comprehensive bibliography of everything that bears upon the subject of concern. In fact, it is the selective bibliography that is usually the most interesting product of the search strategy. For most purposes, the intelligent researcher seeks to limit the amount of information that is gathered to that which can reasonably be processed. No one working on an area concerned with bureaucratic dysfunction could ever read all the theoretical approaches to this that have been written. No intelligent researcher would ever seek to do so. The object would instead be to attempt to consider those approaches that are considered to be outstanding, most influential to the study of large-scale organizations, or otherwise relevant to the particular problem to be studied. An important part of the search strategy addresses the many bibliographic tools that provide theoretical overviews.

The problems and the importance of this stage are best appreciated in considering just what it is investigators are doing when they engage in research. Researchers preparing term papers will limit their analyses to the application of the published findings of others on the problem at hand, using the insights of others to fuel their own creativity. Researchers working on dissertations must accomplish a great deal more than this. They certainly use the findings and theories of others to demonstrate, among other things, a thorough familiarity with previous work relevant to the topic. In this case, however, analysis of particular theoretical models or processes prefaces the testing of them against some body of primary data or is otherwise used to explain or interpret patterns in the data.

In both the term paper and the dissertation, insights gleaned from the work of others are extremely important in the analysis. For the dissertation researcher, however, the paramount concern is to demonstrate an ability to conduct original research by analyzing a body of raw data in such a way as to make a contribution to some larger theoretical framework.

This process of original research, at least as it is currently defined in the social and policy sciences (the behavioral and pure sciences subscribe to rather different models), in essence requires the detailed examination of a little slice of the world and fitting it within an appropriate broad perspective. This task is, in what seems to be the universal opinion of everyone who has undertaken it, an extremely difficult thing to do. Successful completion requires imagination and a knowledge of theory as well as of sources and methods.

The bibliographic needs of the dissertation researcher or the writer of the ambitious term paper will be on two initial levels. First, a bibliography must be developed to cover all potentially interesting aspects of the narrow object of study. This bibliography will probably be as comprehensive as can be managed. Second, a selective bibliography must be constructed on the framework of the analysis. This framework may be on theoretical approaches that could be applied to the analysis; it may also address structural factors used in the interpretation of the data. It may even address psychological approaches of potential significance in explaining the motivation and behavior of actors in the scenario being examined. The researcher may also prepare other selective bibliographies to support different aspects of the subject that intuition and previous reading suggest may be of value in analyzing and interpreting the data.

These bibliographies must be achieved through systematic means. The sense of their importance and purpose will emerge from the evaluation of materials identified at each point in the information-gathering process. This sense is sharpened as the project develops because it is continually informed by the researcher's improved perceptions. It will always be a product of a level of understanding moved by a formal and systematic process of information-collecting. For example, let us say that you intend to investigate factors related to occupational stress among frontline workers in emergency medical services. The first question to answer is why you have chosen this particular aspect of the psychology of work. An acceptable answer cannot simply reflect a general interest in theories of job stress or some particular interest in this occupational group. You must have some interesting and meaningful idea about the chosen setting. It must be *interesting* in the sense that you can use it to explore some question of concern to students of stress in general. It must be *meaningful* in the sense that you believe that you can offer propositions about stress that are testable or otherwise amenable to systematic analysis within the research design and setting adopted. At this stage of the game, you then have a good idea of what you propose to do and some idea of the broader implications of your proposed research and anticipated findings. Of course, you still have a substantial amount of work to do in formulating a detailed research design, isolating a population or sample to examine, and determining methodological techniques for examining it. The point is that you have what seems to be a viable idea and some sense of how it can be implemented in a research setting. You are at least started, and although the original idea and plans for its implementation may well be subject to later modification, the game is in play.

Stages in the search strategy are outlined in the following sections. Although the complexity of each stage is obviously greater for a dissertation or other original research enterprise than for a term paper, the substance of the decisions made remains the same.

1. TOPIC SELECTION

Development of a valid notion of how some narrow study can be devised for the purpose of gaining insight into broader social phenomena is fundamentally a creative process. It involves the derivation of new linkages between settings and theoretical interpretations of them. Because it is a product of original thinking, development of such notions is neither mechanical nor predictable. The ability to come up with new interpretations of social settings is far from being "the supreme grace bestowed upon the few 'elected and anointed' creative geniuses."[1] It is an ability that constitutes the main qualification for all who undertake original research. As such, its achievement is the main objective of any graduate program in the social and policy sciences. Creativity in social research is more than a personal characteristic shared by a few lucky individuals. A capacity for it is symptomatic of the human condition, and this can be nurtured, if not instantly mobilized. It is fuelled and stimulated by the understanding that comes with knowledge obtained through academic study of research settings and, above all, of theoretical perspectives. For this reason, the researcher's own background knowledge and reading are often the best and certainly the most logical starting point for the choice of an appropriate topic.

At this initial step few formal rules apply. Reading, browsing, thinking, and talking to colleagues are all grist for the mill. All viable ideas will reflect some schema incorporating the examination of a body of data, representing a real-world setting, through the lens of some theoretical perspective and the application of an appropriate methodology. The main contribution of the work can address any of these areas. Any chosen setting must be amenable to some productive theoretical interpretation. No problematic or otherwise interesting theory can be tested properly unless it is applied to a worthy body of data. Methodological expertise, no matter how sophisticated, is valueless unless it is suitably applied to a problem in the real world. For these reasons, the dissertation student's difficulty is three-dimensional. Like the writer of the term paper, the dissertation student must look for a research project that is interesting and problematic. Unlike the term-paper writer, the latter must also find a narrow and manageable setting in which to examine the problem, a theoretical perspective from which to analyze it, and methods for isolating and manipulating the data of analysis. This stage of the process should be approached carefully and slowly. The wise graduate student who has not yet reached the dissertation stage should devote as many term papers as course work allows to exploring future dissertation possibilities.

There are ways to make the selection of the topic somewhat easier, although these ways are the more effective the more narrowly you identify your field of interest. (Yet none offers a satisfactory substitute for thorough knowledge of a particular area of endeavor.) The first involves the use of what are collectively referred to as *annual reviews*, which exist in all fields and in many subspecialties within the social, policy, and behavioral sciences. The lists in appendix 1 indicate several dozen that are of potential interest to the student of public administration. These sources generally provide current overviews of disciplines and specialties. Other sources of this nature are identified in later chapters.

Annual reviews are issued by a variety of publishers and differ according to whether the articles are original pieces or are reprints of previously published articles. These reviews usually address narrow specialties within a discipline and, in a series of timely and authoritative articles, selectively review recent developments. They frequently address "hot topics" currently attracting attention in the field, as well as topics that have become arenas for debates over theoretical and other issues of concern to the discipline. Not all annual reviews are subject-driven. *Sociological Methodology*, for example, addresses a variety of methodological developments and considerations of potential interest to the student of large-scale organizations. *Studying Organizations* would be an even more promising choice. (Annual reviews addressing explicitly methodological concerns are grouped with section 11 of appendix 1). The principal function of annual reviews is to provide scholars and practitioners with a means of assessing the direction of current research and of current problems in their fields. By extension, these sources are of great value to the student seeking to isolate a subject for research in the mainstream of current research in a field.

Journals are not always appreciated by those in search of dissertation topics. You are strongly advised to identify a group of a dozen or more journals relevant to your specific area of concern. This group will probably include both major journals in public administration and management and specialized journals in the narrow field of interest. A couple of hours a week spent browsing through current issues can be invaluable, both as a guide to current concerns in an area and as a potential indicator of dissertation topics that have some currency in addressing important issues, helping you obtain a fuller understanding of just what researchers and theoreticians consider when they engage in scholarly debate in the area. Chapter 7 provides a selective, annotated list of journals in public administration and tangential disciplines. Problematic and otherwise interesting concerns are addressed in journal articles before they are picked up in annual reviews. Only much later do they filter down to textbooks and monographs.

Annual meetings of scholarly and professional associations provide an earlier forum in which scholars exchange ideas, discuss issues, and present papers based on research that may not be complete. In these settings they can present their research for comment and criticism without subjecting themselves to the trauma of having their published work criticized in print. The annual meeting is important to scholars as a vehicle through which they can expose an unfinished product to the world. The papers presented at these meetings are an early reflection of ongoing research in a discipline. These papers are usually products of research that is continuing, as well as that recently completed. This research may take several years to get published in journal-article form. The selective publishing agendas of prestigious journals conspire with time lags of one or two years or more to ensure that several years may pass before a completed piece of research appears in print. If authors are not dedicated enough or persistent enough, their pieces may never appear at all. At a typical annual meeting of a large scholarly or professional association, such as the American Society for Public Administration, hundreds of papers will be presented. Only a small proportion of these will ever be published.

Identifying papers given at recent meetings of appropriate scholarly associations is clearly an excellent way of learning what is going on in the way of current research in a field. It is also an excellent route to a research topic or approach.[2] The best way to identify papers of this sort is to be a member of relevant organizations and to attend their annual meetings. Unfortunately, not all of us can spare the time or the money to attend week-long annual meetings in Hawaii or San Francisco. However, these papers are also obtainable through conference catalogs that provide quite lengthy abstracts of the papers presented. Citations to the papers invariably give the names and affiliations of presenters, who usually respond positively to requests for papers. (See chapter 15, section 4, for sources of information for products of scholarly associations.) Some of the databases included in systems described in chapter 9 have a policy of providing citations and abstracts for papers presented at such meetings, as do a few of the printed indexing and abstracting services. *Sociological Abstracts*, for example, regularly includes information on papers presented at the annual meetings of the American Sociological Association and the Society for the Study of Social Problems. Printed abstracts have the advantage of permitting scanning through a broad category; databases do not. Some associations publish their proceedings, including the full texts of papers presented, on microfiche. (Papers delivered at the annual American Society for Public Administration conferences are regularly published in this way by University Microfilms.) These can be identified by contacting the organizations concerned, through guides to publications in microform (see chapter 15), or through computerized searches (see chapter 9).

Nonetheless, the best source for determining what is going on in a field, and what are potential dissertation and term-paper topics, remains the library book collection. Chapters 5 and 6 give detailed accounts of how this can be exploited to the full. Browsing through the stacks and even within the library catalog (whether in card or computerized form) can also provide excellent results. This is especially true for the dissertation seeker. A thorough search of the catalog can only be made through use of the formal techniques discussed later.

2. TOPIC DEFINITION AND REFINEMENT

At this point the researcher will have a potential topic that addresses some particular setting, yet has some broader implications. The researcher will have read a good deal about the setting and will have some thoughtful view of broader considerations. This will have been obtained from prior knowledge of the area and reading in and around it, using materials identified through the library catalog and through any other sources used to select the topic. In other words, the researcher has what seems to be a reasonable idea, based on his or her current knowledge of the topic. This perception cannot be stronger than this, for the simple reason that the researcher does not yet know enough about the topic to make a properly informed decision about whether or not it is viable in its present form. Has the question or setting already been addressed adequately by someone else? Are the proposed theoretical and methodological perspectives appropriate? Are there data available to support the kind of questions the researcher intends to ask?

At this stage of the enterprise answers to these questions can only be tentative. A thorough search of the literature has not yet been done. The theoretical implications of the project have not yet been fully explored. The researcher may not yet know the full range of sources that could be used to support the project. For these reasons, the exact nature of the enterprise is not yet fully formed, nor will it be for some time to come. For reasons noted earlier, it will be redefined and reassessed in a process that will continue through the life of the project. It is the beauty and attraction of social research that researchers never know just what they have until the final stage of the project. As everyone who has gone through the process knows, the data acquire a power of their own, and the researcher's analysis of them, if it is of any value, comes to reflect a reality beyond any individual's own influence on it.

Here you are especially concerned with giving some *form* to the subject matter. You need to know not just what you want to study, but also how you should study it. For example, you might be interested in the modernization of the legal system in 19th-century America. Presumably, you will be modest enough or realistic enough to limit your attention to only one of these United States, such as the sovereign state of Nuevo Albion. What do you need to know in order to construct an acceptable research project? An important thing, of course, will be to first determine if the work proposed has ever been done, either for Nuevo Albion or any other state—or, indeed, any other Anglo-American jurisdiction. If it has, then all is by no means lost. One can always build on another's research by testing earlier findings on records of another state or another period; use the records of Nuevo Albion to examine some other proposition; or extend the analysis to investigate the implications of legal modernization on social life in Nuevo Albion or, indeed, the United States as a whole. The point is that if yours is a well-thought-out proposition, based on some interesting area of social concern, you will find a home for it.

However, before you can start to explore the world of social and legal research done on the chosen state, you must have some idea of the kind of research proposed. When one talks of the "modernization" of a legal system, one is talking of a progression from a prebureaucratic to a bureaucratic system of organization, with all that this implies. All students of large-scale organizations appreciate the strength of the bureaucratic system of organization. As a 19th-century phenomenon, it was successful in many settings as a vehicle for transferring power from the partial hands of an aristocratic class to the more democratic, though perhaps more manipulable and certainly more powerful, public institutions. In the instance of the law one could analyze changes of this nature in terms of factors such as the development of an efficient system of published case law ensuring uniform application of established legal principles, a recognized hierarchy of courts, formal and elaborate rules of criminal procedure, a clear system of appellate review, and so on. Any interesting analysis of these factors would surely relate them to such movements as the rise of the middle classes, their related institutions and political power, the urban way of life, and the relative fall of the old landed class and traditional ways of doing things. Such, for better or worse, is modernization.

As a potential student of legal change in Nuevo Albion, you must obviously determine just what research has been done on the legal history of this state in the 19th century. You must also investigate general trends in legal history covering the United States and other countries in the Anglo-American world during this period. Next, movements in power relations between the social classes must be examined. Finally, if the project is a dissertation and not a term paper, you should obtain some assurance that the primary sources exist that can be expected to document the kinds of legal and social changes being examined.

The search is now on several levels. If you are engaged in this project, you will search for different kinds of things at different levels of intensity. You will certainly seek to find everything that has been written on the legal system of Nuevo Albion in the 19th century. This intensive search will, however, come later. We will suppose for now that you have made something of an investigation and that it appears that this aspect of this state's social and legal history has not been adequately explored. An intensive search on this topic will be left for stage three, as will the search for suitable primary sources.

What you are concerned with now is to ensure that you have an adequate grasp of what has gone on in the way of theoretical interpretations of "modernization" in the legal context. You also need to know what social and organizational theories can be applied to the interpretation of the general drift of institutional change that background reading suggests will be uncovered. Here you do not want a comprehensive bibliography on these aspects. You need overviews of theoretical approaches to the historical study of legal institutions and of the emergence of bureaucracies in modern societies. You need sources that provide selective reviews that will both help you understand what approaches can be taken and how they have been applied in actual studies. There are several ways this kind of information can be found, if background reading in the area has not lead to it, as it often does not.

The first involves the identification of *dissertations* in the area. Dissertations usually include a chapter detailing the theoretical model applied; this can be the starting point for exploring interesting approaches and examining the findings of others. Writers of dissertations are expected to demonstrate a thorough familiarity in their chosen areas. This presumed familiarity is not considered as limited to work done in the immediate area of study. Persons working in the area exemplified here would be expected to be acquainted with different approaches taken in similar areas of study, whether this concerned the modernization of the law in an American state in the 19th century or in a West African country in the 20th. They would also be expected to be familiar with other social and political aspects of the processes of modernization and industrialization. Dissertations commonly include a chapter discussing other approaches to the kind of problem specifically addressed and a chapter providing a critical review of the literature of the particular setting of the study. The bibliography generally includes all works of relevance, whether discussed in the text or not.

A few libraries have policies of collecting dissertations from other institutions and catalog them as they catalog other monographs. Other libraries keep dissertations from their own institutions only and house and catalog them in separate collections. However, a number of computerized databases (see chapters 9 and 15) routinely include dissertations. Once identified, dissertations are fairly accessible through interlibrary loan. Methods and sources for carrying out intensive searches for dissertations are discussed elsewhere. At this point it is sufficient to note that there is an abstracting service, *Dissertation Abstracts International*, with a database equivalent (see chapters 9 and 15), that includes lengthy abstracts of most dissertations accepted for doctorates in the United States. However, this source is extremely difficult to search because subject access to it is limited and general searches by method of approach are also unhelpful. Comments on the ways access to this source can be achieved are included in later chapters.

A further way of looking for background material is through *review articles* in journals. Many prestigious journals frequently include articles reviewing developments in a particular field, and these can be found with some difficulty through periodical indexes. Review articles can sometimes be isolated through computerized databases, if the topic is sufficiently narrow. A few databases allow the product of the search to be limited according to whether it is a review article. In this way large computerized systems can yield fairly general information, provided they categorize articles in this way.

A different approach, attractive to someone who has a potential idea but is not sure just how to locate it in the broader world of social research, is represented by the *specialized social science encyclopedia.* These are not intended to offer comprehensive surveys of the topics covered; instead, they provide *selective* reviews of theoretical and research developments. Overviews of a field serve a similar purpose in providing guides to reading on selected topics. At their best, these sources represent authoritative overviews; their focus is generally theoretical; and they can retain their value for years, even decades, after publication. The *International Encyclopedia of the Social Sciences* (see chapter 3 for full annotation), for example, is an 18-volume set that limits itself to coverage of theory in the social sciences. Its several articles addressing interpretations of the functioning (and malfunctioning) of large-scale organizations are thorough and generally at least 10 pages long. They are authoritative, written by acknowledged experts. Appended to them are excellent selected bibliographies of the major works addressing these fields. In sum, they present informed overviews of the major theoretical issues raised and the major research studies that have helped elucidate and perhaps modify these issues.

Sources such as these have a number of important uses. For those concerned with the term paper, they can be the easiest means of determining the *parameters* of a topic: how people have approached it, what problems they have encountered with it, and how the practice of research has helped in the understanding and possible resolution of these problems. Overviews of this nature are clearly of value in selecting a topic. Criteria for a research topic, whatever its level, indicate that it should be manageable in size and involve issues that are identifiable and interesting. A good social sciences encyclopedia can often provide this information fairly painlessly. For the dissertation student, such works have an additional use. As mentioned earlier, one of the hardest tasks in picking a dissertation topic is to find a problematic setting that is promising and that can also be fitted within some existing explanatory structure. Exploration of a research setting without any guiding interpretative framework is like mining for gold without a clear idea of how precious metals are identified when found. Valuable things may be turned up in the diggings, but the miner who cannot separate base minerals from gold or silver or diamonds will be the last to hit pay dirt. An appropriate social sciences encyclopedia can serve as a guide to those existing frameworks that have possibilities for shaping the analysis. Specialized encyclopedias usually provide a range of structural possibilities upon which the choice of a theoretical perspective can reasonably be based. This is important in formulating a well-designed research project.

Use of sources of this nature is, unfortunately, subject to qualification. Not all academic disciplines are equally served in this regard. History and anthropology, for example, do not yet have many worthwhile encyclopedias of the theoretical kind discussed here. However, both these disciplines now rely heavily on theoretical developments elsewhere in the social sciences and are reasonably well covered by the general specialized encyclopedias listed at the beginning of chapter 3. Public administration and its immediate satellites, as this section shows, are also quite well served in this way.

A further concern is the age of the source. Many of the better specialized encyclopedias are now old. This may not matter so much for theory, as many theories that currently attract attention were first developed many decades ago. However, these specialized encyclopedias are naturally guides to research findings, as well as to theory. One cannot discuss theory properly without addressing how it has been applied in actual research settings. In examining older sources, the user should be aware that they may provide good coverage of theory, but give outdated overviews of how these theories have been applied. Moreover, there are areas in which theory itself has changed dramatically in the last decade or two. Someone seeking perspectives on occupational stress would, or should, appreciate that most of the interesting thought on this topic is a product of the last 15 years. The modernization process, the object of our earlier example, began to attract intensified attention from both theoreticians and researchers following the Western world's recent and belated postcolonial concern for the economic development of the Third World. The interest of social historians and others has been one of relatively short duration.

Specialized encyclopedias provide starting points and not definitive statements of the art. The value of the discussion in an older source depends to some extent on the nature of the topic being researched. The newer the field, the more critical one must be of older reviews. This qualification can be overstated. Most fields within the social and policy sciences rely upon a theoretical base that is long-standing. Knowledge of older concepts often provides the researcher with a theoretical overview based upon established, perhaps more reliable, perceptions. In any case, the researcher has the opportunity to update the overview using other sources. The *International Encyclopedia of the Social Sciences* was published in 1968. Its much less ambitious successors, *The Social Science Encyclopedia* (1985) and the *Encyclopedia of Sociology* (1992), record dramatic changes that have taken place in the ways in which more traditional theory is now interpreted.

A more serious reservation about sources of this kind concerns the fact that all are by no means of equal quality. In public administration many encyclopedic works are geared to the policymaker and the practitioner rather than to the academic researcher. Some of them present the potted quasi-academic fix rather than overviews of the issues aimed at the scholarly researcher. Specialized encyclopedias, extremely valuable as they can be, must be evaluated as what they are and what they purport to do. At best they can help researchers at a critical stage in their endeavors; at worst they are just not helpful. Whatever they are, they will never provide more than taking-off points of varying utility to those at the planning stage of a research project.

3. DEFINITION OF THE BIBLIOGRAPHY

Having identified the topic to be addressed, at least provisionally, you will have a good idea of the scope of the project, what you intend to do, and how projected findings can be interpreted within some preliminary theoretical framework. The body of knowledge used to define the topic in this way is based on your awareness of current research on the narrow setting and your understanding of the theoretical implications of the study that is planned.

Your narrowing of the areas of concern is still tentative. It is based on much reading and much thought about what the topic means and what analysis of it could mean in broader social terms. As a potential investigator of legal change in Nuevo Albion, you are concerned about modernization, that is, the process by which a preindustrial society is transformed into a modern one, using traditional definitions of what "modern" means in social and institutional terms. You are particularly interested in how the law is a contributor to this process and have done some reading on how the process has occurred in the United States in the past and how it is occurring in non-Western countries in the present.

You also have a good knowledge of the sources that reflect the legal history of Nuevo Albion. You know how extensive they are: the detail of trial and reported cases and how far back records of them go, the amount of legislation affecting the functioning of the courts, and the detail of the documentation of this legislation and how this is accessible. However, you have not begun to examine any of these primary sources except for the purpose of ascertaining their detail and historical depth. At this stage you have obviously invested a great deal of time in reading and in attempting to focus your ideas. You are not yet completely committed to anything except the idea that you want to use the law to investigate modernization. Your hope is that you can do this using the records of Nuevo Albion. This is, however, a hope and not a certain belief.

You still describe your project using words like "possible," "provisional," and "tentative" until you are assured that your project is a viable one that applies either a new approach to a set of records already studied or a traditional approach to a set of records never studied in quite this way. In other words, there must be a determination that the proposed study is both unique and of interest to academics in the social sciences. A good piece of research, based on a thoughtful and well-informed approach to some data set, almost always adds to understanding. If you are clear about what you want to do, you can usually use the given setting to come up with something worthwhile. If it turns out that the records of Nuevo Albion have been extensively mined, attention can always be turned to one of its sister states.

Things are still flexible at this point. The purpose of this stage in the search strategy is to crystallize a hope into a reality. A search of the literature must be undertaken to ensure that no one has taken quite your approach to your chosen setting. In this search several bibliographies will be sought. Some will be *selective*; at least one will be *comprehensive*. Here you must define the *scope* of your search and the tactics you will use to implement it. In the example described, you will certainly seek to find everything you can on the legal history of Nuevo Albion, and also everything on its social history, at least in the period of its legal and social modernization. You therefore need to develop comprehensive bibliographies in these areas. You also want to gain a more thorough knowledge of how scholars, especially legal scholars, have approached the subject of modernization. However, you do not want to read everything written in this area but will seek only outstanding contributions of this kind. You might also be interested in general trends in how uses of the law have aided social researchers in settings somewhat similar to yours. If so, you will seek a selective bibliography in this area also.

Several searches at several different levels are clearly in order. At the more selective level the researcher will find effective ways to exploit the library book catalog fully. Determination of the existence of recent journal articles of interest will be the next priority. These can be identified through use of those indexes and abstracts (see chapters 8 and 9) covering the major journals in the areas of concern.

For those researching term papers, decisions about what to search probably end here. It only remains to search the limited number of bibliographic tools identified under appropriate headings. However, a comprehensive search on the narrow area of concern requires more. You must identify and search indexes and abstracts covering a broad range of journals in law, history, and the social sciences, together with the various sources covering dissertations, and standard bibliographies in the area. The search could also be extended in other ways.

There are indexes that focus on the less well known journals in public administration and in other fields (see chapter 8 for a full discussion of bibliographic sources of this nature). There are those that focus on management in both the public and the private sectors. Others address narrower areas such as personnel issues, fire protection management, urban affairs, and criminal justice.

More important to many researchers are sources that focus on a particular bibliographic *form*. Many sources do not address any given subject area but instead aim at identifying materials published in a specific way. There are indexes covering a variety of published forms, including newspapers, government documents (separate indexes cover these at the federal, state, and local levels), technical reports funded by federal and other grants, pamphlets, and separately published bibliographies. At this point you must decide what kinds of bibliographies, and at what levels, are needed. Using annotated lists of available indexes and abstracts included in this book and other guides to the literature of particular social science disciplines, you should draw up inventories of indexes to be searched.

The inventory for the selective bibliographies needed will probably be short. Indeed, an appropriate theory or model may have been found through sources of the kind already noted or through general reading. Similarly, a search for contextual or background reading may be limited to current books found through the library catalog and other sources of books published recently and to examination of volumes of a couple of relevant indexes published over the last three or four years. You might also browse through recent issues of appropriate annual reviews just to discover any recent developments or studies of interest.

The search on the narrow object of inquiry will certainly be more extensive. The choice of indexes will be broader, and the search should extend over a longer period of time. For example, articles on the legal system of Nuevo Albion could have been published any time, and there is no known reason why this system should have attracted special attention in any particular period. The *Index to Legal Periodicals* has been published periodically and continuously since 1908 and, for this project, should be searched in its entirety.

Particular forms of publication and the indexes that cover them may well have a particular interest. Research on the enactment of a federal statute calls for identifying congressional hearings on the bill, as well as other elements of its legislative history. The *CIS Index* specializes in providing detailed coverage of all publications emanating from Congress (see chapter 13). In such a project, this service would clearly be given high priority in the list of indexes to be searched. Research involving an important event or public reactions to it should cover articles in newspapers or popular magazines at the time of its occurrence. There are a number of indexes of materials of this kind published in English. Some go back to the 19th century and one or two to the 18th.

Selection of indexes at this level will be done with care and with an appreciation of the nature of the topic and the ways in which materials relating to it are likely to be published. The dissertation student will obviously devote more attention to this part of the endeavor than will the researcher of the term paper. The former is concerned with all bibliographic sources likely to yield information of direct relevance to the topic. The latter usually reviews the available sources selectively. Nonetheless, this difference of approach is largely one of degree—especially given the assumption that the term paper of today can be thought through as a possible scenario for the dissertation of the future.

4. LIMITATION OF THE BIBLIOGRAPHY

No person of discernment should allow the search for secondary sources to dominate the time spent in the research process. Time is a finite entity for all of us, and that spent reading the material found or engaging in research of an original nature is more rewarding than that spent at the library catalog or in the search of indexes. Moreover, there are hundreds of indexing and abstracting services currently being published (chapter 8 includes only a very selective list). At this stage the strategy is to whittle down the length of the search and the number of bibliographic sources used to manageable proportions, while yet ensuring that a thorough job has been done.

The key lies in thinking through the nature of the project and gaining some understanding of how and when information on it is likely to be published. This understanding can be used to limit the list of indexes to be consulted, as well as to expand it. Limiting the scope of the projected bibliography can be done by applying a number of criteria:

Time. Certain topics have attracted attention at specific times. For example, anyone undertaking, a study of court diversion programs would quickly realize that very little research on this subject was conducted before the 1970s. This reflects concerns for the overloading of the criminal justice system that were not as apparent before this decade. There are interesting historical precedents for court diversion. However, unless these precedents are of pressing concern to the study, the researcher would be well advised to limit searching of bibliographic sources to those covering the early 1970s onward. Often the decision as to how far back a search should go will be an intuitive one influenced by background knowledge and the amount of thought that has gone into the decision.

Language and Country. Decisions about whether to concentrate on materials published in English or in a particular group of countries, English-speaking or otherwise, require some consideration. Frequently, such decisions will be based on common sense. Someone researching a particular agency of the U.S. federal government, for example, would exclude indexes that focus on non-English-language journals. Also excluded would be sources such as the *British Humanities Index* that address journals published in the Anglophone world outside of the U.S. unless an overseas viewpoint is important to the perspective of the study. For instance, the person studying court diversion systems might take the tack of examining how the fundamental problem at issue is handled elsewhere in the world.

Form. The previous stage in the search strategy is used to determine which indexes covering specific forms of publication are relevant to the project. This stage is used to *exclude* indexes that either do not seem of value or are duplicated by other sources that will be searched. Weed out unpromising sources ruthlessly at this stage, realizing that the object of this exercise is not to compile an exhaustive list of bibliographic tools. Bibliographic searching is but a means to an end and has no intrinsic value in itself. The object is to compile a list of sources with the greatest potential value for unearthing information relating to the project but one that is short enough to prove manageable in the time schedule allotted to this stage of the enterprise.

5. PREPARING FOR THE SEARCH

At this point you have selected and defined the topic, modified it through preliminary reading, and developed a plan of campaign through a list of indexes, standard bibliographies, and other bibliographic tools rated according to their expected productivity. Now is the moment to reevaluate the thrust of the project briefly, stepping back from it and assessing it critically and with an awareness that you know more about it at this point than at the last time it was assessed. This stage is not, however, just a reflective one. It will probably involve rereading some preliminary material covered to refine existing ideas or to open up new lines of inquiry. It will also involve looking up items in the bibliographies of significant works read and seeing if their findings influence the nature of the proposed study.

Of particular importance are dissertations in related fields. These, identified through the library catalog or through indexes, may help on several levels. First, because a successful dissertation candidate is obliged to demonstrate to his or her committee a thorough knowledge of the research process, dissertations usually provide extensive documentation of methods and sources. Dissertations therefore usually include one or more chapters detailing the theoretical model, hypothesis, or research question. They discuss how their perspectives fit into the general body of theory addressed. They also discuss the methodology by which the proposition is examined or tested, and they describe the sources of primary data used. All this can be of tremendous value to the novice. Even though one may disagree with the theory, methods, or findings of a dissertation, it may nonetheless be helpful. Just seeing how someone else has tackled a similar problem may be a great stimulus to your own creative process. Many a reader has been piqued into creative action in this way. Examining masters' theses and doctoral dissertations in one's area from a fairly well informed perspective can be an excellent way to begin a critique of one's own research plan.

Sources of this nature may be valuable in other ways. Every successful dissertation candidate must demonstrate a familiarity with all significant research findings of relevance to the chosen topic. This familiarity is demonstrated in two ways. The dissertation's bibliography includes citations to all relevant literature, whether or not this is discussed in the text. Second, the dissertation will usually include one or more chapters showing that there is a problem to be addressed and will review earlier published research in order to make the point that the dissertation attempts to fill some gap or to address some problematic area revealed in the literature. This "review of the literature" section of an existing dissertation, as noted earlier, can be an absolute bonanza, both as a source of bibliography and as a critical guide to the literature of an area. Before embarking on the literature-searching process proper, the student is therefore well advised to assess his or her project once again in the light of the kind of reading and thinking recommended here. Only then should examination of the selected bibliographic sources, the written form of the search strategy, be put into effect.

6. THE SEARCH IN PRACTICE

This stage embodies the legwork of the operation: the systematic searching of bibliographic sources considered appropriate, the identification of relevant items, and their location in the university library or their access through interlibrary loan. When these materials have been read and assessed in terms of their value to the project, something approaching a final bibliography can be prepared.

Although this process sounds mechanical, it is not. Reading new material and deciding whether to incorporate its findings into the study in some way are not limited to the initial stages of a project but continue throughout the life of the enterprise. Conducting original research and at the same time continuing to read new and related material naturally go hand in hand. One's interpretation of what is going on in the research is continually affected by this reading and by the better-informed reflective processes that go with it. Once analysis of original data has begun, options regarding the direction of the research become more limited the further the research progresses. Nonetheless, the process of continually rethinking the project proceeds through all stages of the project, and the final product of the research can be influenced substantially as a result. The cost of failure to conduct periodic audits of one's current research activities can be high and can be paid in the wasted time of misdirected and extraneous activity.

The most radical refinement of a project is best done at the earlier stages in the project. Ideally this is when secondary sources are being identified and examined. This is why the legwork of the project is so important and why its intellectual component is so necessary. This stage, more than any other, involves a process of *continuous feedback*. Materials are identified, located, and read. Their findings are then incorporated into some slightly new version of the project, and, if they are dramatic enough, they influence the production of a revised project and a new search strategy.

7. SEARCH STRATEGY AND THE COMPUTERIZED BIBLIOGRAPHIC SEARCH

Once you have exhausted conventional bibliographic tools and the works identified from them have been read critically, a computerized bibliographic search (CBS) should be conducted. This, as chapter 9 shows in some detail, provides the means of identifying electronically further material on the narrow subject of concern. The computerized search is the final step in preparing the closest you will come to a comprehensive bibliography on your topic.

A computerized search is not usually conducted on general areas of interest. The databases accessed in these searches are so large and their products so unselective that they cannot be useful as critical guides to theory or method. Unlike humans, computers have no judgment and cannot separate wheat from chaff. The wise researcher seeks such information largely by the other means discussed earlier. There are exceptions that prove any rule. Someone who has fixed upon some fairly obscure social theory or psychological test might reasonably wish to know who else has invoked this particular concept. In such a case, a computerized search would be in order. Except in such instances, however, the qualifications stated here apply.

If it is accepted that probably the only computerized search someone wishes to do will be on the narrow research setting (such as the legal system of Nuevo Albion), an immediate question is raised. Why, one might ask, should someone wait until this point to have the literature searched by computer? Why should the researcher spend many laborious hours wading through volumes of *Sociological Abstracts*, the *Current Law Index*, and their like when the job can be done in minutes by electronic means? The answer to such questions is simple. It is not until you have made a thorough literature search and read the products extensively that you really know that the narrow topic chosen is your final one. You might well have retained your interest in modernization and the law but have decided along the way that Nuevo Albion is not the appropriate setting.

Perhaps the legal history of this state has already been thoroughly examined. Perhaps its early records are scanty and not amenable to the kind of research proposed. Perhaps a more promising setting has been identified and its records are easily accessible on microfilm. Dramatic changes of this kind in research venue are not at all uncommon. A good knowledge of modernization theory may have been linked to a setting of convenience. The fact that you live in Nuevo Albion and perhaps in close proximity to its court archives does not mean that this is necessarily the best setting for your study. Definition of the final topic is informed by knowledge as well as considerations of interest and convenience.

If a computerized search had been conducted at the outset, the researcher would have been denied perceptions of this kind. The search would probably have been ill conceived and ultimately of little value. The principal characteristic of computerized searches is that they can only be done on very narrow topics, usually those involving linkages of two or more variables (in this case, "Nuevo Albion" combined with descriptors relating to the law and perhaps to a particular historical period). Computerized searches cannot be used as fishing expeditions. Databases, which can include millions of citations, are too large. Expansive searches are costly and turn up unmanageable numbers of citations. Computerized searches are effectively used by those who know exactly what they want. Unless you have a very good understanding of the literature, you cannot possibly know that the setting chosen is the ideal one or even if it is a viable one. Such an understanding is provided by earlier stages in the search strategy. It is usually only when this understanding has been achieved that a computerized search is appropriate.

8. SEARCH STRATEGY AND THE DISSERTATION

So far, pride of place has been given to the needs of those preparing for the kind of original research project required for a dissertation. However, these needs are different from those engaged in lesser projects in a matter of degree, rather than in kind. Writers of term papers and dissertation researchers have at many levels similar interests in determining effective means for literature searching. The former will presumably design and apply these means less rigorously than will the latter. Of course, this is not to say that the objectives of the two are the same. Far from it. The former prepares for a project that may reflect original thinking but that will usually be based only on secondary sources. The latter prepares a research project of an original and unique nature, and the compilation of a comprehensive bibliography on the narrow topic of concern is certainly an important concern. But the compelling concern lies in other areas. The main problem encountered here is to develop a fine and manageable research project that will illuminate some larger area of social endeavor. Thus attention is given to ways in which suitable theoretical frameworks can be identified without requiring a mastery of new areas of theoretical concern in their entirety.

Apart from this, the dissertation student has other obstacles to face and must identify a research *setting*, that is, a body of primary data that is amenable to the kind of research proposed. such a body of data can consist of published records of agencies, manuscripts, legal materials, newspapers, or, indeed, any other kind of source that is collected by an organization or individual in the normal course of business, or that otherwise naturally documents a particular event, activity, agency, or individual. These data may be printed, in manuscript, on microfilm, or in some machine-readable form. The researcher may "create" this setting in the shape of the results of survey research, psychological testing, or of direct observation. Once obtained, the database is subject to analysis through the application of a variety of qualitative or quantitative techniques, selected by researchers according to their skills and, above all, to the demands of the project.

The dissertation researcher must think in several dimensions at every stage in the search strategy. It is not sufficient to concentrate attention on the particular topic of interest and its theoretical dimensions. The researcher must also give continual attention to the sources to be used to extract the data and the methods by which these data are to be analyzed. The search strategy must be expanded to take these important considerations into account. A brilliant research concept is limited in value if its originator can find no practical setting for its examination. Translating an abstract idea into an explicit research plan is a very difficult thing to do in itself. Moreover, most graduate students are ill prepared for it since their methods courses tend to stress the learning of statistical skills and provide little instruction in research design. Regardless of this, the ability to plan a research project from a practical and methodological point of view, as well as a theoretical standpoint, is essential. If this ability is lacking, there will be no dissertation. No precise rules for doing this can be given, as there is no cookbook that includes recipes for creativity. There are, however, many useful hints that, if followed, can at least ease the burden of this very difficult essence of the research task.

The student must get into the habit of reading published studies with an eye to their methods and sources. All graduate students are trained to read critically for theory and findings; those preparing a dissertation must learn to combine these two perspectives—and very different perspectives they are, too. A study undistinguished in its contribution to the understanding of a field may be tremendously valuable if it provides the reader with a new approach to a problem or an improved knowledge of the kinds of data that can be used to examine it. The earlier in the student's graduate career this facility is learned, the better. Here is yet one more reason why the self-protective graduate student will begin thinking about future dissertation topics at the very beginning of his or her coursework. Earlier in this chapter, reference was made to the importance of looking at other dissertations in one's field. As guides to approaches to research, sources of this nature should never be overlooked. Even a poorly articulated dissertation may be of inestimable value in guiding the reader to a particular survey instrument, testing device, or group of statistical techniques. A historical dissertation will almost certainly include a discussion of the nature and value of the records used. Other dissertations based on groups of existing records, statistics, or other data will do the same. There is nothing wrong with using other people's work for insights of this nature, although proper credit should, of course, always be given. The research process is one of building upon, perhaps modifying, work that has gone before. No points are awarded for the reinventing the wheel.

A further way of helping oneself in this regard is to adopt the standard practice of thinking a project through by imagining what kinds of data could reasonably be used in its analysis and then attempting to determine whether such data actually exist. Such a practice will improve the quality of the student's term papers, as well as being excellent preparation for the development of a viable dissertation topic.

Many published sources provide extensive coverage of compilations of primary data. Later chapters point to sources of statistical and other primary data available in various forms. Chapter 13 identifies government documents that may qualify as primary sources and can be used as the raw material for original research. Primary sources in the form of published government documents include reports of court cases, hearings and reports of legislative committees, annual reports of agencies, and a variety of other records published by governmental bodies in the normal course of their business. The forms and use of other types of primary sources are discussed in chapters 11 through 16.

There is a widespread, but mistaken, belief among graduate students that collecting one's own data is an integral part of the research process and one essential to the successful dissertation. An indicator of the strength of this belief is the very high proportion of dissertations based on analysis of the results of surveys by questionnaire. In fact, no one cares where and how the data are obtained as long as they are adequate for the purpose. Using existing data collections is quite in order. Indeed, most of the better dissertations are produced by students who use such collections because they have chosen, in effect, to concentrate their effort in the analysis and interpretation of the data, rather than in the time-consuming process of collecting it. People producing quantitative studies are attracted to this approach partly because they gain access to far larger samples than they could collect themselves and partly because the ease of access to the data allows them to spend their time in developing sophisticated techniques for their analysis.

It is quite permissible to use data collected by other scholars for research purposes providing that the provenance of the data is properly acknowledged.

Many scholars now send their raw data to various clearinghouses once they have finished using them so that they can be analyzed by others in some new ways. Since these data sets are usually computerized and are often supported by codebooks and computer programs, they are attractive to those who cannot spare the many months needed to collect, code, and computerize their own data. Chapter 12 discusses data sets of this kind.

Before ending this formal discussion of the search strategy, a couple of important qualifications must be made. The student, especially the term-paper student, must take steps to avoid the "blind-alley" outcome. One usually ends up with a much narrower topic than anticipated, having underestimated the scope of the project and overestimated the volume of material deemed manageable. This is quite normal. Dissertation students usually experience a more dramatic narrowing of their topics than do writers of term papers, but the phenomenon is common to both. It sometimes happens, however, that the reverse occurs and that even the most conscientious literature search fails to yield much information. This is not a particularly serious problem for a dissertation. It simply means that the researcher is truly about to set foot on untrodden ground. It does mean that he or she will have to broaden his or her reading and modify the search strategy in order to ensure that the topic is defined within an appropriate situational perspective. For example, someone who somehow knows exactly how to gather the relevant primary data for a study of decision making in the health-care system of present-day Iran would not be surprised to find a certain lack of secondary resources addressing this issue. He or she would, however, presumably have a thesis regarding this that in some way relates to factors such as the expectations and responsibilities of the new Iranian state, its attitudes toward resource allocation, or some other larger issue. Secondary reading would then focus on these and other areas.

A term-paper student addressing this topic would probably be in an impossible situation and would probably land in the position of having done a lengthy search of the literature to no avail. It would, however, be a position that should have been avoided. Reflecting upon and reevaluating the topic are activities that have been discussed as essential at each point in the search strategy. If this had been done, the topic would surely have been revised at an early stage in the game. Application of common sense as well as preliminary knowledge can also help avoid this scenario.

A second, related point concerns the desirability of always working with a topic that is inherently *flexible*. The usual way to do this is to carry two topics in mind: the narrow one of choice, and a rather broader version of it. For instance, someone interested in the development of economic planning in Jamaica might also consider addressing this topic in the context of some larger entity, perhaps the English-speaking Caribbean as a whole. If the first choice proves too narrow, the second may fit the bill. At the same time, a researcher might also consider such related issues as the development of state responsibility in the economic sphere, again, in the country of choice in some larger geographical setting. A topic that proves too broad can usually be pared down to manageable size in some obvious way; it is much harder to expand one that proves too narrow.

One final comment on all this: As has been suggested, the idea of the comprehensive bibliography is one that generally only applies in dissertation research (and other original research endeavors) and only in certain aspects of such research. Most people never want more than a selective bibliography of the outstanding works addressing an area. If a particular event or very limited setting is the focus of the work, then perhaps the researcher should try to uncover everything relating to it. The search for theoretical issues or approaches intended to locate the object of study within some social context will almost certainly be a selective one. Search strategies should be developed and implemented with this factor constantly in mind.

NOTES

1. Sorokin, Pitirim A. (1974). How Are Sociological Theories Conceived and Validated? In Denisoff, R. Serge, Callahan, Orel, & Levine, Mark H. (Eds.), *Theories and Paradigms in Contemporary Sociology* (pp. 84–93). Itasca, IL: Peacock, at p. 92.

2. As they are not usually subject to peer review before presentation, the findings of these papers must be assessed more critically than usual. It is the publishing process that generally provides quality control through formal review. However, as sources of topical approaches they are unaffected by this limitation.

3

OVERVIEWS OF THEORY AND CURRENT DEVELOPMENTS[1]

This chapter covers specialized encyclopedias and handbooks, literature surveys, and annual reviews addressing theoretical disciplines. Those concerned with applied areas are considered in the next chapter. For the sake of convenience, annual reviews, an important resource for the theoretician as well as the practitioner, are also discussed in chapter 4 and are cited in appendix 1.

Listings are necessarily selective. The much-referred-to promiscuity of public administration, in regard to its perspectives and theoretical links, ensures that its body cannot be captured within any single group of works. Wise researchers will note in chapter 4 the bibliographic guides that relate most closely to their interests. All should become aware of the following works, which together constitute the most important bibliographic group in the literature of the social sciences. The relative importance of these guides to the public administration researcher is indicated in the annotations.

Daniells, Lorna M. (1985). *Business Information Sources* (rev. ed.). Berkeley, CA: University of California Press. 673 p.

Excellent for its coverage of bibliographic approaches to administration in the private sector. Includes valuable guides to the major works in the field. Important, indeed indispensable, for anyone with a concern for administrative theory in any of its contexts.

Holler, Frederick L. (1986). *Information Sources of Political Science* (4th ed.). Santa Barbara, CA: ABC–Clio. 417 p.

One chapter deals explicitly with the literature of public administration. Others address comparative organizations, political theory, and American politics and public law. Excellent for its general coverage, but limited in the attention given to administration and its many public and private-sector linkages.

Li, Tze–Chung. (1990). *Social Science Reference Sources: A Practical Guide* (2nd ed.). Westport, CT: Greenwood. 590 p.

A more selective guide than Webb, (below) and lacking its discussion of the major works in each of the disciplines covered. Notable as the most current reference source of its kind.

Sheehy, Eugene P., et al. (1986). *Guide to Reference Books* (10th ed.). Chicago: American Library Association. 1,560 p.

The standard guide published in the United States to reference books. Annotations are, like those in the two works cited below, critical and informed. Updated by supplements and by a column regularly published in the periodical *College and Research Libraries*. A supplement covering the years 1985 through 1990 was published in 1992.

Walford, A. J., et al. (1989–91). *Walford's Guide to Reference Material* (5th ed.). London: The Library Association. 3 vols.

The British counterpart to Sheehy. Volume 2 addresses "Social and Historical Sciences, Philosophy, and Religion." Overlaps with Sheehy to a great extent, but interesting differences make neither one of them the replacement of the other.

Webb, William H., et al. (1986). *Sources of Information in the Social Sciences: A Guide to the Literature* (3rd ed.). Chicago: American Library Association. 777 p.

The principal single reference work in the bibliography of the social sciences. Covers many more sources than do Sheehy and Walford. In addition, discusses major works in the disciplines it covers and is therefore a review of the literature, as well as a bibliographic guide. An indispensable resource for any serious student in the social sciences. Should certainly be used to offset the many limitations of the work you have in hand.

Because the social sciences represent a group of interrelated and often-inseparable concerns and because similar theories are often invoked by different disciplines and applied in different contexts, researchers should combine their use of specialized encyclopedic sources with discussions offered by more general sources. This approach can be the beginning of a truly interdisciplinary venture.

Some confusion occasionally arises in discussion of which sources should be designated as "encyclopedias" and which "handbooks." Traditionally, the first term has denoted an extensive, multivolume work and the latter a one-volume compilation of short discussions. In fact, this distinction has long since eroded. There are short "encyclopedias" and extensive "handbooks." No useful distinction can now be made between the two.

The lists that follow are selective, including only sources that either take sustained theoretical approaches of interest to those concerned with the study of large-scale organizations, or that are otherwise of direct relevance to the study of public administration. For this reason, the sources noted in each section reflect only a fraction of those available in the disciplines covered. The main criterion for inclusion is therefore *theoretical concern*. Practitioner-oriented works are largely considered in chapter 4 as are those in areas (such as social work) that are largely applied in their focus. Public administration being what it is, a few less-than-scholarly works are necessarily cited here. Not all works are equal in quality, as demonstrated by the titles or annotations of works cited. When appropriate, dictionaries, as guides to specialized terms peculiar to a field, are listed at the end of each section.

1. GENERAL SOCIAL SCIENCE ENCYCLOPEDIAS

Deutsch, Karl W., Markovits, Andrei S., & Platt, John (Eds.). (1986). *Advances in the Social Sciences, 1900–1980: What, Who, Where, How?* Lanham, MD: University Press of America. 460 p.

A collection of seventeen essays addressing broad developments common to all the social sciences. The biggest focus is on methodology, but sociology, political science, and economics are singled out for special attention. Not intended as a reference work, but especially valuable when used in this way.

Encyclopaedia of the Social Sciences. (1930–35). New York: Macmillan. 15 vols.

The predecessor of the *International Encyclopedia of the Social Sciences* (below). Still valuable for the depth of its coverage, its historical perspective, and its provision of alternative approaches. No subject index.

Handwörterbuch der Sozialwissenschaften. (1952–65). Stuttgart: Gustav Fischer. 12 vols.

Probably the most extensive work of this kind published in a language other than English. Presents a different perspective on the social sciences and connections within them from other sources discussed here.

Handwörterbuch der Wirtschaftswissenschaften. (1976–83). Stuttgart: Gustav Fischer. 9 vols.

The successor to the previous item. Defines its subject matter more narrowly than its predecessor and addresses political economy, rather than the social sciences in general.

International Encyclopedia of the Social Sciences. (1968). New York: Macmillan and Free Press. 19 vols.

The most comprehensive source of its kind, with long articles prepared by experts. Since its major emphasis is on the historical and developmental aspects of the social sciences, as these are broadly defined, it has not lost its relevance as a basic source for orientation to the general area. Has a one-volume subject index, a biographical supplement (1979), and a dictionary of quotations (1991).

Kuper, Adam, & Kuper, Jessica (Eds.). (1985). *The Social Science Encyclopedia.* Boston: Routledge & Kegan Paul. 916 p.

Not quite as ambitious as its illustrious forebears, but nonetheless a major source of current discussion. Intended for a sophisticated readership. Most valuable when used to update information given in other sources noted here. The principal author is an anthropologist, and this perspective is reflected in the text.

Gould, Julius, & Kolb, William L. (Eds.). (1964). *A Dictionary of the Social Sciences.* New York: Free Press. 761 p.

More of a concise encyclopedia than a dictionary. Explanations are clear and extend to one page or more. Also includes short bibliographies. By far the best source of its kind.

2. SPECIALIZED ENCYCLOPEDIAS

2.1. Public Administration

Auerbach, Alan J., & Feldstein, Martin (Eds.). (1985–87). *Handbook of Public Economics.* Amsterdam: Elsevier. 2 vols.

Individual essays address a field defined to include public finance and aspects of public planning and accounting.

Caiden, Gerald E., & Alexander, Herbert E. (Eds.). (1983). *American Public Administration: A Bibliographical Guide to the Literature.* New York: Garland. 201 p.

Primarily a guide to sources, but does include discussion of trends and developments within the field and relates these to specific works and patterns of publication.

Coleman, James R., & Dugan, Robert E. (1990). *Public Administration Desk Book.* Newton, MA: Government Research Publications. 270 p.

An annotated list of sources arranged in seven parts according to form of publication. More suitable for the practitioner, but includes some discussion of information-finding techniques.

DeSario, Jack P. & Bolotin, Fredric N. (Eds.). (1989). *International Public Policy Sourcebook.* Westport, CT: Greenwood. 2 vols.

Presents descriptive accounts of arrangements surrounding a limited number of policy areas in eight Western countries. Considered are health, social welfare, education, and the environment.

Dunn, William N. & Kelly, Rita M. (Eds.). (1992). *Advances in Policy Studies Since 1950.* New Brunswick, NJ: Transaction. 542 p.

Sixteen chapters are grouped within five sections, each addressing policy studies in one context: political science; multidisciplinary approaches; normative theory; policy utilization; future developments. A volume of the *Policy Studies Review Annual* and one of several issues with a distinctive focus and title.

Loewenberg, Gerhard, Patterson, Samuel C., & Jewell, Malcolm E. (Eds.). (1985). *Handbook of Legislative Research.* Cambridge: Harvard University Press. 810 p.

Presents "extensive bibliographical essays, offering disinterested surveys of the principal subfields of legislative research." Approaches generally assess recent studies in the light of a variety of theoretical perspectives from several disciplines. Probably the best starting point for research in this subject.

Marshall, Marion B. (1987). *Public Finance: An Information Sourcebook.* Phoenix, AZ: Oryx. 287 p.

A bibliography of works, primarily those published in the 1980s. Arranged by topic and with short annotations. Not at its best in covering theoretical or analytical works.

Martin, Daniel W. (1989). *The Guide to the Foundations of Public Administration.* New York: Marcel Dekker. 454 p.

Examines theory in the field through discussion of the major literature. Includes bibliographies listed within 19 chapters. Annotations are very informative. This book has been widely acclaimed as the closest thing to an intellectual history of the field, presented through selective examination of its benchmark works.

Mosher, Frederick C. (Ed.). (1976). *Basic Documents of American Public Administration, 1776–1950.* New York: Holmes & Meier. 225 p.

Presents the texts (usually excerpts) of classic works in the field. Each is preceded by a short discussion of the context of the work. Very valuable as a survey of the area through its classic literature. Extended by Stillman (below).

Nagel, Stuart S. (Ed.). (1983). *Encyclopedia of Policy Studies.* New York: Dekker. 914 p.

A collection of articles that analyze the basic issues in the field of policy studies. The editor defines policy studies as the study of the nature, causes, and effects of alternative public policies for dealing with specific social problems. Specific areas of discussion include criminal justice, health, environmental protection, labor, and education. Conceptual stages, analysis of policy formation, and implementation are also discussed. Discussion is general, but the focus is on the public sector.

Nagel, Stuart S. (Ed.). (1980). *The Policy-Studies Handbook.* Lexington, MA: Lexington Books. 221 p.

Includes many references to case studies and is in this sense a useful guide to research. Limited in its consideration of appropriate methods and now dated.

Nagel, Stuart S. (Ed.). (1984-88). *Public Policy Studies: A Multi-Volume Treatise.* Greenwich, CT: JAI Press. 10 vols.

Each volume is a collection of essays addressing some particular aspect of this subject. The following ten aspects of public policy are addressed: social institutions, policy formulation, policy implementation, environmental issues, political institutions, perspectives and concepts, state and local issues, international concerns, reform, and economic institutions.

Perry, James L. (Ed.). (1989). *Handbook of Public Administration.* San Francisco: Jossey–Bass. 660 p.

A collection of 43 essays arranged under eight broad headings: "Public Administration in a New Era", "Effective Administrative and Organizational Systems," "Strengthening Relationships with Legislatures, Elected and Appointed Officials, and Citizens," "Establishing Successful Policies and Programs," "Effective Budgeting and Fiscal Administration," "Managing Human Resources," "Improving Operations and Services," and "The Professional Practice of Public Administration." As these section headings suggest, this work is directed at the practitioner rather than the scholar. It is nonetheless very valuable, as most of the essays do address theoretical issues when these are relevant.

Rabin, Jack, Hildreth, W. Bartley, & Miller, Gerald J. (Eds.) (1988). *Handbook of Public Administration.* New York: Dekker. 1,095 p.

The first real encyclopedia of public administration, this volume is set up to organize and summarize the relevant literature that has accumulated in the field. The handbook is arranged in 13 subfields, such as public budgeting and financial management, decision making, public law and regulation, judicial administration, public economy, public personnel administration, and labor relations. Each section contains two bibliographic essays by a different author. The first traces the history of the subfield's ideas and theories; the second analyzes emerging ideas and issues of the topic relevant to current policies and programs. Over the course of the book, the full picture of organization theory and public administration emerges. There is a detailed index, and each essay includes an extensive bibliography.

Rabin, Jack, Miller, Gerald J., & Hildreth, W. Bartley (Eds.). (1989). *Handbook of Strategic Management.* New York: Dekker. 457 p.

Intended "to provide broad-based bibliographic essays concerning strategic management . . . [bringing] together in one forum literature from the private and public sectors."

Rouse, John E. (Ed.). (1980). *Public Administration in American Society: A Guide to Information Sources.* Detroit: Gale. 553 p.

An annotated bibliography, not an encyclopedia, but included here for its wealth of citations and relevance of its subject-matter.

Rowat, Donald C. (Ed.) (1988) *Public Administration in Developed Democracies; A Comparative Study.* New York: Dekker. 493 p.

Presents essays, with long bibliographies, describing the admnistrative structures of twenty Western countries. Also includes several essays analyzing common trends.

Stillman, Richard J. (Ed.). (1982). *Basic Documents of American Public Administration since 1950.* New York: Holmes & Meier. 311 p.

A continuation of Mosher (above).

Subramaniam, V. (Ed.). (1990). *Public Administration in the Third World: An International Handbook.* Westport, CT: Greenwood. 447 p.

Presents essays grouped within five geographical areas: Asia, the Middle East, North Africa, sub-Saharan Africa, and the West Indies. Discussions are historical, but more descriptive than analytical.

Chandler, Ralph C., & Plano, Jack C. (1988). *The Public Administration Dictionary* (2nd ed.). Santa Barbara, CA: ABC–Clio. 430 p.

Definitions are grouped around major themes that reflect both the theory and the practice of the field.

Fry, Gerald M., & Martin, Galen R. (1991). *The International Development Dictionary*. Santa Barbara, CA: ABC–Clio. 445 p.

An excellent source that organizes its definitions in four sections, relating to people, basic concepts, analytical concepts, and movements and organizations.

Kruschke, Earl R., & Jackson, Byron M. (1987). *The Public Policy Dictionary*. Santa Barbara, CA: ABC–Clio. 159 p.

Over 200 terms are discussed within five thematic chapters.

Shafritz, Jay M. (1986). *The Facts on File Dictionary of Public Administration*. New York: Facts on File. 610 p.

Provides short definitions of current terms. Especially useful for identification of legal citations to prominent cases and statutes.

2.2. Business and Management

Altman, Edward I., & McKinney, Mary J. (Eds.). (1987). *Handbook of Financial Markets and Institutions*. New York: Wiley. 1,197 p.

Long chapters document the many recent changes in banking and elsewhere in the financial world. The best source of its kind.

Balachandran, Sarojini. (1987). *Decision Making: An Information Sourcebook*. Phoenix, AZ: Oryx. 208 p.

A comprehensive bibliography grouped into four main areas: methodology, applications, decision aids, and quantitative techniques. Cites government documents and dissertations as well as books and articles.

Baughn, William H., Storrs, Thomas I. & Walker, Charls E. (Eds.). (1988). *The Bankers' Handbook* (3rd ed.). Homewood, IL: Dow Jones–Irwin. 1,347 p.

The most comprehensive one-volume guide to this area. Includes over 80 substantial essays, grouped within broad sections.

Bittel, Lester R., & Ramsey, Jackson E. (Eds.). (1985). *Handbook for Professional Managers*. New York: McGraw–Hill. 1,000 p.

Practitioner-oriented, but its articles are substantive and occasionally theoretical in orientation. Prepared by experts in each field. Has good bibliographies.

Brady, George S. & Clauser, Henry R. (Eds.). (1986). *Materials Handbook: An Encyclopedia For Managers, Technical Professionals, Purchasing and Production Managers, Technicians, Supervisors, and Foremen* (12th ed.). New York: McGraw–Hill. 1,038 p.

The latest edition of the outstanding handbook intended for those involved in the organizational purchase of materials.

Connors, Tracy D. (Ed.). (1988). *The Nonprofit Organization Handbook* (2nd ed.). New York: McGraw–Hill. 740 p.

Essays address all aspects of management in nonprofit organizations in the private sector.

Fallon, William K. (Ed.). (1983). *AMA Management Handbook* (2nd ed.). New York: American Management Association. 1,586 p.

Extensive in scope, this book must be regarded as a basic reference source for many aspects of the management of corporations and small businesses. General topics include management of research and technology, marketing, risk and insurance management, employee benefits, public relations, information systems, and administrative services. There are over 200 short essays in this thoughtful, though concise, work. Useful for scholars as well as practitioners.

Finch, Frank (Ed.). (1985). *The Facts on File Encyclopedia of Management Techniques* (rev. ed.). New York: Facts on File. 323 p.

A rather limited source better used as a dictionary than as an encyclopedia. Rather superficial in its scope.

Frederiksen, Lee W. (Ed.). (1982). *Handbook of Organizational Behavior Management*. New York: Wiley. 604 p.

A good overview of the new management approach, OBM, which brings new means of assessing the human factor in organizational behavior. Includes a section discussing the application of OBM to particular organizational problems.

Goldhaber, Gerald M., & Barnett, George A. (Eds.). (1988). *Handbook of Organizational Communication*. Norwood, NJ: Ablex. 502 p.

Basically a guide to the practical applications of applied psychology in this area. Has little concern for relationships between organizational structure and means of communication.

Heyel, Carl (Ed.). (1982). *The Encyclopedia of Management* (3rd ed.). New York: Van Nostrand Reinhold. 1,371 p.

A competitor to Bittel and Ramsey, Fallon, and others as a general guide to management theory. The articles range from a few paragraphs to over 30 pages in length and are enhanced by excellent bibliographies and cross-references. Each article contains background material designed to brief the reader on the essential theories and outlines the major research already done in the field.

Mali, Paul (Ed.). (1981). *Management Handbook: Operating Guidelines, Techniques, and Practices*. New York: Wiley. 1,522 p.

Intended for both professional managers and academics. The 67 chapters included are lengthy and address theoretical as well as practical concerns. Probably the best of the one-volume handbooks in this field.

Meltzer, H., & Nord, Walter R. (Eds.). (1981). *Making Organizations Humane and Productive: A Handbook for Practitioners*. New York: Wiley. 510 p.

Useful for its applications of theory in the form of case studies.

Minor, Robert S., & Fetridge, Clark W. (Eds.). (1984). *The Dartnell Office Administration Handbook* (6th ed.). Chicago: Dartnell. 974 p.

A convenient guide to all aspects of administration in the office setting, including the physical and technological setting.

Schmalensee, Richard, & Willig, Robert D. (Eds.). (1989). *Handbook of Industrial Organization*. New York: Elsevier. 2 vols.

A source of broad scope addressing most aspects of economics, behavior, and management. Many of the essays give considerable attention to the influence of public policy concerns of this organizational environment.

Stessin, Lawrence, & Heyel, Carl (Eds.). (1984). *The Encyclopedia of Managerial Performance Appraisal*. New York: Business Research Publications. 277 p.

A guide to practical, and often informal, evaluation techniques. Of limited value to the researcher.

Walter, Ingo, & Murray, Tracy (Eds.). (1988). *Handbook of International Management*. New York: Wiley. 1 vol., various pagings.

This sourcebook presents a thorough overview of all managerial issues confronting firms doing business internationally. Topics emphasize labor relations, organizational design, and variations in governmental structure.

Banki, Ivan S. (1986). *Dictionary of Administration and Management: Authoritative, Comprehensive*. Los Angeles: Systems Research. 1,369 p.

By far the most extensive dictionary of its kind.

Rosenberg, Jerry M. (1983). *Dictionary of Business and Management* (2nd ed.). New York: Wiley. 631 p.

Gives brief definitions of a large number of terms. One of the best of the many dictionaries of its kind.

2.3. Political Science

Andrews, William G. (Ed.). (1982). *International Handbook of Political Science.* Westport, CT: Greenwood. 464 p.

Quite lengthy articles explore the development of research in political science in some 30 countries since 1945. Other essays explore international developments in the discipline.

Bogdanor, Vernon (Ed.). (1987). *The Blackwell Encyclopaedia of Political Institutions.* Oxford, UK: Blackwell. 667 p.

Gives overviews of the central ideas in the study of political organization in modern societies. Articles are short (rarely more than one page), but meaty, and present up-to-date bibliographies. Intended as a companion to Miller 1987 (see below).

Buhle, Mari J., Buhle, Paul, & Georgakas, Dan (Eds.). (1990). *Encyclopedia of the American Left.* New York: Garland. 928 p.

An extensive compilation of short articles, all of which seem authoritative and based on current sources. Most useful for its historical perspective.

Cook, Chris, Kirk, Tim, & Moore, Bob. (1933–92). *Sources in European Political History.* New York: Facts on File. 3 vols.

Constituent volumes are entitled "The European Left," "Diplomacy and International Affairs," and "War and Resistance." Important for its indications of the existence of personal papers and other primary material relating to the events documented.

DeConde, Alexander (Ed.). (1978). *Encyclopedia of American Foreign Policy: Studies of the Principal Movements and Ideas.* New York: Scribner. 3 vols.

Long articles address ideas and principles, rather than events. The standard work in this area.

DeLancey, Mark W. (Ed.). *Handbook of Political Science Research on Sub-Saharan Africa: Trends from the 1960s to the 1990s.* Westport, CT: Greenwood. 427 p.

A collection of review and bibliographic essays, most of which have a regional focus.

Dent, David W. (Ed.). (1990). *Handbook of Political Science Research on Latin America: Trends from the 1960s to the 1990s.* Westport, CT: Greenwood. 448 p.

Includes 17 bibliographic essays, each of which presents a critique of the research literature addressing a single region or country. The essays are thorough and their bibliographies extensive.

Greene, Jack P. (Ed.). (1984). *Encyclopedia of American Political History: Studies of the Principal Movements and Ideas.* New York: Scribner. 3 vols.

Extensive articles (10 pages or more) on all aspects of political thinking in the U.S. since the 17th century. Emphasis is on ideas rather than events, although the latter are explained in context. Because its subject matter is expanded to include social aspects of political life, this work is important for researchers outside this immediate discipline.

Greenstein, Fred I., & Polsby, Nelson W. (Eds.). (1975). *Handbook of Political Science.* Reading, MA: Addison–Wesley. 9 vols.

Individual volumes address the scope of political theory, micro- and macropolitical theory, political processes inside and outside the context of governmental institutions, policy-making, and methods of inquiry. Lengthy articles, extensive bibliographies, and a one-volume index. The most important encyclopedic work in the discipline, and a major one in the social sciences.

The Greenwood Encyclopedia of American Political Institutions. (1977–). Westport, CT: Greenwood. Irregular.

Each of the 10 volumes published so far in this series presents detailed consideration of some organizational aspect of American life. *Government Agencies,* for example, includes over 100 signed articles discussing the organizational and political development of selected federal agencies. Other volumes include *Foundations, Fraternal Organizations, Labor Unions, Political Parties, Social Service Organizations, Farmers Organizations, Private Colleges, Public Colleges, and Research Institutions.*

Hawkesworth, Mary, & Kogan, Maurice. (Eds.). (1992). *Encyclopedia of Government and Politics.* London: Routledge. 2 vols.

An important and ambitious work presenting a series of analytical and theoretical discussions on all aspects of the political process. The 84 essays are lengthy and are grouped within 10 broad categories (one of which is "Policy Making and Policies"). A major source for the theoretician.

Katz, Alan N. (Ed.). (1986). *Legal Traditions and Systems: An International Handbook.* Westport, CT: Greenwood. 450 p.

Included here because its essays, written by political scientists, are concerned with the ideas expressed in different legal traditions, and not with the substance or mechanics of particular legal systems.

Kernig, C.D. (Ed.). (1972-73). *Marxism, Communism, and Western Society: A Comparative Encyclopedia*. New York: Herder & Herder. 8 vols.

A very encompassing source that intends to address ideological differences between East and West through the thinking and findings of all of the social sciences. Extensive in addressing cultural as well as social and political factors.

Maisel, L. Sandy. (ed.). (1991). *Political Parties and Elections in the United States: An Encyclopedia*. New York: Garland. 2 vols.

A compilation of statistical data, biographies, and historical discussions. Bibliographies and definitions are included. Best used as a guide to sources.

Miller, David (Ed.). (1987). *The Blackwell Encyclopaedia of Political Thought*. Oxford, UK: Blackwell. 570 p.

As a companion to Bogdanor 1987 (above), covers Western political theory from the Greeks onward. Articles are of equal quality to those in its companion. Bibliographies included are selective and excellent.

Nicholson, Frances (Ed.). (1990). *Political and Economic Encyclopaedia of Western Europe*. Harlow, UK: Longmans. 411 p.

Strauss, Leo, & Cropsey, Joseph (Eds.). (1987). *History of Political Philosophy* (3rd ed.). Chicago: University of Chicago Press. 966 p.

Provides lengthy articles on the thought of 40 of the West's outstanding political thinkers from Thucydides to Heidegger. A good starting point when this approach is called for, but none of the essays constitutes more than a basic introduction to the theories and theorists considered.

White, Stephen (Ed.). (1990). *Political and Economic Encyclopaedia of the Soviet Union and Eastern Europe*. Harlow, UK: Longmans. 328 p.

A survey (already out of date, of course) of key political and economic developments since 1945.

Elliot, Jeffrey M., & Ali, Sheikh R. (1988). *The State and Local Government Political Dictionary*. Santa Barbara, CA: ABC–Clio. 325 p.

Focuses on the mechanics and not the theory of the political process. A complement to Smith and Klemanski (below).

Plano, Jack C., & Greenberg, Milton. (1989). *The American Political Dictionary* (8th ed.). New York: Holt, Rinehart & Winston. 608 p.

Arranged by broad concept, with short discussions addressing aspects of each. Articles routinely cite major court decisions in point. The latest edition of a standard tool.

Robertson, David. (1985). *A Dictionary of Modern Politics*. Philadelphia: Taylor & Francis. 341 p.

Limited in scope, as not many terms are covered. Useful for one-page summaries of modern ideas. No bibliographies.

Scruton, Roger. (1982). *A Dictionary of Political Thought*. New York: Harper & Row. 499 p.

Emphasis is on political ideas rather than events or political figures or entities.

Shafritz, Jay M. (1988). *The Dorsey Dictionary of American Government and Politics*. Chicago: Dorsey. 661 p.

Short discussions of topics relating to government at federal, state, and local levels.

Smith, John W., & Klemanski, John S. (1990). *The Urban Politics Dictionary*. Santa Barbara, CA: ABC–Clio. 613 p.

Gives lengthy discussions of terms usually associated with political interaction at the state and local levels. Complements Elliot and Ali (above).

2.4. Sociology

Borgatta, Edgar F., & Borgatta, Marie L. (Eds.). (1992). *Encyclopedia of Sociology*. New York: Macmillan. 4 vols.

The most recent and the most important of the encyclopedic works in this discipline. Also essential as a reference for other social scientists. Almost 400 articles present a wide-ranging view of the discipline and include many discussions of organizational theory and related specialties.

Chemers, Martin, & Ayman, Roya (Eds.). (1993). *Leadership Theory and Research: Perspectives and Directions*. Boston: Academic Press. 347 p.

Thirteen chapters review current theoretical and methodological perspectives in the area. Two address cross-cultural and integrative approaches explicitly and others do so in context. Intended for the scholar informed in this field, and not for the novice.

Christensen, Harold T. (Ed.). (1964). *Handbook of Marriage and the Family.* Chicago: Rand McNally. 1,028 p.

The standard theoretical review of this area. Twenty-four chapters are arranged within five sections, one of which addresses theoretical perspectives and another methodologies. Update using Sussman and Steinmetz, and Hawes and Nybakken.

Dubin, Robert (Ed.). (1976). *Handbook of Work, Organization, and Society.* Chicago: Rand McNally. 1,068 p.

An interesting volume that gathers together essays that discuss the nature of work in relation to society and social systems. The topics include work and the individual, socialization to work, motivation and compensation, and individual chapters on societal influences presented in different countries.

Faris, Robert E.L. (Ed.). (1964). *Handbook of Modern Sociology.* Chicago: Rand McNally. 1,088 p.

Includes some 27 essays surveying the discipline. Many are now outdated, but the several relating to organizational theory are still excellent. An important source, though one that should now be used with care.

Hare, A. Paul. (1976). *Handbook of Small Group Research* (2nd ed.). New York: Free Press. 781 p.

A major source in its field because of its integrated discussion of theory, findings, and methods. Strong for its attention to commonly used research techniques and for its consideration of research applications.

Hawes, Joseph M., & Nybakken, Elizabeth I. (Eds). (1991). *American Families: A Research Guide and Historical Handbook.* Westport, CT: Greenwood. 435 p.

Includes ten essays, each reviewing the field from a particular temporal or thematic concern.

Lindzey, Gardner, & Aronson, Elliot (Eds.). (1985). *Handbook of Social Psychology* (3rd ed). New York: Knopf. 2 vols.

One of the best-known reference works in the social sciences and a classic starting point for research in this field. Volume 1 addresses theories and methods. Volume 2 includes a series of detailed examples of how particular ones have been applied in specific research settings. The chapter on organizational theory (1:379–440) is of major importance as a review and interpretation of the influence of social psychology in this area.

Lorsch, Jay W. (Ed.). (1987). *Handbook of Organizational Behavior.* Englewood Cliffs, NJ: Prentice–Hall. 430 p.

A strong collection of essays that emphasizes the realities of how people act in organizations, rather than how they are supposed to act. Several general overview essays provide excellent syntheses of behavioral and social sciences findings in the area. Other essays pay considerable attention to managerial issues. One covers research methodologies to some extent. Only two specifically address the public sector.

Mann, Michael (Ed.). (1984). *The International Encyclopedia of Sociology*. New York: Continuum. 434 p.

Less than an encyclopedia, more like a dictionary. Does, however, provide very clear explanations of theoretical concepts.

March, James G. (Ed.). (1965). *Handbook of Organizations*. Chicago: Rand McNally. 1,247 p.

Includes very detailed articles, often of 30 pages or more, on methodological as well as theoretical approaches to the study of organizations. Addresses the private and public sectors equally. Old, but still a very important source.

Mohan, Raj P., & Martindale, Don (Eds.). (1975). *Handbook of Contemporary Developments in World Sociology*. Westport, CT: Greenwood. 493 p.

Attempts to provide sweeping reviews, country by country, of the development of the discipline since World War II. Theory, methodology, and teaching are all covered. Many of the discussions address organizational theory and other topics of concern to public administration.

Nystrom, Paul C., & Starbuck, William H. (Eds.). (1981). *Handbook of Organizational Design*. New York: Oxford University Press. 2 vols.

Presents a total of 45 long chapters. Those in volume 1 address the effect of the environment on the structure and functioning of the organization. Volume 2 discusses organizational structure and processes of internal change.

Smelser, Neil J. (Ed.). (1988). *Handbook of Sociology*. Newbury Park, CA: Sage. 824 p.

Articles are quite lengthy, although they address broad topics. Especially recommended for its discussions of organizational theory and of recent theoretical developments within the discipline.

Stogdill, Ralph M., & Bass, Bernard M. (1981). *Stogdill's Handbook of Leadership: A Survey of Theory and Research* (rev. ed.). New York: Free Press. 856 p.

The standard encyclopedic work in this field. Several chapters present a detailed chronological account of the development of theory and research. The remainder discuss the area through the contributions of small group study and other areas of research. Includes a chapter on research possibilities for the future and a definitive bibliography.

Sussman, Marvin B., & Steinmetz, Suzanne K. (Eds.). (1987). *Handbook of Marriage and the Family*. New York: Plenum. 915 p.
One of a number of overviews of a specialty whose theoretical focus and assumptions have changed recently and dramatically.

Bardis, Panos D. (Ed.). (1985). *Dictionary of Quotations in Sociology*. Westport, CT: Greenwood. 356 p.
Entries arranged by subject and indexed by cited author.

Boudon, Raymond, & Bourricaud, François. (1989). *A Critical Dictionary of Sociology*. Chicago: University of Chicago Press. 438 p.
Provides lengthy definitions and short articles addressing concepts in mainstream sociology. Based on a larger French work and reflects a European perspective. Does not supplant Gould and Kolb (section 1).

Jary, David, & Jary, Julia. (1991). *The Harper Collins Dictionary of Sociology*. New York: Harper Perennial. 601 p.
Probably the dictionary in this discipline most concerned with presenting short introductions to theory. Provides a detailed approach to a more limited group of ideas than presented by Boudon and Bourricaud.

2.5. Economics

Ashenfelter, Orley, & Layard, Richard (Eds.). (1986). *Handbook of Labor Economics*. New York: Elsevier. 2 vols.
A theoretical work that addresses theoretical aspects of labor as a cost of production and does not concern itself with personnel issues as a factor in managerial decisions.

Cambridge Economic History of Europe from the Decline of the Roman Empire. (1941–). Cambridge, UK: Cambridge University Press. Irregular.
Each volume is a collection of thematic essays addressing both economic and social movements in a particular setting. Eight volumes have been published so far; the latest in 1989. These cover "Agrarian Life of the Middle Ages," "Trade and Industry in the Middle Ages," "Economic Organization and Policies in the Middle Ages," "The Economy of Expanding Europe in the 16th and 17th

Centuries," "The Economic Organization of Early Modern Europe," "The Industrial Revolutions and After," and "The Industrial Economies:

Chenery, Hollis, & Srinivasan, T. N. (Eds.). (1988–89). *Handbook of Development Economics*. New York: Elsevier. 2 vols.

Intended as "a definitive source, reference, and teaching supplement for use by professional researchers and advanced graduate students." The field is surveyed in 33 chapters, authored by what one reviewer called "a stunning array of economics researchers."

Davidson, Sidney, & Weil, Roman L. (Eds.). (1983). *Handbook of Modern Accounting* (3rd ed.). New York: McGraw-Hill. 1,358 p.

Organized into extensive chapters. Intended for the practitioner, but articles often refer to debates in the area and have good bibliographies. A supplement was published in 1987.

Deane, Phyllis, & Kuper, Jessica (Eds.). (1988). *A Lexicon of Economics*. New York: Routledge, Chapman & Hall. 388 p.

Provides short essays on theoretical subjects written by experts in their fields.

Eatwell, John, Milgate, Murray, & Newman, Peter (Eds.). (1987). *The New Palgrave: A Dictionary of Economics*. New York: Stockton. 4 vols.

In spite of its title, an encyclopedia including substantial essays on all aspects of economic theory and its development, interpreted to include "political economy." A revision of a classic first published in the 1890s. See also Newman, Milgate, and Eatwell.

Encyclopedia of American Business History and Biography. (1988–). New York: Facts on File.

Seven volumes in a projected 10-volume set have so far been published. These address banking and finance, the railroads, and the iron and steel, airline and automobile industries. Coverage is detailed and impressive, although volumes published so far have been criticized for lack of an integrated historical perspective.

Greenwald, Douglas (Ed.). (1982). *Encyclopedia of Economics*. New York: McGraw–Hill. 1,068 p.

A good one-volume encyclopedia, with an emphasis on economic theory, including econometrics and statistics. Articles are often lengthy and usually well written.

Higgs, Henry (Ed.). (1923–26). *Palgrave's Dictionary of Political Economy* (rev. ed.). London: Macmillan. 3 vols.
Still valuable for its coverage of traditional theories and concepts.

Magill, Frank N. (Ed.). (1991). *Survey of Social Science: Economics Series*. Pasadena, CA: Salem Press. 5 vols.
Intended to provide "the general reader with insight into topics [that] are often accessible only to academicians and experts [and] with essential views of areas that are increasingly important to the layperson as well as to the specialist." The first of a series of four multivolume works addressing several of the social sciences.

Munn, Glenn G., Garcia, F. L., Woelfel, Charles J. (1991). *Encyclopedia of Banking and Finance* (9th ed.). Boston: Bankers Publishing. 1,097 p.
Short articles oriented toward the practitioner in all areas of private-sector finance. Discussions are well documented with current statistical and other data. The latest edition of a standard work.

Newman, Peter, Milgate, Murray, & Eatwell, John. (Eds). (1992). *New Palgrave Dictionary of Money and Finance*. New York: Stockton. 3 vols.
A collection of over 1,000 essays addressing a broad range of issues at a sophisticated level notable for its historical as well as theoretical perspective. The companion to Eatwell, Newman, and Milgate.

Porter, Glenn (Ed.). (1980). *Encyclopedia of American Economic History: Studies of the Principal Movements and Ideas*. New York: Scribner. 3 vols.
Interprets its field quite broadly to include topics of general social concern.

Greenwald, Douglas (Ed.). (1983). *The McGraw-Hill Dictionary of Modern Economics: A Handbook of Terms and Organizations* (3rd ed.). New York: McGraw–Hill. 632 p.
Probably the best of the many short dictionaries in this discipline. Includes an appendix listing organizations in the discipline.

Knopf, Kenyon A. (1991). *A Lexicon of Economics*. New York: Academic Press. 314 p.
Includes about 800 terms and primarily intended for the general reader or undergraduate.

Rutherford, Donald. (1992). *Dictionary of Economics*. London: Routledge. 539 p.
Notable for its coverage of terms relating to international economics and its related theory.

Shim, Jae K., & Siegel, Joel G. (1989). *Dictionary of Accounting and Finance.* Englewood Cliffs, NJ: Prentice–Hall. 504 p.
Presents short essays, not definitions.

Terry, John V. (1990). *Dictionary for Business and Finance* (2nd ed.). Fayetteville: University of Arkansas Press. 399 p.
Mainly concerned with applied issues but does pay some attention to theories and terms relating to theories of management.

2.6. Psychology

Adams, Henry E., & Sutker, Patricia B. (Eds.). (1984). *Comprehensive Handbook of Psychopathology.* New York: Plenum. 1,091 p.
A very thorough overview of clinical practice, research, and theory. Articles are arranged within five broad themes.

Altman, Irwin, & Christensen, Kathleen (Eds.). (1990). *Environment and Behavior Studies.* New York: Plenum. 2 vols.
A thorough review of intellectual history in a specialty of increasing interest to those concerned with the influence of environment on work and social planning.

Arieti, Silvano. (Ed.). (1974–86). *American Handbook of Psychiatry* (2nd ed). New York: Basic Books. 8 vols.
The classic work in its field. The last two volumes are especially valuable as reviews of recent trends in the discipline.

Atkinson, Richard C., et al. (Eds.). (1988). *Stevens' Handbook of Experimental Psychology* (2nd ed.). New York: Wiley. 2 vols.
A very technical work most useful to advanced researchers. Chapters are organized around the four themes of perception, motivation, learning, and cognition. The standard work in its specialty.

Borgatta, Edgar F., & Lambert, William W. (Eds.). (1968). *Handbook of Personality Theory and Research.* Chicago: Rand McNally. 1,232 p.
Includes 24 detailed chapters grouped within five thematic areas. Although old, still a major source.

Corsini, Raymond J. (Ed.). (1984). *Encyclopedia of Psychology.* New York: Wiley. 4 vols.

This set is the most general encyclopedia in this discipline and gives equal attention to all specialties within psychology, excluding, perhaps, those with a therapeutic bias. Articles are detailed, but intended for the nonspecialist.

Drenth, P. J. D., et al. (Eds.). (1984). *Handbook of Work and Organizational Psychology*. New York: Wiley. 2 vols.

One of the best reviews of theory and practice in this area. Articles are detailed and ambitious in their scope. Especially valuable in presenting a largely European perspective.

Dunnette, Marvin, & Hough, Leaetta M. (Eds.). (1990–91). *Handbook of Industrial and Organizational Psychology* (2nd ed.). Palo Alto, CA: Consulting Psychologists Press. 2 vols.

An authoritative text that includes extremely well documented essays on every aspect of the field. Each article includes detailed references to experiments, tests, theories, and methods of research and evaluation. Its three parts address theory and methodology, work management and job measurement, and behavioral aspects of organizational theory.

Eysenck, Michael W. (Ed). (1990). *The Blackwell Dictionary of Cognitive Psychology*. Oxford, UK: Blackwell. 390 p.

Eysenck, Michael W. (Ed.). (1984). *A Handbook of Cognitive Psychology*. Hillsdale, NJ: Erlbaum. 417 p.

These two works by Eysenck are encyclopedic in nature and offer essays rather than definitions intended "to provide the reader with the scope and diversity of contemporary cognitive psychology." Different issues are emphasized in each and the two volumes are complementary.

Gilgen, Albert R., & Gilgen, Carol K. (Eds.). (1987). *International Handbook of Psychology*. Westport, CT: Greenwood. 629 p.

Essays survey the recent development of theory in countries throughout the world; Western and non-Western. A very good introductory discussion addresses the development of psychology as a product of culture, economics, and political structure.

Goldberger, Leo, & Breznitz, Shlomo (Eds.). (1982). *Handbook of Stress: Theoretical and Clinical Aspects*. New York: Free Press. 804 p.

Takes a more clinical approach than does Sethi (see below). Especially valuable as a guide to tests, questionnaires, and other survey instruments in the field. Heavy in its focus on occupational stress.

Goldenson, Robert M. (Ed.). (1970). *The Encyclopedia of Human Behavior: Psychology, Psychiatry, and Mental Health.* Garden City, NY: Doubleday. 2 vols.

Important for its broad interpretation of its subject field. Because of its age, information included should be used with care.

Gregory, Richard L., & Zangwill, O. L. (Eds.). (1987). *The Oxford Companion to the Mind.* New York: Oxford University Press. 856 p.

An ambitious work that is probably the best one-volume reference work in this discipline. An inadequate index makes it rather difficult to use.

Honig, Werner K., & Staddon, J. E. R. (Eds.). (1977). *Handbook of Operant Behavior.* Englewood Cliffs, NJ: Prentice–Hall. 689 p.

Essays address theoretical and experimental aspects of that branch of psychology that deals with the analysis of behavior induced by external stimuli. One of several handbooks in this specialty.

Kagehiro, D., & Laufer, W. (Eds.). (1992). *Handbook of Psychology and Law.* New York: Springer–Verlag. 628 p.

A series of essays that emphasize current issues in this rapidly growing field.

Knutson, Jeanne N. (Ed.). (1973). *Handbook of Political Psychology.* San Francisco: Jossey–Bass. 543 p.

Articles by psychologists, sociologists, and political scientists present the first attempt to synthesize research and theory addressing the political context of human motivation and development. Sections on methods are also included.

Koch, Sigmund (Ed.). (1959–63). *Psychology: A Study of a Science.* New York: McGraw–Hill. 6 vols.

The most authoritative and extensive general overview in English of this discipline. Volumes 5 and 6 address applications of psychological theory.

Landy, Frank J. (1989). *Psychology of Work Behavior* (4th ed.). Belmont, CA: Brooks/Cole. 715 p.

Focuses on recent theories of human performance, motivation, leadership, job satisfaction, stress, and personnel psychology. Use in conjunction with Dunnette and Hough (above).

Lerner, Richard M., Peterson, Anne C., & Brooks–Gunn, Jeanne (Eds.). (1991). *Encyclopedia of Adolescence.* New York: Garland. 2 vols.

Essays are often lengthy (up to 15 pages) and review current theory and research findings relating to development and dysfunction in this age group in Western society.

The Marshall Cavendish Encyclopedia of Personal Relationships: Human Behavior. Bellmore, NY: Marshall Cavendish. 19 vols.

A massive collection of essays on social and behavioral aspects of a rather vaguely-defined field. Contributions vary considerably in quality.

Mussen, Paul H. (Ed.). (1983). *Handbook of Child Psychology* (4th ed.). New York: Wiley. 4 vols.

Each volume addresses a defined area: history, theory, and methods; infancy and developmental psychobiology; cognitive development; and socialization, personality, and social development. The standard reference work in its field.

Popplestone, John A., & McPherson, Marion W. (1988). *Dictionary of Concepts in General Psychology*. Westport, CT: Greenwood. 380 p.

More of a short encyclopedia than a dictionary, with brief review essays and bibliographies on selected topics. Best used only as an introduction to the terms discussed.

Sethi, Amarjit Singh, & Schuler, Randall S. (Eds.). (1984). *Handbook of Organizational Stress Coping Strategies*. Cambridge, MA: Ballinger. 319 p.

Brings together the contributions of many scholars in the field of stress management and acts as a useful introduction to the literature through its extensive bibliographies.

Stokols, Daniel, & Altman, Irwin (Eds.). (1987). *Handbook of Environmental Psychology*. New York: Wiley. 2 vols.

Offers a detailed overview of environmental psychology in terms of its major theoretical, methodological, and empirical contributions. The range of topics is very broad and includes such areas as territoriality, work environments, community psychology, and environmental cognition. There is an extended section on applications of environment-behavior concepts and findings along with analysis of community problems and public policy. There is also a section on international research studies and the prospects for future research in the field.

Walker, C. Eugene (Ed.). (1983). *The Handbook of Clinical Psychology: Theory, Research, and Practice*. Homewood, IL: Dow Jones–Irwin. 2 vols.

A thorough survey of theory, research findings, diagnostics, and therapy.

Watson, Robert I. (Ed). (1976). *Eminent Contributors to Psychology.* New York: Springer. 2 vols.

One of a number of works introducing concepts in this area through discussion of their outstanding theorists.

Weiner, Irving B., & Hess, Allen K. (Eds.). (1987). *Handbook of Forensic Psychology.* New York: Wiley. 725 p.

Addresses all aspects of the connections between psychology and the law, ranging "from highly conceptual issues concerning the implications and intent of the law to very practical matters involving the evaluation and rehabilitation of those who break the law."

Wolman, Benjamin B. (Ed.). (1977). *International Encyclopedia of Psychiatry, Psychology, Psychoanalysis, and Neurology.* New York: Van Nostrand Reinhold. 12 vols.

The most extensive encyclopedic source in the discipline. Articles are scholarly, lengthy, and well documented. Ambitious in its coverage of psychiatry, as well as psychology, but the latter field does not suffer for this. Updated by a *Progress Volume* published in 1983.

Wolman, Benjamin B., & Stricker, George (Eds.). (1982). *Handbook of Developmental Psychology.* Englewood Cliffs, NJ: Prentice–Hall. 960 p.

A good overview of a subdiscipline of marginal interest to researchers primarily concerned with organizations and their functioning.

Goldenson, Robert M. (Ed.). (1984). *Longman Dictionary of Psychology and Psychiatry.* New York: Longman. 815 p.

Useful for its inclusion of the terminology of psychiatry and mental health.

Harre, Rom, & Lamb, Roger (Eds.). (1983). *The Encyclopedic Dictionary of Psychology.* Cambridge, MA: MIT Press. 718 p.

Among the best of the many specialized dictionaries in this discipline.

2.7. Anthropology

There is no good encyclopedic work covering the theoretical development of this discipline, although some aspects of it are considered by the sources noted below. Much better coverage of anthropological theory is given by the general social science encyclopedias and by those in political science and sociology. In contrast to this, there is a database of anthropological literature, the Human

Relations Area Files (HRAF), which is of great consequence to all in the social sciences. This is discussed in section 7 of chapter 14.

Akoun, André (Ed.). (1974). *L'Anthropologie*. Verviers, France: Marabout. 690 p.

Basically a dictionary, but also includes some 13 survey articles. Written in French.

Brown, Samuel R. (Comp.). (1987). *Finding the Source in Sociology and Anthropology; A Thesaurus-Index to the Reference Collection*. Westport, CT: Greenwood. 269 p.

A detailed index to a limited number of reference works, including some in anthropology. No annotations. Less interesting than the title suggests.

Dorson, Richard M. (Ed.). (1983). *Handbook of American Folklore*. Bloomington: Indiana University Press. 584 p.

An excellent survey of an expanding specialty of anthropology. Essays included present a heavy focus on research methods and the interpretation of data. (For sources addressing popular culture, see "History" below.)

Encyclopedia of World Cultures. (1991–). Boston: G. K. Hall. Projected in 10 vols.

Intended to provide "cultural summaries" of elements within societies throughout the world. Based on the contents of the enormous Human Relations Area Files. Summaries are short, documented, and often technical. Volumes so far issued are *North America* and *Oceania*, and *South Asia*.

Honigmann, John J. (Ed.). (1973). *Handbook of Social and Cultural Anthropology*. Chicago: Rand McNally. 1,295 p.

Although limited in scope and now fairly old, the closest thing to a comprehensive review of theory and research findings in this discipline. See also Manners and Kaplan (below).

Hunter, David E., & Whitten, Phillip (Eds.). (1976). *Encyclopedia of Anthropology*. New York: Harper & Row. 411 p.

Despite its title, more of a dictionary than an encyclopedia. Articles vary greatly in length. At their best, they do address concepts and theories.

Johnston, R. J., & others. (Eds.). (1981). *Dictionary of Human Geography*. New York: Free Press. 411 p.

Includes short articles with bibliographies. Many have relevance to social anthropology.

Manners, Robert A., & Kaplan, David (Eds.). (1968). *Theory in Anthropology, A Source-Book.* Chicago: Aldine. 578 p.

Represents a somewhat limited view of theory in this discipline and includes good essays by specialists. Use in conjunction with Honigmann (see above).

Munroe, Ruth H., Munroe, Robert L., & Whiting, Beatrice B. (Eds.). (1981). *Handbook of Cross-Cultural Human Development.* New York: Garland. 888 p.

Reflects recent concerns for assessing the influence of culture on the development of psychological processes. Very detailed articles usually include reviews of the literature of their topics.

Seymour-Smith, Charlotte. (1986). *Dictionary of Anthropology.* Boston: G. K. Hall. 305 p.

Definitions emphasize the contributions of major Western anthropologists.

Triandis, Harry C., & Draguns, Juris G. (Eds.). (1980). *Handbook of Cross-Cultural Psychology.* Boston: Allyn & Bacon. 6 vols.

A very unusual work addressing research on the psychological attributes associated with different cultural settings. A very detailed treatment of a very particular area.

Winthrop, Robert H. (1991). *Dictionary of Concepts in Cultural Anthropology.* Westport, CT: Greenwood. 347 p.

Presents extensive essays on about 80 theoretical areas. A detailed subject index provides access to narrow terms discussed in these essays.

2.8. History

In keeping with the focus of this book, the sources that are cited here are mainly theoretical. (A few other kinds of works are also cited when these present information of immediate value to the beginning researcher in the field.) For information on the many encyclopedic works dealing with particular periods and settings, see the bibliographic guides cited in section 4.9 of the following chapter. Works on economic and political history are cited in sections 2.3 and 2.5.

Adams, James T., & Ketz, Louise B. (Eds.). (1976). *Dictionary of American History* (rev. ed.). New York: Scribner. 8 vols.

Articles are short, but are written by experts and provide bibliographies. Good coverage of social and economic history and of popular culture. The last volume is the index to the set.

Cayton, Mary K., Gorn, Elliott, J., & Williams, Peter W. (Eds.). (1993). *Encyclopedia of American Social History*. New York: Scribner's. 3 vols.

The first sustained attempt to synthesize the approaches and findings of this growing historical specialty in the American context. One hundred eighty lengthy essays are grouped within broad thematic and periodic categories. Important if only for its contribution to the definition of this yet amporphous field.

Foner, Eric, & Garraty, John A. (Eds.). (1991). *The Reader's Companion to American History*. Boston: Houghton Mifflin. 1,226 p.

Includes thematic essays as well as biographical sketches and short, factual pieces. Important for its discussions of the findings of recent research in social cultural history.

Gilbert, Felix, & Graubard, Stephen R. (Eds.). (1972). *Historical Studies Today*. New York: Norton. 469 p.

A collection of essays aimed at assessing the current state of theory and method in history. Pays particular attention to developments then considered new in the field. Updated by Iggers and Parker (below).

Greene, Jack P., & Pole, J. R. (Eds.). (1991). *The Blackwell Encyclopedia of the American Revolution*. Cambridge, MA: Blackwell. 845 p.

Offers 75 lengthy surveys of various issues surrounding the topic, together with short biographical sketches and a chronology of events. One of the many encyclopedic sources limited to a particular geographical and temporal setting.

Hall, Kermit L. (Ed.). (1989). *United States Constitutional and Legal History*. New York: Garland. 25 vols.

Each volume includes collections of previously published essays related to a particular theme. The subject matter of the set is interpreted quite broadly to incorporate many aspects of social and political history. Cited here as an example of one of the many excellent specialized encyclopedias in the discipline of history.

Horn, Pierre (Ed.). (1991). *Handbook of French Popular Culture*. Westport, CT: Greenwood. 307 p.

Each of the 13 chapters presents a survey of a particular aspect of mass culture, e.g., advertising, music, sports. Areas covered are necessarily chosen selectively.

Iggers, Georg G., & Parker, Harold T. (Eds.). (1979). *International Handbook of Historical Studies: Contemporary Research and Theory*. Westport, CT: Greenwood. 452 p.

A direct descendant of Gilbert and Grabaud (see above) and similar in structure and objectives.

Inge, M. Thomas (Ed.). (1989). *Handbook of American Popular Culture* (2nd ed). Westport, CT: Greenwood. 3 vols.

An indispensable source for anyone undertaking research in this rapidly growing field. Most of the essays address cultural artifacts in printed form. Others deal with art, music, theater, film, television, radio, and also with institutional aspects of American life and their relation to popular values.

The International Military Encyclopedia. (1992–). Gulf Breeze, FL: Academic International. Project in 50 vols.

Strongly historical focus. By the end of 1992 only one volume had been published. Additional volumes are planned at a rate of two or three a year.

Janosik, Robert J. (Ed.). (1987). *Encyclopedia of the American Judicial System: Studies of the Principal Institutions and Processes of Law.* New York: Scribner. 3 vols.

Concerned with the development of jurisprudence as a social as well as a legal phenomenon. Articles were prepared by scholars and demonstrate a strong historical sense. Cited here as an example of a specialized guide to the understanding of historical process. See also Levy (below).

Kellogg, Jefferson B., & Walker, Robert H. (Eds.). (1983). *Sources for American Studies.* Westport, CT: Greenwood. 766 p.

Includes a series of bibliographic essays addressing a number of topics including, but not limited to, historical approaches to popular culture. A sequel to Walker (see below).

Lee, R. Alton, & McDonald, Archie P. (Eds.). (1983–). *Encyclopedia USA: The Encyclopedia of the United States of America Past and Present.* Gulf Breeze, FL: Academic International Press. Vols. 1–.

At the time of writing, the first 17 volumes of this projected 50-volume set have been published. Although articles vary substantially in length, this encyclopedia promises to be a standard in its area.

Levy, Leonard W. (Ed.). (1986). *Encyclopedia of the American Constitution.* New York: Macmillan. 4 vols.

A guide to constitutional history that seeks to incorporate the understanding of historians and political scientists, as well as jurists. See also Janosik (above).

Nelson, William E., & Reid, John P. (1985). *The Literature of American Legal History*. New York: Oceana. 356 p.

An important work that focuses on published primary as well as secondary sources. Considerable discussion of sources at both the state and the federal level.

The New Cambridge Modern History. (1957–79). Cambridge, UK: Cambridge University Press. 14 vols.

The standard history of the development of the West between the Renaissance and 1945. Strongly, but not overpoweringly, European in its perspective. Of particular interest here is the *Companion Volume* (vol. 13), which includes long essays on social and economic themes in the period covered (see, for example, the essay "Bureaucracy"). A revised edition of this work will begin publication early in the 1990s under the general editorship of the renowned scholar G. E. Elton.

Thernstrom, Stephan (Ed.). (1980). *Harvard Encyclopedia of American Ethnic Groups*. Cambridge, MA: Belknap. 1,076 p.

Includes scholarly essays reviewing different ethnic experiences in American life. Presents broad social science perspectives but retains a historical focus. Cited here as an example of the many excellent specialized tools in this discipline.

Walker, Robert H. (Ed.). (1976). *American Studies: Topics and Sources*. Westport, CT: Greenwood. 393 p.

Similar in form and coverage to Kellogg and Walker (see above).

Cook, Chris. (1989). *Dictionary of Historical Terms* (2nd ed.). London: Macmillan. 364 p.

Unsurpassed for short explanations of historical concepts.

Morris, Richard B. (Ed.). (1982). *Encyclopedia of American History*. (6th ed.). New York: Harper & Row. 1,285 p.

Basically a chronology of events and not an encyclopedia. Emphasis is on political history, and coverage is up to 1981. The standard work of its kind.

Ritter, Harry. (1986). *Dictionary of Concepts in History*. Westport, CT: Greenwood. 490 p.

Good discussions of almost 100 terms used in historical thought. These include those peculiar to history (e.g., "historiography") and more general social science concepts that have been applied by historians in particular ways.

Stevenson, John (Ed.). (1992). *The Columbia Dictionary of European Political History Since 1914*. New York: Columbia University Press. 437 p.

Excellent as a survey of developments affecting both Eastern and Western Europe with coverage through the middle of 1990.

2.9. Philosophy

Becker, Lawrence C., & Becker, Charlotte B. (Eds.). (1992). *Encyclopedia of Ethics*. New York: Garland. 2 vols.

A collection of over 400 extensive essays reviewing the major concepts, thinkers, and theories in this area. Essays usually include excellent bibliographies.

Bowman, James S., & Elliston, Frederick A. (Eds.). (1988). *Ethics, Government, and Public Policy: A Reference Guide*. Westport, CT: Greenwood. 341 p.

A collection of essays that review the current research in significant ethical issues of government. The topics address both individual ethics and organizational morality and are concerned with local, national, and international governmental policies.

Burr, John R. (Ed.). (1980). *Handbook of World Philosophy: Contemporary Developments Since 1945*. Westport, CT: Greenwood. 641 p.

The most up-to-date of the surveys of theory in this discipline. Essential to supplement the more extensive, but older, sources cited here.

Carman, John, & Juergensmeyer, Mark. (Eds.). (1991). *A Bibliographic Guide to the Comparative Study of Ethics*. Cambridge, UK: Cambridge University Press. 811 p.

Each of the 15 essays is devoted to ethical concerns within a particular tradition, religious, intellectual, or social.

Copleston, Frederick C. (1946–75). *A History of Philosophy*. London: Burns, Oates, & Washbourne. 9 vols.

One of several encyclopedic approaches to the history of this discipline published since World War II. Recommended here as possibly the best of those written in English.

Edwards, Paul (Ed.). (1967). *The Encyclopedia of Philosophy*. New York: Macmillan and Free Press. 8 vols.

The principal encyclopedic work in the field. Articles are often quite sophisticated in approach, are always written by scholars, and include good bibliographic introductions to the topics addressed.

Klibansky, Raymond (Ed.). (1958–59). *Philosophy in the Mid-Century*. Florence: Nuova Italia. 4 vols.

Klibansky, Raymond (Ed.). (1968–71). *Contemporary Philosophy: A Survey*. Florence: Nuova Italia. 4 vols.

Between them, these two works attempt to cover the state of the discipline throughout the world and developments within it between World War II and the end of the 1960s. About half the articles are in English.

Reich, Warren T. (Ed.). (1978). *Encyclopedia of Bioethics*. New York: Free Press. 4 vols.

A high quality work devoted to ethical issues raised in the delivery of services related to health. This subject matter is defined broadly, and considerable attention is given to public policy aspects of the issues under consideration.

Tice, Terrence N., & Slavens, Thomas P. (1983). *Research Guide to Philosophy*. Chicago: American Library Association. 608 p.

Part 1 includes review essays of theory, with pride of place given to 20th-century developments. Part 2 covers particular areas of inquiry. Especially valuable is part 3, which presents a thorough discussion of the bibliographic tools in this subject.

Tobey, Jeremy L. (1975–77). *The History of Ideas: A Bibliographical Introduction*. Santa Barbara, CA: Clio. 2 vols.

Limited in coverage to the classical, medieval, and early modern periods. Use to supplement Tice and Slavens (see above).

Wiener, Philip P. (Ed.). (1973–74). *Dictionary of the History of Ideas: Studies of Selected Pivotal Ideas*. New York: Scribner. 5 vols.

Limited in the range of concepts addressed, but traces these through history and across cultures. Organized around seven themes, one of which is "the historical development of economic, legal, and political ideas and institutions, ideologies and movements."

Angeles, Peter A. (1981). *Dictionary of Philosophy*. New York: Harper & Row. 326 p.

The most recent and one of the most extensive dictionaries of its kind.

Bullock, Alan, & Stallybrass, Oliver (Eds.). (1977). *The Harper Dictionary of Modern Thought.* New York: Harper & Row. 684 p.

A step up from Angeles (above). Definitions are more detailed and the scope of the work is broader. Edited by two outstanding thinkers in modern philosophy.

Encyclopedias in more specialized areas are considered in the following chapter, together with annual reviews and bibliographic guides.

2.10. Other Areas

Dunbar, Gary S. (Ed.). (1991). *Modern Geography: An Encyclopedic Survey.* New York: Garland. 219 p.

A brief survey of a field generally defined to include only 20th century cultural geography.

Encyclopedia of World Problems and Human Potential (3rd ed.). (1991). Munich: K. G. Saur. 2 vols.

An unusual collection of articles on a strange array of topics of global concern. Valuable, but exasperating to use because of the seemingly arbitrary choice of topics and form of arrangement.

Humm, Maggie. (1990). *Dictionary of Feminist Theory.* Columbus: Ohio State University. 278 p.

Has the perspective of presenting modern feminist thought in relation (often in contrast) to traditional modes of approach.

Spender, Dale (Ed.). (1983). *Feminist Theorists: Three Centuries of Key Women Thinkers.* New York: Pantheon. 402 p.

Theory is presented largely through biographies of individual thinkers.

Tierney, Helen (Ed.). (1989–91). *Women's Studies Encyclopedia.* Westport, CT: Greenwood. 3 vols.

Each volume presents 100 or so lengthy essays addressing a particular focus: "Views From the Sciences," "Literature, Arts, and Learning," "History, Philosophy, and Religion." Valuable for its cross-disciplinary focus and considerable range of coverage.

NOTE

1. Chapters 3 and 4 were prepared with the assistance of Professor Robert P. Grappone of the John Jay College of Criminal Justice Library.

4

OVERVIEWS OF THEORY IN APPLIED CONTEXTS; ANNUAL REVIEWS; GUIDES TO THE LITERATURE

1. APPLIED SPECIALIZED ENCYCLOPEDIAS

These encyclopedic works which focus more on the application than on the nature of theory. Although important, they should be used by the social researcher in conjunction with the more theoretical works cited in chapter 3.

1.1. Personnel and Human Resources Management

Blum, Albert A. (Ed.). (1980). *International Handbook of Industrial Relations: Contemporary Developments and Research.* Westport, CT: Greenwood. 698 p.
A collection of essays dealing generally with relations between workers and managers in some 27 countries. The areas addressed include unionism, employer organizations, personnel administration, and labor laws. Discussions are usually presented in some historical context.

Famularo, Joseph J. (Ed.). (1986). *Handbook of Human Resources Administration* (2nd ed.). New York: McGraw–Hill. 1,514 p.
Lengthy chapters, each written by a specialist. This latest edition pays more attention to legal issues. Written for the manager, but perspectives taken reflect the theoretical underpinnings of the field.

Filipelli, Ronald L. (Ed.). (1990). *Labor Conflict in the United States: An Encyclopedia.* New York: Garland. 609 p.
Short essays document several hundred conflicts from the 17th century onward. Narratives include brief bibliographies.

Fink, Gary M. (Ed.). (1977). *Greenwood Encyclopedia of American Institutions: Labor Unions*. Westport, CT: Greenwood. 520 p.

Offers historical sketches of more than 200 national unions and labor federations that have been part of the American labor movement. Attempts to include unions representative of most minority groups, trades, industries, time periods, and ideological movements.

Nadler, Leonard, & Nadler, Zeace (Eds.). (1990). *The Handbook of Human Resource Development* (2nd ed.). New York: Wiley. 1 vol., various pagings.

One of the more interesting handbooks in this group in focusing as much on theories and concepts as on practice. Includes 31 chapters grouped into five main sections: the general field of human resource development, program areas, international developments, related human resource areas, and the agenda for the future.

Parmeggiani, Luigi (Ed.). (1983). *Encyclopaedia of Occupational Health and Safety* (3rd ed.). Geneva: International Labour Office. 2 vols.

This encyclopedia is intended as an information source for all administrators responsible for safeguarding workers' health and safety. Each article contains a bibliography, and the references are to various international journals published in many languages. Topics include occupational hygiene, the impact of industrialization on health and safety, psychosocial problems and mental health of workers, pesticides, and fire prevention. Very wide-ranging and well indexed. Includes an appendix of recommendations and guidelines adopted by various international organizations.

Rabin, Jack, Hildreth, W. Bartley, Miller, Gerald, & Vocino, Thomas (Eds.). (1983). *Handbook on Public Personnel and Labor Relations*. New York: Dekker. 671 p.

Rabin, Jack, & Steinhauer, Marcia B. (Eds.). (1988). *Handbook of Human Service Administration*. New York: Dekker. 604 p.

Probably the two best-known reference works in their areas. The first emphasizes a legal and practical approach; the second includes some theoretical discussion of group dynamics and other aspects of applied psychology.

Scheer, Wilbert E. (Ed.). (1985). *The Dartnell Personnel Administration Handbook* (3rd ed.). Chicago: Dartnell. 1,124 p.

Organized within a number of broad chapters with discussions addressing particular aspects of each theme covered.

Shafritz, Jay M. (1985). *The Facts on File Dictionary of Personnel Management and Labor Relations* (2nd ed.). New York: Facts on File. 534 p.

Apart from the definitions it offers, useful for its listings of journals, publishers, and other organizations in the field. Especially useful summaries of relevant legislation and court cases.

Slote, Lawrence. (1987). *Handbook of Occupational Safety and Health.* New York: Wiley. 744 p.

More of a practical guide than that of Parmeggiani (above). Covers topics related to safety and health in all types of corporations and agencies, including training programs, economics of occupational safety, and workplace litigation. Appendixes list relevant journals, organizations, and other information sources.

Tracey, William R. (Ed.). (1985). *Human Resources Management and Development Handbook.* New York: American Management Association. 1,550 p.

Probably the most authoritative recent guide of its kind. Includes over 100 chapters arranged within 18 sections. Each chapter is written by an expert. Valuable for both professional and researcher.

Tracey, William R. (1991). *The Human Resources Glossary: A Complete Desk Reference for HR Professionals.* New York: American Management Association. 416 p.

Presents careful and contextual definitions of over 3,000 terms related to personnel management.

1.2. Education

For some reason, this discipline is especially well served in this area; the researcher is very fortunate. The excellence of encyclopedic sources in this discipline, compared with the dearth in other social sciences, may reflect the fact that more than 80 percent of doctorates currently awarded in the social sciences are in education.

Alkin, Marvin C. (Ed.). (1992). *Encyclopedia of Educational Research* (6th ed.). New York: Macmillan. 4 vols.

A thorough overview that also cites findings in the related area of child psychology. Arranged by broad subject and well indexed. Very good coverage of statistical methods and research techniques.

Altbach, Philip G. (Ed.). (1991). *International Higher Education: An Encyclopedia.* New York: Garland. 2 vols.

Essays are largely descriptive and cover 52 countries and 15 cross-cultural topics. Use to supplement Knowles.

Boyan, Norman J. (Ed.). (1988). *Handbook of Research on Educational Administration*. New York: Longman. 767 p.

Obviously applied in its focus, but does include reference to administrative theory.

Cameron, J., et al. (Eds.). (1983–84). *International Handbook of Education Systems*. New York: Wiley. 3 vols.

Provides worldwide coverage, with the notable exception of the United Kingdom, the United States, and the then USSR. A guide to practice rather than theory.

Clark, Burton R., & Neave, Guy R. (Eds.). (1992). *The Encyclopedia of Higher Education*. New York: Pergamon. 4 vols.

Volume 1 includes descriptions of about 135 national systems. Two other volumes analyze broad issues reaching across national boundaries. The last volume reviews trends in the development of education within individual disciplines and can be used as a guide to evolving definitions of these disciplines.

Deighton, Lee C. (Ed.). (1971). *The Encyclopedia of Education*. New York: Macmillan. 10 vols.

Aimed at providing a detailed guide to educational practice, primarily in the United States. In fact goes far beyond this and includes many articles on administrative and many other aspects of the field.

Gutkin, Terry B. & Reynolds, Cecil R. (Eds.). (1990). *The Handbook of School Psychology* (2nd ed.). New York: Wiley. 1,056 p.

Intended for the practitioner. Important for its discussions of assessment techniques and instruments.

Husen, Torsten, & Postlethwaite, T. Neville (Eds.). (1985). *International Encyclopedia of Education: Research and Studies*. New York: Pergamon. 10 vols.

An excellent overview of research and theory in this area. Most of the articles address aspects of learning theories or other psychological concerns. Administration, however, is well covered. Especially valuable for its coverage of systems outside of the United States. Supplementary volumes (two published so far) keep the work up-to-date.

Knowles, Asa S. (Ed.). (1970). *Handbook of College and University Administration*. New York: McGraw Hill. 2 vols.

Very much a guide to practice rather than theory. Considerable attention is given to everything related to planning.

Knowles, Asa S. (Ed.). (1977). *International Encyclopedia of Higher Education*. San Francisco: Jossey–Bass. 10 vols.

Comparable in scope and depth to the other works in this discipline. Labor relations and other faculty-related issues are given a good deal of attention. Update using Altbach (above).

Thomas, R. Murray (Ed.). (1990). *The Encyclopedia of Human Development and Education: Theory, Research, and Studies*. New York, NY: Pergamon. 519 p.

Presents excellent overviews of topics that go beyond their educational context. Organized by theme and includes lengthy bibliographies.

Walberg, Herbert J., & Haertel, Geneva D. (Eds.). (1990). *The International Encyclopedia of Educational Evaluation*. New York, NY: Pergamon. 796 p.

Articles are grouped within eight broad sections. Each is further subdivided, and considerable attention is paid to methodological issues. The definitive work of its kind.

Good, Carter V. (Ed.). (1973). *Dictionary of Education* (3rd ed.). New York: McGraw–Hill. 681 p.

Definitions are lengthier and more scholarly than those in Rowntree (see below).

Rowntree, Derek. (1982). *A Dictionary of Education*. Totowa, NJ: Barnes & Noble. 354 p.

The most extensive of the recent dictionaries in this subject area.

1.3. Criminal Justice

This field (scarcely a discipline) is considered here as a recent offshoot of a yet-uneasy relationship between criminology, as a branch of sociology, social work, and public administration. It is addressed here as an example of the kind of amalgam of disciplines that most researchers in public administration have to contend with. Perhaps more than any other situation, it illustrates the need of the student in public administration to acquire a familiarity with ways of thought of an array of perspectives. For this reason alone, it is worthy of attention here.

Bailey, William G. (Ed.). (1989). The *Encyclopedia of Police Science*. New York: Garland. 718 p.

Best for its descriptions of police agencies and of concepts used in police administration. Does, however, make some effort to incorporate the theories and findings of social researchers who have studied the police as an institution.

Fennelly, Lawrence J. (2nd ed.). (1989). *Handbook of Loss Prevention and Crime Prevention*. Boston: Butterworths. 721 p.

A source of practical information on the related topics of physical security and loss prevention. Emphasis is on innovative crime-prevention programs and security systems, new technologies, investigative techniques, legal questions in security, and specific security and crime-prevention applications.

Glaser, Daniel (Ed.). (1974). *Handbook of Criminology*. Chicago: Rand McNally. 1,180 p.

Long essays with good bibliographies. Grouped around four themes: criminological theory, police and the courts, corrections, and crime prevention. Still competes well with Kadish (below).

The Guide to American Law: Everyone's Legal Encyclopedia. (1983). St. Paul, MN: West. 12 vols.

All that its name suggests. Very good for the person who needs to dip into the world of legal theory. No good at all for the researcher with a serious interest in legal research, who should be reading one of the several guides to legal research cited in section 3 of chapter 13. Updated by an annual yearbook.

Johnson, Elmer H. (Ed.). (1987). *Handbook on Crime and Delinquency Prevention*. Westport, CT: Greenwood. 402 p.

Unlike most other works on this topic, this is much concerned with the theoretical aspects of it and how these relate to the findings of criminological research. Essays are well documented, and a "Supplementary Bibliography" is also included.

Johnson, Elmer H. (Ed.). (1983). *International Handbook of Contemporary Developments in Criminology*. Westport, CT: Greenwood. 2 vols.

Essays do include short descriptions of criminal justice systems in the countries addressed. Their main value, however, lies in their assessments of trends in research and in theoretical developments. Volume 1 is subtitled *General Issues and the Americas*; volume 2, *Europe, Africa, the Middle East, and Asia*.

Kadish, Sanford H. (Ed.). (1983). *Encyclopedia of Crime and Justice*. New York: Free Press. 4 vols.

The only work of its kind. Includes articles on all aspects of criminal justice. Useful as a background source for most topics in the field and as a reference guide to related areas through its extensive bibliographies. Good as far as it goes, but is most valuable to the beginning researcher.

Kurian, George T. (1989). *World Encyclopedia of Police Forces and Penal Systems*. New York: Facts on File. 582 p.
Essentially a descriptive work. Occasionally provides statistics and mentions sources for the study of the countries addressed.

Williams, Vergil L. (1979). *Dictionary of American Penology: An Introductory Guide*. Westport, CT: Greenwood. 530 p.
Although it purports to address "ideological disputes" in contemporary American penology, a large proportion of the entries constitute descriptions of particular systems and institutions. Does present good short treatments of theoretical concerns.

Black's Law Dictionary: Definitions of the Terms and Phrases of American and English Jurisprudence, Ancient and Modern. (1990). (6th ed.). St. Paul, MN: West. 1,657 p.
The standard one-volume legal dictionary.

Walsh, Dermot, & Poole, Adrian (Eds.). (1983). *A Dictionary of Criminology*. London: Routledge & Kegan Paul. 242 p.
Entries vary in length and in quality, but this remains the only recent dictionary that addresses ideas as well as terms in criminology.

1.4. Social Work

Encyclopedia of Social Work. (1987). (18th ed.). New York: National Association of Social Workers. 2 vols.
Written for practitioners, but includes strong discussions of theoretical approaches and of the organizational settings of social work practice. Updated between editions by annual supplements.

Romanofsky, Peter (Ed.). (1978). *Greenwood Encyclopedia of American Institutions: Social Service Organizations*. Westport, CT: Greenwood. 2 vols.
Provides historical profiles of over 200 organizations, many of which are considered in less detail in the *Encyclopedia of Social Work*. Discusses their activities and publications and includes critical bibliographies.

Barker, Robert L. (2nd ed.). (1991). *The Social Work Dictionary*. Silver Spring, MD: National Association of Social Workers. 287 p.

Concentrates on providing short, technical definitions.

1.5. Other Areas

Ashworth, William (Ed.). (1991). *The Encyclopedia of Environmental Studies*. New York: Facts on File. 470 p.

Includes short articles emphasizing definitions in a wide range of technical fields including the pure and applied sciences and the law.

Bright, William (Ed.). (1992). *International Encyclopedia of Linguistics*. New York: Oxford University Press. 4 vols.

About 750 articles present a comprehensive survey of all major branches of this field, including those relating to areas such as psychology, developmental studies, and language studies. Well indexed and with extensive bibliographies.

Covington, Paula H. (Ed.). (1992). *Latin America and the Caribbean: A Critical Guide to Research Sources*. Westport, CT: Greenwood. 924 p.

Essays describe and explain relevant theoretical approaches and their attendant bibliography. Some discussion of outstanding special library collections is included, but no attention is given to the techniques of bibliographic searching.

Lowery, Charles D., & Marszalek, John F. (Eds.). (1992). *Encyclopedia of African-American Civil Rights From Emancipation to the Present*. Westport, CT: Greenwood. 672 p.

Malmkjaer, Kirsten, & Anderson, James M. (Eds.). *The Linguistics Encyclopedia*. London: Routledge. 575 p.

A limited competitor to Bright. Particularly good for its coverage of applied linguistics but limited in its discussions of languages and language groups. Includes a glossary of terms.

Nam, Charles B., Serow, William J., & Sly, David F. (Eds.). (1990). *International Handbook on Internal Migration*. Westport, CT: Greenwood. 438 p.

An interdisciplinary effort that presents comparative data on social, legal, and demographic aspects of population movements. Also addresses important issues regarding the study of these as social phenomena. See also Serow (below).

Nijkamp, Peter & Mills, Edwin S. (Ed.). (1986). *Handbook of Regional and Urban Economics*. Amsterdam: Elsevier. 2 vols.

Volume 1 is entitled *Regional Economics* and is specifically concerned with the methods and sources for undertaking comparative studies. The title of volume 2 is *Urban Economics* and has a similar focus.

Rabin, Jack (Ed.). (1992). *Handbook of Public Budgeting*. New York: Dekker. 735 p.

A technical work addressing applied financial aspects of public management including legal issues of accountability and fiscal responsibility.

Rabin, Jack, & Dodd, Don (Eds.). (1985). *State and Local Government Administration*. New York: Dekker. 446 p.

A generally descriptive account that does include some reference to organizational history in this area.

Rabin, Jack, & Jackowski, Edward (Eds.). (1988). *Handbook of Information Resource Management*. New York: Dekker. 567 p.

The only guide of its kind addressing new and important problems concerning the great proliferation of public information and the difficulties of both managing and consuming it.

Rowat, Donald C. (Ed.). (1980). *International Handbook on Local Government Reorganization: Contemporary Developments*. Westport, CT: Greenwood. 626 p.

Presents comparative accounts of governmental structures at the local and regional levels in both developed and developing nations.

Schmid, Alex P., & Jongman, Albert J. (1988). *Political Terrorism: A New Guide to Actors, Authors, Concepts, Data Bases, Theories and Literature* (rev. ed.). New Brunswick, NJ: Transaction. 700 p.

Presents broad-ranging discussions of theories and concepts in this area which emphasize the definitional problems peculiar to this area. An important section discusses the existence and characteristics of databases of primary data. An important work in a field rapidly generating its own bibliography.

Schultz, Marilyn S., & Kasen, Vivian L. (Eds.). (1984). *Encyclopedia of Community Planning and Environmental Management*. New York: Facts on File. 475 p.

Includes less coverage of historical and international developments than does Whittick (below). Better for its consideration of the situation in the United States, including policy development.

Serow, William J. (Ed.). (1990). *Handbook on International Migration.* Westport, CT: Greenwood. 385 p.

The companion to Nam, Serow, and Sly (above). Similar in form and structure.

Washnis, George J. (Ed.). (1980). *Productivity Improvement Handbook for State and Local Government.* New York: Wiley. 1,492 p.

Deals with effective methods for improving productivity in government and addresses areas such as organization, techniques of management, and functional operations of federal and state agencies.

Waugh, William L., & Hy, Ronald J. (Eds.). (1990). *Handbook of Emergency Management: Programs and Policies Dealing with Major Hazards and Disasters.* Westport, CT: Greenwood. 336 p.

Each chapter addresses a particular disastrous circumstance (for example, drought, fires, earthquakes). Based on case studies rather than any more general perspective.

Whittick, Arnold (Ed.). (1974). *Encyclopedia of Urban Planning.* New York: McGraw–Hill. 1,218 p.

A substantial work that concentrates on theoretical aspects. Includes about 400 articles, many of which address problems commonly encountered throughout the world.

2. ANNUAL REVIEWS

The list given in appendix 1 includes those annual reviews that are, in the opinion of the author, likely to be of greatest value to the student of public administration. Given the spread of this field, it is always possible that there may be other reviews relevant to the research topic in point. Additional sources of this nature can be identified through the several sources noted in this appendix.

The nature and organization of annual reviews has already been commented upon. Differences between them, other than subject bias, are fairly minor. As noted, some include only original articles commissioned especially and not published elsewhere. Others are compilations of what are thought to be the best or the most representative articles published recently in standard journals. Some attempt to review current developments in an area in their entirety. Others limit coverage to a single important, usually controversial, current issue in the area.

Annual reviews can be searched in ways more formal than simple browsing. Quite a few of them are covered by standard indexing and abstracting services. Those listed in appendix 1 are primarily compilations of original articles, supplemented by extensive bibliographies, specifically intended to acquaint the reader with current developments in the field under consideration. They usually also include book reviews or extensive review essays that can be used as critical evaluations of recent works. Most usually include some documentation of recent trends and developments in the field. All publications listed are annual unless indicated otherwise. Monographs in series are excluded, as these usually have distinct titles and can be identified in conventional ways (see chapter 9).

In accordance with the general thrust of this work, the reviews cited in appendix 1 are generally theoretical or methodological in their orientation. For others, the reader is directed to the several works cited at the beginning of the previous chapter, especially Webb, et al. (1986).

3. OVERVIEWS OF THE FIELD

Overviews can be considered as broad introductions to a subject area that, like the other types of source discussed in this chapter, guide the reader to an understanding of current developments and debates and of the scope and complexity of such issues. It is not easy to distinguish between overviews and encyclopedias, although the latter usually address specific issues, while the former are more concerned with general trends. In addition, overviews are usually as much guides to reading as they are providers of informational substance.

With this in mind, the following list includes good selective bibliographies and some other sources that serve these functions. Like the other materials cited in this chapter, only those addressing broad themes within public administration are included. Techniques for locating bibliographies relating to one's narrow topic are discussed in chapter 10. Because currency is a very important characteristic of overviews, the following list is limited by date. Nothing published before 1980 has been included. This list is but a partial one. No attempt has been made to include those review essays regularly included in many of the yearbooks and annual reviews cited in appendix 1.

Bergerson, Peter J. (1988). *Ethics and Public Policy: An Annotated Bibliography*. New York: Garland. 200 p.

Citations accompanied by long abstracts are preceded by a good review article. A very good survey of this topic.

Borgatta, Edgar F., & Cook, Karen S. (Eds.). (1988). *The Future of Sociology*. Newbury Park, CA: Sage. 422 p.

A collection of essays reviewing topics and methods on the cutting edge of this discipline.

Brown, J. Cudd. (1980). *A Selective Bibliography and Specific Bibliographies Relevant to Management Improvement and Productivity Enhancement in the United States Government in Compliance with the Civil Service Reform Act of 1978*. Washington, DC: U.S. Office of Personnel Management. 54 p.

Butcher, Tony. (1984). Public Administration and Policy Studies. In Englefield, Dermot, & Drewry, Gavin (Eds.), *Information Sources in Politics and Political Science: A Survey Worldwide* (pp. 189–208) London: Butterworths. 509 p.
An excellent short overview of writings, although British in its orientation. Other interesting essays in this volume address local government and the judiciary and government.

Caiden, Gerald E. (Ed.). (1983). *American Public Administration: A Bibliographical Guide to the Literature*. New York: Garland. 201 p.
Includes chapters either reviewing the field or discussing bibliographic access to it. One in the former category includes an essay on the scope of the field. Another presents a lengthy bibliography of the most influential works in it. See also McCurdy (below).

Cullen, Finnuala. (1984). A Selective Bibliography of Publications on Management in Government from 1979 to 1984. *Management in Government, 39*, (May), 153–56.

Finifter, Ada W. (Ed.). (1983). *Political Science: The State of the Discipline*. Washington, DC: American Political Science Association. 614 p.
A collection of some 19 papers that address the discipline as a whole. A substantial proportion of them are concerned with policy or otherwise address public agencies and the political process.

Goehlert, Robert U., & Martin, Fenton S. (1985). *Policy Analysis and Management: A Bibliography*. Santa Barbara, CA: ABC-Clio. 398 p.
Divided into seven sections: concepts, theories, and economic, political, social, science and technology, and environmental policy issues. No annotations, but an extensive and well-organized guide to the current literature.

Gunn, Elizabeth M. (1980). *Ethics and the Public Service: An Annotated Bibliography and Overview Essay*. Norman, OK: University of Oklahoma, Bureau of Government Research. 47 p.
The "overview essay" constitutes a good review of this topic.

Hero, Rodney E. (1986). The Urban Service Delivery Literature: Some Questions and Considerations. *Polity, 18* (Summer), 659–77.

A review that is most critical of recent research studies for their general characterization of citizens as passive consumers and their failure to appreciate both the full range of urban services and the power of public agencies in the creation of policy. Methodological criticisms of these studies are also made.

Herron, Nancy L. (Ed.). (1989). *The Social Sciences: A Cross-Disciplinary Guide to Selected Sources*. Englewood, CO: Libraries Unlimited. 287 p.

Cited here for its review essays, which collectively attempt to present a current assessment of the social sciences and the relationships between them. These essays are valuable only if very general perspectives are needed.

Holzer, Marc, & Halachmi, Arie. (1988). *Public Sector Productivity: A Resource Guide*. New York: Garland. 166 p.

Covers articles, books, and government documents. Also includes listings of relevant journals and associations.

Huddleston, Mark W. (1984). *Comparative Public Administration: An Annotated Bibliography*. New York: Garland. 245 p.

Addresses an area that has come to affect the mainstream of thought in administration research. The bibliography "consists mainly in selected references to English language books and articles published from 1962 through 1981." Over 600 entries.

Kass, Henry D., & Catron, Bayard L. (1990). *Images and Identities in Public Administration*. Newbury Park, CA: Sage. 266 p.

Essays included are very much concerned with conceptions of the field held by those within and without it. Valuable for these latter perceptions alone.

Lovrich, Nicholas P., & Neiman, Max. (1984). *Public Choice Theory in Public Administration: An Annotated Bibliography*. New York: Garland. 122 p.

A quite selective, but very good, listing of sources both supportive and critical of this increasingly important approach to public decision making. Preceded by a good discussion of dilemmas in the area.

Lynn, Naomi B., & Wildavsky, Aaron (Eds.). (1990). *Public Administration: The State of the Discipline*. Chatham, NJ: Chatham House. 540 p.

Reviewers have used the term "self-conscious" in describing this book and have done so in a positive sense. Chapters are organized within six parts. One of these addresses theory; others concern methodological and historical approaches.

McCurdy, Howard E. (1986). *Public Administration: A Bibliographic Guide to the Literature*. New York: Dekker. 311 p.

Presents a long review of theoretical development, followed by long summaries of each of the almost 200 books that "are the principal knowledge base upon which the practice of public administration is based." The final section is a classified bibliography, without annotations, of the 1,200 books considered to be most influential. Essential reading for even the experienced researcher. The first two chapters constitute the best discussion I have encountered of the development of public administration as an object of study.

McCurdy, Howard E. & Cleary Robert E. (1984). Why Can't We Resolve the Research Issue in Public Administration? *Public Administration Review, 44*, January/February, 49-55.

A critical analysis of scholarship in this field through examination of published research. The general finding suggests that public administration has yet to develop rigorous standards of scholarly practice. See also the two 1986 articles by White (below).

McInnis, Raymond G. (1982). *Research Guide for Psychology*. Westport, CT: Greenwood. 604 p.

A thorough guide to recent literature. A model work of its kind. Includes an entire section on applied psychology (pp. 425–70) that gives an excellent survey of psychological issues in the workplace. Essential reading in this area.

Miewald, Robert D. (1984). *The Bureaucratic State: An Annotated Bibliography*. New York: Garland. 601 p.

A very extensive bibliography preceded by a short interpretative essay. Items are in classified order, and annotations, although very short, are often analytical.

Morgan, David, & Stanley, Liz (Eds.). *Debates in Sociology*. Manchester, UK: Manchester University Press. 256 p.

Reviews current issues considered to be central to this discipline through a collection of articles reprinted or excerpted from *Sociology*, the official journal of the British Sociological Association. This collection attempts to present competing views that reflect the substance of recent debate.

Murin, William J., Greenfield, Gerald M. & Buenker, John D. (Eds.). (1981). *Public Policy: A Guide to Information Sources*. Detroit: Gale. 283 p.

An extensive listing of sources, but with little discussion of their value.

Nagel, Stuart S. (1984). *Basic Literature in Policy Studies: A Comprehensive Bibliography*. Greenwich, CT: JAI Press. 453 p.

A thorough guide to this specialty. Good annotations are provided in entries.

Nagel, Stuart S. (1985). An Overview of the Policy Studies Literature, 1970–1985. *Behavioral and Social Sciences Librarian, 4* (Summer), 49–59.

A short critical review of this rapidly growing field through literature that emphasizes its links to public administration. Limited almost entirely to books.

Obern, A. Gaylord, & Nunez, Richard I. (1983). *Annotated Bibliography on Staff Training and Development in the Public Sector and on Public Finance Management, Accounting, and Audit: Developing Countries*. New York: United Nations, Department of Technical Cooperation for Development. 102 p.

Presents over 550 annotated citations to works published in a variety of forms. Most of the references are to works published in English in the 1960s and 1970s.

Overman, E. S., & Garson, G. D. (1983). Themes of Contemporary Public Management. *Public Administration Quarterly, 7* (Summer), 139–61.

Dominant themes are assessed from a survey of current practice, not from an analysis of the literature. Results emphasize continuing links with traditional perspectives such as scientific management, allied with increased concern for policy analysis.

Paul, Samuel. (1983). *Training for Public Administration and Management in Developing Countries: A Review*. Washington, DC: World Bank. 132 p.

A review of current practices and current needs. Identifies key areas where improvements are especially needed and makes recommendations as to how these needs can be met.

Payad, Aurora T. (1986). *Organization Behavior in American Public Administration: An Annotated Bibliography*. New York: Garland. 264 p.

An important bibliography on an important subject. Entries are taken from the major journals in administration from the mid-1970s onward.

Peters, B. Guy. (1981). Comparative Public Policy. *Policy Studies Review, 1* (August), 183–97.

Robey, John S. (1984). Policymaking, Analysis, and Evaluation: A Topical Bibliography of Recent Research (1977–81). *Policy Studies Review, 3* (May), 521–8.

A more selective review than that given in Robey's *Public Policy Analysis* (see below). Reports of research projects only are included.

Robey, John S. (1984). *Public Policy Analysis: An Annotated Bibliography.* New York: Garland. 195 p.

The first 11 chapters address policy analysis in given settings. The last 2 are especially valuable for their consideration of theoretical and conceptual approaches.

Rosenbloom, David H. (1983). *Public Administration and Law: Bench v. Bureau in the United States.* New York: Dekker. 236 p.

A good review of the area, but now dated due to ongoing developments in aspects such as the law relating to personnel actions.

Stallings, Robert A., & Ferris, James M. (1988). Public Administration Research: Work in *PAR*, 1940–1984. *Public Administration Review, 48* (January/February), 580–87.

Analyzes the contents of research articles in this journal according to five characteristics: approach, research design, topic, level of organization studied, and researcher characteristics. Concludes that research continues to be geared to practical rather than theoretical concerns.

Wamsley, Gary L. (1990). *Refounding Public Administration.* Newbury Park, CA: Sage. 333 p.

Essays included in this work present a strong defense of public administration as an independent area of study. Worth reading for the integrity of its position, even though this may not be one supported here.

White, Jay D. (1986). Dissertations and Publications in Public Administration. *Public Administration Review, 46*, 227–34.

An update of McCurdy and Cleary (1981). On the basis of an examination of 305 dissertation abstracts published in 1980 and 1981, found that a high proportion of these do not appear to meet accepted standards of social research. This finding supports the 1981 conclusion that the quality of scholarly research in the field still lags behind that in the other social sciences.

White, Jay D. (1986). On the Growth of Knowledge in Public Administration. *Public Administration Review, 46*, 15–24.

Presents the opinion that a new theory of public administration is developing based on some presumed and necessary connection between theory and practice. Discusses different "modes" of social research and provides a strong critique of their application in this subject area.

4. BIBLIOGRAPHIC GUIDES

The works cited here are the principal guides to the literature and to information-finding methods in the various subject areas that relate to public administration. A researcher undertaking a project that relates to one or another of these areas should take the precaution of examining the appropriate guides in order to at least identify sources of potential value not considered here.

There are also bibliographic guides that do not address particular subject specialties, but instead focus on materials published in specific forms. Such forms include technical reports, dissertations, conference papers, and, of most import, documents issued at the various levels of government. Specialized guides of this nature are discussed at different points in this book.

Some fields are served by several guides of a similar nature. In compiling the following list an effort has been made to include only the most comprehensive guides and those most suitable for someone preparing to undertake original research. Guides that focus on the location, use, or manipulation of *primary* sources are discussed at appropriate points in this book.

4.1. General

The major guides are those crucial six discussed at the beginning of the previous chapter. None of those mentioned in this section supplants them. More specialized guides are, however, of great value, particularly in directing their users to sources of primary data and methodologies of peculiar interest to their disciplinary perspective.

The existence of guides in areas not mentioned here may be determined through the work by Sable, cited below. This in turn can be updated using standard sources of current reference works, such as *American Reference Books Annual*.

Carter, Sarah, & Ritchie, Maureen. (1990). *Women's Studies: A Guide to Information Sources*. Jefferson, NC: McFarland. 278 p.

An interdisciplinary guide most useful as a supplement to Searing (below) because of the currency of its references.

McNeil, Robert A., & Valk, Barbara G. (Eds.). (1990). *Latin American Studies: A Basic Guide to Sources* (2nd ed.). Metuchen, NJ: Scarecrow. 458 p.

An important and extensive guide indispensable to anyone preparing to engage in any aspect of social research addressing this area. Intended to meet the needs of the scholar concerned also with primary sources.

Sable, Martin H. (1986). *Research Guides to the Humanities, Social Sciences, Sciences, and Technology: An Annotated Bibliography of Guides to Library Resources and Usage Arranged by Subject or Discipline of Coverage.* Ann Arbor, MI: Pierian. 181 p.
Discusses over 160 guides, almost all of which were published after 1970.

Searing, Susan E. (1985). *Introduction to Library Research in Women's Studies.* Boulder, CO: Westview. 257 p.
Cited here as one example of a number of guides addressing popular interdisciplinary approaches to academic research. This work, like others that incorporate movements across traditional boundaries, cannot do full justice to the range of its subject matter and should only be used in conjunction with guides in relevant disciplines. Use in conjunction with Carter and Ritchie (above).

4.2. Public Administration

Cutchin, D. A. (1981). *Guide to Public Administration.* Itasca, IL: Peacock. 159 p.
In essence a rather limited dictionary of related terms. Also includes annotated bibliographies of research resources (that is, general reference books) and journals and abstracting services.

Rouse, John E. (Ed.). (1980). *Public Administration in American Society: A Guide to Information Sources.* Detroit: Gale. 553 p.
Essentially an annotated bibliography concentrating on books and articles addressing the growth of the public sector in recent decades and its impact upon society. The 11 chapters address all major areas of public administration. A valuable general bibliography in the field that discusses reference tools as well as secondary sources.

Wasserman, Paul, Kelly, James R., & Vikor, Desider L. (Eds.). (1988). *Encyclopedia of Public Affairs Information Sources.* Detroit: Gale. 303 p.
Like similar works published by Gale, basically a bibliography of reference sources, arranged by narrow topic. There are no annotations, and the work is extremely broad in the scope of its coverage.

Wright, Martin. (1977). The Literature and Sources of Public Administration. In Roberts, N. (Ed.), *Use of Social Sciences Literature* (pp. 192–218). London: Butterworths. 326 p.
A good short guide that emphasizes approaches to British sources.

4.3. Business and Management

Bakewell, K. G. B. (Ed.). (1977). *Management Principles and Practice: Guide to Information Sources*. Detroit: Gale. 519 p.

One of the few guides devoted exclusively to administration as a theoretical study. Annotations are very brief; attention is more on identification of sources than on their use.

Lavin, Michael R. (1992). *Business Information: How to Find It, How to Use It* (2nd ed.). Phoenix, AZ: Oryx. 499 p.

Best for its discussions of sources of information on companies, markets, and financial indicators.

Strauss, Diane W. (1988). *Handbook of Business Information: A Guide for Librarians, Students, and Researchers*. Englewood, CO: Libraries Unlimited. 537 p.

Not as extensive as Daniells (see chapter 3) in materials covered, but a valuable supplement to it because of its discussions of information-finding techniques and use of sources.

Thompson, Marilyn T. (1981). *Management Information, Where to Find It.* Metuchen, NJ: Scarecrow. 272 p.

Essentially a bibliography of sources, with little discussion as to their content or use. However, cites the major bibliographic tools in the area.

Vernon, K. D. C. (Ed.). (1984). *Information Sources in Management and Business* (2nd ed.). London: Butterworths. 346 p.

Combines discussion of methods with literature reviews of six related areas.

4.4. Political Science

Brock, Clifton. (1969). *The Literature of Political Science: A Guide for Students, Librarians, and Teachers*. New York: Bowker. 232 p.

Too old now to be reliable for some of its sources. Still the best discussion of methodology in this area.

Englefield, Dermot, and Drewry, Gavin (Eds.). (1984). *Information Sources in Politics and Political Science: A Survey Worldwide*. London: Butterworths. 509 p.

A series of review essays on a variety of topics that pays some attention to the finding of information. Despite its title, emphasizes British sources. The first chapter is entitled "Library and Bibliographical Aids to the Study of Politics."

Holler, Frederick L. (1986). *Information Sources of Political Science* (4th ed.). Santa Barbara, CA: ABC–Clio. 417 p.

The best single listing of reference tools in this area. Discussion of particular subject areas is preceded by an essay addressing search techniques. Includes strong sections dealing with public administration. The best guide of its kind.

York, Henry E. (1990). *Political Science: A Guide to Reference and Information Sources*. Englewood, CO: Libraries Unlimited. 249 p.

Not as comprehensive as Holler (above), but an important supplement to it because it focuses on reference and other works published during the 1980s.

4.5. Sociology

Aby, Stephen H. (1987). *Sociology: A Guide to Reference and Information Sources*. Littleton, CO: Libraries Unlimited. 231 p.

An excellent guide to reference works in this area. Limited by its lack of discussion of the research process.

Bart, Pauline, & Frankel, Linda. (1986). *The Student Sociologist's Handbook* (4th ed.). New York: Random House. 291 p.

The most extensive of a fairly weak group of guides in this discipline. Concerned with methods as well as sources, but primarily concerned with the needs of the undergraduate student. Should be used in conjunction with Aby.

Guttsman, W. L. (1977). The Literature of Sociology. In Roberts, N. (Ed.), *Use of Social Sciences Literature* (pp. 56–79). London: Butterworths. 326 p.

A very good discussion of the place of sociology and its literature in the social sciences. Too limited to address more than the principal sources.

4.6. Economics

Fletcher, John (Ed.). (1984). *Information Sources in Economics* (2nd ed.). London: Butterworths. 339 p.

A collection of 22 essays addressing recent and historical trends in the literature and bibliographic methods. Also addresses some types of primary sources, including statistics. Like other books in this series, heavily British in its orientation.

Melnyk, Peter. (1971). *Economics: Bibliographic Guide to Reference Books and Information Sources*. Littleton, CO: Libraries Unlimited. 263 p.
Goes well beyond economic theory and into areas such as public finance, labor economics, and economic conditions. Now old; should be used in conjunction with the works cited in section 2.5 of chapter 3 above.

4.7. Psychology

Borchardt, D. H., & Francis, R. D. (1984). *How to Find Out in Psychology: A Guide to the Literature and Methods of Research*. Oxford, UK: Pergamon. 189 p.
A thematic guide to the discipline and its literature. Short, but informative, and excellent for its discussions of research methods.

Reed, Jeffrey G., & Baxter, Pam M. (1992). *Library Use: A Handbook for Psychology* (2nd ed.).Washington, DC: American Psychological Association. 179 p.
Good as an introduction, but intended for the beginner and limited in the sources covered. Strong on topic selection and refinement. Use with McInnis (see section 3 of this chapter).

4.8. Anthropology

Brunvand, Jan H. (1976). *Folklore: A Study and Research Guide*. New York: St. Martin's. 144 p.
One chapter discusses reference works in this specialized area. Others review major theories and research studies.

Currier, Margaret. (1976). Problems in Anthropological Bibliography. *Annual Review of Anthropology, 5*, 15–34.
A valuable discussion of the major reference works and of techniques for negotiating the limitations of the bibliographic sources in this discipline.

Frantz, Charles. (1972). *The Student Anthropologist's Handbook: A Guide to Research, Training, and Career*. Cambridge, MA: Schenkman. 228 p.
A dated work that only covers library research as one of a number of issues.

Haas, Marilyn L. (1977). Anthropology: A Guide to Basic Sources. *Reference Services Review, 5* (Winter), 45–51.

The best introduction to bibliographic research in this discipline. Much of the discussion addresses sources that are outside of anthropology, but that are important for its documentation.

Kibbee, Josephine Z. (1991). *Cultural Anthropology: A Guide to Reference and Information Sources*. Englewood, CO: Libraries Unlimited. 205 p.

Despite its title, addresses all related branches of this discipline (archeology, ethnology, folklore, linguistics, and applied, physical, and psychological anthropology). A good competitor to Weeks (below), but not satisfactory in its discussions of archives.

Smith, Margo L., & Damien, Yvonne M. (Comps.). (1981). *Anthropological Bibliographies: A Selected Guide*. South Salem, NY: Redgrave. 307 p.

Lists a large number of bibliographic sources published in a variety of forms. No discussion of techniques, but does provide a starting point for research in this rich, but poorly documented discipline. The preface lists major reference works.

Urry, J. (1977). The Literature of Social Anthropology. In Roberts, N. (Ed.), *Use of Social Sciences Literature* (pp. 101–17). London: Butterworths. 326 p.

Defines the field fairly narrowly, but provides discussion of the standard bibliographic tools and of information-gathering techniques.

Weeks, John M. (1991). *Introduction to Library Research in Anthropology*. Boulder, CO: Westview. 281 p.

Similar to Kibbee (above) in scope and currency but refers to many more sources.

4.9. History

Guides in this discipline tend to focus on particular regional and/or temporal settings, and only a few examples of them are given below. Other specialized works may be found through the six major bibliographic guides to the social sciences, noted early in chapter 3.

Freidel, Frank B. (Ed.). (1974). *Harvard Guide to American History* (rev. ed.). Cambridge, MA: Belknap Press. 2 vols.

The basic reference bibliography in its area and one long overdue for revision. Entries are arranged chronologically and by topic and include published primary sources as well as secondary works. The first volume includes chapters addressing research methods and sources.

Howe, George F. (Ed.). (1961). *Guide to Historical Literature.* New York: Macmillan. 962 p.

Like Freidel (above), presents topical bibliographies of major works. Despite its age, still a major resource in the discipline. Should be used as a starting point and supplemented by a more specialized guide, if an appropriate one exists.

Jessup, John E., & Coakley, Robert W. (1979). *A Guide to the Study and Use of Military History.* Washington, DC: Center of Military History. 507 p.

Cited here as an example of an excellent guide to research in one of the many specialized areas well covered bibliographically.

Mitterling, Philip I. (Ed.). (1980). *U.S. Cultural History: A Guide to Information Sources.* Detroit: Gale. 581 p.

Interprets its subject matter broadly to include popular culture and economic, political, and social thought. A bibliography, but has good chapters and sections on reference sources.

Prucha, Francis P. (1987). *Handbook for Research in American History: A Guide to Bibliographies and Other Reference Works.* Lincoln, NE: University of Nebraska Press. 289 p.

The only up-to-date guide of its kind. Discussion of general sources followed by sections dealing with particular periods and subjects. Does not address methodology.

Trask, David F., & Pomeroy, Robert W. (Eds.). (1983). *The Craft of Public History; An Annotated Select Bibliography.* Westport, CT: Greenwood. 481 p.

More than a bibliography, this is a topical introduction to methods and sources in this rapidly growing field. All aspects of public history are considered, and the emphasis is very much on the practical concerns of the researcher and archivist.

4.10. Philosophy

De George, Richard T. (1980). *The Philosopher's Guide to Sources, Research Tools, Professional Life and Related Fields.* Lawrence, KA: Regents Press. 261 p.

Probably the most comprehensive guide available. Also valuable for its coverage of bibliographic tools in related areas. The second edition of a standard work.

Matczak, Sebastian A. (1975). *Philosophy: Its Nature, Methods, and Basic Sources*. New York: Learned Publications. 280 p.

A good competitor to De George, with annotations and descriptions that are sometimes more extensive.

4.11. Personnel and Human Resources

Franklin, Jerome L. (Ed.). (1978). *Human Resource Development in the Organization: A Guide to Information Sources*. Detroit: Gale. 175 p.

Hanson, Agnes O. (Ed.). (1976). *Executive and Management Development for Business and Government: A Guide to Information Sources*. Detroit: Gale. 357 p.

Like other works in this series by Gale, the above two are bibliographies rather than bibliographic guides. Useful given their age. The researcher in this field would be better off using the guides in the broader areas of business and management to gain an understanding of the range of resources in this field.

4.12. Education

Berry, Dorothea M. (1990). *A Bibliographic Guide to Educational Research* (3rd ed.). Metuchen, NJ: Scarecrow. 500 p.

Less critical than Woodbury (below) and more suited to the beginning researcher and the practitioner.

Buttlar, Lois J. (1989). *Education: A Guide to Reference and Information Sources*. Englewood, CO: Libraries Unlimited.
258 p.

The most current of the three guides listed here and the one that emphasizes bibliographic techniques most strongly.

Woodbury, Marda. (1982). *A Guide to Sources of Educational Information* (2nd ed.). Arlington, VA: Information Resources. 430 p.

Especially good for its discussion of research methods and sources of tests and other research instruments. Includes a chapter addressing educational finance and government. More than a guide to printed sources, as it discusses government agencies and other institutional sources of information.

4.13. Criminal Justice

Lutzker, Marilyn, & Ferrall, Eleanor. (1986). *Criminal Justice Research in Libraries*. Westport, CT: Greenwood. 167 p.

Addresses the methods of library research, as well as the tools and sources in this field, and is intended mainly for the undergraduate. Includes a chapter on the problems of finding materials on other countries and one on historical research. The chapter on legal research should be used with care.

O'Block, Robert L. (1986). *Criminal Justice Research Sources* (2nd ed). Cincinnati: Anderson. 183 p.

Often good for its annotated listings of sources, but includes little discussion of techniques. An uneven work that should be used in conjunction with Lutzker and Ferrall (above).

4.14. Other Areas

Fishburn, Katherine. (1982). *Women in Popular Culture: A Reference Guide*. Westport, CT: Greenwood. 267 p.

Primarily a review of the field through bibliographic essays. Some attention is paid to information-finding aids and archival sources.

Landrum, Larry N. (1982). *American Popular Culture: A Guide to Information Sources*. Detroit: Gale. 435 p.

Mendelsohn, Henry N. (1987). *A Guide to Information Sources for Social Work and the Human Services*. Phoenix, AZ: Oryx. 136 p.

Interprets its subject-matter broadly to include the approaches of many of the social and behavioral sciences. Because of this, quite selective in its coverage. Best used as a guide to the applied social sciences.

Propas, Sharon W. (1992). *Victorian Studies: A Research Guide*. New York: Garland. 334 p.

A cross-disciplinary guide which emphasizes the humanities but also addresses relevant sources for conventional historical research.

5

THE CONVENTIONAL LIBRARY CATALOG AND SOURCES OF CURRENT BOOKS

The emphasis thus far has been on the *identification* of published works likely to provide information relevant to the research project. The *location* of books and other separately published materials on the same topics is found through catalogs of libraries and library systems.

Researchers should survey the library collection as a whole at different levels of intensity at each stage of the search. At an early point, researchers may simply want to get a general idea of the range and currency of works on a provisional topic. Later, they may wish to explore a topic in more detail, using works discussed in earlier chapters and otherwise extending the bibliographies provided by these sources. Finally, a time will come when a thorough search of the literature will be required on a topic that has now been refined and restructured.

Whatever the situation, researchers need to acquire at an early stage in the endeavor the skills for exploiting the book collection of a large research library to the full. These skills are usually the most important in the information seeker's repertoire because library catalogs invariably address "monographs" rather than "books"; the former is a more expansive term covering any separately published item, including pamphlets, reports, dissertations, and government documents as well as books. Published materials traditionally excluded from catalogs are articles in journals and other periodical articles and essays in collections. For these, a separate search must be made (see chapters 8 and 9). Fortunately, these skills are readily transferable from one library to the next. They are standardized since most academic libraries today use the subject headings and classification systems established by the Library of Congress (LC).[1] Libraries indeed have compelling reasons for doing so. The Library of Congress catalogs (that is, sets up entries and assigns subject headings and call numbers) to almost all books and many other types of monographs published in English and to a high proportion of those published in other Western countries. Libraries that accept LC copy for the books they acquire thereby save themselves the considerable expense that the cataloging process requires. The organization of library materials tends to follow a constant pattern; techniques and approaches learned in one academic library are universal and easily applied in another. Public libraries usually follow a different system of classification, the Dewey Decimal System, which is also a by-product of LC cataloging. Libraries using it, however, also subscribe to standard LC subject-headings.

Potential problems for the user lie in the fact that many of the larger research libraries and some small specialized libraries have developed unique systems of organization that must be learned for effective use. The situation is not, however, a serious one. The Library of Congress has been cataloging books for other libraries since 1898. Most research libraries have long relied upon its subject headings, and subject searches in their catalogs are standard in form. Moreover, even the biggest institutions are converting rapidly to the LC classification system. The pace of this conversion is accelerating as many develop computerized catalogs (see the following chapter) that further encourage standardization of library practice. The situation is not as critical in the United States, as elsewhere, for example, in Western Europe, where the user of a major research library often must cope with a quite different concept of subject access. Many European libraries do not acknowledge responsibility for subject access through their catalogs, and users must use the catalog only to search works identified through bibliographies. Here again, technology is making rapid inroads and with computerization comes standardization to the American model.

Card and computerized catalogs are similar in structure and content, but quite different in form. The ways that they can be searched are also quite different. For these reasons, they are considered separately here. Knowledge of both types is essential because many libraries, particularly the larger ones, document recently acquired holdings in computerized catalogs and older collections in card form. Although such libraries are endeavoring to recatalog their entire collections in electronic form, it will be many years before this has been accomplished universally.

1. THE CARD CATALOG

Traditional card catalogs take either the "separate" or the "integrated" form. In the former, works are listed by author and title in one part of the file and by subject in the other. In the latter, entries are arranged by author, title, and subject in one integrated alphabetical listing. Whatever the case, author and title searches are straightforward, although the accomplished user must learn to appreciate certain apparently bizarre, but again standardized, rules of alphabetizing.[2]

Searching by either author or title is always an option, and the decision on which approach to take is governed by practical considerations. Government documents, for example, are often difficult to search by author if this is not a person but an agency. Unless the title looks problematic (if it was simply *Report* or *Hearings*), a title search is usually in order. A combination of author and title searching often solves the problem of searching citations that are incomplete or wrong. Many works are distinguished by "added entries" integrated in the catalog, identifying works by characteristics such as coauthor(s), editor(s), series, and sponsor.

Figure 1 ("The Library Catalog Card") illustrates the structure of entries and the nature of the information provided in them. The figure shows the various entries (author, title, and subject) for the same work; in other words, the different ways it can be located through the catalog. The card, under whichever entry it is found, shows that the library has the item and where it is to be found. The card also provides other valuable information about the work, for example, length, type of work, and existence and scope of a bibliography.

Other information provided may also help the user assess the potential value of the work before he or she actually looks at it: date of publication (indicating timeliness of the work in reviewing other theories and findings of relevance) and provenance (the nature, interests, and reputation of the sponsor or publisher). In these ways the catalog entry can go beyond its usual function of helping the user locate a known work.

2. SUBJECT SEARCHING AND THE LC SYSTEM

Subject searches are not just mechanical exercises. They are not influenced entirely by local rules of alphabetization or universal rules of common sense. The key to an effective search is the isolation of headings that are the most relevant and most precise. Often one can guess the headings in the catalog that are relevant to a topic, but seldom can one guess the most precise and appropriate heading. A detailed guide to headings established by the Library of Congress is published and revised more or less annually; the latest edition of this work (commonly referred to as the *Red Book* or the *LCSH*), now in three volumes, is cited below:[3]

U.S. Library of Congress. Office for Subject Cataloging Policy. (1992). *Subject Headings* (15th ed.). Washington, DC. 3 vols.

All libraries keep one or more copies of the latest edition of this set in close proximity to their catalogs. Its main purpose is to enable the reader, first, to identify all relevant headings on the topic, and, second, to locate the most

Figure 1
The Library Catalog Card

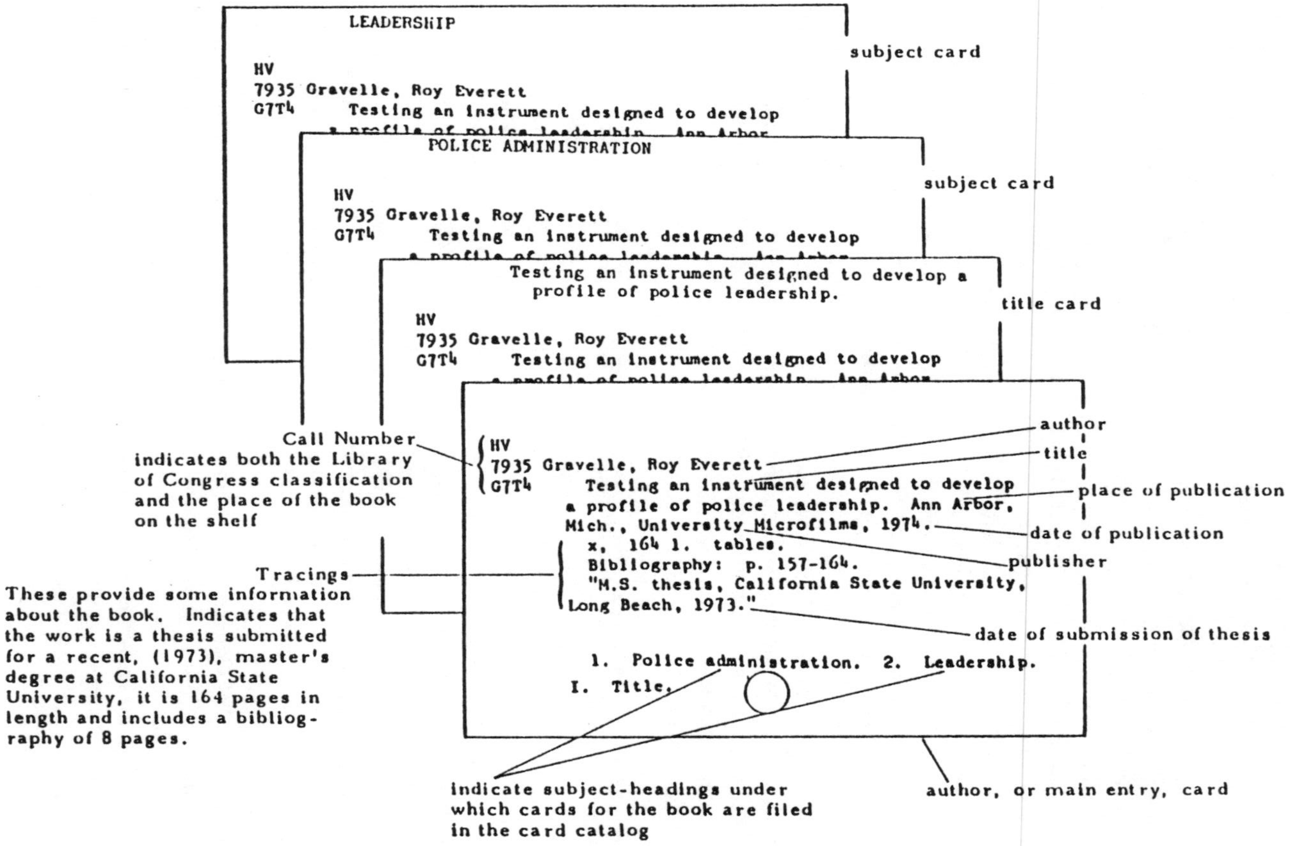

LEADERSHIP
HV
7935 Gravelle, Roy Everett
G7T4 Testing an instrument designed to develop
subject card
POLICE ADMINISTRATION
HV
7935 Gravelle, Roy Everett
G7T4 Testing an instrument designed to develop
subject card
Testing an instrument designed to develop a profile of police leadership.
HV
7935 Gravelle, Roy Everett
G7T4 Testing an instrument designed to develop
title card
HV
7935 Gravelle, Roy Everett
G7T4 Testing an instrument designed to develop
a profile of police leadership. Ann Arbor,
Mich., University Microfilms, 1974.
x, 164 l. tables.
Bibliography: p. 157-164.
"M.S. thesis, California State University,
Long Beach, 1973."
1. Police administration. 2. Leadership.
I. Title.
author
title
place of publication
date of publication
publisher
date of submission of thesis
Call Number
indicates both the Library of Congress classification and the place of the book on the shelf
Tracings
These provide some information about the book. Indicates that the work is a thesis submitted for a recent, (1973), master's degree at California State University, it is 164 pages in length and includes a bibliography of 8 pages.
indicate subject-headings under which cards for the book are filed in the card catalog
author, or main entry, card

precise headings. Figure 2 shows a list of accepted terms and headings in the catalog designated in boldface type. Following the boldface entry, valuable information about the heading is usually given. This can include a brief explanation of the scope of the heading together with an indication of the call-number areas most clearly associated with it.[4]

The example in figure 2 tells exactly what field the heading **Personnel management** is defined to cover; how, for example, it excludes supervision of employees. The designation "UF" (meaning "Use For") further illustrates the limits of coverage of this term. You are also given the range of call numbers that generally address this topic. The information "May Subd Geog" simply tells you to expect to find geographic subheadings under the topic, **Personnel management—Alabama**, for example.

The entries below this suggest related subject headings that are also used in the catalog. Those designated "BT" are "Broader Terms" that incorporate the heading of interest, but extend beyond it. "SA" ("See Also") references guide the user to other entries under which works relating directly to personnel management can be found. Most interesting is the list (in this example, a very long list), of "Narrower Terms" ("NT"). In a broad subject area such as this, few people would wish to search under a heading as general as **Personnel management**. The NT designations direct the user to more specific headings addressing particular aspects of this subject. Given the principle that the more precise the heading the better, this part of the entry is often of the greatest value to the user.

Specificity is also served by recognition of subdivisions of the heading, other than those that are geographical. Here, the *Red Book* is helpful, but less than candid, pointing to any subject-driven subdivisions that are particular to this heading. Figure 3 describes the existence of a heading **Evaluation research (Social action programs)—Utilization**. You are not told of subdivisions that are standard and may be applied to any subject. Instead, you are pointed to important aspects of the subject such as **Bibliography**, **Case studies**, or **Psychological aspects**. It is not easy to identify from the *Red Book* which subject subdivisions could exist, nor are you advised to try. The best solution to this problem is to first use the *Red Book* to determine the major headings of interest. Then locate the heading in the catalog. Before examining the entries under it, quickly flick through the body of entries to determine the existence of any subdivisions of special concern.

One other problem exists that is resolved by the *Red Book*, by and large. This concerns terms that are used as subject headings, but also as subdivisions. For example, figure 3 shows that the terms **Evaluation** and **Evaluation research** are major headings in the catalog. The first entry directs you to broader, narrower, and related terms. It provides the general call-number range for this subject ("AZ191–AZ193"). A moment's thought suggests that limiting your activities to searching under this heading and looking through this call-number range will not

Figure 2
Subject Entry with Scope Note

— **Salaries, etc.** *(May Subd Geog)*
UF Wages—Personnel directors
Personnel management *(May Subd Geog)*
[*HF5549-HF5549.5*]
Here are entered works on that field of management which has the fundamental responsibility for recruiting, hiring, training, compensating, developing and caring for the general welfare of employees. Works on the managing of employees by their supervisors so that duties are performed according to instructions are entered under Supervision of employees. Works dealing with employer-employee relations in general are entered under Industrial relations.
UF Corporations—Personnel management
Employment management
Human resource management
Manpower utilization
Personnel administration
BT Management
Public administration
RT Employees
SA *subdivision* Personnel management *under names of individual corporate bodies and under types of industries and organizations, e.g.* United States. Navy—Personnel management; Construction industry —Personnel management; Hospitals —Personnel management
NT Affirmative action programs
Alcoholism and employment
Applications for positions
Career development
Church personnel management
Civil service—Personnel management
Communication in personnel management
Compensation management
Drugs and employment
Employee assistance programs
Employee competitive behavior
Employee morale
Employee motivation
Employee rules
Employee selection
Employees—Recruiting
Employment references
Employment stabilization
Employment tests
Goal setting in personnel management
Grievance procedures
Incentives in industry
Industrial sociology
Interviewing
Job analysis
Job enrichment
Job evaluation
Job postings
Job security
Labor discipline
Labor turnover
Library personnel management
Manpower planning
Motion study
Outplacement services
Performance awards
Personnel departments
Personnel procedure manuals
Personnel research
Promotions
Psychology, Industrial
Seniority, Employee
Supervision of employees
Time study
Timekeeping
Wages—Psychological aspects
— Information storage and retrieval systems
USE Information storage and retrieval systems—Personnel management
— Research
USE Personnel research
Personnel management in the civil service
USE Civil service—Personnel management
Personnel management libraries
(May Subd Geog)
[*Z675.P46*]
UF Libraries, Personnel management
BT Business libraries
Personnel managers
USE Personnel directors
Personnel procedure manuals
BT Personnel management
Personnel programs, Intergovernmental
USE Intergovernmental personnel programs
Personnel records *(May Subd Geog)*
UF Personnel records in industry
BT Records
SA *subdivision* Personnel records *under names of individual corporate bodies, e.g.* United States. Navy—Personnel records
NT Labor passports
— **Access control**
BT Confidential communications—Personnel records
Privacy, Right of
— **Law and legislation** *(May Subd Geog)*
BT Labor laws and legislation
NT Confidential communications—Personnel records
Personnel records in education
[*LB2845.7*]
UF Report cards
School children—Personnel records
Student records
Students—Personnel records

Source: US Library of Congress. Office for Subject Cataloging Policy. (1992). Library of Congress Subject Headings (15th ed.). Washington, DC. Vol. 3, pages 3,458-59.

Figure 3
Subject Entry with Subdivision Note

Evalt family
USE Ewald family
Evaluation *(May Subd Geog)*
[AZ191-AZ193]
BT Research
SA *subdivision* Evaluation *under names of individual corporate bodies and under subjects*
NT Disability evaluation
Educational evaluation
Evaluation research (Social action programs)
Job evaluation
Risk assessment
Self-evaluation
Student evaluation of curriculum
Student evaluation of teachers
Task analysis
Universities and colleges—Departments—Evaluation
Evaluation, Job
USE Job evaluation
Evaluation, Nondestructive
USE Non-destructive testing
Evaluation of curriculum
USE Curriculum evaluation
Evaluation of literature
USE Bibliography—Best books
Books and reading
Criticism
Literature—History and criticism
Evaluation of orthopedic disability
USE Orthopedic disability evaluation
Evaluation of psychiatric disability
USE Psychiatric disability evaluation
Evaluation of seedlings
USE Seedlings—Evaluation
Evaluation of social action programs
USE Evaluation research (Social action programs)
Evaluation research (Social action programs)
(May Subd Geog)
UF Evaluation of social action programs
Evaluative research (Social action programs)
BT Evaluation
Social action
Social sciences—Research
Social service—Research
SA *subdivision* Evaluation *under individually named programs or projects and under various types of programs or projects, e.g.* Economic development projects—Evaluation
—Utilization
UF Utilization of evaluation research (Social action programs)
Evaluation research in education

<u>Source</u>: US Library of Congress. Office for Subject Cataloging Policy. (1992). <u>Library of Congress Subject Headings</u> (15th ed.). Washington, DC. Vol. 2, page 1,552.

be satisfactory. The material found through such approaches will probably address the theory and techniques of evaluation in general and will certainly be helpful in this regard. However, most people engaged in this kind of research do so in particular contexts that have their own problems of data reliability, measurement, and criteria of expectation and judgment. The entries under the headings recognize this and expect you to look first under the major subject of concern and then under the subdivision **Evaluation**. In one instance, you are directed to see also the "subdivision **Evaluation** under names of individual corporate bodies and under subjects." In the other, slightly different wording includes as an example **Economic development projects—Evaluation**.

The subject-headings directory is more than just a listing of legal headings. "See" references are also incorporated directing the user from that word or phrase to the correct form of the heading. For example, if you look under the letter *H* to determine whether "Human resource management" is recognized as a heading in the catalog, you will find a "see" reference that will tell you that this is not an established heading and will direct you to the heading that is (**Personnel management**). This simple feature of this directory is invaluable.

You will find that careful use of the *Red Book* is essential to full exploitation of the library catalog, whether this is in card or computerized form. The more you know about your subject and the more clearly you define it, the better you can build upon your knowledge. Assessment of how best to approach the subject catalog is greatly informed by a knowledge of the field and common approaches to it.

Time spent with the subject-headings list is therefore rarely wasted and has value beyond using the catalog. Many, though by no means all, kinds of indexing and abstracting services addressed in chapter 8 and the databases addressed in chapter 9 also subscribe to the LC system or some version of it. Those who have determined the best subject headings to search in the catalog will also apply these same headings in their searches of at least some of the sources covering journals and other forms of published material generally excluded from the library catalog.

The catalog is an important and a sophisticated tool. As with any research instrument, its use is sometimes problematic. One obvious difficulty concerns the ways in which works are assigned their subject headings. Books cataloged by the Library of Congress are processed by subject specialists whose professional task it is to ensure that the several (usually three or four) subject headings assigned to a work are an accurate reflection of its substance. However, as with any human process, decisions reached by catalogers may reflect the interests of a particular individual or social perspective, and the headings that result may not be easily comprehensible to someone with a different worldview. Although the master list of LC headings is constantly revised to reflect new developments and changing scholarly perceptions, the fact is that not all subject areas are equally well served by this schema.

Thus it is difficult to know just which of numerous interesting-looking, but not quite accurate, headings should be searched. The computerized catalog (see the next chapter) solves this problem best. However, subject card catalogs commonly include "guide cards." These are nothing more than cards bearing "see" and "see also" references and filed appropriately. As with cross-references in the *Red Book*, they serve to direct the user from an unacceptable to a valid heading, and from a valid heading to narrower and other relevant terms. Useful as these are, they rarely provide the full range of options available in the complete lists of broader, narrower, and related headings given in the Red Book.

A different, and sometimes more valuable, approach is provided through the information given in the body of individual catalog cards. As discussed, figure 1 presents a diagrammatic representation of a set of catalog cards representing the author, title, and subject entries for a single work. The card for each entry is identical, except that on top of each is typed the particular word or phrase under which that card is to be filed. Attention has been given to ways in which the information on the body of the card can be used advantageously. Note the information given on the second-last line of the card, which indicates subject headings to which this work, and therefore other works of interest, have been assigned. A search under each and all of these headings will identify all pertinent sources included in the catalog. If one relevant book is known, this can be searched by author or title. A catalog card for it will indicate its location and will also provide a shortcut to the determination of the correct subject headings (and call-number areas) to search.

Although this technique is generally an effective second line of attack on the subject catalog, again it does not provide a cast-iron guarantee of success. Researchers should explore subject access to the catalog to the fullest and with techniques that knowledge and imagination suggest. Let us say, for example, that you have a general interest in theories of bureaucracy, but are especially interested in informal means of communication within this structural form. Your purpose will therefore be to find both analytical and case studies comparing classic theory with actual practice. At first, things may look promising. There are a number of appropriate headings in the LC list, including **Communication in organizations** and **Communication in Management**. A search, however, may produce a disappointingly small number of entries, and these may generally seem to address just the mechanics of formal communication. It is disturbing that these headings exclude works known to be classics in the field. The work of Michel Crozier, for example, has been assigned to the very broad headings **Bureaucracy** and **Industrial management**.[5]

The LC subject list often does not help to isolate a topic in the catalog. What should you do next? There are several possibilities. The first is to search the subject-headings list more imaginatively. Headings such as **Management** and **Organizational behavior** can be expected to include works referring to the ways that different management styles can influence all aspects of the functioning of a bureaucracy, including communications within it. It may be necessary to extend the search in this way.

Second, the very broad headings attached to seminal works in the field (like those of Crozier) suggest that similar works may have been cataloged consistently. The idea of searching the card catalog of a large research library under the general heading **Bureaucracy** and its many subdivisions may not be very appealing, but it would seem necessary in such a case. Before undertaking a time-consuming project of this nature, the researcher would be well advised to search other important works (previously identified through the sources discussed in chapters 3 and 4) to determine which subject headings have been assigned to them.

Next, round out the task in the old-fashioned way by conducting author or title searches of works identified in bibliographies. Locate these through relevant journal articles and through specialized encyclopedias, annual reviews, and other sources discussed in other chapters. Finally, try to shortcut the process through the valuable and time-honored technique of browsing (see the next section).

The occasional limitations of the subject approach to the card catalog, and indeed to the journal literature, have been demonstrated. These problems reflect the fact that no schematic outline of the social sciences can do justice to every perspective and every interest. Indeed, the situation can be even more complicated. To resurrect an example used in chapter 2, the concept of "modernization" has many dimensions—economic, political, social, legal, and cultural. There may be no subject heading that addresses any one of these dimensions properly, and there may be none that addresses the concept generally. However, our purpose is not to overemphasize the difficulties of using the subject catalog. The LC subject-headings list usually serves the researcher better than this, and most situations are straightforward. But no system of organizing information works for everything. The more narrow and personalized an interest, the more frequently is this problem encountered. Subject catalogs are designed for those who seek a unidimensional approach to a topic. They do not always work well for those who are custom-tailoring their own topics by taking perspectives not usually assumed and making links between issues that are not usually made. Use whatever system is at hand to the best advantage, and remedy its deficiencies by other means. The best catalog technique is the one that works best at the time.

No one should end this analysis of the search process without becoming informed as to exactly what the catalog includes and just what is to be searched. Although library catalogs have traditionally included monographs published in a variety of forms, many institutions have policies of not including certain collections. They might exclude federal documents, rare books, or dissertations for degrees awarded by the institution. This tendency has become more pronounced in recent years with the wide availability of published collections in microform of both primary and secondary sources (see chapter 16). Even small libraries now routinely buy such collections. Collections in microform represent a comparatively cheap way of building library subject strengths. These collections usually come with their own finding guides, an important matter because individual items are not always included in the purchasing library's main catalog. It has never been more important for the library user to be aware of what collections and published forms the catalog excludes and to learn how to access them by other means. This important addendum to catalog searching applies equally to the conventional card catalog and the one in computerized form.

3. THE LIBRARY OF CONGRESS SYSTEM AND BROWSING

One further technique exists that depends on the fact that the LC classification system, by which call numbers are assigned and by which books are arranged on the shelves, is a rigorously subject-oriented system. As figures 2 and 3 show, annotations in the subject-headings list frequently provide the general call-number area for books on a given subject. Appendix 2 includes the LC classification schedules for the general fields of sociology, the general social sciences, and political science. Included within them are the schedules for the policy sciences, public administration, and general management. These call-number schedules are hierarchical; that is, the call numbers for most areas in public administration lie within the schedule for the general area of political science, the "J" schedule. Management theory and practice generally lie within the schedule for the study of organizations and group behavior, the "H" schedule. Those who need the schedules for other areas within the social and behavioral sciences may go to the source from which appendix 2 was drawn.[6]

It follows that if one knows the approximate call-number area, browsing can be tremendously valuable in libraries with open stacks. To follow the example given in figure 2, if your topic relates to personnel management, go to the general call-number area that relates to it (HF5549) and browse through it. One can usually find the call-number range from the subject-headings list. If you are more ambitious, you can go to the relevant call-number schedule (see in appendix 2). This will indicate not just the general area but also any related areas of potential value.

Browsing is a priceless technique and one never to be ignored. Even if a book on your topic has been rendered inaccessible to you by the nature of its subject cataloging, the chances are that its call number will keep it close to similar studies. Every researcher has found important secondary sources by general browsing that would perhaps never have been uncovered by other means. Browsing is a particularly good way of assessing the scope of a subject or of stimulating the development of new lines of thought usually required in selection of the topic. It is also a valuable adjunct to searching when the subject catalog proves uncooperative.

Browsing is important even when you have successfully and accurately identified the appropriate subject headings. This is because of the wide-ranging nature of the research process and the fact that even the narrowest research project must somehow be tied to some larger world. To illustrate this, let us consider an earlier example of a legal historian interested in bureaucratic changes in the courts of a particular state of the United States in the 19th century, and how these changes related to other social and policy issues of the time. Such a person will obviously intend to read the quite massive literature on the subject in its time and place as well as works addressing the theory of legal systematic change. Other historical settings would, however, also be of interest. If similar (or radically different) changes were going on at the same time in other common-law jurisdictions, such as Virginia or England, then consideration of them would provide a titillating comparative perspective to the analysis. Searching for such items of ancillary interest could be done through the catalog, but this would be an extremely arduous business. Simple knowledge of the LC schedules would tell the historian that such materials would probably be housed in three principal areas of the stacks: KD, KFA through KFV, and sections of HV. Browsing through these areas would probably be the most productive means of approach.

Similarly, in investigating a particular theory of management by applying it to a determined setting, search for everything on both the theory and the setting. In addition, undertake a very selective search for material on the method of intended approach. Attempt to get at least a familiarity with other theories and related debates. In a large library, one way this familiarity could be gained is by browsing through the appropriate classifications in the stacks. Browsing is not a precise method of exploring a library's resources, but herein lies its strength as well as its weakness.

Browsing should not be used as an alternative to formal searching of the library collection. The reason for this lies in the nature of the book-cataloging process. As we have seen, a given book is usually assigned three or four subject headings and may therefore be located in three or four different ways (in addition to author and title) through the catalog. It is not usual to assign fewer headings to a book, simply because most books address several different aspects of a topic. A book is, of course, a finite item and cannot be in more than one physical place at one time. It can therefore have only one location symbol (call number). Although the nature of this call number will presumably address the main content of the work, it will not reflect every aspect of it. We know from earlier discussion that most works addressing personnel management will be in the HF series. However, a work addressing legal or psychological aspects of personnel might be in a different area. A work with a legal focus would probably have a K call number, this being the call-number schedule for law. Similarly, a work with a psychological concern would likely be in the BF series, the schedule for psychology. The decision on this would rest on the possibly fine question of whether personnel management itself or some subject approach to it was the main focus of the book. A work on personnel management which alluded in passing to legal areas would presumably be given an HF call number. One that emphasized legal areas would be assigned a call number in the legal (KF) series. The researcher should never assume a relationship between physical subject arrangement and intellectual thought.

Because of this important fact, browsing through a given area of the stacks, while a valuable (perhaps indispensable) activity, can never guarantee that you will identify the library's entire monograph holdings on a topic. For better or worse, proper access to the library collection must be achieved through its catalog. The techniques discussed in this chapter provide the key to this.

4. SOURCES OF CURRENT BOOKS

The ability to identify recently published books in a field is of obvious importance. You cannot rely upon even a large library to acquire the most current books comprehensively and promptly. The sources cited below are the principal ones for locating recent works. Most focus on commercially published books, but some also cover monographs published in different forms. Listings given here are limited primarily to sources covering works published in English. Several general guides to reference books cited previously describe those covering other and older source materials. The reader should note that many of the sources cited in the remainder of this chapter are now available in electronic forms, of the kinds discussed in chapters 6 and 9.

Books in Print: An Author-Title-Series Index to the Publishers' Trade List Annual. (1948–). New York: Bowker. Annual, with a midyear supplement.

Includes only books published commercially or sold by the major publishing houses in the United States.

Subject Guide to Books in Print. (1957–). New York: Bowker. Annual.

The companion to *Books in Print.* Subject categories are broad and not always easy to fathom.

Forthcoming Books. (1966–). New York: Bowker. Bimonthly.
An author and title listing of books recently published or projected for publication in the succeeding five months. Issues overlap in their coverage.

Subject Guide to Forthcoming Books. (1967–). New York: Bowker. Bimonthly.
Complements *Forthcoming Books.*

Cumulative Book Index. (1898–). New York: H. W. Wilson. Eleven issues a year, with regular cumulations.
Broader in scope than the previous four sources, covering books and other monographs published throughout the English-speaking world. Most reliable, however, for publications from the United States. Entries arranged by author, title, and subject. Easier to search by subject than the above, as the CBI now uses standard LC subject headings.

Bowker's Law Books and Serials in Print. (1984–). New York: Bowker. Annual.
Updated by occasional supplements.

Canadian Books in Print: Author and Title Index. (1975–). Toronto: University of Toronto Press. Annual.
Not reliable for its coverage of Canadian books published in French.

Canadian Books in Print: Subject Index. (1976–). Toronto: University of Toronto Press. Annual.

BNB: The British National Bibliography. (1950–). London: The British National Bibliography. Quarterly, with regular cumulations. Documents all works cataloged by the British Library. Formerly the *British National Bibliography.* Now available on computer and on CD.

Whitaker's Books in Print; The Reference Catalogue of Current Literature. (1874–). London: Whitaker. Now published annually.
An author, title, and keyword subject listing. Formerly *British Books in Print.*

Whitaker's Cumulative Book List. (1924–). London: Whitaker.
Quarterly, with regular cumulations.
A dictionary arrangement by author, title, and broad subject. One of the two standard sources of books currently published in the United Kingdom.

Whitaker's Books of the Month and Books to Come. (1970–). London: Whitaker. Monthly.
The British equivalent of *Forthcoming Books.*

5. PUBLISHED LIBRARY CATALOGS

Although the searching of the various sources noted here, together with specialized bibliographies (see chapter 10) and databases such as OCLC and RLIN,[7] is recommended as the best way to offset the limitations of the local library, the reader should be aware of the value of published library catalogs. When these allow for subject access, they are invaluable as guides to holdings of major libraries that may or may not be amenable to computerized searching. Even when subject access is not available, they can provide locations of books otherwise identified and can thereby make them accessible through interlibrary loan. The catalogs of two of the greatest libraries in the English-speaking world, the Library of Congress and the British Museum (now officially, although not colloquially, known as the British Library), are cited immediately below. Limited versions of these catalogs are available in computerized form.

U.S. Library of Congress. (1968–80). *The National Union Catalog, Pre-1956 Imprints: A Cumulative Author List Representing Library of Congress Printed Cards and Titles Reported by Other American Libraries*. London: Mansell. 685 vols.

Includes author entries for books published before 1956 catalogued by the Library of Congress, those held by it, and those reported held by about 700 participating libraries. The term "union list" indicates that locations of works are given. Supplements list works published before 1956, but only identified or reported since 1980.

U.S. Library of Congress. (1970–72). *The National Union Catalog: A Cumulative Author List Representing Library of Congress Printed Cards and Titles Reported by Other American Libraries*. Washington, DC. 125 vols. Updated by monthly, quarterly, annual, and quinquennial supplements.

Coverage similar to the previous item, but for books published since 1955.

U.S. Library of Congress. (1950-). *Library of Congress Catalog—Books: Subjects: A Cumulative List of Works Represented by Library of Congress Printed Cards*. Washington, DC. Quarterly, with annual and quinquennial cumulations.

More limited in its coverage than the previous two sources, this work primarily includes works cataloged by the Library of Congress represented by printed cards. Covers works published since 1950.

U.S. Library of Congress. (1983–). *National Union Catalog. Books*. Washington, DC. Monthly, with regular cumulations.

This microfiche publication serves, among other things, to update the three sources cited previously by providing access by author, title, and LC subject heading to works cataloged by the library. Also includes maps and a variety of materials in nonprint form. (For discussion of the rather complex array of published catalogs produced by the Library of Congress, see Nelson 1982, below.)

British Museum. Department of Printed Books. (1979–). *General Catalogue of Printed Books to 1975*. London: Clive Bingley. In progress.

Basically an author and name listing that is the major source of works published in the United Kingdom. It may never be revised beyond 1975, as later works are cataloged in machine-readable form. Limited subject access is provided by the following sources.

British Museum. Department of Printed Books. (1902–03). *Subject Index of the Modern Works Added to the Library of the British Museum in the Years 1881–1900*. London. 3 vols. Updated by quinquennial supplements.

Difficult to use because of the unique nature of the subject headings and the large number of supplements that must be searched.

BNB. (See above).

Complements *Forthcoming Books* in that it cites copyrighted works in advance of their publication.

A London Bibliography of the Social Sciences. (1929). London: Mansell Information. 4 vols. Updated by supplements issued every two or three years.

A subject index to the acquisitions of a group of libraries associated with the British Library of Political and Economic Science. A very worthwhile source, but supplements lag by several years.

Subject access to the older contents of major libraries such as the British Museum and the Library of Congress will always be problematic. As noted earlier, the wise researcher will negotiate such problems by searching author or title entries identified from bibliographies. Searching of these libraries' acquisitions over the last few years can also be difficult because of the arrangement of some of the sources that document them and because of the tardiness of some of these sources.

For those with an interest in the social sciences and in works published primarily in English, the situation has been made a great deal easier by a series of annual bibliographies, many of which are published in Boston by G. K. Hall, addressing books and monographs cataloged by the Library of Congress and by other major libraries. These annuals cite works by author, title, and subject. Their subject entries have the advantage of being those assigned by the Library of Congress and will therefore be familiar to the researcher at this stage of the endeavor.

As sources for identifying recent books written in English on the topic of concern, the annuals cited below are generally fully adequate for the purpose. Their limitations are those of the LC subject-headings system, considered earlier. They are also limited in the nature of the material covered and cannot be relied upon for the identification of government documents or other nontrade-published forms (see chapters 13 and 15). With these qualifications in mind, the G. K. Hall series should be considered as the basic source of current books in the field of interest. Annotations to individual titles in this annual series are limited to mention of those libraries, in addition to the Library of Congress and the member libraries of the OCLC consortium, whose recent acquisitions have contributed to the bibliographies presented. Full bibliographic information is given only when the publisher is one other than G. K. Hall.

Bibliographic Guide to Anthropology and Archaeology. (1987–).
A guide only to the materials acquired and cataloged by the Tozzer Library of Harvard University.

Bibliographic Guide to Black Studies. (1975–).
Materials acquired by the Schomburg Center for Research in Black Culture.

Bibliographic Guide to Business and Economics. (1975–). New York: New York Public Library. Research Libraries.

Bibliographic Guide to Education. (1978–).

Bibliographic Guide to Latin American Studies. (1978–).

Bibliographic Guide to Law. (1975–).

Bibliographic Guide to North American History. (1977–). New York: New York Public Library. Research Libraries.
"North America" is defined to include only the United States and Canada.

Bibliographic Guide to Psychology. (1975–). New York: New York Public Library. Research Libraries.

PsycBOOKS: Books & Chapters in Psychology. (1987–). Arlington, VA: American Psychological Association. Annual in 5 vols.

Abstracts of recent books and chapters within book are organized within four broad categories: experimental; development, personality, and social; professional and clinical; educational and health psychology. An offshoot of *Psychological Abstracts* (see chapter 8) and one of the few indexing or abstracting services providing good coverage of monographs.

There are as yet no series of this kind that address the social sciences in their entirety. New books in disciplines not covered by the G. K. Hall and related series can be identified through sources identified earlier in this chapter, through annual reviews, through the indexing and abstracting services discussed in chapter 8, and through large computerized library networks of the kind discussed in chapter 6.

Many other library catalogs have been published and are generally available in the reference collections of large libraries. Relatively few are kept up to date, as the current trend toward computerization and associated terminal access makes redundant the idea of constantly revising them. Published catalogs that exist are still valuable for a number of reasons: They permit the identification of library holdings that have not been put into computerized form, they allow for "browsing" through entries (behavior the electronic world does not encourage), and they enable the user to identify individual collections that he or she may find it profitable to visit.

Many large research libraries have published their catalogs. The most comprehensive discussion and listing of them is given by Nelson (below). Its first chapter discusses the characteristics and strengths of research library catalogs, including those of the Boston Public Library, New York Public Library, Columbia University, Harvard University, the Universities of California and Chicago, and the numerous works that give access to the resources of the Library of Congress. The remaining 32 chapters discuss catalogs listed according to subject categories. These include "government, public administration and law"; "general social science and sociology"; "business and economics"; "labor." Descriptions are long and clear.

Nelson, Bonnie R. (1982). *A Guide to Published Library Catalogs.* Metuchen, NJ: Scarecrow. 342 p.

In the future, few library catalogs will be published in conventional form. Libraries both large and small are increasingly inclined toward making information on their holdings accessible through one or more of the large library electronic networks (see chapter 6).

6. BOOK REVIEWS

With all these resources, the isolation of current books relevant to the topic may be rather time-consuming, but it is not a difficult task. In certain of the social sciences it may be eased somewhat by the many serial publications specifically intended to provide book reviews. The most relevant are cited below. These include both book reviews and review essays comparing recent works on particular topics. All are well indexed, with most having cumulative author, title, and subject indexes. Their value lies in their selectivity. None makes any attempt at comprehensive coverage. Instead, each attempts to review only the outstanding, or at least attention-getting, recently published books in its areas of coverage. Because of this, these sources are best used to keep abreast of a general, rather than a specific, area of interest. In terms of our earlier example, the student of 19th-century legal and bureaucratic change would use these sources to keep abreast of new books in related areas such as theory of legal development, 18th- and 19th-century social history, relations between culture and the law, legal history in other jurisdictions, and anything else that is likely to pique the researcher's interest. Awareness of new literature on the precise subject in point would be maintained by more systematic means.[8]

Use of sources of book reviews, such as those noted below, will be helpful but is probably not essential. Most annual reviews and journals include book reviews. A student who makes a point of regularly examining that group of journals and annuals of greatest relevance, together with relevant volumes of the G. K. Hall and related series (above), will most likely identify new books of interest. The book-review sources cited here are likely to be of greatest value in identifying new works of peripheral significance and also those published in disciplines outside of the researcher's immediate point of reference.

American History: A Bibliographic Review. (1985–). Westport, CT: Meckler. Annual.

Each volume presents review essays based on a single theme; the 1988 volume, for example, is concerned with methodological issues surrounding the use of computerized techniques by historians. Primary sources and their access are routinely discussed.

Annual Bulletin of Historical Literature. (1911–). London: Historical Association.

Presents lengthy, detailed, and sometimes idiosyncratic essays reviewing recent literature. Emphasizes European history, but recent volumes also address other regions as well as methods and sources.

Book Review Digest. (1905–). NY, NY: H. W. Wilson. Ten issues a year, with annual cumulations.

Includes excerpts of published reviews, with indications of their source. General in coverage and not limited to the social sciences. Early volumes entitled *Cumulative Book Review Digest.*

Book Review Index. (1965–). Detroit: Gale. Monthly, with quarterly and annual cumulations.

Indexes a much larger number of reviews than does the *BRD* (above). No abstracts. Also general in coverage. A 10-volume cumulation covers the years 1965 through 1984.

Social Sciences Index. (1907–). New York: H. W. Wilson. Quarterly, with annual cumulations.

Includes a separate section covering only book reviews. One of the major periodical indexes in the social sciences. Reviews in the various indexes that predated the *SSI* are accessible through the next two sources cited below.

Book Review Index to Social Science Periodicals. (1978–81). Ann Arbor, MI: Pierian Press. 4 vols.

Covers the period 1964–74.

Combined Retrospective Index to Book Reviews in Scholarly Journals, 1886-1974. (1979–82). Arlington, VA: Carrollton. 15 vols.

Indexes over one million reviews published in almost 500 journal titles in the social sciences over the best part of a century.

Current Anthropology: A World Journal of the Sciences of Man. (1960–). Chicago: University of Chicago Press. Five issues a year.

Includes both critical reviews and review essays. Notable for its regular inclusion of the feature "Documentation in Anthropology." This lists important bibliographies and other information-finding tools recently published.

Reviews in Anthropology. (1974–). Westport, CT: Redgrave. Bimonthly.

Publishes about 60 lengthy reviews a year.

Business Library Review. (1973–). New York: Gordon & Breach. Quarterly.

Now incorporates *Economics and Business* and *Wall Street Review of Books.* Emphasizes business, economics, finance, and management.

Educational Studies: A Journal in the Foundations of Education. (1970–). Austin, TX: American Educational Studies Association. Quarterly.

Groups reviews by theme.

The Review of Education. (1975–). Pleasantville, NY: Redgrave. Quarterly.
Reviews new books, teaching materials, research reports, and other monographs.

Review of Educational Research. (1931–). Washington, DC: American Educational Research Association. Quarterly.
Includes reviews of individual books and review essays on particular topics.

Contemporary Sociology: A Journal of Reviews. (1972–). Washington, DC: American Sociological Association. Bimonthly.
Reviews and review essays of major recent books. Covers about 700 books a year.

Current Sociology/La Sociologie Contemporaine. (1952–). Newbury Park, CA: Sage. 3 issues a year.
Each issue is devoted to a "trend report" in which are reviewed "current trends and tendencies in all areas of sociological work—theories, methods, concepts, substantive research and national or regional developments." Extensive bibliographies are provided.

Sociology: Reviews of New Books. (1973–). Washington, DC: Heldref. Bimonthly.
Short review articles.

Progress in Human Geography: An International Review of Geographical Work in the Social Sciences and Humanities. (1977–). London: Edward Arnold. Quarterly.
Reviews and review articles of varying length. Has a counterpart entitled *Progress in Physical Geography.*

Perspective: Monthly Review of New Books on Government Politics International Affairs. (1972–). Washington, DC: Heldref. Bimonthly.
Several hundred reviews in eight categories, most of which address international affairs and comparative studies.

History: Reviews of New Books. (1972–). Washington, DC: Heldref. Quarterly.
Numerous short reviews.

Reviews in American History. (1973–). Baltimore: Johns Hopkins University Press. Quarterly.

Reviews are few and critical.

Journal of Management: An International Quarterly of Management Research. (1975–). College Station, TX: Southern Management Association.
Includes a "Yearly Review of Management (Books)."

Management Bibliographies and Reviews. (1975–). Bradford, UK: MCB University Press. Bimonthly.
Most issues include a major review essay on a particular topic with a related annotated bibliography.

Michigan Law Review. (1902–). Chicago: Michigan Law Review Association. Eight issues a year.
One issue in the year is devoted to a very extensive "Survey of Books Relating to the Law."

Political Science Reviewer. (1971–). Bryn Mawr, PA: Intercollegiate Studies Institute. Annual.
Each issue includes a dozen or so review essays, each of which discusses a new title, or titles, in a bibliographic and theoretical perspective.

Trends in History: A Review of Current Periodical Literature in History. (1979–). New York: Institute for Research in History. Quarterly.
Bibliographic essays review selected topics.

7. OTHER LIBRARIES

Many of the sources discussed in this chapter not only identify publications of interest but also tell the researcher their locations, a matter of interest if they are not held by the home library. An unspoken implication of this is that works so located may readily be obtained on interlibrary loan (ILL). This is true, but only up to a point. Libraries do subscribe to formal ILL networks, and these are heavily used. However, ILL operations are costly to libraries in labor and paperwork. Given dwindling academic resources, libraries, whether they are borrowers or lenders, simply cannot afford to allow their patrons unrestricted access to ILL. The user can expect to obtain a couple of books every few weeks in this way, but a research bibliography cannot be based on the fruits of such borrowing.[9] Moreover, the ILL process is a leisurely one, and it can easily take three or four weeks to acquire an item. (Many academic libraries are obliged to shut down ILL operations in the summer, the time when most academics accelerate their research activities.) The realistic user will recognize that a research project will use some materials from the home library, some will have to be bought, and some will be acquired on ILL. Access to the remainder will require trips to other libraries. On-site use of a library that is strong in the areas of concern can have unexpected bonuses. Many large libraries have special or archival collections that are either uncataloged or not easily accessible through usual means.

The main directories listing academic libraries and their specialties are cited below. Most of them provide fairly detailed information on their holdings. Included in the guides cited below are a number that cover libraries and other information sources in a particular geographic area. These are particularly valuable to those with limited geographic mobility. Others, particularly those covering governmental institutions, are also valuable in their discussions of nonlibrary information services offered. The reader is cautioned that some libraries (usually those supported by private funds) do not always welcome outsiders. Visiting privileges can, however, usually be obtained through the intervention of one's own library.

Excluded from the directories listed here are those covering collections of government documents and archives and other primary sources. Discussion of these is given elsewhere in this volume.

American Library Directory: A Classified List of Libraries in the United States and Canada, with Personnel and Statistical Data. (1923–). New York: Bowker. Annual.
Listings by state, city, and county, with no subject access.

Ash, Lee, Miller, William & McQuitty, Barbara J. (Comps.). (1985). *Subject Collections: A Guide to Special Book Collections and Subject Emphases as Reported by University, College, Public, and Special Libraries and Museums in the United States and Canada* (6th ed.). New York: Bowker. 2 vols.
The major guide of its kind. Descriptions by narrow category.

Christo, Doris H. (Comp.). (1990). *National Directory of Education Libraries and Collections.* Westport, CT: Meckler. 269 p.

Coatsworth, Patricia A. (Ed.). (1980). *Directory of Planning and Urban Affairs Libraries in the United States and Canada, 1990* (5th ed.). Chicago: Council of Planning Librarians. 98 p.

Darnay, Brigitte T., Leighton, Holly M., & Southward, Carol (Eds.). (1987). *Subject Directory of Special Libraries and Information Centers 1987: A Subject Classified Edition of Material Taken from "Directory of special libraries and information centers," Tenth Edition, Covering Approximately*

18,000 Special Libraries, Research Libraries, Information Centers, Archives, and Data Centers Maintained by Government Agencies, Business, Industry, Newspapers, Educational Institutions, Nonprofit Organizations, and Societies in the United States and Canada. (10th ed.). Detroit: Gale. 5 vols.
One volume includes a section listing urban and regional planning libraries.

Dubno, Denise (Comp.). (1982). *Information Resources of New York State Agencies.* Albany, NY: New York State. Department of State. 149 p.

Evinger, William R. (Ed.). (1987). *Directory of Federal Libraries.* Phoenix, AZ: Oryx. 271 p.

Geist, Christopher D. (Ed.). (1989). *Directory of Popular Culture Collections.* Phoenix, AZ: Oryx. 234 p.
Covers the U. S. and Canada.

Hellman, Ronald G., and Pfannl, Beth K. (Eds.). (1988). *Tinker Guide to Latin American and Caribbean Policy and Scholarly Resources in Metropolitan New York.* New York: City University of New York. Bildner Center for Western Hemisphere Studies. 217 p.

Jennings, Margaret S. (1979). *Library and Reference Facilities in the Area of the District of Columbia* (10th ed.). White Plains, NY: Knowledge Industry Publications. 258 p.

Lewanski, Richard C. (Comp.). (1978). *Subject Collections in European Libraries* (2nd ed.). New York: Bowker. 495 p.

Macdonald, Roger, & Travis, Carole (Eds.). (1988). *Libraries and Special Collections on Latin America and the Caribbean: A Directory of European Resources* (2nd ed.). Atlantic Highlands, NJ: Athlone. 339 p.

National Library of Canada. (1974–). *Canadian Library Directory.* Ottawa. Annual.
Volume 1 covers federal libraries; volume 2, academic and other libraries.

Reed, Monica, Perry, Paula J., & Nelson, Bonnie R. (Eds.). (1979). *Directory of Anthropological Resources in New York City Libraries.* New York: Wenner-Gren Foundation. 64 p.

Roberts, Stephen A., Cooper, Alan, & Gilder, Lesley. (Comps.). (1978). *Research Libraries and Collections in the United Kingdom: A Selective Inventory and Guide.* Hamden, CT: Linnet Books. 285 p.

Rostenberg, Leona, & Stern, Madeleine B. (Eds.). (1989). *Special Collections in College and University Libraries.* New York: Macmillan. 639 p.

Stafford, Beth (Ed.). (1990). *Directory of Women's Studies Programs and Library Resources.* Phoenix, AZ: Oryx. 154 p.

U.S. Department of the Interior. Office of Library and Information Services. (1976–). *Libraries and Information Services Directory.* Washington, DC. Annual.

World Guide to Libraries: Internationales Bibliotheks-Handbuch. (10th ed). (1990). New York: K. G. Saur. 2 vols.
Probably the most extensive worldwide guide to libraries and their holdings.

NOTES

1. Subject headings are the arrangement according to which materials are listed in the catalog. Classification systems are the arrangement according to which materials are physically arranged on the shelves. The location symbol of an individual item within this arrangement is its call number.

2. For example, authors with last names that are patronymics beginning with the prefix "Mac" and its variants are integrated alphabetically as though they were all spelled in this way: MacNaughton, McNaughton, M'Naughton. A detailed discussion of the rules governing alphabetization of the catalog can be found in the first volume of the *Red Book*, cited in section 2 of this chapter.

3. As up to 10 percent of these headings are revised each year, it is obviously of great importance that the most recent edition of this work be used. The most current version of this is maintained on compact disk (CD-ROM).

4. "Scope notes," as definitions of the topic addressed, and indications of call-number ranges are given in one-third or more of the entries.

5. Crozier, Michel. (1967). *The Bureaucratic Phenomenon.* Chicago: University of Chicago Press.

6. U.S. Library of Congress. Office for Subject Cataloging Policy. (1990). LC Classification Outline (6th ed.). Washington, DC. Cultural anthropology is generally call number GN; education is L; history is D and E; law is K; psychology is BF; and so on. This *Outline* is a much-abbreviated version of a set revised annually: *Library of Congress Classification Schedules Combined with Additions and Changes.* (1987–). Detroit: Gale. This set is massive, with several volumes sometimes devoted to one letter in the classification, and is of little value to people other than library catalogers. Its sheer size,

however, draws attention to the extremely detailed nature of the LC system. An abbreviated and more manageable version of it is provided by Chan, Lois M. (1990). Immroth's Guide to the Library of Congress Classification (4th ed.). Englewood, CO: Libraries Unlimited.

7. Descriptions of the organizations represented by these acronyms are given in the next chapter.

8. Through scanning of current journals and abstracting services, and through close familiarity with recent issues of journals and annuals such as *Criminal Justice History* and the *American Journal of Legal History*.

9. For qualifications of this statement, see section 6 of chapter 6.

6

THE COMPUTERIZED LIBRARY BOOK CATALOG

Until the beginning of the 1980s, the terms "library catalog" and "card catalog" were virtually interchangeable. Things are quite different now. The pace of change in libraries has traditionally been slow, but the dramatic emergence of the catalog in database form, accessible through a computer terminal, has shown that tradition can very quickly be turned on its head. At the present time, most libraries, whether academic, public, or special, have either become computerized or are actively planning for computerization.

The holdouts now are the largest institutions. The very size of their collections and the fact that many are faced with converting their own systems of classification to that of the Library of Congress make computerization more expensive. It may be years before the largest libraries have all their holdings online. (This is one reason why so much attention has been given so far to the use of the card catalog.) Nonetheless, the computer is a fact of life even in these institutions. Many are computerizing recent acquisitions, doing retrospective conversions as time and money permit. Users must now and in the near future be familiar with both systems.

The speedy advancement of modern technology requires some explanation. It would be nice to observe that the change occurs due to a desire to serve patrons more effectively. This may be true up to a point, but if it was the only reason, the rate of change would be exceedingly slow. In fact, the moving force is money. It is very expensive, primarily in terms of labor costs, to maintain a card catalog. Catalog cards must be prepared or acquired from the Library of Congress. Filing must be done slowly, accurately, and under close supervision. This is a costly and labor-intensive operation. Computerization is also expensive, but the bulk of the expense lies in the start-up costs. Once conversion of existing holdings is complete, and the database is in place, unit costs fall dramatically.

Database maintenance, or the periodic adding to its contents, is much cheaper than adding to a card catalog particularly because catalog copy for most works, even in the largest libraries, is available from the Library of Congress in machine-readable form.

Most user reactions to computerized catalogs are negative. This is due in part to lack of user familiarity with computers in the library setting. There is undoubtedly a certain comfort in leafing through a drawer of catalog cards that even the most computer-literate person tends to miss. There are also deficiencies in the electronic catalog that are often very readily apparent. Computer systems, especially new ones, tend to be down a lot, thereby causing frustration to one and all. One cannot browse through entries on a terminal screen as well as in a catalog drawer. There are usually no "guide cards" with "see" and "see also" references, and it is no good trying out an unacceptable subject heading on the computer; it will respond with something like "No entries found." Subject approaches to the card catalog can sometimes be hit-and-miss affairs. Use of the computer catalog requires extensive and routine use of the list of subject headings, and the heading used must be fed into the computer exactly as it appears in the list. The computer catalog is more demanding, although it only mandates in the new what made life a great deal easier in the old.

Furthermore, entries must be precise; a misspelled word or a slightly incorrect subject heading will produce a blank screen. In this sense, the computerized catalog seems to be the only recent innovation in the academic world intolerant of poor spelling.[1] In fact, the electronic catalog, if used knowledgeably, is very sophisticated. This new tool is the means for much more effective library searching. It can produce results that could never be achieved using a card catalog.

Computerized catalogs come in different forms that are searched using rather different commands. For this reason, the particular search techniques described here should be taken as exemplifying principles only. The mechanics of their application must be learned in the local situation. Whatever else they can do, these catalogs can be searched in all conventional ways: by author, title, and subject. Particular care must be taken in these searches. An author name or book title must be verified. The subject heading fed in must be the right one. Unacceptable spacing, as well as inaccurate or misspelled terms, generally results in the negative response, "no entries found."

The catalog discussed here is CUNYPLUS, the catalog designed for the 22 constituent colleges of the City University of New York. This is, like many of its fellows, a *union catalog* in the sense that it covers the contents of a number of libraries. Cooperative efforts between libraries in cataloging and acquisition policies are much easier to implement when compatible technologies are involved. For this reason, computerized catalogs will be likely to include the holdings of more than one institution.

1. AUTHOR AND TITLE SEARCHING

This quite straightforward type of search must conform to the local rules of the system. As systems almost invariably have a number of "help" screens to assist the user in the several different approaches to searching, no undue difficulties should be encountered.

Figure 4 illustrates the results of different ways of searching for Emile Durkheim's classic, *The Rules of Sociological Method.* In 4A I have used the appropriate command for an author search and have entered "A=Durkheim Emile." This pulls up every entry for any edition of any title by this author in any college in the system. The list of entries produced includes the first letter of the first substantive word in the title of each work. By pulling up entry 148, "Durkheim Emile R," you can get a list of those titles in the system by Durkheim beginning with this letter (see figure 4B). Further selections after this point enable you to select whichever edition, in whichever college collection, most suits your preference. The net result will be the bibliographic entry, illustrated in 4C, giving you all the information needed to locate the book. (If it is charged out to another patron, the entry should also tell you this, and you will be able to put a hold on it at the circulation desk.)

One does not have to spell the entire names of authors to retrieve their works. If the last name of the author is unusual, entering a first name is probably unnecessary. Typing in "A=Durkheim" or "A=Durkheim E" would probably have produced the same result. This is because Emile is probably the only author named Durkheim in the system. If his last name had been "Smith," searching in this abbreviated way would be, if not impossible, then certainly time-consuming.

In the case of an author who is prolific, like Durkheim, or whose last name is common, it is probably much easier to search by title. To do this, the general rule is that the title is entered under the first *substantive* word. The first word is ignored if it is an article: "a," "an," "the," "le," "el," and so on. A search for the Durkheim title by using the command "T=Rules of Sociological Method" will bring up all editions of works with this title in the system. Again, abbreviate your search by cutting off the title at any point. "T=Rules of S" would retrieve all titles beginning with this entry. It would take less time to type and would almost certainly bring up a manageable number of items (see figure 4D).

The computer catalog can, however, serve you much better than this, should the need arise. A common circumstance is when you know only the last name of an author and have only a vague notion of the title. Unless this last name is a truly unusual one, all the card catalog has to offer to resolve this problem is the prospect of a wearisome search by author or subject. A computerized system is made for solving this kind of problem. For example, a man called Robson wrote an important book about immigration to Australia that, predictably enough, had the word "Australia" in the title. Rather than search through the large

Figure 4A
Author and Title Searching

```
CUNY+ SEARCH REQUEST: A=DURKHEIM EMILE
 AUTHOR/TITLE GUIDE -- 211 ENTRIES FOUND
   1      DURKHEIM EMILE +D
  42      DURKHEIM EMILE +E
  91      DURKHEIM EMILE +F
  93      DURKHEIM EMILE +I
  97      DURKHEIM EMILE +J
  98      DURKHEIM EMILE +M
 120      DURKHEIM EMILE +O
 126      DURKHEIM EMILE +P
 148      DURKHEIM EMILE +R
 171      DURKHEIM EMILE +S
 209      DURKHEIM EMILE +V
```

Figure 4B
Author and Title Searching

```
CUNY+ SEARCH REQUEST: A=DURKHEIM EMILE
 AUTHOR/TITLE INDEX -- 211 ENTRIES FOUND, 148 - 165 DISPLAYED
148 BC:DURKHEIM EMILE +READINGS FROM EMILE DURKHEIM <1985
149 BB:DURKHEIM EMILE +READINGS FROM EMILE DURKHEIM <1985
150 QC:DURKHEIM EMILE +READINGS FROM EMILE DURKHEIM <1985
151 KB:DURKHEIM EMILE +REGLAS DEL METODO SOCIOLOGICO <1969
152 QC:DURKHEIM EMILE +REGLES DE LA METHODE SOCIOLOGIQUE <1927
153 HC:DURKHEIM EMILE +REGLES DE LA METHODE SOCIOLOGIQUE <1981
154 BB:DURKHEIM EMILE +RULES OF SOCIOLOGICAL METHOD <1938
155 CC:DURKHEIM EMILE +RULES OF SOCIOLOGICAL METHOD <1938
156 QC:DURKHEIM EMILE +RULES OF SOCIOLOGICAL METHOD <1938
157 GC:DURKHEIM EMILE +RULES OF SOCIOLOGICAL METHOD <1938
158 BC:DURKHEIM EMILE +RULES OF SOCIOLOGICAL METHOD <1950
159 BM:DURKHEIM EMILE +RULES OF SOCIOLOGICAL METHOD <1950
160 HC:DURKHEIM EMILE +RULES OF SOCIOLOGICAL METHOD <1950
161 SI:DURKHEIM EMILE +RULES OF SOCIOLOGICAL METHOD <1958
162 JJ:DURKHEIM EMILE +RULES OF SOCIOLOGICAL METHOD <1964
163 NY:DURKHEIM EMILE +RULES OF SOCIOLOGICAL METHOD <1964
154 GC:DURKHEIM EMILE +RULES OF SOCIOLOGICAL METHOD <1964
165 CC:DURKHEIM EMILE +RULES OF SOCIOLOGICAL METHOD <1964

TYPE m FOR MORE ENTRIES. TYPE LINE NUMBER FOR FULL RECORD WITH CALL NUMBER.
TYPE g FOR GUIDE. TYPE r TO REVISE SEARCH, h FOR HELP, e TO START OVER.
TYPE COMMAND and PRESS ENTER==>  154
```

Figure 4C
Author and Title Searching

```
CUNY+ SEARCH REQUEST: A=DURKHEIM EMILE
BIBLIOGRAPHIC RECORD -- NO. 154 OF 211 ENTRIES FOUND

Durkheim, Emile, 1858-1917.
  The rules of sociological method, by Emile Durkheim.  8th ed., translated
by Sarah A. Solovay and John H. Mueller and edited by George G. E. Catlin.
New York, Free Press, c1938.
  lx, 146 p. 22 cm.
 SUBJECT HEADINGS (Library of Congress; use s= ):
     Sociology.

LOCATION: Baruch Stacks 7th Floor
CALL NUMBER:  HM24 .D962 1938b
     Not charged out. If not on shelf, ask for assistance at Service Desk.
```

Figure 4D
Author and Title Searching

```
CUNY+ SEARCH REQUEST: T=RULES OF S
 AUTHOR/TITLE GUIDE -- 19 ENTRIES FOUND
  1     RULES OF SLEEP POEMS *MOSS HOWARD <1984
  2     RULES OF SOCIOLOGICAL METHOD *DURKHEIM EMILE <193
  3     RULES OF SOCIOLOGICAL METHOD *DURKHEIM EMILE <195
 10     RULES OF SOCIOLOGICAL METHOD *DURKHEIM EMILE <196
 18     RULES OF SOCIOLOGICAL METHOD *DURKHEIM EMILE <198
 19     RULES OF STYLE <1974
```

number of Robson author entries, use commands that search for entries that include the words "Robson" and "Australia," in any field and in any order. Search for these words as *keywords* and enter the command, "K=Robson and Australia." It would be almost certain that the only product of this search would be L. L. Robson's classic *The Convict Settlers of Australia.*

In this example, the computer has done something that only it can do effectively. It has searched for entries that include a specified word or phrase that also include another specified word or phrase. The profound implications of this for constructing tailor-made subject searches are considered in section 3.

2. SUBJECT SEARCHING

Searching by subject is not problematic once you understand that only established headings can be searched in this way and that use of the *Red Book* is an indispensable preliminary. Let us say that you are interested in some aspect of change as a natural process within bureaucracies. Your first step will be to identify, through the *Red Book*, what appears to be the major heading, which turns out to be **Organizational change**. Use this source to identify any interesting-sounding related headings; the computerized catalog, unlike the card catalog, will not direct you to them. Armed with this information, you can search each identified heading directly.

Figure 5 shows the immediate product of using the "S" command ("S" for "Subject") to enter the instruction "S=Organizational Change." This pulls up the set number of the general heading, together with those for the various subdivisions of this heading. Now go through the process of investigating the contents of whichever sets look promising. This screen will certainly be of great interest since it will tell you things that the *Red Book* will not. The latter indicates which subject headings are subdivided geographically (most are) and which subdivisions of a special nature have been assigned to that heading (**Evaluation research (Social action programs)—Utilization**, for example). It will not explain which of the so-called "standard" subdivisions have been applied to that subject.

As noted earlier, it is not easy to determine just what these standard subdivisions are. The information in figure 5 obviates the need to find this out since it shows all subdivisions assigned to those works on organizational change included in the collections covered by the catalog. A card catalog provides such information, but its access requires, at the very least, the scanning of all the cards under a possibly general subject heading. Figure 5 gives the information at one fell swoop.

From the screen represented by figure 5 you can proceed with the search as usual. Individual subdivisions are called up, and entries for individual works

Figure 5
Subject Searching

```
CUNY+ SEARCH REQUEST: S=ORGANIZATIONAL CHANGE
 SUBJECT HEADING GUIDE -- 31 HEADINGS FOUND. 1 - 18 DISPLAYED
 1  ORGANIZATIONAL CHANGE
 2  --ADDRESSES ESSAYS LECTURES
 3  --BIBLIOGRAPHY
 4  --CARIBBEAN AREA
 5  --CASE STUDIES
 6  --CATALOGS
 7  --COLLECTED WORKS
 8  --COLOMBIA -CASE STUDIES
 9  --CONGRESSES
10  --CROSS-CULTURAL STUDIES
11  --DEVELOPING COUNTRIES
12  --EUROPE -CASE STUDIES
13  --EVALUATION
14  --EVALUATION - ADDRESSES ESSAYS LECTURES
15  --EVALUATION -BIBLIOGRAPHY
16  --HANDBOOK MANUALS ETC
17  --INDIA
18  --JAPAN

TYPE m FOR MORE SUBJECT HEADINGS. TYPE LINE NO. FOR TITLES UNDER A HEADING.
TYPE r TO REVISE SEARCH, h FOR HELP, e TO START OVER.
TYPE COMMAND and PRESS ENTER==>
 CUNY+ SEARCH REQUEST: s=ORGANIZATIONAL CHANGE
  SUBJECT HEADING GUIDE -- 31 HEADING FOUND, 19 - 31 DISPLAYED
    ORGANIZATIONAL CHANGE
19  --JAPAN -HISTORY -CASE STUDIES
20  --JAPAN -LONGITUDINAL STUDIES
21  --MANAGEMENT
22  --MATHEMATICAL MODELS
23  --MORAL AND ETHICAL ASPECTS
24  --NEW YORK STATE
25  --PERIODICALS
26  --PROBLEMS EXERCISES ETC
27  --PUBLIC OPINION
28  --UNITED STATES
29  --UNITED STATES -ADDRESSES ESSAYS LECTURES
30  --UNITED STATES -BIBLIOGRAPHY
31  --UNITED STATES -CASE STUDIES


TYPE LINE NO. FOR TITLES UNDER A HEADING.
TYPE r TO REVISE RESEARCH, h FOR HELP, e TO START OVER.
TYPE COMMAND and PRESS ENTER==>
```

within them are examined. From this, other promising headings can be identified, and the search is generally under way. Use of the full potential of the catalog in this way depends on the creative selection of established subject headings. Further exploration of the catalog must come from a deeper appreciation of its potential as a database.

3. KEYWORD SEARCHING AND "BESPOKE TAILORING"

Any disadvantages of the electronic catalog pale before the considerable advantages of the new ways of searching that technology now permits. To understand this, one must appreciate the computer catalog for its form rather than its content. It is a *database*; its function in life is to be *manipulated*. Searches in card catalogs must, by the nature of their form, be unilinear. You search one heading at one time. If you have an idea linking two concepts, you make two separate searches, and you must keep an eye out for studies that appear to relate the concepts of interest. In a computer system linkages can be made instantly. The earlier example of the author/title keyword search for a book by one Robson, first name unknown, is a case in point. Figure 6 is a conceptual diagram of this search. The instruction "k=Robson and Australia" requires the system to carry out three separate operations. It first identifies every instance in the database in which the word "Robson" appears (set A), and then every instance in which "Australia" appears (set B). Set C, the one in which we are interested, represents everything in set A that is also in set B. The terminal does not show each of these operations as it does them. It only shows us set C, the net product of the search.

Robson's monumental study could probably be identified easily in this simple search. You could, however, focus the search more finely if desired. In keyword searching you can search a word or phrase in a specified *field*; that is, in an author, title, or subject entry. The computer will do this readily given the appropriate command. In the CUNYPLUS system, entering "k=robson.au. and australia.ti." (the case of the letters does not matter) tells the system to search "Robson" in the author field and "Australia" in the title field. In other words, if Australia (or Robson) is included only in a publisher name, place of publication, or other field, this item will be excised from the search product. You could probably achieve much the same result if you specified that the term "Australia" be in a subject heading: "k=robson.au. and australia.su." If you really wanted to cover all bases, but yet exclude unwanted items, combine Robson as an author entry with Australia in a title or a subject entry: "k=robson.au. and (australia.ti. or australia.su.)." Here you have *nested* the command and told the system to first create a set including either "australia.ti." or "australia.su." and then to combine

Figure 6
Author/Title Keyword Search

" k = Robson and Australia "

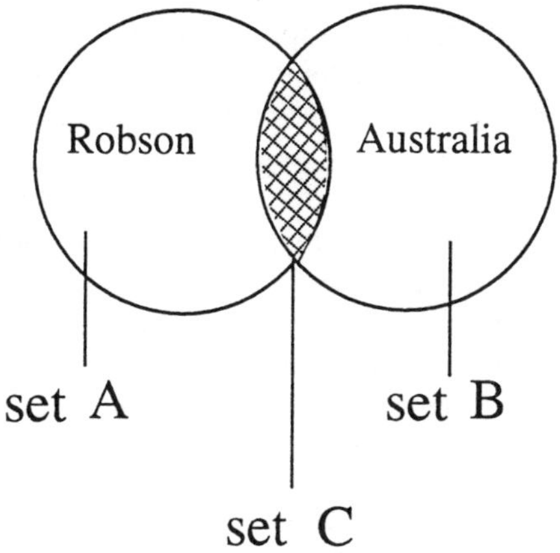

this with a set that includes "robson.au." (If you omitted the brackets, the system, mindless thing that it is, would create a set that included Robson as an author and Australia as a title. It would then create a larger set that included anything that was in this set or that had been assigned a subject heading that included the term "Australia." In other words, you would turn up everything in the database that included a Robson as an author entry and Australia in its title, or that had Australia as a subject heading, not what you want at all.)

To tune the search even more finely, suppose the existence of a Fred C. Robson, who writes extensively on the moral perils of gold-mining in Australia. If his publishing activities suggest a complication, design a search intended specifically to exclude his efforts. The "Ballentyne" (named from the logo of a well-known brewer) configuration of figure 7 shows the results of this search. Here you have initially created three sets: "robson" (set A), "australia" (set B), and a new set (D) that includes a variety of subject headings related to mining and to gold. Your instruction is "k=((robson.au.) and (australia.au. or australia.su.)) NOT (gold.su. or mines.su. or mining.su.)." This rather more complicated nesting arrangement tells the system to first create two sets and to combine them Robson in an author field and Australia in a title or subject field; (set A+B=C). Second, the system is told to create set D, which includes everything in the system with a subject heading related to mining or to gold. Set E, your object of interest, is created by the third implied command to *exclude* items in set C that address any of the concerns of set D—made as if by order, which indeed it was.

Figure 7, clearer visually than in its written explication, incorporates the essence of all you need to know to manipulate a library database to full advantage. It shows how you can define terms, specify fields, or search free-text (that is, for a word or phrase appearing anywhere in the entry), and exclude (with the "NOT" command). The example given was selected for its ease of presentation. Use of such techniques for the simple identification of a single work is perhaps self-indulgent and more appropriate to the hacker's concern with technique than to the scholar's concern with the outcome. The publications of Fred C. Robson would not really complicate the task of finding Robson's work on the transport of convicts to Australia. Exclusion of them lends a certain beauty to the search but has a negligible impact on its outcome.

The virtue and the strength of such techniques lie in their application to the construction of custom-made subject searches. "Bespoke tailoring" is an expensive, perhaps justifiable, route to a stylish garment from Savile Row. In the library catalog it is a route to a truly customized subject search. This can be fairly simple in its nature. If you are doing a case study on bureaucratic change and would like to find other studies, regardless of where they were conducted, the most relevant heading is **Organizational Change**, with **Case Studies** as the appropriate subdivision. You can certainly find this subdivision through the

Figure 7
Author/Title Keyword Search with "NOT" Command

"k = ((Robson.au. and (Australia.ti. or Australia.su.)) NOT (gold.su. or mines.su. or mining.su.)"

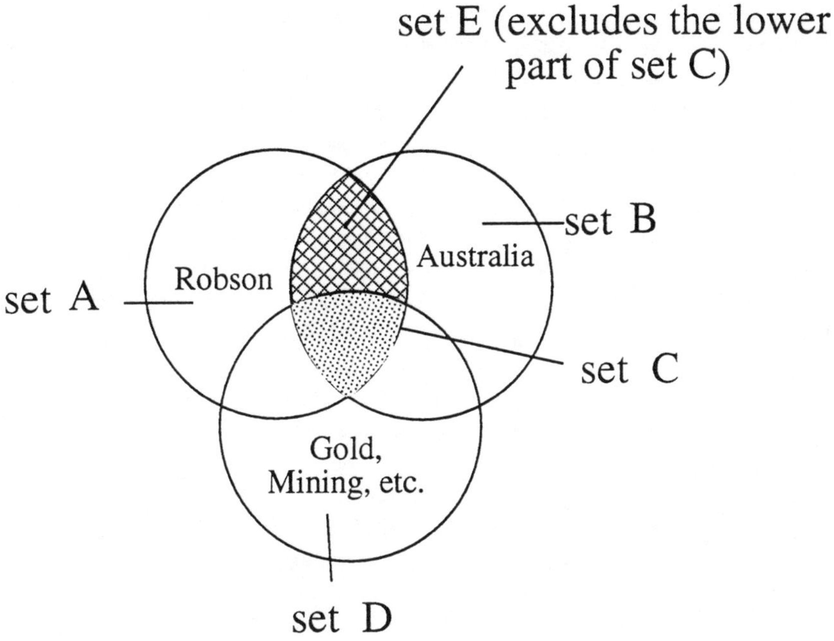

straightforward, unilinear, approach to the catalog, as illustrated in figure 5. This, however, would involve searching through each and every geographical subdivision within the catalog: **Organizational change—Colombia—Case studies, Organizational change—Europe—Case Studies**, and the like. Through keyword searching, you can simply enter the command: "k=organizational adj change.su. and case adj studies.su." to retrieve works of potential interest, regardless of whether their setting was Atlanta or Zanzibar.[2]

Processes like this can be developed more ambitiously and for more than two concepts. One can search for studies addressing three or more linked concepts at the same time (but it is rare that one can productively make linkages involving more than three concepts). Illustration of this is best preceded by a brief discussion of the principle of *truncation*. This allows you to search a term, whether author, title, subject, or free text, by its beginning symbols. In the above example, searching "Australi?.ti. or Australi?.su." allows for the picking up of any titles or subject headings beginning with the letters specified. (The "?" sign being here the indicator of truncation). These would here include "Australia's" and "Australian," as well as "Australia," in the fields specified.

A more significant application of the great flexibility of the system allows you to search *subdivisions* as though these were subject headings. For example, the *Red Book* provides the information that **Job Stress** is not only a subject heading, but, more important, it is used as a subdivision for other major subject headings (**School administrators—Job stress**). The keyword capability means that you can combine headings and subheadings at will. You can, for example, command the system to search "k=job adj stress.su. and case adj studies.su." This will yield case studies in the area of interest in any subject or geographic context. Anyone concerned with planning or evaluating such a study would probably have little interest in the provenance of interesting examples. A search of this nature would certainly preclude the impossible task of wading through examples of this phenomenon among the myriad of entries covering job stress among corrections officers in New Caledonia and school administrators in Newfoundland. Without keyword searching, no one could exploit these relationships between the substance and the method without searching almost the entire library catalog.

The strength of this capability of the catalog is best explained by example. Let us suppose that you have decided to do a dissertation relating in some way to the evaluation of treatment programs for violent juvenile offenders. You have gone through earlier chapters of this book, have obeyed all the rules, and have a strong-enough grasp of the areas to which your proposed research relates to have made a well-informed decision about the topic. At this point, you are beginning an exhaustive search that will cover the very narrow area of study. You intend also to gain information about current thinking on the etiology of juvenile violence in general.

First go through the subject-headings list to determine if there are any headings that address your concerns directly. There are headings of interest, although limited in age group and in setting: **Violence in children** and **School violence**. After searching them, you probably find some good material but feel that there are other areas to exploit. A thorough search of the list reveals four groups of headings of interest. Without giving the exact forms of entry, these may be grouped as they deal with

1. juveniles (as distinguished from the younger age group "children");
2. violence;
3. rehabilitation (in institutional settings) and treatment (in an out patient facility or otherwise outside of an institution).
4. evaluation of social programs.

If you are working with the card catalog and want to be thorough, you will search each heading in each group (for example, **Juvenile delinquency**, **Juvenile delinquents**, **Juvenile justice, administration of**," etc.), a daunting enterprise, especially when one remembers that each of these is certainly itself subdivided in various ways: **Juvenile delinquency—Alabama**," and so forth. With a database, you create data sets and combine them at will, typing in established subject headings identified through the *Red Book*, entering them in groups, and then combining one or more groups. You can also truncate subject headings. Entering "Juvenil?.su." will pick up headings such as **Juvenile delinquency** and **Juvenile delinquents**. Entering this heading in this way will abbreviate the search process.

You might also, and for methodological rather than theoretical reasons, be anxious to find studies and techniques on the evaluation of rehabilitation/treatment programs in general. These could be located through a search combining sets 3 and 4. In all likelihood you will wish to read at least the major works dealing with the apparently accelerating interest of juveniles in violence. A bibliography on this topic would be created by combining sets 1 and 2. You might also identify studies and discussions addressing the evaluation of rehabilitation programs for juvenile delinquents, whether their offenses are against persons or property. Alternatively, you might see what is written on the evaluation of rehabilitation programs for violent offenders in general, regardless of their age. Appropriate manipulation of sets should achieve what is needed.

So far, you have combined established subject headings. In the example just discussed, the headings were clear, but not situationally specific. The problem was limited to one of linking existing headings to create a narrow one of your own devising. If there appear to be no headings that properly address the subject matter of concern, the computerized system can also help resolve this. The system, being a database, is not limited to searches by author, title, or subject; it can also search *keywords* or *key phrases*, words or phrases that appear anywhere in titles of books, or even, depending on the system, in essay or chapter titles within books. Keyword searching can be combined with other forms of searching and can be used in many ways. There are often situations in which keyword searching can be used to compensate for the inadequacies of the subject-headings system.

Suppose you are exploring the timely subject of bureaucratic dysfunction. A search of the subject-headings lists yields only the most general headings for the first variable and none at all for the second. You cannot combine two subject headings because you do not have two to combine. Even searching seminal works on the subject is not much help. One major work in this area, for example, has been assigned the headings **Administrative responsibility**, **Political ethics**, **Public officers**, **Public administration**, and **Civil service**.[3] The problem may well be solved by a combination of searching under general headings, informed browsing, and the checking of bibliographies. Before doing this, try one more step. Combine the various subject headings for large-scale organizations with entries such as "dysfunctio?.ti." (picking up dysfunction, dysfunctional, dysfunctioning, dysfunctions) and "malfunctio?.ti.," as these appear in titles. Your choice of title keywords is limited only by your imagination. The result may not solve the problem entirely.[4] It will surely be a step on the way.

A more dramatic example of the application of this approach is provided by a topic that has recently attracted the attention of social scientists, but does not appear to have been in any way recognized within the LC subject-heading system. "Modernization," as alluded to earlier, is a concept that reflects the changes, cultural and institutional as well as technological and economic, that accompany the transformation of a primarily rural economy into an industrial state. No subject heading exists for it. A promising-looking heading **Modernism** relates to particular doctrinal developments in modern theology. Similar headings address recent movements in aesthetics and in the arts, but these are no help either. A keyword search using "moderniz?" or "modernis?" is clearly in order.[5] This must obviously be qualified in important ways; otherwise, the end product of the search will be loaded down with uses of the term in a variety of unwanted contexts. This could be done using the "NOT" command; for example: "k=(moderniz?.ti. or modernis?.ti.) NOT modernism.su." However, it is unlikely to solve the problem. It removes discussions of theology, but not the many other unwanted contexts in which our chosen term is used.

A better way to achieve the desired result would be to combine the targeted keywords with others likely to appear in the kind of entry that is of interest. Let us say that your intention is to locate works addressing modernization in any social setting, regardless of time, context, or place, and to limit the search using a number of variables related to the economic developments associated with modernization. Figure 8 illustrates some of the more interesting products of a search intended to find references to the concept associated with urbanization and/or industrialization: "k=(moderniz? or modernis?) and (industria? or urban?)."

Several things about this exercise exemplify some of the potential pitfalls of this kind of search. In the first place, the search was conducted *free-text*, that is, without specifying the *field* (author, title, or subject) of search. This is just as well, as figure 8 shows that the book by Shelley has, surprisingly enough, been assigned no subject headings related to either industrialization or urbanization. Subject cataloging is like keyword searching, a far-from-exact science. If you had searched the two qualifiers in a subject field ("industria?.su. or urban?.su."), you would have failed to retrieve Shelley's work. For our hypothetical student of legal modernization in Nuevo Albion, this would be a serious loss.

The obvious relevance of the 3 works cited in figure 8 does not obviate the fact that they were drawn from almost 200 works retrieved through CUNYPLUS by this search. A high proportion were of little or no interest for reasons that are clear once you view the titles.[6] Keyword searching is therefore not always a precise technique. Retrieving a high proportion of irrelevant items should not be seen as a problem as long as some desired works are also retrieved. A third and related point to be made is that a search that produces a number of precisely relevant works is not necessarily an adequate search. The command described above would, for example, omit Joseph Lee's *The Modernisation of Irish Society, 1848–1918*, and S. C. Dube's *Modernization and Development: The Search for Alternative Paradigms*, as neither includes either of the second group of qualifiers ("industria?" or "urban?") in a subject of title entry.[7] Works of this nature would be identified only through a more elaborate, or perhaps a separate, search.

Modernization is not the only topic poorly-served by the LC subject-headings system. There are many areas in which existing heading serve to confound rather than to illuminate. For example, the "vignette" technique in social research refers to a means of gauging respondents' beliefs and attitudes by exposing them to constructed scenarios of relevant situations. The LC subject heading "vignettes" refers to a typographical term which may be familiar to book designers, but which is unfamiliar to most social researchers.

Before ending these general comments on the database catalog, some important, though perhaps obvious, qualifications on its use must be made. First, not all such catalogs can yet accept all of the routines mentioned here, although by the mid-1990s they all surely will have this capability. Second, sophisticated techniques of combining terms are of little use in a library with a small collection. If a college library has little material on "modernization" (as defined here) in general, there is little to be gained from constructing a narrow search

Figure 8
The Keyword Search as Subject Search

"K=(moderniz? or modernis?) and (industria$ or urban?)"

Martin, Benjamin, 1917-
The agony of modernization : labor and industrialization in Spain / Benjamin Martin. -- Ithaca, NY : ILR Press, School of Industrial and Labor Relations, Cornell University, c1990.
xvii, 570 p. : ill. ; 24 cm. -- (Cornell international industrial and labor relations report : no. 16)
Includes bibliographical references (p. 427-539) and index.
SUBJECT HEADINGS (Library of Congress; use s=):
Labor movement--Spain--History--20th century.
Trade-unions--Spain--History--20th century.
Spain-Industries--History--20th century.
Labor policy--Spain--History--20th century.

LOCATION: Brooklyn Stacks
CALL NUMBER: HD8584 .M28 1990
Not charged out. If not on shelf, ask for assistance at Service Desk.

Germani, Gino.
The sociology of modernization : studies on its historical and theoretical aspects with special regard to the Latin American case / Gino Germani. New Brunswick, N.J. : Transaction Books, c1981.
266 p. ; 24 cm.
Includes bibliographical references and index.
SUBJECT HEADINGS (Library of Congress; use s=):
Social change.
Industrialization.
Secularization.
Urbanization--Latin America.

LOCATION: Brooklyn Stacks
CALL NUMBER: HN18 .G43
Not charged out. If not on shelf, ask for assistance at Service Desk.

Shelley, Louise I.
Crime and modernization : the impact of industrialization and urbanization on crime / Louise I. Shelley. Carbondale : southern Illinois University Press.
c1981.
xxii. 186 p. ; 24 cm. (Science and international affairs series)
Includes index.
Bibliography: p. 165-177.
SUBJECT HEADINGS (Library of Congress; use s=):
Crime.
Underdeveloped areas--Crime and criminals.
Technology--Social aspects.

LOCATION: John Jay Stacks
CALL NUMBER: HV6025 .S458
Not charged out. If not on shelf, ask for assistance at Service Desk.

on one aspect of it. The techniques discussed here are clearly designed for use in research libraries with extensive collections.

Fortunately, library conversions to database systems have encouraged the development of *union catalogs*, or databases covering the holdings of more than one institution. In addition, all academic libraries now have electronic access to networks documenting the contents of hundreds, in some cases thousands, of institutions. The user can access them at least to determine what published works of concern exist, as well as those that are immediately available. Further discussion of these networks is given in section 6.

Finally, the reader should be aware of some technical limitations on keyword searching. "Stopwords" are those used so frequently in records that they are excluded from the keyword index. Typical stopwords include "a," "an," "by," "in," "of," "on," "the," and "with." In addition, words that are used in the system as *commands* (AND, NOT, OR, SAME) are similarly excluded.

4. KEYWORD SEARCHING AND METHODOLOGICAL CONCERNS

So far, the emphasis on keyword searching has been on its potential for subject access, and the focus has been on keywords or key phrases as they appear in author, title, or subject entries. In many systems, however, a free-text search will search all entries, including these three, but not be limited to them. You may, for example, wish for some reason to limit the search by date of publication of the works retrieved. Adding the qualifier "197?" to the search will pull up anything in the database that includes, in any field, sequences beginning with the numbers "197." Most of these sequences will be dates (1970, 1971, and so on), and the majority will be dates of publication. Undoubtedly some will reflect other meanings of this sequence (a book 197 pages long, for example, would be retrieved by this command), but this circumstance should not unduly distort the search outcome.

In the same way, qualifiers can be added to searches to isolate works in particular series or issued by particular publishers. Sage Publications, for instance, produces two excellent series of short monographs that between them provide guides to most aspects of qualitative and quantitative research, especially the latter. These series are entitled "Qualitative Research Methods" and "Quantitative Applications in the Social Sciences." Someone interested in finding out quickly whether either includes a guide of interest to the method being considered can simply search the appropriate series title free-text, perhaps qualifying it with the term "sage." This can, of course, only be done if the protocols of the system permit this.[8]

These applications aside, the most important use of the keyword, other than in subject and title searching, lies in the access it can provide to *method.* As noted earlier, anyone engaging in original research should define and address a problem through three dimensions: A *setting* (body of data) must be analyzed from some *theoretical perspective* by application of an appropriate *method.* In planning such a difficult enterprise, the researcher must be qualified to select an appropriate method from the large menu of available choices. Effective planning as to just how the chosen methodology will be implemented requires some knowledge of how similar situations have been handled by others working in related fields.

Conventional library techniques will be of little help in this regard. Library cataloging systems are notoriously subject-oriented. They deal mostly with the products of research and little with the means by which these products are obtained. The Library of Congress often does assign subdivisions of subject headings which recognize the nature of the methodologies applied. Unfortunately, such assignation is somewhat arbitrary. One cannot search for ethnographic approaches to a setting through subject headings because the Library of Congress does not recognize this as a method.[9] On the other hand, it does use a subdivision **Cohort analysis** to designate studies applying this particular way of approaching populations of interest. However, the library cataloging entry for what is probably the most often cited work in criminology using this approach includes no recognition of the method employed.[10] A subject approach to the identification of cohort analyses applied in particular settings would therefore be of limited help. It would, in fact, be of negative value because its results would encourage the unwary user in the mistaken belief that a thorough search had been conducted.

Aside from the variability of their deployment, a problem with method-oriented subject headings is that it is often difficult to determine just what they are. Scouring the *Red Book* over an extended period of time would doubtless serve to resolve such issues, but this is not an option likely to be attractive to even the most dedicated researcher. It is, moreover, an unnecessary option. Free-text searching will yield method-driven words or phrases in any field, and the reader is advised to use only this approach. In doing this, the rule of thumb is to enter the method term, or terms, in as short a form as possible. Searching "cohort analysis" as a phrase would not produce the criminology book mentioned in the preceding paragraph because the second word in the phrase appears nowhere in the entry. Someone searching for this method in this context would probably find it by a search such as "k=(crim? or delinquen? or prisone? or inmat?) and cohor?."

Terms intended to yield applications of method should, in the spirit of the free-text principle, be applied creatively and knowledgeably. Someone planning, for instance, an ethnographic study of social and work-related interactions in a large hospital would combine a series of subject headings and free-text terms intended to reflect the range of terminology this approach might suggest: "ethnograph? or participant or observ? or field or fieldwork."

Many libraries have acquisition policies that include the collection of theses and dissertations accepted for higher degrees.[11] Some collect them sporadically and some systematically.[12] When acquired, they are usually cataloged with other monographs and are therefore accessible through standard search techniques. Dissertations can be problematic as sources, but they can be of tremendous value if used correctly. They are problematic because their findings vary considerably in quality and usefulness (this is why some libraries choose not to acquire them in great numbers). Nonetheless, they are potentially valuable for reasons other than the originality of their findings.

The importance of dissertations to those preparing to engage in original research has already been emphasized. They are expected to cite and review all major published works relevant to their subject, and, at their best, their bibliographies can be used as starting points. They can sometimes be even more valuable as sources of method and data. Dissertations are the only published forms that provide exhaustive detail on the characteristics of data used and the methods and instruments used to analyze them. For this detail alone they can be most helpful to other researchers. Scholars have some interest in making a special effort to identify relevant dissertations.

The library catalog card shown in figure 1 identifies a monograph of this type as a standard feature of the catalog entry for it. One need only search free-text, combining the keywords "dissertation or thesis" with a subject qualifier, to find all the works in this genre related to the subject in point. It is clear that this subject (and/or methodological) qualifier should be broader than the narrow topic of interest. Finding dissertations on a particular topic suggests either extraordinary luck or, more likely, that it has already been mined extensively, perhaps exhaustively.[13]

5. GENERAL REFLECTIONS ON THE SEARCH PROCESS

Clearly there are no absolute rules of the search process that guarantee success. The process itself is like a fishing expedition: Luck is something whose influence no participant would underestimate. On the other hand, one's chances of being lucky are greatly improved by good planning, good judgment, and a detailed knowledge of local conditions. The moving force behind a good search is the same as that applicable to research design in general: The better one's knowledge of the subject matter, its contexts, and the methods and theoretical perspectives associated with it, the better the search and the more productive its results.

A good search will also reflect an awareness of the capabilities and limitations of the database system. Keyword searching can be used in most systems, but the fields of entry to which it can be applied vary. Search of a database that excludes certain collections, as many do, must be supplemented accordingly. Databases that are union catalogs, linked to large systems, are the most receptive to sophisticated search techniques. A complicated search carried out on a small database has much less chance of success.

Finally, the thoughtful researcher will appreciate that the primary objective is to *include* desired items, not to *exclude* unwanted ones. The number of entries retrieved must be manageable, a criterion often imposed by the technology since many systems will only permit the display of the first 200 or so of the items found. Nonetheless, undue attention should not be given to limiting the presence of extraneous material. In doing so, one runs the risk of losing the baby (or some of its parts) with the bathwater. Experienced researchers understand that finding needed entries compensates for a great deal of exposure to entries that are unwanted.

6. COMPUTERIZED LIBRARY NETWORKS

Most libraries now have electronic access to large networks that may be searched in all the ways so far described. Membership in these networks is important for technical operations in libraries because their contents provide ready-made cataloging copy for new acquisitions. Library interest in these networks is driven primarily by operational considerations, so they do not always publicize their research potential and availability. Still, these networks are usually fully accessible to patrons for their very different purposes.

Libraries do vary in the ways that they make their systems physically accessible. As with bibliographic databases covering journal articles and other materials (see chapter 9), some libraries permit patrons to conduct searches themselves. Users must then master particular system-oriented commands and techniques. (The larger systems publish reference manuals that take some of the pain out of this.) Other libraries accept written or verbal requests from patrons and assign their implementation to qualified librarians. In this kind of situation the researcher is well advised to direct, or at least assist in, the planning of the search. No amount of technical expertise with a database can compensate for academic knowledge of the characteristics and scope of the subject being searched. Lack of access to such expertise will present more of a problem in the future. Computerized library and other bibliographic systems are increasingly available through electronic bulletin boards (EBBs) that are instantly accessible through computers with modem linkages (see section 9 of chapter 15). All the systems described below are presently searchable by this means, as are several hundred others. As searching shifts from the library terminal to the home or office PC, users will be moved further from the source of technical searching expertise. The wise among them make the effort to become their own experts.

Three major database systems of this sort are described below. All are massive in terms of the volume of works they cover, and all are updated regularly, sometimes even weekly. At least two (OCLC and RLIN) are generally accessible through college and university libraries in the United States. In the past these systems could be searched only by author and title and in certain other limited ways. Now all are capable of being searched by subject.

BLAISE (British Library Automated Information Service). This system is based on entries acquired or cataloged by the British Library (popularly still known as "the British Museum") and its affiliates, but now includes the contents of 19 separate databases originating in various parts of the world. Its particular strengths are works published in Europe, including theses, dissertations, government documents, and other material not always well covered by other sources. As with the other databases described here, it is only comprehensive in its coverage of recently published works (from about 1980 onward), although retrospective cataloging continually makes earlier works accessible. In addition, some of its subfiles focus upon particular areas that do provide extensive historical coverage. The National Serials Data Centre (NSDC), for example, records British serials dating back to the 17th century. The Eighteenth Century Short Title Catalogue (ESTC) includes more than 220,000 books, pamphlets, chapbooks, and other items published in that century. It represents the collections of over 1,000 libraries worldwide, as well as that of the British Museum.

Online Computer Library Center (OCLC). This presently includes over 2 million bibliographic records, reflecting the holdings of over 10,000 libraries throughout the world. However, it is best used as a source of the contents of academic libraries in the United States, excluding the very largest. More than 20,000 entries are added to this database each week, and a growing proportion of them represent older works (that is, works published before 1968, when OCLC began its operations) and those in languages other than English.

Research Libraries Information Network (RLIN). This is a group of six related databases that together include over 32 million entries and represent a growing proportion of the holdings of a number of large research libraries in the United States. It also includes subfiles that cover works cataloged by the Library of Congress and the National Library of Medicine and those published by the Government Printing Office, as well as at least some of the special and subject collections of member institutions. An important feature of this network is its coverage of nonprint materials. These include conventional archives, sound and visual recordings, and a variety of machine-readable files.

There is no single computerized library network that has achieved primacy. Various networks complement each other. The research libraries represented by RLIN, for example, have much stronger collections of historical and esoteric materials than do the smaller academic libraries represented by OCLC. On the other hand, many libraries on OCLC have been entirely computerized, and their possession of unusual works, if they have any, is determined easily. A library in RLIN may hold a particular item, but since research libraries are generally nowhere near computerizing their entire catalogs, this information may not be included in the database. A search of both OCLC and RLIN, whether by author, title, or subject, is frequently appropriate.

In chapter 5 mention was made of the benefits of interlibrary loan (ILL), but in a qualified way. The existence of library networks, which of course always identify all institutions in their systems holding the works listed, clearly makes it easy to locate, as well as to identify, items of interest. This in turn has increased pressures on libraries to act as ILL agents, whether as lenders or borrowers. The net result is that most libraries are now inclined to ration these services fairly severely. Requests for two or three books or articles a month might be seen as reasonable in this light, but no library is likely to provide all or most of the published materials needed to support a research project in this fashion.

OCLC and RLIN also complement one another in this regard. Most large research libraries charge hefty fees, $20 or more, to process a single ILL request; most smaller libraries charge nothing. Research libraries may discourage use by outsiders; smaller libraries may be more welcoming. Most libraries take several weeks to process ILL requests; larger libraries generally take more time than smaller ones. For these reasons alone it might be worthwhile to search a title on OCLC, even though it has already been located through RLIN.

Cost considerations aside, there is no doubt that reliance on interlibrary loan to gain access to more than a small number of promising works identified can be time-consuming and frustrating. The fact is that electronic modes of literature searching have not been matched by systems of document delivery. At its worst, the doubtful advantage of a sophisticated search is that, in the cynical words of Laurie Taylor, "instead of all those hours mooching along the (library) shelves, you now simply key in the topic that interests you and this database immediately tells you the number of interlibrary loan forms you will need to complete in order to obtain the necessary information."[14]

This situation will be most acute for those without at least occasional access to large research libraries. However, the imbalance is to some extent being corrected by accelerating efforts to publish books and other materials in an electronic form, free of charge and accessible to almost everyone. Project Gutenberg, for example, is an electronic network (see section 9 or chapter 15) which aspires to issuing the full texts of 10,000 monographs electronically by the end of the decade. If this is a wave of the future, the problems of accessing the contents of a bibliography obtained through the systems mentioned here will soon be eased considerably. Even if they are not, computerized library systems cannot be ignored. Difficulties of access cannot be used to justify the avoidance of important materials.

Usually the librarian knows which major systems are available locally. There may, however, be available systems and subfiles of which the librarian is unaware, either because they are rarely used or because they are accessible by first entering one of the large systems. The directories cited below are the most important resources for identifying promising systems. They provide detailed descriptions of several thousand organizations that are in some way in the business of generating information in computerized form. Library networks of the kind discussed here are included, and the information given often relates to any specialized subfiles that they may include. Other directories of this nature are cited in section 3 of chapter 9 and sections 5 and 6 of Chapter 12.

Dempsey, Lorcan. (Ed.). (1992). *Library Bibliographic Networks in Europe: A LIBER Directory*. The Hague: NBLC. 110 p.

Also discusses continuing efforts to make access to these networks easier through standardization of related software.

Information Industry Directory. (1971–). Detroit: Gale. 2 vols. Now annual in 2 vols.

Earlier entitled *Encyclopedia of Information Systems and Services*.

Neubauer, Karl W., & Dyer, E. R. (Eds.). *European library networks*. Norwood, NJ: Ablex, 1990. 448 p.

Describes contents and access of large networks in nine European countries, including four in Germany and four in the United Kingdom.

This approach aside, the most convenient means of accessing the catalogs of other libraries by computer is often through the several electronic networks discussed in section 9 of chapter 15. Direct access to several hundred library catalogs is now available in this way, and this number is likely to increase dramatically in the immediate future.

NOTES

1. There are search programs that will allow for this by responding with words or phrases close to those searched. At the present time, these are not generally used in library catalogs.

2. "Adj" ("adjacent to") is a command within the CUNYPLUS system that must be added, in any command after the first, to direct the search of any two words as a phrase. It is a local command and has no relevance to any other system. The reader is advised that other systems have other local idiosyncrasies.

3. Burke, John P. (1986). *Bureaucratic Responsibility*. Baltimore: Johns Hopkins University Press.

4. It would, for example, exclude John Burke's important book.

5. This search recognizes use of spellings such as "modernise" in most English-speaking countries other than the United States.

6. For example, *The Maintenance and Modernisation of Urban Housing; Deposit Insurance Reform and Financial Modernization.*

7. This is so for good reason. Lee's work is mainly concerned with political and governmental aspects of the process. Dube's work addresses modernization, not as a natural process, but as a part of a strategy for planned change.

8. Some systems include the series field in a free-text search; others do not. Others appear to include it in a selective, and therefore unsatisfactory, fashion. CUNYPLUS is one of these.

9. It includes it within the larger and more subject-oriented category of **Ethnology**.

10. Wolfgang, Marvin E., Figlio, Robert M., & Sellin, Thorsten. (1972). *Delinquency in a Birth Cohort*. Chicago: University of Chicago Press. The solitary and generally unhelpful subject heading assigned to this work is Juvenile delinquency—Pennsylvania—Philadelphia—Case studies.

11. The two terms are sometimes used interchangeably, but the convention is to associate the word "thesis" with work accepted for a master's degree, and "dissertation" with the doctoral degree. As it is dissertations, being generally more ambitious products, that are of most concern here, this is the term that will be used.

12. Because the user has little way of knowing the strengths of a library collection in this regard, other means of accessing materials in these forms are discussed elsewhere in this book.

13. For some reason, the topic of "police cynicism" seems to continually attract the attention of graduate students. This is perhaps because the survey instruments associated with such studies are now fairly standard. This makes the topic relatively easy to address; it does not make the end products correspondingly interesting or easy to read.

14. Quoted in Law, Derek. (1993, February). Opening Up the Networks. *Library Association Record, 95*, 93.

7

THE JOURNAL LITERATURE

The importance of the periodical literature to an adequate bibliography on a topic of concern is obvious enough to require little in the way of its justification. Articles in journals and other periodicals are vital for several important reasons.[1] On the day of its publication, the information in a book may be well over a year old, because it can take the publisher at least this long to put the manuscript through the processes of editing, production, and marketing. There are time lags in publishing journal articles, too, but these are usually measured in months rather than years. Articles are therefore sources of current information. Articles are generally much narrower in scope than are books and explore issues more thoroughly. In many areas of study, the crucial literature is entirely, or almost entirely, in journal-article form, and the book literature is of concern only insofar as it summarizes and interprets experiments and other research studies that are reported fully in the journal literature. The contents of journals are easily accessible. Indexing and abstracting services of the kinds discussed in chapters 8 and 9 are specialized and sophisticated, whether they are in printed or computerized form. Few, if any, journals of consequence are not accessible in this way.

Finally, the number and range of journals in existence has accelerated dramatically as the publishing world has sought to address new subdisciplines and interdisciplinary perspectives. This trend has been most notable in the pure and applied sciences, but it has also had a substantial effect on the behavioral, policy, and social sciences. A further boost to the greater availability of specialized journals published in English has been given by the increased willingness of many countries to switch to the English language for purposes of scholarly communication. As English becomes more of a world language, this trend is likely to become even more pronounced.

The volume of periodical literature available even on narrow topics can be massive. One volume of even a specialized index may include hundreds or thousands of journal citations. For this reason, a systematic search of the journal literature is imperative once the project assumes a recognizable shape and is not likely to be changed dramatically by some new revelation from the literature. This time is, of course, only reached when the researcher has a sound grasp not only of the literature on the narrow topic in point but upon its theoretical associations and the methodological approaches that have been taken to it. This stage is reached when a thorough search of the library catalog and published bibliographies has been made and, more important, after the products of this search have been read and digested.[2] A selective search of the periodical literature will have been made at this point, as the conscientious worker will have followed through in looking up items in the bibliographies and notes of important works found.[3]

It is at this point that a more thorough search of the periodical literature—and other sources not likely to be covered by the library catalog—should be made. The vast body of periodical literature should only be coaxed into yielding a narrow and focused bibliography when a sound grounding of knowledge has been attained. Contrary to popular belief, this is achieved through thoughtful reading, and not through the preliminary process of applying sophisticated information-finding techniques.

At this moment, the researcher's way is clear. A list of indexes and abstracts covering materials in potentially valuable forms, including periodical articles, is prepared. This list will include indexes and abstracts in both printed and computerized form and will be drawn from those items mentioned below, as well as from the sources noted. A competent, that is, well-informed, search of these indexes and abstracts will produce the end product wanted. This product is an exhaustive bibliography of journal articles and other materials on the subject specified, constrained only by the known limits of the indexes and, of course, by the knowledge and creativity of the searcher.

It is important to recognize at this point that the search will have been a narrow one, but will almost certainly not have addressed all the interests of the researcher. Someone interested in the "modernization" (as this has been earlier defined) of legal institutions would undoubtedly conduct a focused search of the periodical literature on this minute topic. This search would probably benefit by being expanded to address public bureaucracies in general). Understanding how the law reacted to "modernization" is surely a function of how society in general reacted to it.

Making the necessary connections between your immediate topic of interest and the broader theoretical and historical world within which it lives is probably the most difficult aspect of the process of original research. Selection of data to be analyzed and means of analysis pale into insignificance beside it. It can only be solved by broad knowledge of the field. Selective use of the indexing and abstracting services covering a general field can certainly help. This is why printed sources of this nature can be of inestimable value. They provide the researcher with the means of browsing through abstracts of somewhat related materials. The scalpel of the computer cuts through to only the precise area of interest. For this reason both printed and computerized indexing and abstracting sources of journal literature are discussed in the chapters that follow, and without prejudice.

Computerized sources are only superior in their ability to hone in on a defined topic when related concerns have been explored or are otherwise of no interest. In the world of research, such a perspective is rarely warranted. Our hypothetical researcher, interested in the modernization of the courts in 19th- century Nuevo Albion, will always want to know anyone else's reports of related developments in public bureaucracies in general, in whatever Anglo-American jurisdiction, and in the 19th century or perhaps in other historical settings. Use of printed abstracting services will perhaps provide this information, if it exists. Computerized searching is designed not to do so, as the variables searched must be defined quite specifically. For this reason, the reader is encouraged to regard computerized and printed indexes and abstracts (often the same sources are issued simultaneously in the two forms) as instruments that *complement* one another. They do not necessarily *compete* with each other.

Use of indexes, in whatever form, is also valuable to cover significant articles from various disciplines. You might assume that the literature you need to survey will be published in the sizeable group of journals that cover the field of public administration. Such an assumption, as anyone with a grasp of the substance of the topic would quickly appreciate, is quite mistaken. Sociologists are interested in this modernization in a variety of contexts, as are psychologists and political scientists. These scholars prefer to report the results of their findings in their own journals. This tendency is quite marked.[4] Anyone who wishes to survey a field of study must recognize this fact. Searching of the established journals in public administration would, in this case, unearth only the products of one limited perspective. A broader search, through indexes and abstracts covering the social sciences in general, would be mandatory.

There is another important reason why scholars should be interested in surveying the current journal literature. This is quite simply to maintain an awareness of the kinds of things that are going on in a field. All scholars survey their own group of journals regularly to determine current developments in an area. As has been mentioned, our hypothetical student of legal "modernization" would undoubtedly scan current issues of periodicals such as *American Journal of Legal History*, *Public Historian*, and various other journals in history and other social sciences. The student more in tune with recent thought and developments within public administration or the policy sciences would undoubtedly plan, as a matter of habit, to browse through important journals in these general areas. This would be done to keep abreast of any developments of even marginal relevance to a particular topic and to keep up with the mainstream of a broad discipline. Selection of such journals would be in addition to those that more directly addressed the more specific area of study.

It is important to know what these journals are and what general developments in the field they report. Major journals in public administration and some of its related fields are listed and described in section 2. Others are noted in the subject-oriented bibliographic guides cited in chapter 4 and in the directories noted below. Most of these directories are guides for budding authors in various fields. They accordingly take some pains to identify the quality, subject strengths, and relative prestige of the journals cited.[5] Of these directories, that by Katz and Katz is the most general, and therefore the most selective. *Ulrich's* is the most comprehensive and the least informative for this purpose.

Newspapers and popular magazines, their sources and potential value as *primary* sources, are discussed in sections 2 and 3 of chapter 15.

1. SOURCES OF JOURNALS

Many of the guides noted here are intended for prospective authors anxious to send their manuscripts to the most appropriate journal. Guides with this purpose are particularly valuable in indicating the precise scope and topical specialties of the serials covered.

Ardell, Donald B., & James, John Y. (Eds.). (1980). *Author's Guide to Journals in the Health Field*. New York: Haworth. 139 p.

Blum, Eleanor, & Wilhoit, Frances G. (1990). *Mass Media Bibliography: An Annotated Guide to Books and Journals for Research and Reference* (3rd ed.). Urbana, IL: University of Illinois Press. 344 p.

Cabell, David W. E. (Ed.). (1990). *Cabell's Directory of Publishing Opportunities in Business and Economics* (5th ed.). Beaumont, TX: Cabell. 3 vols.

Collins, Mary E. (Comp.). (1988). *Educational Journals and Serials: An Analytical Guide*. Westport, CT: Greenwood. 355 p.

Economics and Business. (1955–). New York: Gordon & Breach.
Quarterly. Formerly *Economics Selections*.

European Directory of Trade and Business Journals. (1990). London: Euromonitor. 293 p.

Documents about 2,000 serial publications including those of associations and institutes.

Fisher, William H. (Ed.). (1991). *Business Journals of the United States*. Westport, CT: Greenwood. 318 p.

Fisher, William H. (Comp.). (1986). *Financial Journals and Serials: An Analytical Guide to Accounting, Banking, Finance, Insurance, and Investment Periodicals*. Westport, CT: Greenwood. 201 p.

Fyfe, Janet (Comp.). (1986). *History Journals and Serials: An Analytical Guide*. Westport, CT: Greenwood. 351 p.

Geahigan, Priscilla C., & Rose, Robert F. (Eds.). (1988). *Business Serials of the U.S. Government* (2nd ed.). Chicago: American Library Association. 86 p.

Grollig, F. X., & Tax, Sol (Eds.). (1982). *Serial Publications in Anthropology* (2nd ed.). South Salem, NY: Redgrave. 177 p.

Harris, Chauncey D. (1980). *Annotated World List of Selected Geographical Serials: 443 Current Geographical Serials from 72 Countries with a Study of Serials Most Cited in Geographical Bibliographies* (4th ed.). Chicago: University of Chicago. Department of Geography. 165 p.

Hellebust, Lynn (Ed.). (1990). *Directory of Political Newsletters*. Washington, DC: Government Research Service. 70 p.

Lists over 140 newsletters concerned with the government and public policy at the federal and state levels. A title listing with a subject index.

Journals in Psychology: A Resource Listing for Authors (3rd ed.). (1990). Washington, DC: American Psychological Association. 133 p.

Katz, William A., & Katz, Linda S. (Eds.). (1992). *Magazines for Libraries* (7th ed.). New York: Bowker. 1,125 p.

Attempts to include the outstanding journals in each of the many subject areas addressed. Includes long descriptions. Valuable for its selectivity and cannot be relied upon as a comprehensive source. Updated by supplements issued between editions.

Loke, Wing H. (1990). *A Guide to Journals in Psychology and Education*. Metuchen, NJ: Scarecrow. 410 p.

Loverd, Richard A., Pavlak, Thomas J., & Wong, Molly M. (1983). Professional Journals in Public Affairs and Public Administration. In Caiden, Gerald E. and Alexander, Herbert E. (Eds.). *American Public Administration: A Bibliographical Guide to the Literature* (pp. 57–122). New York: Garland.

Markle, Allan, & Rinn, Roger C. (Eds.). (1977). *Author's Guide to Journals in Psychology, Psychiatry, and Social Work.* New York: Haworth. 214 p.

Mendelsohn, Henry N. (1987). *An Author's Guide to Social Work Journals.* (2nd ed.). Silver Spring, MD: National Association of Social Workers. 153 p.

Mersky, Roy M., Berring, Robert, & McCue, James K. (Eds.). (1978). *Author's Guide to Journals in Law, Criminal Justice, and Criminology.* New York: Haworth. 243 p.

Miller, A. Carolyn, & Punsalan, Victoria J. (Comps.). (1988). *Refereed and Nonrefereed Economic Journals: A Guide to Publishing Opportunities.* Westport, CT: Greenwood. 252 p.

O'Brien, Nancy P., & Fabiano, Emily. (1991). *Core List of Books and Journals in Education.* Phoenix, AZ: Oryx. 125 p.

Oxbridge Communications. (1981). *Legal and Law Enforcement Periodicals, A Directory.* New York: Facts on File. 238 p.

Persson, Dorothy M. (1990). *Psychology and Psychiatry Serials: A Bibliographic Aid for Collection Development.* New York: Haworth. 121 p.

Ruben, Douglas H. (Comp.). (1985). *Philosophy Journals and Serials: An Analytical Guide.* Westport, CT: Greenwood. 147 p.

Santora, Joseph C. (1987). *Planning: A Selected Guide to Periodical Literature, 1975–1985.* Monticello, IL: Vance. 28 p.

The Serials Directory: An International Reference Book. (1986–). Birmingham, AL: EBSCO. Annual.

Includes subject listings of well over 100,000 titles. At least as comprehensive as *Ulrich* (below) for English-language sources and, given this limitation, easier to use.

Sichel, Beatrice, & Sichel, Werner (Comps.). (1986). *Economics Journals and Serials: An Analytical Guide.* Westport, CT: Greenwood. 285 p.

Sova, Harry W., & Sova, Patricia L. (Eds.). (1992). *Communication Serials: An International Guide to Periodicals in Communication, Popular Culture, and the Performing Arts*. Virginia Beach, VA: Sova Comm. 1,041 p.
A thorough guide to English-language periodicals which is most valuable because of its transition of traditional disciplinary boundaries.

Spiceland, J. David, & Agrawal, Surendra P. (1988). *International Guide to Accounting Journals*. New York: Wiener. 291 p.

Sussman, Marvin B. (Ed.). (1978). *Author's Guide to Journals in Sociology and Related Fields*. New York: Haworth. 214 p.

Ulrich's International Periodicals Directory. (1932–). New York: Bowker. Annual.
The most comprehensive guide to periodicals of all kinds published throughout the world. Listings are by subject. Because of the great volume of sources covered, and the fact that no descriptions of entries are given, it is not always easy to use this work as a guide to suitable browsing materials. Updated by the quarterly *Ulrich's Update*. Also available in database form.

UNESCO. Social Science Documentation Centre. (1991). *World List of Social Science Periodicals* (8th ed.). Paris. 1,264 p.

Vaughn, Michael, & del Carmen, Rolando V. (1992). An Annotated List of Journals in Criminal Justice and Criminology: A Guide for Authors. *Journal of Criminal Justice Education, 3*, 93-142.

Vocino, Michael C., & Cameron, Lucille W. (Comps.). (1989). *Labor and Industrial Relations Journals and Serials: An Analytical Guide*. Westport, CT: Greenwood. 214 p.

Wang, Alvin Y. (1989). *Author's Guide to Journals in the Behavioral Sciences*. Hillsdale, NJ: Lawrence Erlbaum Associates. 481 p.

Wepsiec, Jan. (1983). *Sociology: An International Bibliography of Serial Publications, 1880–1980*. London: Mansell. 183 p.

Williams, John T. (Comp.). (1986). *Anthropology Journals and Serials: An Analytical Guide*. Westport, CT: Greenwood. 182 p.

2. MAJOR JOURNALS IN PUBLIC ADMINISTRATION AND RELATED FIELDS

The very selective lists provided in this section include only those journals in the field of public administration and in areas directly related to it. In most cases the sources listed are those addressing the needs and interests of academic and other researchers. Those intended for a practitioner audience are described as such in the annotations. Virtually all the journals cited here are indexed in one or more, usually several, of the indexing and abstracting services discussed in chapter 8 and the computerized data banks discussed in chapter 9.

2.1. Sources of General Theory

The journals listed here represent the major periodical sources providing current general discussions of theoretical developments in the field. The reader's attention is also drawn to journals in sociology, economics, and especially political science, which regularly include articles of interest to the student of public administration and the policy sciences.

Administrative Science Quarterly. (1956–). Ithaca, NY: Cornell University. Graduate School of Business and Public Administration. Quarterly.
Emphasizes empirical and theoretical studies relevant to administration as a theoretical discipline applied to both the public and private sectors. Regularly includes lengthy book reviews and review articles.

American Academy of Political and Social Science. *Annals*. (1891–). Newbury Park, CA: Sage. Bimonthly.
Articles are frequently grouped around single issues, often policy-related issues. Includes many critical book reviews of works of general interest to the social sciences.

American Behavioral Scientist. (1957–). Newbury Park, CA: Sage. Bimonthly.
Each issue focuses on a particular issue, usually one with some relevance to public policy. Aspects of it are addressed by social (as well as behavioral) scientists.

American Political Science Review. (1906–). Washington, DC: American Political Science Association. Quarterly.
Perhaps the most prestigious journal in this discipline and cited here as a reminder that many journals in political science frequently include important

articles relevant to theoretical and methodological issues relating to public administration.

Journal of Public Administration Research and Theory. (1991–). Lawrence, KA: University of Kansas. Department of Public Administration. Quarterly.

An "interdisciplinary quarterly devoted to building the body of knowledge of public administration through empirical research and theoretical inquiry."

Philosophy and Public Affairs. (1971–). Princeton, NJ: Princeton University Press. Quarterly.

An academic journal in philosophy aimed at addressing matters of public concern that have "an important philosophical dimension."

Public Administration. (1923–). London: Royal Institute of Public Administration. Quarterly.

The major British journal of its kind and perhaps the oldest English-language journal in the field. Not surprisingly, the emphasis is very much on Commonwealth institutions, but the coverage of other countries, as well as coverage of general theory, is substantial. Book reviews and listings of documents and pamphlets received are included in each issue.

Public Administration Review. (1940–). Washington, DC: American Society for Public Administration. Bimonthly.

Intended as a general theoretical journal for scholars and practitioners. Includes lengthy book reviews and annotated checklists of trade and non-trade materials recently published.

Public Affairs Quarterly. (1987–). Bowling Green, OH: Bowling Green State University. Philosophy Documentation Center.

"Intended to provide a forum for the philosophical scrutiny of public policy issues." Aims to present "philosophical case studies of ethical and justificatory aspects of particular issues [and] . . . also make some place for discussions that relate theory to practice."

Public Manager. (1972–). Washington, DC: American Society for Public Administration. Quarterly.

Intended for both scholars and practitioners and designed to "assist the decision-making process by raising public policy questions, analyzing the implications, and suggesting possible alternative solutions for consideration." Most issues include a bibliographic or review essay on one specific topic. Earlier the *Bureaucrat*.

Social Forces. (1922–). Chapel Hill: University of North Carolina Press. Bimonthly.

Reports research efforts on topics of public concern that are usually empirical and sociological in focus. Contents of individual issues are frequently grouped around a unifying theme.

2.2. State and Local Issues

Most of the journals in this category are written expressly for the public manager. When the focus is scholarly, this is noted.

American City and Country. (1909–). Pittsfield, MA: Morgan-Grampian. Monthly.

Intended for those actively involved in management at the municipal level of government. Articles emphasize problems of local concern. Includes regular sections on recent "Legal Notes and Decisions" and "Municipal and Civic Publications." Previously *American City*.

The American Review of Public Administration. (1967–). Parkville, MO: Midwest Review of Public Administration. Quarterly.

Seeks to address the needs of both scholars and practitioners primarily concerned with state and local issues. Emphasizes commentaries and research on pressing issues, reviews and syntheses of research, and discussions of changing boundaries of the field. Formerly entitled *Midwest Review of Public Administration*.

City: Magazine of Urban Life and Environment. (1967–). Washington, DC: National Urban Coalition. Bimonthly.

Each issue includes a valuable column entitled "Chronicle of Urban Events and Ideas." Emphasizes topics of general interest to the student of urban affairs.

Intergovernmental Perspective. (1975–). Washington, DC: U.S. Advisory Commission on Intergovernmental Relations. Quarterly.

Most useful as an informational guide to recent developments in the United States and to the activities and publications of the commission.

The Journal of State Government. (1926–). Lexington, KY: Council of State Governments. Quarterly.

Articles are short and descriptive. Useful for its concern for recent federal developments affecting the states. Earlier titles include *State Government*, *American Legislator* and *Legislator*.

Local Government Studies. (1971–). Birmingham, UK: University of Birmingham. Institute of Local Government Studies. Bimonthly.

Scholarly research articles address policy concerns primarily in British settings, but occasionally in those of other countries.

Municipal Management: A Journal. (1978–). Montpelier, VT: Municipal Management. Quarterly.

Practitioner-oriented and with a focus on the interests of managers in small- or medium-sized communities.

National Civic Review. (1912–). New York: National Municipal League. Monthly.

Devoted to local government affairs. Each issue includes news announcements and a section entitled "Researchers' Digest." In this, research reports of concern to local government are abstracted and reviewed. Reviews are often quite lengthy. Formerly the *National Municipal Review*.

Nation's Cities Weekly. (1963–). Washington, DC: National League of Cities. Monthly.

Intended for those making decisions at the municipal level rather than for the scholar.

PM: Public Management. (1918–). Washington, DC: International City Management Association. Monthly.

Formerly *Public Management* and *City Manager Magazine*. Concentrates on governmental problems at the municipal level. An important source because of its emphasis on urban problems. Practitioner-oriented, but includes the occasional short research article.

Publius: The Journal of Federalism. (1971–). Denton, TX: University of North Texas. Center for the Study of Federalism. Quarterly.

Published by "an interdisciplinary research and educational institute dedicated to the study of federal principles, institutions and processes as practical means of organizing political power in free societies." Addresses federalism and intergovernmental relations worldwide.

State and Local Government Review. (1968–). Athens: University of Georgia. Institute of Government. Three issues a year.

"A journal of research and viewpoints on state and local government issues." Articles address problem-oriented research of concern to scholars and practitioners.

2.3. Comparative Administration

Administration and Society. (1969–). Newbury Park, CA: Sage. Quarterly.
Entire issues are devoted to discussions of one particular topical concern or geographical area. Review articles and book reviews are often included. Formerly entitled *Journal of Comparative Administration*.

Annals of Public and Cooperative Economy. (1908–). Liege, Belgium: International Centre of Research and Information on Public and Cooperative Economy (CIRIEC). Quarterly.
Primarily a vehicle for scholars to address economic aspects of public enterprises in a variety of national contexts.

Comparative Political Studies. (1968–). Newbury Park, CA: Sage. Quarterly.
An academic journal focusing on all comparative aspects of political systems at the national level throughout the world. Articles frequently address administrative and policy issues.

Comparative Politics. (1968–). New York: City University of New York. Graduate Center. Quarterly.
Articles examine political institutions and political behavior in both Western and developing societies.

Electoral Studies. (1982–). Guildford, UK: Butterworths. Quarterly.
International and often comparative in its coverage. Regularly features a "Guide to Journal Articles."

Growth and Change: A Journal of Regional Development. (1970–). Lexington: University of Kentucky. College of Business and Economics. Quarterly.
Articles are written primarily by academics specializing in economics, geography, political science, and different approaches to planning.

International Journal of Public Administration. (1979–). New York: Dekker. Bimonthly.
Each issue is substantial and devoted to one quite narrow topic, for example, "Public Administration and Decision-aiding Software." Offers theoretical as well as comparative perspectives.

International Organization: A Journal of Political and Economic Affairs. (1947–). Cambridge, MA: MIT Press. Quarterly.
Sponsored by the World Peace Foundation and concerned with cooperative mechanisms between nations and their institutions.

International Review of Administrative Sciences. (1928–). Brussels: International Institute of Administrative Sciences. Quarterly.

Probably the outstanding journal in its area. Has its own index, which cumulates every five years. The entire text of this edition is in English.

Journal of Developing Areas. (1966–). Macomb: Western Illinois University Press. Quarterly.

Focuses on Third World settings and is concerned with all aspects of the development process.

Journal of Development Studies. (1964–). London: Frank Cass. Quarterly.

"A quarterly journal devoted to economic, political and social development."

Public Administration and Development: A Journal of the Royal Institute of Public Administration. (1962–). Chichester, UK: John Wiley. Quarterly.

Early issues concentrate almost exclusively on institutions and systems within the British Commonwealth. Has more recently come to emphasize the Third World in general. Includes book notes and a section listing events of current interest. Formerly entitled *Journal of Local Administration Overseas* and, more recently, *Journal of Administration Overseas.*

Social and Economic Studies. (1953–). Kingston, Jamaica: University of the West Indies. Institute of Social and Economic Research. Quarterly.

Includes research articles in all areas relating to the problems of developing societies throughout the world, but has a special concern for the Caribbean.

Studies in Comparative International Development. (1964–). New Brunswick, NJ: Transaction Periodicals. Quarterly.

An interdisciplinary journal that emphasizes theoretical issues associated with policy development and social change in developing societies.

2.4. National Journals

In addition to the journals already cited, many theoretical journals also focus on the problems and concerns of individual countries. A selection of these is given here.

Administration. (1953–). Dublin: Institute of Public Administration. Quarterly.

Has its own index, which cumulates every five years.

Australian Journal of Public Administration. (1937–). Sydney, Australia: Royal Australian Institute of Public Administration. Quarterly.
Formerly entitled *Public Administration.*

Bangladesh Journal of Public Administration. (1987–). Savar Dhaka: Public Administration Training Centre. Quarterly.

Canadian Public Administration/Administration Publique du Canada. (1958–). Toronto: Institute of Public Administration of Canada. Monthly.
Strong in its listings of current non-trade publications and is a major source for identifying relevant Canadian publications of this kind.

Indian Journal of Public Administration. (1955–). New Delhi: Indian Institute of Public Administration. Quarterly.

Israel Annual of Public Administration and Public Policy. (1959–76). Jerusalem: Israel Institute of Public Administration.
Formerly *Public Administration in Israel and Abroad.*

Offentliche Verwaltung: Zeitschrift für Verwaltungsrecht und Verwaltungspolitik. (1948–). Stuttgart: Kohlhammer Verlag. Semimonthly.
One of the two principal German-language journals in this field.

Philippine Journal of Public Administration. (1957–). Manila: University of the Philippines. Quarterly.

Public Administration. (1960–). Riyadh, Saudi Arabia: Institute of Public Administration. Semiannual.

Public Sector. (1938–). Wellington: New Zealand Institute of Public Administration. Semiannual.
Formerly entitled *New Zealand Journal of Public Administration.*

Quarterly Journal of Administration. (1966–). Ile-Ife, Nigeria: University of Ife. Institute of Administration. Quarterly.

Revista de Administración Pública. (1950–). Madrid: Instituto de Estudios Politicos. Three issues a year.

Revista de Administración Pública. (1964–). Río Piedras: Universidad de Puerto Rico. Semiannual.

Revue Administrative. (1948–). Paris: Bourse de Commerce. Bimonthly.

Revue Française d'Administration Publique. (1967–). Paris: Institut International d'Administration Publique. Quarterly.
Formerly entitled the *Bulletin* of the institute. Major emphasis is on the institutions of Francophone countries in general. Each issue includes an "Information bibliographique" section that provides extensive annotated listings of recently published material.

Sudan Journal of Administration and Development. (1965–). Khartoum: Sudan Institute of Public Administration. Annual.

Verwaltung: Zeitschrift für Verwaltungswissenschaft. (1968–). Berlin: Duncker & Humblot. Quarterly.

2.5. General Management

Journals in this category are those that present theoretical developments and research findings of interest to scholars and professionals in the public sector, although largely originating outside of it.

Academy of Management Journal. (1958–). Mississippi State: Academy of Management. Quarterly.
Reports research largely carried out by academicians. Articles have an empirical focus.

Academy of Management Review. (1976–). Mississippi State: Academy of Management. Quarterly.
An offshoot of the *Academy of Management Journal* that emphasizes theoretical concerns. (A third journal in this series, the *Academy of Management Executive*, addresses practical applications.)

Advanced Management Journal. (1935–). New York: Society for Advancement of Management. Quarterly.
Intended primarily for practitioners, but articles generally present some theoretical perspective. Reviews or cites recent books.

Business Horizons. (1958–). Bloomington: Indiana University. Graduate School of Business. Bimonthly.
Articles by both academics and managers address all aspects of the administrative process in the private sector.

California Management Review. (1958–). Berkeley, CA: University of California. Graduate School of Business Administration. Quarterly.

Intended to introduce managers to ideas and theoretical concepts in the area.

Harvard Business Review. (1922–). Boston: Harvard University. Graduate School of Business Administration. Bimonthly.

Probably the best known of the management journals and addressed to both scholars and professional managers. Has an annual index that cumulates into a moving 10-year index.

International Studies of Management and Organization. (1971–). Armonk, NY: M. E. Sharpe. Quarterly.

Includes translations of major articles appearing in languages other than English throughout the world. Each issue is devoted to a particular topic or theme.

Journal of General Management. (1974–). Henley, UK: Braybrooke Press. Quarterly.

Articles address the needs and interests of the professional manager. Useful to the scholar for its discussions of the applications of theory to practice.

Journal of Management Studies. (1964–). Oxford, UK: Blackwell. Three issues a year.

Presents scholarly articles emphasizing organizational theory and its application to management practice. A major British source.

Management Science. (1954–). Providence, RI: Institute of Management Sciences. Monthly.

An outstanding journal in an area otherwise known as operations research. Addresses both new methods and the problems of converting theory into practice.

Sloan Management Review. (1959–). Cambridge, MA: Massachusetts Institute of Technology. Sloan School of Management. Quarterly.

With the *Harvard Business Review*, one of the two outstanding journals in management. Combines theoretical perspectives with case studies and other practical applications. Formerly the *Industrial Management Review.*

2.6. Policy Sciences

Canadian Public Policy/Analyse de Politiques. (1975–). Guelph, Ont.: University of Guelph. Quarterly.

Addresses problems of particular concern to all levels of Canadian government. Primarily practitioner-oriented.

Decision Sciences. (1970–). Atlanta: Decision Sciences Institute. Quarterly.

Highly technical articles focus on the application of quantitative techniques to administrative decisions, with a particular concern for the business enterprise.

Economic Systems Research. (1989–). Abingdon, UK: Carfax. Quarterly.

Includes theoretical discussion, but emphasizes "tools and data for modeling, policy analysis, planning and decision-making in large economic environments."

Futures: The Journal of Forecasting and Planning. (1968–). Guildford, UK: IPC Science and Technology. Bimonthly.

Futurics. (1976–). Minneapolis: Future Systems. Quarterly.

Futurist. (1967–). Washington, DC: World Future Society. Bimonthly.

These three journals generally address mixed audiences of the academic and general public on a broad range of issues concerned with some aspect of social forecasting. Most articles are closely concerned with policy implications.

Governance: An International Journal of Policy and Administration. (1987–). Oxford, UK: Blackwell. Quarterly.

Subject matter is defined as "executive politics," that is, the translation of legislated policy into bureaucratic practice.

Journal of Policy Analysis and Management. (1981–). New York: Wiley. Quarterly.

A scholarly journal that also addresses the interests of policymakers. The official journal of the Association for Public Policy Analysis and Management.

Journal of Policy History. (1989–). University Park: Pennsylvania State University Press. Quarterly.

"Aims to encourage research into the formation and development of public policy [and] the application of diverse methods and theories to public policy and their politics within a historical perspective."

Journal of Policy Modeling. (1979–). New York: Elsevier. Quarterly.

The official journal of the Society for Policy Modeling and explicitly concerned with "questions of critical import to the world community as a whole . . . and the economic, social, and political interdependencies between national and regional systems." A high proportion of the contents address the public sector.

Journal of Political Economy. (1892–). Chicago: University of Chicago Press. Bimonthly.
A scholarly source that emphasizes the application of economic analysis to the understanding of the behavior and policies of organizations and groups.

Journal of Public Policy. (1981–). Cambridge, UK: Cambridge University Press. Quarterly.
The major British journal in this area. International in its interests.

Journal of Social Policy. (1972–). Cambridge, UK: Cambridge University Press. Quarterly.
Analytical rather than quantitative articles that tend to address United Kingdom settings. A regular feature is "Social Policy Digest," which cites and summarizes recent governmental and other publications of interest.

Law and Policy. (1979–). Oxford, UK: Blackwell. Quarterly.
Articles are geared to the interests of scholars and legal professionals and provide critical discussions of specific policy areas. Formerly entitled *Law and Policy Quarterly.*

Mathematics of Operations Research. (1976–). Providence, RI: Institute of Management Sciences and Operations Research Society of America. Quarterly.
A highly technical journal intended primarily for mathematicians concerned with applications in this specialized area.

Operations Research. (1952–). Providence, RI: Operations Research Society of America. Bimonthly.
Concerned with all aspects of the field and includes discussions of applications as well as research articles.

Policy and Politics. (1972–). Bristol, UK: University of Bristol. School for Advanced Urban Studies. Quarterly.
Addresses an audience of academics and policymakers and intended to illuminate the structure and mechanics of policy formulation.

Policy Sciences: An International Journal Devoted to the Improvement of Policy Making. (1970–). Dordrecht, Holland: Kluwer. Quarterly.

International in its coverage and in its concerns. Perhaps the premier scholarly journal in this area. "An international journal devoted to the improvement of policy making."

Policy Studies Journal. (1972–). Urbana, IL: Policy Studies Organization. Quarterly.

Articles are frequently grouped around broad issues (for example, "judicial review and public policy") and often have a comparative perspective. Review essays are regularly included.

Policy Studies Review. (1981–). Urbana, IL: Policy Studies Organization. Quarterly.

An offshoot of the *Policy Studies Journal* that focuses more on reviewing important developments in the field, including analyses of major government reports.

Public Choice. (1962–). Blacksburg, VA: Virginia Polytechnic Institute. Center for Study of Public Choice. Quarterly.

Emphasizes political and economic influences on policy-making in the public sector. Intended for a broad educated audience.

Public Interest. (1965–). New York: National Affairs. Quarterly.

Intended for a well-informed but nonspecialist audience, this journal examines aspects of U.S. domestic policy from a rather conservative stance.

Public Welfare. (1943–). Washington, DC: American Public Welfare Association. Quarterly.

This journal attempts to review developments across the spectrum of U.S. welfare policy and does so through articles of research and review and through comments on recent legislation and policy, court decisions, and other events of note.

Social Problems. (1953–). Buffalo, NY: Society for the Study of Social Problems. Quarterly.

A scholarly journal sponsored by the major organization in the United States concerned with the application of sociological analysis to contemporary social problems.

Technology Analysis and Strategic Management. (1988–). Abingdon, UK: Carfax. Quarterly.

"A quarterly international research journal linking the analysis of science and technology with the strategic needs of policy makers and management." Methodological and empirical research is emphasized.

2.7. Public Finance

Government Accountants Journal. (1952–). Arlington, VA: Association of Government Accountants. Quarterly.
As its earlier title (*Federal Accountant*) indicates, mainly concerned with financial operations of the U.S. federal government. Articles are mainly by and for professionals, but some research studies are included.

Government Finance Review. (1985–). Chicago: Government Finance Officers Association. Bimonthly.
Articles are short and informational in content. Primarily addresses the concerns of governments at the state and local levels in the United States and elsewhere.

Government Finance Review. (1926–). Chicago: Government Finance Officers Association. Quarterly.
Intended for the practitioner rather than the academic, with articles emphasizing financial issues at the local levels of government. Several earlier titles include *Governmental Finance, Government Financial Management Resources in Review,* and *Municipal Finance.*

Journal of Accounting and Public Policy. (1982–). New York: Elsevier. Quarterly.
Includes articles, theoretical or empirical, that address some aspect of the relationship between accounting systems and public policy.

Journal of Accounting, Auditing, and Finance. (1977–). Westport, CT: Greenwood. Quarterly.
Exists to provide a vehicle for publishing academic research for the benefit of an audience of scholars and practitioners. Affiliated with the New York University School of Business.

Journal of Financial and Quantitative Analysis. (1966–). Seattle: University of Washington. Graduate School of Business. Five issues a year.
Many of the issues addressed are market-driven, but articles of interest to those concerned with the public sector are sometimes included. Sponsored by the Western Finance Association.

Journal of Law and Economics. (1958–). Chicago: University of Chicago. Law School. Semiannual.

Articles have a strong emphasis on those interfaces between these two disciplines that are important for the development or implementation of public policy.

Journal of Public Economics. (1972–). Lausanne: Elsevier. Quarterly.

Concerned with a broad range of issues relating to the creation and application of policy. International in its coverage. Emphasizes academic approaches to public policy modeling.

Municipal Finance Journal. (1980–). Greenvale, NY: Panel Publishers. Quarterly.

Publishes contributions "to professional practice and substantive knowledge concerning municipal finance, including tax-exempt financing. Interdisciplinary approaches . . . address legal, financial, economic, and political aspects."

National Public Accountant. (1955–). Alexandria, VA: National Society of Public Accountants. Monthly.

Short, informational articles are intended to interpret government systems and otherwise assist practitioners.

National Tax Journal. (1948–). Columbus, OH: National Tax Association-Tax Institute of America. Quarterly.

The major journal of its kind, with the mostly empirical articles representative of the interests of practitioners and academics.

Public Budgeting and Finance. (1981–). New Brunswick, NJ: Transaction Periodicals Consortium. Quarterly.

Addresses the broad spectrum of public financial management. Articles are written by and for both scholars and practitioners. Sponsored by the American Association for Budget and Program Analysis.

Public Finance and Accountancy. (1974–). London: Chartered Institute of Public Finance and Accountancy. Monthly.

The journal of the major professional association in Britain for senior financial managers in the public sector. Former title: *Local Government Finance.*

Public Finance/Finances Publiques. (1946–). The Hague: Netherlands Public Finance. Three issues per year.

"Devoted to the study of fiscal theory and policy and related problems." Articles are scholarly and usually quantitative. International in scope. In English with summaries in English, French, and German.

Public Finance Quarterly. (1973–). Newbury Park, CA: Sage.
Scholarly and concerned with the theory and practice of financial allocation at all levels of government. Emphasis is on assessment of current policies. Articles are technical and usually quantitative.

2.8. Personnel

Human Resource Management. (1961–). Ann Arbor, MI: University of Michigan. Bureau of Industrial Relations. Quarterly.
Like those in several other journals listed in this category, articles are short and intended for the working professional, rather than the academic. Earlier title: *Management of Personnel Quarterly.*

Human Resource Planning. (1978–). New York: Human Resource Planning Society. Quarterly.
Concentrates on presenting new developments or findings relevant to planning. Includes some reports of original research.

Industrial and Labor Relations Review. (1947–). Ithaca, NY: Cornell University. School of Industrial and Labor Relations. Quarterly.
Scholarly articles reflecting both empirical and theoretical concerns. Extensive book reviews in each issue.

Industrial Relations. (1961–). Berkeley, CA: University of California. Institute of Industrial Relations. Three issues a year.
A "journal of economy and society" that emphasizes quantitative research on a broad range of topics linking changes in the labor force to economic factors.

Industrial Society. (1918–). London: Industrial Society. Bimonthly.
Covers management/worker relations from a generally management (and British) perspective. Previously entitled *Industrial Welfare.*

International Labour Review. (1921–). Geneva: International Labour Office. Bimonthly.
A journal of major significance to academics and managers for the variety of its coverage of issues relating to the labor force and for the international nature

of its concerns. Articles are usually academic and frequently empirical in approach.

Journal of Collective Negotiations in the Public Sector. (1972–). Amityville, NY: Baywood. Quarterly.

Addresses procedural, legal, and other aspects of public labor negotiation. Concerns are cross-national.

Journal of Counseling and Development. (1921–). Falls Church, VA: American Personnel and Guidance Association. Ten issues a year.

Perhaps the major practitioner-oriented journal in this area. Valuable for its critical assessments of recent theoretical developments. Better known under its old title, the *Personnel and Guidance Journal.*

Journal of Employment Counseling. (1963–). Washington, DC: National Employment Counselors Association. Quarterly.

Primarily a vehicle for articulating the needs and interests of professionals concerned with employee guidance and training. Some research articles are included.

Journal of Human Resources. (1966–). Madison, WI: University of Wisconsin Press. Quarterly.

Primarily reports empirical studies of a variety of behavioral and social studies related to the workplace. Published under the auspices of the University of Wisconsin's Industrial Relations Research Institute.

Labor Law Journal. (1949–). Washington, DC: Commerce Clearing House. Monthly.

Provides commentary and documentation of legal developments in this area. Articles are always informational and frequently academic.

Personnel Administrator. (1955–). Berea, OH: American Society for Personnel Administration. Monthly.

About half the articles in each issue are grouped around a single theme. As with many journals in this area, articles are a mixture of the scholarly and the professional.

Personnel Journal. (1922–). Santa Monica, CA: Personnel Research Federation. Monthly.

A practitioner's journal intended to provide "a source of contemporary ideas, both theoretical and practical, for professionals in the personnel management and labor relations field." Earlier entitled *Journal of Personnel Research.*

Personnel Management. (1969–). London: Business Publications. Monthly.
The journal of the (British) Institute of Personnel Management. In substance and structure, very like its U.S. counterpart (see previous entry). Formed from a union of *Personnel* and *Personnel and Training Management.*

Personnel Psychology. (1948). Durham, NC: Personnel Psychology. Quarterly.
A "journal of applied research" written by and for behavioral scientists concerned with this area. Includes extensive book reviews.

Public Personnel Management. (1940–). Washington, DC: International Personnel Management Association. Quarterly.
One of the few journals concerned exclusively with managerial or scholarly aspects of personnel issues in the public sector. Includes book reviews and listings of recent publications. Formerly entitled *Personnel Administration and Public Personnel Review.*

Relations Industrielles/Industrial Relations. (1945–). Montréal: Université Laval. Département des Relations Industrielles. Quarterly.
The major journal focusing primarily on labor relations concerns in Canada. Addresses the interests of both professionals and academics.

Review of Public Personnel Administration. (1980–). Columbia, SC: University of South Carolina. Bureau of Governmental Research and Service. Three issues a year.
A strictly scholarly journal that includes articles relating the interaction between personnel issues and larger policy formulation.

Training and Development. (1947–). Madison, WI: American Society for Training and Development. Monthly.
Concerned with the practical needs of managers in this area. Formerly entitled *Training Directors Journal* and *Training and Development Journal.*

Work and Occupations. (1974–). Newbury Park, CA: Sage. Quarterly.
Articles reflect social, rather than managerial, concerns, and emphasize theoretical insights over empirical findings. Formerly entitled *Sociology of Work and Occupations.*

2.9. Productivity and Evaluation

Assessment and Evaluation in Higher Education. (1975–). Bath, UK: University of Bath. School of Education. Three issues a year.

Educational Evaluation and Policy Analysis. (1979–). Washington, DC: American Educational Research Association. Quarterly.

These two titles are presented as examples of the many journals of narrow focus addressing evaluation in a particular public setting.

Evaluation and Program Planning. (1978–). Elmsford, NY: Pergamon. Quarterly.

An interdisciplinary journal essentially concerned with practical aspects of evaluation research. Considerable attention is paid to the public sector.

Evaluation and the Health Professions. (1978–). Newbury Park, CA: Sage. Quarterly.

One of a small group of journals concerned with evaluation in a specific public context. Articles are primarily case studies.

Evaluation Review. (1977–). Newbury Park, CA: Sage. Quarterly.

A more scholarly source, but one that also retains a concern for applications in public-sector settings. Presented as "a forum for researchers, planners, and policymakers engaged in the development, implementation, and utilization of studies aimed at the betterment of the human condition." Includes "Research Briefs" and methodological "Craft Notes." Former title: *Evaluation Quarterly.*

National Productivity Review: The Journal of Productivity Management. (1981–). New York: Executive Enterprises. Quarterly.

Articles address concepts and techniques in both private and public settings.

Public Productivity and Management Review. (1975–). San Francisco: Jossey-Bass. Quarterly.

The only journal devoted exclusively to productivity in the public sector. Includes regular features dealing with current research, meetings and conferences, and other matters of concern to academics and practitioners. Most of the articles report research findings. Formerly entitled *Public Productivity Review.*

2.10. Legal Issues

Legal aspects of public administration are addressed in articles published in the standard law reviews, listed in Mersky, Benning, and McCue (see section 1) and indexed in sources such as the *Current Law Index* (see chapter 8). The journals cited here are those that focus mainly on the area of public law or on legal aspects of important public concerns.

Administrative Law Review. (1949–). Denver, CO: American Bar Association. Administrative Law Section. Quarterly.

Intended for jurists and legal scholars and presents original scholarly articles as well as comments on recent legal decisions and other matters of interest. Earlier title: *Administrative Law Bulletin.*

Fordham Urban Law Journal. (1972–). New York: Fordham University. School of Law. Quarterly.

Articles address current issues important to the judiciary of the United States, especially New York State. Also includes a section presenting summaries of recent developments.

Harvard Journal of Law and Public Policy. (1978–). Cambridge, MA: Harvard Society for Law and Public Policy. Three issues a year.

Usually addresses important public issues with groups of articles discussing their social and legal implications, for example, "The Future of Civil Rights Law." One issue presents papers from an annual symposium on law and philosophy.

Harvard Journal on Legislation. (1964–). Cambridge, MA: Harvard University. School of Law. Semiannual.

"Specializes in the analysis of legislation and the legislative process. It focuses on legislative reform and on organizational and procedural factors that affect the efficiency and effectiveness of legislative decisionmaking."

Journal of Law and Politics. (1983–). Charlottesville, VA: University of Virginia. School of Law. Quarterly.

"An interdisciplinary publication devoted to the analysis of the legal aspects of politics and the impact of politics on law."

Journal of Law and Society. (1974–). Oxford, UK: Blackwell. Quarterly.

Addresses current policy issues from a British legal perspective. Includes regular feature articles on legal philosophy.

Journal of Legislation. (1974–). Notre Dame, IN: University of Notre Dame. School of Law. Semiannual.

"A law review specializing in legislation, public policy, administrative law, and regulatory affairs."

Law and Contemporary Problems. (1933–). Durham, NC: Duke University. School of Law. Quarterly.

Issues usually consist of articles grouped around a single issue. This is usually topical and controversial, for example, "Freedom and Tenure in the Academy."

Law and Society Review. (1966–). Amherst: University of Massachusetts. Five issues a year.

A publication of the Law and Society Association, "whose purpose is the stimulation and support of research and teaching on the cultural, economic, political, psychological, and social aspects of law and legal systems." Frequently includes extensive review essays.

Legislative Studies Quarterly. (1976–). Iowa City: University of Iowa. Comparative Legislative Research Center.

Emphasizes cross-national and comparative approaches to all aspects of the legislative process.

Notre Dame Journal of Law, Ethics, and Public Policy. (1984–). Notre Dame, IN: University of Notre Dame. School of Law. Semiannual.

"Seeks to build upon Notre Dame's religious tradition by translating Judeo-Christian principles into imaginative yet practical proposals for legislative and judicial reform."

University of Michigan Journal of Law Reform. (1983–). Ann Arbor: University of Michigan. School of Law. Quarterly.

Each issue presents essays grouped around a single theme. Most of these reflect moral and philosophical, as well as legal, concerns, for example, "Comparable Worth" and "Legal Issues in Scientific Research."

Washington University Journal of Urban and Contemporary Law. (1968–). St. Louis, MO: Washington University. School of Law. Semiannual.

Articles mainly report and interpret court decisions and other recent legal developments relating to legal aspects of the functioning of public institutions. Otherwise known as the *Journal of Urban and Contemporary Law.*

Yale Journal on Regulation. (1983–). New Haven, CT: Yale University. School of Law. Semiannual.

"A unique forum for debate on regulation in a wide range of disciplines, including finance, environmental law, health care policy, public utilities, and administrative law."

2.11. Criminal Justice Administration

British Journal of Criminology. (1950–). London: Stevens. Quarterly.

Sponsored by the Institute for the Study and Treatment of Delinquency. Also addresses the broader subject fields of "delinquency and deviant social behavior." Early volumes were entitled *British Journal of Delinquency.*

Crime and Delinquency. (1955–). Newbury Park, CA: Sage. Quarterly.

Established as the journal of the major private research institute in this area, the National Council on Crime and Delinquency. Special issues often address single topics. Articles are always research-oriented.

Crime, Law, and Social Change. (1976–). Boston: Kluwer. Bimonthly.

Seeks understanding of "the interplay between crime, development and legal change; between class structures and crime, policing and punishment; and on comparative crime control." Formerly entitled *Contemporary Crises.*

Criminal Justice and Behavior. (1974–). Newbury Park, CA: Sage. Quarterly.

A scholarly journal devoted to the approaches of psychologists and other behavioral scientists. Sponsored by the American Association of Correctional Psychologists.

Criminal Justice Policy Review. (1986–). Indiana, PA: Indiana University of Pennsylvania. Quarterly.

Issues are thematic. All address the development, implementation, or interpretation of policy.

Criminologie. (1968–). Montréal: Presses de l'Université de Montréal. Semiannual.

A scholarly journal that addresses aspects of the sociology of law as well as criminology. Issues frequently address a single topic. Articles are in French with English summaries. Early volumes were entitled *Acta Criminologica.*

Criminology: An Interdisciplinary Journal. (1963–). Newbury Park, CA: Sage. Quarterly.

Despite the subtitle, its perspective is primarily sociological, reflecting that of its organizational sponsor, the American Society of Criminology. Early volumes were entitled *Criminologica.*

International Journal of the Sociology of Law. (1973–). London: Academic Press. Quarterly.

Articles are theoretical, often philosophical, and address law creation and application as social processes. Formerly entitled *International Journal of Criminology and Penology.*

Journal of Criminal Justice. (1973–). New York: Pergamon. Quarterly.
The premier journal addressing all aspects of the criminal justice system and the links between its constituent parts.

Journal of Criminal Law and Criminology. (1910–). Baltimore: Williams & Wilkins. Quarterly.
Articles are devoted primarily to social aspects of criminal law. Few address criminology. An offshoot of the *Journal of Criminal Law, Criminology and Police Science.*

Journal of Police Science and Administration. (1910–). Gaithersburg, MD: International Association of Chiefs of Police. Quarterly.
The major scholarly journal addressing social and administrative aspects of policing. Before 1973, combined with the *Journal of Criminal Law and Criminology* as the *Journal of Criminal Law, Criminology, and Police Science.* No issues have appeared for several years.

Justice Quarterly. (1984–). Omaha, NE: Academy of Criminal Justice Sciences.
The official journal of one of the two principal scholarly associations in this area, whose interests are also to some extent practitioner-oriented.

Justice System Journal. (1974–). Denver, CO: National Center for State Courts. Quarterly.
Concerned mainly with the functioning of the criminal courts. Review essays are frequently included.

Police Journal. (1928–). Chichester, UK: Justice of the Peace. Quarterly.
Articles are diverse and reflect research, commentary, or opinion. Written by and for both practitioners and academics. Advertised as international in its concerns, but British settings are strongly emphasized.

Police Studies. (1978–). New York: John Jay Press. Quarterly.
The major journal addressing policing in comparative perspective. Articles are short, but generally scholarly.

Prison Journal. (1845–). Philadelphia: Pennsylvania Prison Society. Semiannual.
One of the oldest continuously published journals in the United States. Articles are short, but scholarly and reflective of the publisher's concern for advocacy,

policy, and management. Formerly entitled *Journal of Prison Discipline and Philanthropy.*

Revue Internationale de Criminologie et de Police Technique. (1947–). Geneva: Centre International d'Etudes Criminologiques. Quarterly.
One of the several major European journals in this area. Includes book reviews and abstracts of current journal literature. Early issues are entitled *Revue de Criminologie et de Police Technique.*

2.12. Historical Perspectives

American Journal of Legal History. (1957–). Philadelphia: Temple University. School of Law. Quarterly.
Extensive essays on a broad range of topics. All are scholarly and generally reflect the approaches of the historian or other social scientist rather than the legal scholar. Reviews about 10 books in each issue.

Comparative Studies in Society and History. (1958–). Cambridge, UK: Cambridge University Press. Quarterly.
"A forum for the presentation and discussion of new research into problems of changes and stability that recur in human societies through time or in the contemporary world."

Congress and the Presidency: A Journal of Capitol Studies. (1972–). Washington, DC: American University. Center for Congressional and Presidential Studies. Semiannual.
"An interdisciplinary journal of political science and history . . . features scholarly articles on Congress, the Presidency, the interactions between the institutions, and national policymaking." Former titles include *Capitol Studies* and *Congressional Studies.*

The Economic History Review: A Journal of Economic and Social History. (1927–). Oxford, UK: Blackwell. Quarterly.
Official journal of the (British) Economic History Society. As with other journals in this category, articles often relate to the development of public institutions. Long book reviews.

Federalist. (1980–). Washington, DC: Society for History in the Federal Government. Quarterly.
Generally addresses historical aspects of federal agencies and functions, rather than the legislative and judicial arms of government.

Journal of Economic History. (1941–). Port Chester, NY: Cambridge University Press. Quarterly.

The journal of the Economic History Association.

Journal of Interdisciplinary History. (1970/71–). Cambridge, MA: MIT Press. Quarterly.

One of the major journals relating history to other social sciences and "spanning all geographical areas related to work in applied fields such as economics and demographics."

Journal of Legal History. (1980–). London: Frank Cass. Three issues a year.

Largely concerned with developments in Anglo-American jurisdictions. Occasionally includes articles addressing other systems of law.

Journal of Social History. (1967–). Pittsburgh, PA: Carnegie-Mellon University. Quarterly.

The principal journal in its field published in the United States. Regularly includes articles on methodology and sources.

Journal of Urban History. (1974–). Newbury Park, CA: Sage. Quarterly.

Concerned with the "history of cities and urban societies in all periods of human history and in all geographical areas of the world." Often devotes an entire issue to one broad topic.

Labor History. (1960–). New York: New York University. Tamiment Institute. Quarterly.

Articles tend to emphasize political aspects of the American labor movement and the relationships of these aspects to social movements.

Past and Present. (1952–). Oxford, UK: Oxford University Press. Quarterly.

The pioneering journal in the now-established fields of social and public history. Has been characterized as "the most influential historical journal."

The Public Historian. (1978–). Santa Barbara, CA: Graduate Program in Public Historical Studies, Department of History. University of California. Quarterly.

The vehicle of the National Council on Public History and very much concerned with documenting the methodology, as well as the findings, of this relatively new field. Has extensive review essays, as well as reviews of books, exhibits, and films.

Urban History Review/Revue d'Histoire Urbaine. (1972–). Toronto: City of Toronto Archives. Quarterly.

Articles and book reviews address "the historical evolution of urban Canada . . . ranging from early Canadian history to contemporary concerns over the evolution of urban policy."

2.13. Organizational Theory and Behavior

Group and Organization Management. (1976–). Newbury Park, CA: Sage. Quarterly.

The "international journal for group facilitators." A professional journal intended primarily for those concerned with training, communication, and other aspects of organizational development. Formerly *Group and Organization Studies.*

Human Organization. (1941–). Washington, DC: Society for Applied Anthropology. Quarterly.

A vehicle for scholarly, mainly ethnographic studies by anthropologists on formal groupings. Formerly entitled *Applied Anthropology.*

Human Relations. (1947–). London: Plenum. Monthly.

An interdisciplinary journal that includes many articles on human relationships in organizational settings.

Journal of Applied Behavior Analysis. (1968–). Ann Arbor, MI: Society for the Experimental Analysis of Behavior. Quarterly.

Most articles are empirical or clinical studies of behavior in organizational or other group settings.

Journal of Applied Behavioral Science. (1965–). Arlington, VA: NTL Institute for Applied Behavioral Science. Quarterly.

Most articles are written by psychologists and address processes of planned change.

Journal of Applied Psychology. (1917–). Washington, DC: American Psychological Association. Bimonthly.

Scholarly articles mainly report empirical research, much of which is of institutional interest.

Journal of Applied Social Psychology. (1971–). Washington, DC: V. H. Winston. Bimonthly.

The objective of this journal is to publish original research by psychologists that some bearing upon social problems. Many of the areas covered concern relationships between individuals and organizations.

Journal of Organizational Behavior. (1980–). Chichester, UK: Wiley. Quarterly.
Articles report original studies by industrial psychologists. Formerly the *Journal of Occupational Behavior.*

Journal of Organizational Behavior Management. (1977–). New York: Haworth. Quarterly.
Has a particular focus on industrial psychology and its concern for work-related research settings.

Organization Studies. (1980–). Berlin: de Gruyter. Quarterly.
Emphasizes the social contexts of organizational behavior and cross-cultural differences that affect this. Sponsored by the European Group for Organizational Studies and the Maison des Sciences de l'Homme, Paris.

Organizational Behavior and Human Decision Processes. (1966–). New York: Academic Press. Bimonthly.
"A journal of fundamental research and theory in applied psychology." All articles are reports of research, primarily of a quantitative nature. Early volumes were entitled *Organizational Behavior and Human Performance.*

Organizational Dynamics. (1972–). New York: American Management Association. Quarterly.
Articles are a mixture of the scholarly and the practitioner-oriented. Public-sector settings are frequently used. Frequently includes review essays.

Small Group Research. (1970–). Newbury Park, CA: Sage. Quarterly.
Articles are limited to empirical, clinical, and theoretical research involving interactions within small groups of people, in work or in experimental settings. Formerly entitled *Comparative Group Studies* and *Small Group Behavior.*

2.14. Planning and Urban Affairs

American Planning Association. *Journal.* (1935–). Washington, DC. Quarterly.
An academic journal for practitioners and academics concerned with the fields of urban and regional planning.

Annals of Regional Science. (1967–). Bellingham, WA: Annals of Regional Science. Three issues a year.

Emphasizes interdisciplinary approaches to problem-oriented issues related to urban affairs. An organ of the Western Regional Science Association.

City and Society: Journal of the Society for Urban Anthropology. (1987–). Washington, DC: American Anthropological Association. Semiannual.

Important here for its regular articles on the methodology of ethnographic research in urban settings.

Community Development Journal. (1966–). Manchester, UK: Oxford University Press. Three issues a year.

Presents articles related to community development and mobilization primarily, but not exclusively, in Third World settings. Earlier *Community Development Bulletin.*

Comparative Urban Research. (1972–). New York: Comparative Urban Research. Three issues a year.

Emphasizes comparative and interdisciplinary research of either a methodological or a theoretical nature and related in some way to the process of urbanization. Sponsored by the American Society for Public Administration and the International Sociological Association.

Development and Change. (1969–). Newbury Park, CA: Sage. Quarterly.

Articles reflect interdisciplinary and scholarly approaches to all aspects of the problems of developing societies. Supported by the Netherlands Institute of Social Studies.

Journal of Urban Affairs. (1978–). Greenwich, CT: JAI Press. Quarterly.

Sponsored by the Urban Affairs Association and concerned primarily with issues related to public planning. Earlier titles were *Urban Interest* and *Urban Affairs Papers.*

Journal of Urban Analysis and Public Management. (1972–). New York: Gordon & Breach. Semiannual.

A policy-oriented journal that focuses on specific topics of concern to those with a professional concern for urban problems. Formerly the *Journal of Urban Analysis.*

Long Range Planning. (1968–). London: Pergamon. Bimonthly.

Addresses the concepts and tools needed to develop planning in both the public and private sectors. Intended for academics and practitioners.

Regional Studies. (1967–). Cambridge, UK: Cambridge University Press. Bimonthly.

Reports the results of original research on social issues (housing, labor mobility, and so on) related to business planning.

Socio-Economic Planning Sciences. (1967–). New York: Pergamon. Quarterly.

Most of the articles reflect the application of systems approaches to the planning of public enterprises. Articles are usually quantitative and technical.

Town and Country Planning. (1904–). London: Town and Country Planning Association. Monthly.

Articles on current developments in Britain and elsewhere are emphasized, especially as these relate to the establishment of new communities. Published for a professional audience.

Town Planning Review. (1910–). Liverpool, UK: Liverpool University Press. Quarterly.

Takes a generally academic approach to an interpretation of planning that includes social aspects of it.

Urban Affairs Quarterly. (1965–). Newbury Park, CA: Sage.

Intended as yet another vehicle for improving communication between the bureaucrat and the scholar. Includes review articles and "research notes" as well as scholarly articles. Tends to focus on the United States.

Urban Anthropology. (1972–). New York: Plenum. Quarterly.

A scholarly journal that largely reports ethnographic studies of the cultural systems of urban areas. Sponsored by the Institute for the Study of Man.

Urban Life. (1972–). Newbury Park, CA: Sage. Quarterly.

Another journal that is largely a vehicle for academics with an interest in ethnographic and other qualitative studies of life in urban areas. Continues *Urban Life and Culture.*

Urban Studies. (1964–). Abingdon, UK: Carfax. Bimonthly.

"An international journal for research in urban and regional studies." Emphasizes multidisciplinary approaches to the study of regional and urban planning. Articles frequently reflect the approaches and interests of economists.

The section on electronic bulletin boards in chapter 15 refers to the future importance of this medium in supplanting conventional modes of publishing. A growth in the number of journals published electronically is indicated by the 900 titles included in the 1992 edition of the following directory, an increase of about 50 percent over the number listed the previous year.

Directory of Electronic Journals, Newsletters, and Academic Discussion Lists. (1991–). Washington, DC: Association of Research Libraries. Annual.

NOTES

1. The vocabulary of the library trade here requires some explanation. A *serial* publication is one that appears at any regular interval. A *periodical* is a serial that appears at least twice a year. *Journals* are periodicals that report original research or are otherwise of a scholarly bent. *Magazines* are periodicals whose purpose is to inform, but whose articles are not held to the same standard of scholarly documentation. *Newsletters* report current information without analysis, and usually in some abbreviated form.

2. See chapter 10 for discussion of published bibliographies.

3. It has been suggested, no more than half in jest, that a scholar is someone who takes pleasure in reading footnotes. The scholarly mind-set certainly views footnotes as potential sources of nuggets waiting to be mined.

4. As a rule, scholars in criminology who wish to report their findings prefer to be published in sociological journals. A search of those indexes and abstracts that cover only the criminological literature would ignore the best work in this area.

5. One crucial gauge of quality is whether or not the journal is *refereed.* A refereed journal is one that only publishes articles that have been vetted by the independent assessment of a group of specialists in the area addressed. In the academic world, a journal that does not use this process is immediately suspect.

8

INDEXES, ABSTRACTS, AND ACCESS TO THE JOURNAL LITERATURE

Familiarity with the principal journals relevant to the researcher's field of interest is of great importance as a source of knowledge of current disciplinary trends. However, the scanning of any fixed group of journals, no matter how extensive this is, cannot be relied upon to yield a thorough literature review of journal articles related to one's field of study. Interdisciplinary approaches to many research topics in the social, behavioral, and policy sciences have now been popular for several decades. A researcher addressing a given topic from a particular disciplinary focus cannot ignore the possibility that illuminating or provocative work on the topic, or on the methods or sources used to study it, may have been undertaken by scholars with very different backgrounds and perspectives.

For example, the student of the dynamics of police/citizen interactions would do well to recognize that it is not just sociologists and criminologists who have been interested in this phenomenon. Political scientists and anthropologists have also addressed it, in rather different ways. As previously noted, academics tend to seek to publish in the journals associated with their own disciplines. A search of the major journals in sociology, criminology, and criminal justice might therefore fail to yield relevant and important literature produced from yet other social and behavioral perspectives. Moreover, searching through back volumes and indexes of even a small group of journals can be arduous and not entirely productive. If your purpose is to conduct a thorough survey of the journal literature on a given topic, a much better approach is to employ appropriate indexes and abstracting services from the many available.

These services provide subject access to the contents of a fixed group of 200 or more journals or other types of material.[1] Very few of them cover books.[2] Most focus upon journals within a single discipline or group of related disciplines and therefore provide a focused approach to literature searching. As a result, you must make an early decision about which disciplines are likely to have produced research articles of interest. As with all activities in the research process, this is done most effectively when based on a good working knowledge of the topic and its related literature. Identify and search the appropriate sources, usually starting with the most recent issues and working back under relevant headings through earlier volumes. Both indexes and abstracts generally appear periodically—monthly or quarterly, in some cases weekly—and cumulate every year. They usually list, in each volume, the titles of those journals covered. In this way the user knows just which journals are so accessed and which are not. "Current contents" services are specialized forms of indexes that aim to provide the most timely coverage of articles by reproducing the tables of contents of journals in the field covered. They are published very frequently (usually weekly) and are intended as guides to only the most recent literature. Their structure and arrangement do not make them suitable for extensive retrospective searches.

The most obvious distinction between an indexing and an abstracting service lies in their rather different objectives and formats. An indexing service seeks only to provide citations to articles on a particular topic; an abstracting service also provides summaries of the articles. The latter service is, on the face of it, a potentially more valuable source because it gives a means of undertaking some preliminary evaluation of the article before it is actually looked up and read. (We are all familiar with the experience of identifying articles with very promising titles, but whose contents fail to live up to expectations).

Despite this, it is usually good practice to search both indexing and abstracting services and not to regard the latter as substitutes for the former. Indexes are usually more comprehensive in their coverage and easier to search because the best of them use standardized subject headings, often Library of Congress headings or some variant of them. Many abstracting services use their own systems of subject access, which must be understood before they can be searched. Searching an index is much easier and quicker. Figures 9 and 10 illustrate the relative structure of indexes and abstracts. Figure 9 shows an example taken from a recent volume of the *Social Sciences Index*, perhaps the outstanding service of its kind. The schema presented in this figure corresponds closely to the structure of the conventional library catalog. The heading, **Legal ethics**, is in fact a standard LC heading. The five (in this case) "see also" headings listed immediately under it are all LC headings related in some way to the topic in point. These provide further possible avenues of investigation. The remaining entries include full bibliographic citations to all articles on the topic published in any issue of any journal indexed by the *SSI* in the time period covered by that issue or volume of the index. Once the relevant subject heading

Figure 9
An Index Entry

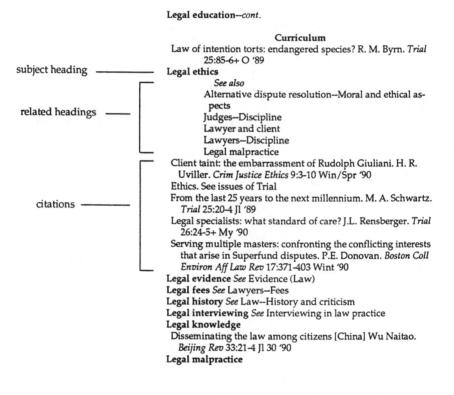

Legal education--*cont.*

Curriculum

Law of intention torts: endangered species? R. M. Byrn. *Trial* 25:85-6+ O '89

subject heading — **Legal ethics**

related headings —

See also

Alternative dispute resolution--Moral and ethical aspects
Judges--Discipline
Lawyer and client
Lawyers--Discipline
Legal malpractice

citations —

Client taint: the embarrassment of Rudolph Giuliani. H. R. Uviller. *Crim Justice Ethics* 9:3-10 Win/Spr '90
Ethics. See issues of Trial
From the last 25 years to the next millennium. M. A. Schwartz. *Trial* 25:20-4 Jl '89
Legal specialists: what standard of care? J.L. Rensberger. *Trial* 26:24-5+ My '90
Serving multiple masters: confronting the conflicting interests that arise in Superfund disputes. P.E. Donovan. *Boston Coll Environ Aff Law Rev* 17:371-403 Wint '90

Legal evidence *See* Evidence (Law)
Legal fees *See* Lawyers--Fees
Legal history *See* Law--History and criticism
Legal interviewing *See* Interviewing in law practice
Legal knowledge
Disseminating the law among citizens [China] Wu Naitao. *Beijing Rev* 33:21-4 Jl 30 '90
Legal malpractice

Source: Social Sciences Index (1990/91), 17, 1058.

or headings have been identified, the mechanics of the search in a well organized index of this sort proceed smoothly and quickly.

Figure 10, using an example taken from *Human Resources Abstracts*, illustrates the results of a two-step process of searching an abstracting service. In the figure, the citation for the article is accompanied by a very detailed summary of the article's findings. Usually, some attention is paid to the methodology applied in the study, if this is an original piece of research. In this case, the characterization of the study as a piece of survey research is implied rather than stated. After reading this summary, the researcher would be in little doubt as to whether this was indeed an important item in the secondary literature of the topic. Locating this abstract might not be a quick process. Issues and volumes of abstracting services usually include entries arranged by abstract number. The numbers of entries associated with a particular topic are found through a separate index. In this particular case, the article was assigned the various headings "group behavior," "job performance," and "social loafing." (We know this because we are so informed by the entry; we would not know this until we had located the entry).

The twofold difficulty here is mechanical and not conceptual in nature. First, not all entries for articles on similar topics are located together; they must be identified through the abstract numbers (or sometimes page numbers) given in the index.[3] Second, the subject headings used in this example—and there are many like it—are certainly problematic. "Job performance" is, in this instance, reasonable. "Group behavior" is very broad; who would imagine "Social loafing?" In abstracting services that may not have rigorous and clear indexing criteria, it may be useful to scan a few recent issues to determine just what kinds of subject arrangement they use and how their subject headings conform to nomenclature commonly used in the field.[4] It may even be useful to isolate a broad category of potentially useful entries and look through them to determine how broad your searching terms should be.

Searching abstracts is a slower process than searching indexes, and, because of the more limited numbers of journals usually covered by abstracting services, the results gained tend to reflect more limited access to the world of secondary literature. The reader is advised to draw up a list of both indexing and abstracting services, based solely on judicious assessment of the subject emphases likely to yield citations of interest. An informed determination should also be made of how far back the search should be taken, given knowledge of the topic and those aspects of it that have attracted scholarly attention at different times.[5]

Search your selected indexing and abstracting services, giving preference to the former. This is recommended due to their greater coverage and ease of use and because the better indexes will also permit a certain spread in the definition of the topic searched. Any studies dealing with comparative, historical, or other

Figure 10
An Abstract Entry

grams and other pertinent groups and individuals. (The term "psychoactive" drug is used for drugs which principally act in the central nervous system; these differ from those used medically to treat disease symptoms, combat disease, or correct bodily malfunctions.)

citation number — **620**

citation — Schnake, Mel E. Equity in effort: the "sucker effect" in co-acting groups. Journal of Management 17(1):41-55, March 1991.

subject-headings — GROUP BEHAVIOR. JOB PERFORMANCE. SOCIAL LOAFING.

abstract — This research investigates the effect of negative social cures on worker quantitative task performance, internal work motivation, and job satisfaction. Negative social cues may create an effect similar to a class of social dilemma phenomena in small groups known as the "sucker effect." The sucker effect was originally identified as a particular form of social loafing and stems from the perceptions that others in the group are withholding, or intend to withhold, effort. Individuals who hold this perception then withhold effort themselves to avoid being played for a "sucker." although most social loafing research has examined the sucker effect in situations where individuals performed additive or disjunctive tasks, this experimental research investigated the degree to which the sucker effect occurs among individuals working in coacting groups. Two common managerial strategies, goal setting and punishment, were examined for their ability to reduce the sucker effect. The results showed that the sucker effect does occur in coacting groups, and that both punishment and goal setting may be used to reduce it. Furthermore, goal setting was found to be a more effective strategy than punishment.

Source: Human Resources Abstracts. (1991), 26, 334.

aspects of the topic will usually be identified in an index as in the conventional library catalog. They are not always identifiable in this way in abstracting services.

The interdisciplinary focus of much current research throughout the various social and behavioral sciences has been emphasized in almost every chapter in this book. Public administration has, of course, always relied more heavily than most disciplines on models, techniques, and theories developed in its sister disciplines. Yet research in all these disciplines is frequently becoming issue-oriented rather than discipline-oriented. Unless the object of study is strictly self-contained or problem-oriented,[6] do not assume that relevant secondary literature will have been focused within any one disciplinary perspective.

The best approach is to consider continually what kinds of disciplines have been, or are likely to have been, represented in analyses of the topic under study. Identify the major indexing and abstracting services in these disciplines and search them properly. The services described below are compartmentalized; most restrict themselves to covering groups of journals associated with particular disciplinary approaches. Human endeavor, however, is not necessarily so restricted. Disciplinary connections provide us with structure and support. They are not intended to limit either our imagination or our efforts.

The selected indexes and abstracts noted below include those from areas that, on the face of it, have little necessary relationship to public administration. Those who decide that their research topics closely devolve upon other disciplines should obviously take note of these sources. They should also use the various guides cited in chapter 4 that provide information on the many other bibliographic resources available in these disciplines.[7]

Only sources of major significance to the general area of public administration are cited below. Those also amenable to computerized searching, with all its advantages and limitations (see chapter 9), are designated by an asterisk (*).[8] Those available on computer disk are designated by an ampersand (&).[9] Services listed below are limited to those that exclusively or primarily provide access to the current journal literature. Those that primarily address other forms of published material are discussed elsewhere in this account. Those that are not open-ended in that they address noncurrent journal literature are considered as separately published bibliographies and are discussed in chapter 9.

With regard to organization of the sources presented, the disciplinary relations of public administration and its allied fields are recognized. The first category includes important indexes and abstracts in the social and policy sciences, such as *Psychological Abstracts*, that, because of their range of journal coverage, have a general importance that belies the narrowness of their titles. Other categories address the general area of public administration and the broader one of administration and management. Next are presented the major sources documenting several of the specialized aspects of management, both public and private. Finally, the major services documenting particular aspects of the social and behavioral sciences are presented. Services that primarily address methodological issues are discussed in chapter 14. Those covering newspapers and popular magazines are considered in chapter 15.

1. GENERAL THEORY IN THE SOCIAL SCIENCES

ASSIA: Applied Social Sciences Index and Abstracts. (1987–). London: Bowker/Saur. Bimonthly, with annual cumulation. (*).

An important source that combines a social science perspective with an interest in public-sector issues. Covers about 550 English-language journals published throughout the world. Most of the issues addressed have implications for policy and its implementation, although these are most usually related to social work.

British Humanities Index. (1962–). London: Library Association. Quarterly.

Continues a series earlier entitled *Subject Guide to Periodicals*, initiated in 1915. Covers journals in the social sciences as well as the humanities.

Bulletin Signalétique. (1947–). Paris: Centre National de la Recherche Scientifique, Institut de l'Information Scientifique et Technique. Usually quarterly, with an annual. (* &).

Of the several dozen works in this series at least twenty address the social and behavioral sciences. The most important of them, from the point of view of the social or organizational researcher, are cited below according to discipline. They are all of concern to the anglophone researcher in that: (1) they include a great many entries (almost one-half) relating to English-language sources; (2) the materials they cite are frequently theses and other "gray" literature; (3) each series has a section devoted to methodology. All series are available online and on CD-ROM (see chapter 9) under the title *FRANCIS.* All present materials within grouped subject specialties. Those few individual titles cited here are presented in appropriate categories and without annotations.

Current Contents: Social and Behavioral Sciences. (1961–). Philadelphia: Institute for Scientific Information. Weekly. (* &).

One of seven subsets. Others address various other fields of scholarly endeavor. One of these concerns "Clinical Practice." The others relate to various pure and applied sciences. Presents the tables of contents of a large number of journals in the fields addressed.

Essay and General Literature Index. (1900–). New York: H. W. Wilson. Semiannual, with annual and quinquennial cumulations. (* &).

An index to "collections of essays and work of a composite nature that have reference value" and the only source that is exclusively concerned with materials of this nature. Covers about 300 collections each year, and these are evenly divided between the humanities and the social sciences.

Fondation Nationale des Sciences Politiques. *Bulletin Analytique de Documentation Politique, Economique et Sociale Contemporaine.* (1946–). Paris: Presses Universitaires de France. Monthly, with annual subject index.

Brief summaries, in French, of articles in French and other European journals. Updates the *Bulletin Bibliographique de Documentation Internationale Contemporaine*, published between 1926 and 1940.

Hispanic American Periodicals Index. (1978–). Los Angeles: University of California. Latin American Center. Annual. (*).

A subject and author index of almost 250 journals published throughout the world which cover some aspect of Latin America or of Latin Americans in North America. The great majority of sources covered are published in Spanish.

Index to Black Periodicals. (1961–). Boston: G. K. Hall. Annual, with a retrospective cumulation for 1950–59.

Provides comprehensive coverage of about 35 journals and selective coverage of many others. Former titles: *Index to Periodical Articles By and About Blacks* and *Index to Periodical Articles By and About Negroes.*

Internationale Bibliographie der Zeitschriftenliteratur aus allen Gebieten des Wissens. (1963–). Osnabrück: Dietrich. Semiannual.

Perhaps the major index for accessing journal articles in the social sciences published in Western languages other than English. Also provides extensive coverage of published forms such as conference proceedings, essays in collections, symposia, and yearbooks.

LLBA: Linguistics and Language Behavior Abstracts. (1967–). San Diego, CA: Sociological Abstracts. Quarterly. (*).

A subset of *Sociological Abstracts* that explicitly addresses articles dealing with the various research approaches to the uses of language. Much broader in scope than its title suggests, and should be used in conjunction with its parent file.

Psychological Abstracts. (1927–). Washington, DC: American Psychological Association. Monthly, with regular cumulations. (* &).

The major abstracting service in psychology and one of the principal bibliographic tools in the social sciences. Covers conference proceedings and other materials as well as journal articles only marginally related to psychology. Supplements the *Psychological Index*, published between 1894 and 1935.

Social Sciences Citation Index. (1969–). Philadelphia: Institute for Scientific Information. Three issues a year, with annual cumulation. (* &).

An author, title, and keyword index to a very large number of journals in the social, behavioral, and policy sciences. There is no controlled subject access to this index. An extremely valuable, indeed essential, source, but one much better searched in its computerized version, *Social SciSearch*, than by hand (see chapter 9, also for discussion of its companion, the *SciSearch*.

Social Sciences Index. (1907–). New York: H. W. Wilson. Quarterly, with annual cumulations. (* &).

Between 1907 and 1965 the *International Index* and between 1965 and 1974 the *Social Sciences and Humanities Index.* Since its new definition in 1974, this index has provided subject coverage of the most prestigious journals in its area. Any search of the recent journal literature of any area related to the social, behavioral, or policy sciences should begin with this source.

Social Work Research and Abstracts. (1965–). Albany, NY: National Association of Social Workers. Quarterly; indexes cumulate. (*).

Includes review articles as well as classified abstracts of articles from about 250 journals. Much of the subject matter addressed has strong policy or other implications, and it is for this reason that this source is included in this section. Earlier entitled *Abstracts for Social Workers.*

Sociological Abstracts. (1953–). San Diego, CA: Sociological Abstracts. Five issues per year, with annual cumulations. (* &).

Abstracts conference papers and book reviews as well as articles. A much more limited resource than *Psychological Abstracts*, and one that should be used in conjunction with it.

The Substance Abuse Index and Abstracts: A Guide to Drug, Alcohol, and Tobacco Research. (1986/7–). New York: Scientific DataLink. Annual in 5 vols.

Very extensive coverage worldwide. Most useful for its focus on the scientific and medical literature.

Women Studies Abstracts. (1972–). Rush, NY: Women Studies Abstracts. Quarterly, with annual indexes.

Abstracts a variety of published forms (including about 350 journals) reflecting the universe of disciplinary approaches. A valuable source, but one far from providing adequate coverage of this wide-ranging area.

Women's Studies Index. (1989–). Boston: G. K. Hall. Annual.
Indexes 78 women's journals in their entirety and other titles selectively. The most comprehensive indexing service in this area.

World Agricultural Economics and Rural Sociology Abstracts: Abstracts of World Literature. (1959–). Slough, UK: Commonwealth Agricultural Bureaux. Monthly.
Included here because of its very extensive coverage of the journal literature. Approximately 2,500 journals and other materials are covered in this source, and a surprising number of them address topics of concern to the student of public administration.

2. PUBLIC ADMINISTRATION AND RELATED ASPECTS OF POLITICAL SCIENCE

ABC Pol Sci: Advance Bibliography of Contents: Political Science and Government. (1969–). Santa Barbara, CA: ABC–Clio. Bimonthly; indexes cumulate regularly. (*).
A current-contents service that reproduces the tables of contents of over 300 journals. Very valuable as a means of scanning recent developments in the general field. Formerly *Advance Bibliography of Contents.*

APAIS: Australian Public Affairs Information Service: Subject Index to Current Literature. (1945–). Canberra: National Library of Australia. Monthly; last issue is the annual cumulation. (*).
Important for its coverage of articles and other published forms concerned with Australasia and the Far East. Formerly the *Australian Public Affairs Information Service.*

Documentation in Public Administration. (1957–). New Delhi: Indian Institute of Public Administration. Quarterly.
Indexes and abstracts a limited number of journals. Useful for its coverage of non-Western English-language journals not indexed elsewhere. Formerly *Public Administration Abstracts and Index of Articles.*

International Bibliography of Political Science. (1952–). London: Tavistock. Annual.

Includes articles, books, and other materials. Interprets its subject matter broadly and includes a great number of citations of direct consequence to public administration and its related fields. Well indexed. The principal source of its kind.

International Current Awareness Services: Political Science. (1990–). London. London School of Economics. British Library of Political and Economic Science. Monthly.

Much better in its coverage of the European literature than parallel sources, such as *ABC Pol Sci* (see above).

International Political Science Abstracts. (1951–). Paris: International Political Science Abstracts. Bimonthly; indexes cumulate.

Arranged in six broad areas, one of which is "Governmental and Administrative Institutions." Abstracts in English for items published in English, and in French for those published in other languages.

PAIS International in Print. (1915–). New York: Public Affairs Information Service. Monthly, with quarterly and annual cumulations. (* &).

Probably the best single index addressing journals of interest to the student of public administration, as it covers most major journals in the field published throughout the world, as well as other forms of materials. A separately published subject cumulation covers the years 1915 through 1974. Before 1991, published in two separate series as the PAIS *Bulletin* and *Foreign Language Index.*

Political Science Abstracts. (1967–). New York: IFI/Plenum. Annual.

Updates the extensive bibliography of the Universal Reference System; (see chapter 10). Usually issued in three volumes, which include many classifications of entries of direct relevance to administrative and policy concerns. Earlier entitled *Political Science, Government, and Public Policy Series: Annual Supplement.*

Royal Institute of Public Administration. Library. (1979–). *Accessions List.* London. Usually three issues a year.

A classified list of periodical articles, books, and other materials included in one of the world's major libraries in this area. No indexes.

Sage Public Administration Abstracts. (1974–). Newbury Park, CA: Sage. Quarterly; indexes cumulate annually.

Covers the contents of over 100 journals, together with many other forms of materials, directly related to the public administration field. Entries are organized within broad categories. Very valuable, but by its own terms of reference cannot be used as a guide to items of interest published in related areas.

United States Political Science Documents. (1975–). Pittsburgh, PA: University of Pittsburgh. Center for International Studies. Annual. (*).

Abstracts the contents of over 100 major journals in political science, plus a number in public administration. Also covers books and some other forms of material. Subject and author indexes are detailed, but not always the easiest to use.

3. GENERAL MANAGEMENT AND ADMINISTRATION

Anbar Management Services Abstracts. (1961–71). Wembley, UK: Anbar. Eight issues a year.

This is now published in five separate series, each of which presents summaries of articles in selected journals. Arrangement is classified, and no detailed indexes are provided. The series now include *Accounting and Data Processing Abstracts*, *Marketing and Distribution Abstracts*, *Personnel and Training Abstracts*, *Top Management Abstracts*, and *Work Study and O and M Abstracts*. Each series is sponsored by the appropriate British professional organization in the field.

Bulletin Signalétique. Part 528: Bibliographie Internationale de Science Administrative. (1947–). Paris: Centre National de la Recherche Scientifique, Institut de l'Information Scientifique et Technique. Quarterly, with annual index. (* &).

See the generalized *Bulletin Signaletique* description in section 1. Formerly *Science Administrative*. Particularly strong in administrative issues relating to the public sector.

Business Index. (1979–). Los Altos, CA: Information Access. Updated monthly.

An index in microfilm form that covers journals and newspapers of a primarily financial nature. The current reel covers the most recent five years or so of citations. Earlier material is available on microfiche.

Business Periodicals Index. (1958–). New York, NY: H. W. Wilson. Monthly, with frequent cumulations. (* &).

The standard index to scholarly journals in the fields of administration and management in both public and private sectors. Selective in its coverage and only indexes the major journals in its field. The administrative equivalent of the *Social Sciences Index* (see section 1).

Canadian Business Index. (1975–). Toronto: Micromedia. Monthly, with annual cumulations. (* &).

Covers newspapers and journals concerned with finance, business, and management in Canada.

Contents Pages in Management. (1972–). Manchester, UK: Manchester Business School. Semimonthly.

Covers well over 100 journals. Formerly entitled *Current Contents in Management.*

DOGE. (1980–). Paris: Centre National de la Recherche Scientifique, Institut de l'Information Scientifique et Technique. Semiannual. (* &).

Addresses French and French-Canadian literature on all aspects of management. Particularly strong on management education. Most of the materials covered are conference papers, theses, and other non-trade forms of publication. Online as *Gestion des Enterprises.*

Indian Management. (1961–). New Delhi: All India Management Association. Monthly.

A journal that now incorporates a section earlier published separately as *Management Abstracts*, and valuable for its coverage of English-language material generated in South Asia.

Management Abstracts. (1973–). Port of Spain, Trinidad: Management Development Centre. Bimonthly.

A "current review of digests and summaries on management" that is one of the few services to give any significant coverage of Caribbean issues.

Management and Marketing Abstracts. (1976–). Oxford, UK: Pergamon. Monthly. (*).

Covers 300 journals, primarily professional ones in marketing.

Management News. (1948–). London: British Institute of Management. Monthly.

An abstracting service that focuses on publications primarily oriented to the practitioner. Covers articles in scholarly journals as well as those in the professional literature, including newsletters. Earlier titles were *Management Abstracts* and *Management Review and Digest.*

SCIMP: European Index of Management Periodicals. (1978–). Helsinki, Finland: European Business School Librarians Group. Monthly, with annual cumulations. (* &).

A major source covering the now-substantial body of managerial literature being generated throughout Europe. Abstracts are in English, although a high proportion of works cited are in other languages. The acronym of the title stands for "Selective Cooperative Index of Management Periodicals."

4. SPECIAL AREAS IN ADMINISTRATION

4.1. Personnel

Human Resources Abstracts. (1966–). Newbury Park, CA: Sage. Quarterly, with annual index.

Articles are summarized within 10 categories. The range of its perspective is indicated by its earlier title *Poverty and Human Resources Abstracts.*

International Labour Office. *International Labour Documentation.* (1965–). Geneva. Monthly. (*).

Annotated subject listings of books and articles received in the ILO library. This collection emphasizes social and political aspects of its field and has a strongly international perspective. Editions of this source are published in English, French, and Spanish. Hard to use, as there are no indexes or cumulations. For this reason the computerized version is to be preferred.

Personnel Management Abstracts. (1955–). Ann Arbor, MI: University of Michigan. Graduate School of Business Administration. Quarterly.

Includes both articles and books. Interprets its subject matter broadly to include various aspects of organizational behavior.

U.S. Office of Personnel Management. Library. *Personnel Literature.* (1941–). Washington, DC: GPO. Monthly, with annual index.

The most comprehensive source in this area. Lists, without annotations, books and articles within 70 subject categories. Citations included are based on the holdings of the OPM Library.

Work Related Abstracts. (1973–). Detroit: Information Coordinators. Monthly, with quarterly and annual cumulations.

A loose-leaf service that summarizes books and articles within 20 broad categories. Has an extensive subject index that is regularly updated. Covers about 250 journals. Formerly *Employment Relations Abstracts.*

4.2. Planning and Urban Affairs

International Development Abstracts. (1982–). Lausanne: Elsevier. Quarterly, with an annual index. (*).

Surveys about 600 journals, primarily for articles addressing development in the Third World.

Journal of Planning Literature. (1985–). Newbury Park, CA: Sage. Quarterly.

Each issue is devoted to literature reviews of particular narrow topics. Included also are citations to several hundred publications in the general area, about half of which are summarized.

LOGA: Local Government Annotations Service. (1966–). London: Havering Public Libraries. Monthly.

An extensive index of articles, books, and British government documents concerned with all aspects of municipal governments and their responsibilities. Indexes about 100 journals.

Recent Publications on Governmental Problems. (1932–). Chicago: Mirriam Center Library. Semimonthly.

A checklist that indexes articles relating to state and local government. Most useful, however, for identifying government documents, research reports, and other nontrade materials. Does not cumulate, has no indexes, and is therefore difficult to use.

Rural Development Abstracts. (1978–). Wallingford, UK: CAB International Centre. Quarterly.

Covers articles in 400 journals as these relate to the planning and implementation of public projects, especially in developing countries.

Sage Urban Studies Abstracts. (1973–). Newbury Park, CA: Sage. Quarterly; indexes cumulate annually.

The companion to *Sage Public Administration Abstracts* (see section 2). Similar in form and organization and should be used in conjunction with it. Expressly concerned with governmental involvement in urban life and urban development.

U.S. Department of Housing and Urban Development. *Housing and Planning References.* (1948–). Washington, DC: GPO. Bimonthly. Indexes cumulate annually.

Indexes articles in journals and other publications received by one of the largest libraries specializing in this area.

Urban Abstracts. (1974–). London: London Research Centre. Monthly. (*).

Originally developed as a current bibliography of books, articles, and other materials received by the Greater London Council Library. Particularly concerned with local government in Great Britain, but includes a great deal of policy-oriented and other material of general interest.

Urban Affairs Abstracts. (1971–). Washington, DC: National League of Cities. Weekly, with semiannual and annual cumulations.

Very broad in its interpretation of its subject matter and includes headings dealing with topics such as private-sector involvement in community development and planning. Indexes about 400 journals.

4.3. Policy Sciences

Social Planning, Policy and Development Abstracts. (1978–). San Diego, CA: Sociological Abstracts. Quarterly. (* &).

A subfile of *Sociological Abstracts.* Because of the diverse nature of the way this area is defined and addressed, it does not include all the relevant information from its parent file.

4.4. Public Finance

ABA Banking Literature Index. (1982–). Washington, DC: American Bankers Association. Monthly, with annual cumulation.

Indexes over 170 periodicals, including some financial newspapers as well as scholarly and professional journals.

Accountants' Index. (1921–). New York: American Institute of Certified Public Accountants. Quarterly, with annual cumulations. (*).

An author, title, and subject listing of articles, books, and many other forms of material. A very comprehensive source.

Accounting Articles. (1963–). Chicago: Commerce Clearing House. Monthly.

This is in a loose-leaf format that is regularly updated. Provides abstracts of books and articles by broad category and includes a fine subject index.

Brown, Lawrence D., Gardner, John C., & Vasarhelyi, Miklos A. (Eds.). (1989). *Accounting Research Directory: The Database of Accounting Literature* (2nd ed.). New York: Wiener. 583 p.

Limited in coverage (provides access to the contents of six journals between 1963 and 1988), but valuable for the depth of its indexing.

4.5. Other Areas

ACM Guide to Computing Literature. (1976–). New York: Association for Computing Machinery. Annual.

An expanded version of *Computing Reviews* which covers books, dissertations, conference papers, and other forms as well as journals articles. Supersedes the ACM's *Bibliography and Subject Index*, published between 1963 and 1976.

Abstracts in Human-Computer Interaction. (1990–). Lawrence, KS: Ergosyst Associates. Quarterly; annual subject index.

Covers published materials in all forms, many of which are probably not indexed elsewhere.

Artificial Intelligence Abstracts. (1984–). New York: Bowker. Monthly.

Covers research reports, conference proceedings, monographs, and the contents of over 100 journals.

Communication Abstracts. (1978–). Newbury Park, CA: Sage. Bimonthly.

Covers over 200 journals concerned with both technological and behavioral aspects of human interaction.

Computer Literature Index. (1970–). Phoenix, AZ: Applied Computer Research. Quarterly, with annual cumulation.

A classified list of books, articles, and other materials that concentrates on applied, rather than research, activities in the area. The former title was *Quarterly Bibliography of Computers and Data Processing.*

Computing Reviews. (1960–). New York: Association for Computing Machinery. Monthly.

Abstracts articles related to "hardware, software, systems theory, systems applications, and computing milieu" appearing in over 500 journals.

Ecology Abstracts. (1975–). Bethesda, MD: Cambridge Scientific Abstracts. Monthly, with annual index.

Covers over 900 journals. Subject matter includes issues related to planning and management. Formerly *Applied Ecology Abstracts.*

Environment Abstracts Annual. (1971–). New York: Environment Center. (*).

Interprets this field very broadly to include scientific, technological, political, and other policy aspects. Books, articles, and other published forms are summarized within over 20 broad headings. Formerly *Environment Index.*

Ergonomics Abstracts. (1969–). London: Taylor & Francis. Quarterly.
Indexes about 250 journals addressing "human-computer interaction, psychology, physiology, biomechanics and work design."

Hospital Literature Index. (1944–). Chicago: American Hospital Association. Quarterly, with annual cumulations. (*).
An author and subject index that demonstrates a strong concern for the administration, planning, and social aspects of health care in institutional settings. One of a number of sources of its kind. These are typically well organized and extensive in coverage, as they are largely offshoots of one or another of the massive medical literature systems. Continues the *Hospital Periodical Literature Index.*

HRIS Abstracts. (1931–). Washington, DC: National Academy of Sciences. Monthly.
Formerly *Transportation Research Abstracts* and *Highway Research Abstracts.* Coverage not limited to journal articles.

Information Science Abstracts. (1966–). New York: IFI/Plenum. Monthly; index cumulates annually. (*).
Published under the sponsorship of the American Society for Information Science and, like this organization, concerned with many aspects of information use and retrieval, including those of concern to industry and government. Formerly *Documentation Abstracts.*

Insurance Periodicals Index. (1963–). New York: Special Libraries Association. Annual. (*).
A subject index to the 50 or so outstanding journals concerned with life, property, and liability insurance. Many of the articles covered address demographic and behavioral features of the population. A cumulation of the monthly lists appearing in *Best's Review.*

Leisure, Recreation, and Tourism Abstracts. (1976–). Wallingford, UK: CAB International Centre. Quarterly.
Covers 400 journals. Formerly *Rural Recreation and Tourism Abstracts.*

5. DISCIPLINES IN THE SOCIAL AND BEHAVIORAL SCIENCES

5.1. Anthropology

Abstracts in Anthropology. (1970–). Westport, CT: Greenwood. Quarterly.
Covers the three standard subfields of this discipline—archeology, physical anthropology, and cultural anthropology, the last of which is of greatest concern to this discussion. No cumulations and therefore somewhat difficult to use.

Anthropological Index to Current Periodicals in the Museum of Mankind Library. (1963–). London: Royal Anthropological Institute. Quarterly.
Covers about 450 specialized journals. Hard to use, as there is no cumulative subject index.

Anthropological Literature: An Index to Periodical Articles and Essays. (1979–). Pleasantville, NY: Redgrave. Quarterly.
A comprehensive index, not limited to periodical articles. Represents the contents of current acquisitions of one of the world's principal libraries in this area, the Tozzer Library of Harvard University's Peabody Museum of Archaeology and Ethnology.

Bulletin Signalétique. Part 529: Ethnologie. (1947–). Paris: Centre National de la Recherche Scientifique, Institut de l'Information Scientifique et Technique. Quarterly, with annual index. (* &).
See the generalized *Bulletin Signaletique* description in section 1. Formerly *Sociologie-Ethnologie.*

Ethnographic Bibliography of North America (4th ed.). (1975). New Haven, CT: Human Relations Area Files. 5 vols.
A product of the monumental HRAF (others are discussed in section 7 of chapter 14). Volumes are arranged geographically: General North America; Arctic and Subarctic; Far West and Pacific Coast; Eastern United States; Plains and Southwest. Updated by supplements, the last covering the years 1973–87 and published in 1990 in three volumes.

Geographical Abstracts: Human Geography. (1966–). Norwich, UK: Elsevier/Geo Abstracts. Monthly.
The most comprehensive source of English-language materials in a discipline defined to overlap with many aspects of ethnography and cultural anthropology.

Covers over 1,000 journals as well as other forms of material. Formerly *Geo Abstracts.*

International Bibliography of Social and Cultural Anthropology. (1955–). Chicago: Aldine. Annual.
Indexes books and articles published in a variety of languages in a field defined to also include folklore and linguistics. Each volume has a subject index in English and French.

International Current Awareness Services: Anthropology and Related Disciplines. (1990–). London: British Library of Political and Economic Science. Monthly.
Covers about 1,500 journals in 30 languages, as well as monographs, conference papers, and other materials. Probably the most extensive service in this discipline.

5.2. Economics

American Economic Association. *Index of Economic Articles in Journals and Collective Volumes.* (1961–). Homewood, IL: Richard D. Irwin. Annual.
The major index in this discipline. Classified in arrangement and covers the contents of all significant journals published since 1886. Essays in collections are also included. A stripped-down version of the *Journal of Economic Literature,* (below), which updates it.

Bulletin Signalétique. Part 617: Economie Genérale. (1947–). Paris: Centre National de la Recherche Scientifique, Institut de l'Information Scientifique et Technique. Quarterly, with annual index. (* &).
See the generalized *Bulletin Signalétique* description in section 1.

Contents Pages of Recent Economic Journals. (1971–). London: HMSO. Weekly.
Covers about 200 journals, primarily published in the English language.

International Bibliography of Economics. (1952–). London: Tavistock. Annual. (*).
A well-organized and well-indexed source of books, articles, and other publications in the discipline. Like other bibliographies in this series, suffers from the disadvantage of not including entries until two or three years after their dates of publication.

International Current Awareness Services: Economics and Related Disciplines. (1990–). London: British Library of Political and Economic Science. Monthly. Similar in scope and structure to its complement in anthropology (section 5.1).

Journal of Economic Literature. (1963–). Nashville, TN: American Economic Association. Quarterly, with annual index. (*).

An important source that indexes relevant articles, but also abstracts recent books and presents review articles of different and sometimes unusual kinds. One section of it provides the tables of contents of major journals in the discipline. Formerly entitled *Journal of Economic Abstracts.*

5.3. History

America: History and Life. (1964–). Santa Barbara, CA: ABC–Clio. Quarterly; indexes cumulate annually and quinquennially. (*).

Abstracts the journal literature of the history of North America only. Often preferable to its online counterpart, as this last often cannot be searched successfully by historical period (see the entry for it in chapter 9, section 4).

Historical Abstracts. (1955–). Santa Barbara, CA: ABC–Clio. Quarterly; indexes cumulate annually and quinquennially. (*).

The companion to *America: History and Life.* Like its companion, often preferable to its online version, and for the same reason. Worldwide in coverage (except for North America). Best for its documentation of Western Europe.

International Bibliography of Historical Sciences. (1926–). Paris: Colin. Annual.

Lists, with no annotations, books and articles on worldwide aspects of the discipline. Classified in arrangement and with subject indexes. Best used for non-Western settings, as the Western world is better served by other sources noted here.

Periodical Source Index. (1986–). Fort Wayne, IN: Allen County Public Library. Annual.

A classified list of the contents of about 2,000 journals in genealogy and local history. Many entries address sources and the methodology of their use. A six-volume retrospective set is in preparation and will extend coverage back to 1847.

Writings on American History: A Subject Bibliography of Articles. (1902–). Millwood, NY: KTO Press. Annual.

The standard tool in its discipline and for many years published by the American Historical Association. Extremely thorough in its coverage of the journal literature. Classified in arrangement and with indexes in each volume. A retrospective index covers the period 1902 through 1940. No abstracts now included.

5.4. Law and Criminal Justice

Criminal Justice Abstracts. (1968–). Monsey, NY: Willow Tree Press. Quarterly; index cumulates annually. (*).

Important for its coverage of English-language materials, including research reports and unpublished papers, as well as journal articles. Each issue usually includes a review essay addressing one controversial aspect of the area. Based on a major library collection, that of the National Council on Crime and Delinquency, now maintained at Rutgers University in Newark, New Jersey.

Criminal Justice Periodical Index. (1975–). Ann Arbor, MI: UMI. Quarterly, with annual cumulations. (*).

Surveys some scholarly journals, but is most important for its extensive coverage of the professional literature, including newsletters, in areas such as policing and security management.

Criminology and Penology Abstracts. (1961–). Amsterdam: Kugler. Bimonthly, with annual indexes.

Exceptional for its coverage of European journals and other materials. Regularly surveys about 350 journals. Earlier titles include *Excerpta Criminologica* and *Abstracts on Criminology and Penology.*

Current Law Index. (1980–). Los Altos, CA: Information Access. Monthly, with quarterly and annual cumulations. (* &).

Indexes the several hundred principal law reviews documenting the Anglo-American system of law, as well as a number in the social sciences. Uses standard LC subject headings. Has the sponsorship of the American Association of Law Libraries.

Index to Canadian Legal Periodical Literature. (1960–). Montreal: Canadian Association of Law Libraries. Quarterly, with regular cumulations. (*).

Important for documenting the literature that address North American law in one of those settings that are not part of the Anglo-American legal tradition.

Index to Foreign Legal Periodicals. (1960–). London: University of London. Institute of Advanced Legal Studies. Quarterly, with annual and quinquennial cumulations.

The major source indexing articles addressing Roman and other legal systems unconnected to the Anglo-American system of law. Somewhat sporadic in the nature and breadth of the law reviews it covers.

Index to Legal Periodicals. (1908–). New York, NY: H. W. Wilson. Monthly, with quarterly, annual, and three-year cumulations. (* &).

Provides very much the same coverage as the *Current Law Index* (see above). Important because of its historic scope, essential to any student of legal history or the sociology of law. Earlier volumes are hard to search because of the very general nature of their subject headings.

Index to Periodical Articles Related to Law. (1958–). Dobbs Ferry, NY: Glanville. Quarterly, with annual cumulations.

Surveys social sciences journals for articles with a legal bias. A useful, if not infallible, index for the legal historian or student of the sociology of law. Covers about 350 English-language journals.

Legal Contents: LC. (1987–). Northbrook, IL: Management Contents. Semi-monthly.

"Reproduces the tables of contents of the most recent issues of all major law reviews and journals, and indexes all articles, case comments, notes, and recent decisions by field of law."

Police Science Abstracts. (1971–). Amsterdam: Kugler. Quarterly; indexes cumulate annually.

International in coverage. Presents long abstracts, arranged within broad subject groups. Of particular note for its interest in the forensic sciences and forensic medicine. Formerly entitled *Abstracts on Police Science.*

5.5. Psychology

Child Abuse and Neglect. (1977–). New York: Pergamon. Quarterly. (*).

A service with a social work orientation and with a particular interest in therapeutic concerns. Important here for its coverage of papers presented at conferences throughout the world and for its interest in the many difficulties of public agency involvement in this problem.

Journal of Addictive Diseases: The Official Journal of American Society of Addiction Medicine. (1981–). Binghamton, NY: Haworth. Quarterly; indexes cumulate annually.

A very extensive service covering all of the many aspects of the social sciences of interest to this area. The primary focus of this source is, however, therapeutic, and for this reason it is included in this section. Abstracts of articles, books, and other publications are arranged by broad area. Issues regularly include literature reviews of narrow aspects of the area. Formerly *Advances in Alcohol and Substance Abuse.*

PASCAL Explore. E65: Psychologie, Psychologie, Psychiatrie. (1961–). Paris: Centre National de la Recherche Scientifique, Institut de l'Information Scientifique et Technique. Ten issues a year. (* &).

Numerous earlier titles include *Bulletin Signalétique. Part 390: Psychologie, Psychopathologie, Psychiatrie.* One of a group in a series broadly addressing the medical sciences.

PsycBOOKS: Books and Chapters in Psychology. (1987–). Arlington, VA: American Psychological Association. Annual. (* &).

One of a number of supplements to the printed *Psychological Abstracts* and drawn from its more extensive computerized form. This one is important for its coverage of essays and chapters in books—forms not generally well covered in printed indexing and abstracting services.

Psychological Abstracts. See section 1.

5.6. Sociology

Bulletin Signalétique. Part 521: Sociologie. (1947–). Paris: Centre Nationale de la Recherche Scientifique, Institut de l'Information Scientifique et Technique. Quarterly. (* &).

See the generalized *Bulletin Signalétique* description in section 1. Formerly *Sociologie–Ethnologie.*

International Bibliography of Sociology. (1952–). Chicago: Aldine. Annual.

Like its companion series in other social sciences, this is well organized with good indexes and provides citations to books and other materials as well as articles. A major resource in this discipline.

International Current Awareness Services: Sociology and Related Disciplines. (1990–). London: British Library of Political and Economic Science. Monthly.

Similar in scope and structure to its complement in anthropology (section 5.1).

Sage Family Studies Abstracts. (1979–). Newbury Park, CA: Sage. Quarterly, with cumulative indexes.

The articles and books abstracted reflect social, psychological, therapeutic, and other aspects of this interdisciplinary area of study.

Sage Race Relations Abstracts. (1975–). Newbury Park, CA: Sage. Quarterly, with annual indexes.

Published on behalf of the London Institute of Race Relations. Articles abstracted frequently have an international focus. Each issue includes a bibliographic essay on one narrow aspect of the area.

Sociological Abstracts. See section 1.

5.7. Education

British Education Index. (1954–). Leeds, UK: University of Leeds. Quarterly, with annual cumulation. (*).

Covers about 300 journals, almost all of which are British or Commonwealth in origin.

Bulletin Signalétique. Part 520: Sciences de l'Education. (1947–). Paris: Centre National de la Recherche Scientifique, Institut de l'Information Scientifique et Technique. Quarterly, with annual index. (* &).

See the generalized *Bulletin Signalétique* description in section 1.

Current Index to Journals in Education. (1969–). Phoenix, AZ: Oryx. Monthly, with regular cumulations. (* &).

CIJE is a product of the federally supported Education Resources Information Center (ERIC) and indexes about 700 journals, more than its competitor, the *Education Index.* Particularly good for coverage of developments overseas.

Education Index. (1929–). New York: H. W. Wilson. Ten issues a year, with regular cumulations. (* &).

Not as comprehensive as *CIJE*, but indexes some journals not covered by this source. Easier to use because of its reliance on LC subject headings.

Educational Administration Abstracts. (1966–). Newbury Park, CA: Sage. Quarterly.

Covers the contents of about 150 journals, as well as many other types of material. Arranged by broad topic.

Higher Education Abstracts. (1965–). Claremont, CA: Claremont Graduate School. Quarterly.

Includes conference papers, research reports, and monographs, as well as journal articles. Formerly entitled *College Student Personnel Abstracts.*

Sociology of Education Abstracts. (1965–). Abingdon, UK: Carfax. Quarterly, with annual author and subject index.

Has a different disciplinary perspective from other sources noted in this section, and the journals covered reflect this.

6. OTHER WAYS OF IDENTIFYING INDEXES AND ABSTRACTS

The sources cited and discussed in this chapter are illustrative and not definitive. Situations frequently occur in which what is needed is an indexing source that covers one narrow area quite intensively. Specialized indexes and abstracts of this nature can be identified in a number of ways. They are listed in the comprehensive *Ulrich's International Periodicals Directory* and in the various published guides to the serial literature of the social sciences noted in section 1 of chapter 7. They are also discussed in the various bibliographic guides to the literature of these areas discussed in chapter 4. The guide cited immediately below is similar in coverage to *Ulrich's*, but is much easier to use.

The Index and Abstract Directory: An International Guide to Services and Serials Coverage. (1989–). Birmingham, AL: EBSCO. Biennial.

Lists over 700 indexes and abstracts and the more than 30,000 serials they cover.

Gorman, G. E., & Mills, J. J. (1992). *Guide to Current Indexing and Abstracting Services in the Third World.* New Providence, NJ: H. Zell. 260 p.

Cites, describes, and evaluates over 200 sources. Probably of value only to those addressing a particular geographical setting but invaluable for this purpose.

NOTES

1. Some services also provide bibliographic access to nonjournal literature. Others cover particular types of material exclusively: federal government documents, theses and dissertations, conference proceedings, and so forth. These are discussed at appropriate points in this book.

2. For sources providing subject access to books as these are published in given periods, see chapter 5.

3. This is because issues of abstracting services appear monthly or quarterly and articles cited in them are arranged according to some sort of subject arrangement. At the end of each year, the indexes to them cumulate, but the entries within them usually do not. What we have at the end of each year, then, is 4 (or 12) issues bound together as they originally appeared, and linked by a single, cumulative index.

4. A number of important services, such as *Psychological Abstracts* and *Sociological Abstracts*, are now searchable by computer and do apply rigorous, clear criteria (see chapter 4). At the moment of writing, these, at least for the student of public administration and public policy, are yet in a minority.

5. "Modernization," for example, was largely considered a purely economic phenomenon until the early 1970s. Only since then have its social correlates been appreciated. One cannot, of course, know this without knowing something of the field. Here, as in all things, research is no substitute for reading.

6. Identifying, for example, uses and critiques of a particular evaluation technique, appropriate indicators of a given social attribute, or studies of a particular agency or organization.

7. Those seeking comprehensive listings of indexing and abstracting services in a given field should consult the latest edition of *Ulrich's International Periodicals Directory*. Only those looking for indexes addressing a very narrow subject area should consult this directory for this purpose. Generally speaking, the specialized bibliographic guides cited in chapter 4 are quite adequate in introducing the user to approaches to the periodical literature of any one of the social and behavioral sciences.

8. The reader should be aware that database equivalents of printed indexes and abstracts sometimes acquire new titles in the transition. The printed *Current Law Index*, for example, becomes the *Legal Resource Index* online. Such title changes often reflect a change in substance, as online versions of printed sources frequently include a great deal more material. All the database catalogs and finding guides discussed in chapter 9 do include subject indexes. The user is advised to examine these carefully to avoid missing resources whose content is familiar but whose name is not.

9. Moves within the computerized world are extensive and rapid. New databases are becoming accessible on disk almost daily. Determination of which files are available on disk should properly be made through use of the latest editions of the directories cited in section 5 of chapter 9.

9

SEARCHING THE LITERATURE BY COMPUTER

Printed indexes and abstracts of the kind discussed in the previous chapter are not the only means of access to the journal literature. Many of these printed sources exist in parallel computerized forms in which citations and abstracts (where these are provided) have essentially been dumped into a database. Entries may be retrieved in a number of ways: through subject headings that generally conform to those used in the printed source and through keywords or key phrases appearing in author, title, subject, or abstract fields. In terms of structure, the relationship between bibliographic databases and printed indexes and abstracts covering journal articles is directly comparable to that between the library card catalog and computerized library book catalogs. Each presents information in ways determined and restricted by physical form and mode of access. Each is searched according to rules determined by structure and informed expectation.

The principles governing searches of printed sources, whether indexes or card catalogs, and computerized tools, whether electronic library catalogs or databases of journal articles, are exactly the same. Those who have not yet internalized these principles are advised to do so them by rereading chapters 5 and 6. An understanding of them is necessary if the user is to appreciate the relative advantages of each type of source, as well as the mechanics of searching them effectively.

Printed indexes and abstracts, like their blood relation the card catalog, are *linear* and generally *hierarchical* in structure. They are linear in that subject or other terms must be searched individually and cannot be combined or otherwise manipulated at the whim of the researcher.[1] Their typically hierarchical structure is permitted by subdivisions within established subject headings. A researcher looking for material on one fine aspect of a broader topic is therefore exposed to related material that may be of value.[2] In the example given in figure 2, someone primarily interested in published information on personnel management is given a very clear idea of the scope and definition of this category and of the many other headings and subheadings that subsume aspects of this subject.[3] Some of the more sophisticated services have developed hierarchical modes of presentation in very useful ways. *Psychological Abstracts*, for example, groups citations and abstracts within 16 broad subject areas, each of which is broken down into standardized subdivisions. Each issue and each volume also includes a subject index organized according only to quite specific terms. This means that the user has the option of searching what amounts to a subfile that deals with all aspects of the general topic of interest.

The bibliographic database is a superb instrument for a precision search, but its inability to permit this kind of browsing is its chief deficiency. Someone who knows exactly what he or she wants can, with adequate preparation, achieve just this; that is, a bibliography of everything in the database on the narrow topic in point that is limited only by the parameters of the search. The important qualifier here is the adjective "narrow." These databases are typically huge and can in some cases include millions of citations addressing a single group of disciplines (even large library catalogs usually include only a small fraction of these numbers of works in similar categories). A search of them must be narrow to avoid generating an unmanageable number of entries.[4]

There are also particular technical reasons that inhibit the ways in which searches in some databases can be limited. For example, the two main databases that specifically address historical works are often very hard to limit successfully by historical period—the very way one usually wants to limit them.[5] In these circumstances, the person planning the search must usually seek to limit the citations generated by making the search more specific in other ways. Inability to limit in one important area requires greater specificity in another.

A similar difficulty might be encountered by someone wishing to limit a search by geographical area. Let us say, following an earlier example, that you wish to examine legal modernization and its social correlates in any 18th- or 19th-century common law jurisdiction. Limiting this search geographically, but without excluding potentially important settings, would be very hard to do. You could not enter all the possibilities as subject terms because there would be too many to enter (New South Wales, Northern Ireland, Idaho, Natal—the list is long). It would also be unrealistic to try to "not out" (see chapter 6) unwanted settings, as the list would be even longer. You would probably decide to ignore geography as a variable. To prevent the printout generated from causing the needless demise of another tree, you would probably seek to define the remaining variables of the search in a tighter fashion.

Computerized searches must necessarily be extremely focused. This is because of the vast range of bibliography involved and because local factors sometimes prevent imposition of the kinds of limits one would like. For these reasons, computerized approaches to the journal literature should only be undertaken as the very last step in the literature-searching process.

When printed and computerized indexing sources are discussed, the question usually hanging in the air, whether spoken or not, is this: "If all these sources are available on computer and can be searched instantly and more effectively, why do I need to go through the laborious manual process of searching through volumes of printed indexes?" The main answer to this is, one hopes, implicit in the preceding paragraphs and refers to the fact that printed and computerized services of this kind are complementary, not competing, sources. They are used in rather different ways and at different stages in the research process.

As has been emphasized throughout this book, topic definition and refinement are activities occurring throughout the research enterprise. One often continually modifies one's conceptions and objectives by what is found in the secondary literature and, after original research has begun, by preliminary findings. Rarely does the project at any point become mechanical. It follows also that a search for literature on the immediate object of study is, whenever possible, carried out with an eye to possible theoretical concerns and methodological applications. This last activity is virtually impossible to do in a computerized search.[6] A search of printed sources, with their typical hierarchical structure, can seek to accomplish these things. For this reason, at least limited use of printed indexes and abstracts usually precedes the move to the computer.

There are other reasons why the computer has not, or at least not yet, come to supplant the printed word in this respect. These are a bit more mundane than those outlined above, but no less important. Computerized searching of journals is a resource that began only in the early 1970s and has soared in the two decades that have followed. A few databases have sought retrospective coverage of their subject areas, but most have not. The fact remains that in the social, behavioral, and policy sciences searching of the literature before about 1970 requires manual searching simply because database coverage for this period is not yet extensive. In addition, the worlds of the computerized database and the printed index or abstract are not mutually inclusive. Many printed services have a database equivalent—one should say "complement," as the computerized version usually includes entries not reflected in the printed versions. Many, however, do not, and for these, electronic access is simply not an alternative. One searches manually or not at all.

The remainder of this chapter presents, first, an explanation of just what these databases are, how they should be approached, and what one can expect of them. Following this, some of the mechanics of their use are described. In section 3, a bibliography of sources for their identification is given. The chapter concludes with a brief discussion of imminent future developments. The tremendous possibilities of the CD-ROM are described briefly in section 5. A grouped and annotated list of the outstanding databases likely generally accessible and likely to be of interest to readers of this book is presented in section 4.

1. THE COMPUTERIZED DATABASE SYSTEM

There are presently several hundred computerized databases easily accessible to those associated with academic institutions. Each is an entity unto itself, with its own form of organization and often with its own system of subject headings. As with printed indexes and abstracts, some use the standardized LC subject headings, or some version thereof, but most do not. Those in this latter category are invariably documented by a published guide to their structure, use, and subject headings. This is the *thesaurus*, which will be available at any library, research center, or other location through which the database is accessible. Discussion in chapters 5 and 6 demonstrates that in the planning of a search extreme care should go into the use of these thesauri to determine just which headings are of import and how they should be combined.[7]

Access to these databases is usually achieved through one or another of the "vendors," or intermediaries that offer these services to institutions. There are four principal systems: BRS, CompuServe, DIALOG, and ORBIT.[8] Each of these offers the institutional subscriber access to the entire contents of its system for a small basic fee.[9] The institution, whether library or research center, then pays according to time used in searching individual databases. Examination of the nature of the databases available is indicative of the provenance of this entire development in the world of information resources. Most are geared to the needs of the pure and applied sciences and to business and the law. This fact is, quite reasonably, a consequence of recognition by the commercial world of the importance of published information as a marketable commodity.

Vendors of this kind usually provide their customers with other valuable services. Most provide a "current awareness" service by which individuals can be provided with periodic bibliographic updates of a "profile" that they themselves define. Someone working on an extensive project with specific and ongoing scholarly concerns may obtain a customized bibliography that will be updated by monthly or other regular searches of the same files, using the same search strategy.

The explosive and ongoing growth of resources in this area is in no way linked to any social recognition of the social or policy sciences as important efforts in human endeavor. New databases continue generally to represent the interests of the business world. The latest trend is for new entrants to be *nonbibliographic* and to present original numeric data, for example, statistical trends in financial markets, the labor force, and elsewhere in the economy. Some of these statistical databases are not passive, but may be manipulated to respond to social questions, a feature giving them considerable potential as primary sources.

Several dozen of the hundreds of databases available are of great potential interest to readers of this book. One clear difficulty relating to the market origins of this system is that the closer the subject matter of a database gets to the needs of the commercial sector, the more expensive is the hourly cost of searching it.[11] Aside from this, the fact remains that this kind of computer searching is never inexpensive. For this reason, institutions are somewhat chary about supporting unrestrained forages in this area.[12] Money is indeed an aspect that disturbs the philosophy as well as the practice of searching. Universities seem to be universally opposed to scholars planning and executing their own searches.[13] They are quite right to be so. Funds for this purpose are typically drawn from an academic library's book budget, and the unavoidable product of a worthless search is, at the very least, one less book in the library's collection.

Unfortunately, because of this circumstance, computerized searches of the journal literature are typically undertaken by proxy. Researchers usually submit a description of their needs to a librarian searcher who then translates the request into a search strategy to be applied to databases of the executive's choice. This translation is sometimes planned following a conversation between patron and librarian, sometimes not. The results of all this may be valuable. They will rarely be all they can be. The reason for this is that only the researcher can discern the headings that should be searched and intuit the ways these can be combined. Only he or she can recognize when promising connections along the way are established or when the outcome indicates a blind alley. In this setting, the functionary who does the search must also second-guess the needs of the recipient. Only when the objective of the search is devoid of theoretical or methodological interest can such a search be taken to be productive.[14]

The best strategy is for researchers to plan their own searches, after carefully examining lists and descriptions of available databases, after thoughtful use of the thesauri that indicate worthwhile subject access to their contents, and after considering suitable title keywords that may be used to qualify generally important subject headings. Providing a detailed search schema to those executing a search is much more valuable than giving them a general expression of need. An important development here is the emergence of the database on CD-ROM, which allows unlimited searching by the ultimate recipient of the product. This development is described in section 5.

Although computerized databases are vehicles for accessing the journal literature, they often cover a variety of other genres of materials. Some focus exclusively on other forms: dissertations, documents of one kind or another, technical reports, newspaper articles, market surveys, patents, legal materials, and so forth. The one thing most of them have in common is that they exclude books. Only important databases that primarily cover the journal literature are addressed here and described in section 4. Those that address other forms of material are noted in other chapters of this account.

2. THE MECHANICS OF THE SEARCH

The mechanics of the search have been described in principle in chapter 6, which addresses the computerized library catalog and related notions of identifying and combining sets of variables within such a catalog. The major point made and illustrated in this chapter concerns the ways in which concepts can be identified, defined through use of title words and subject headings, and combined in ways that create a custom-tailored search.[15]

Searches of databases covering journal articles for the most part involve no new principles. However, implementation of these searches is materially affected by one or two technical factors. The first concerns the size of the resources being searched. As noted earlier, some of these databases are massive. A database of journal articles that includes several million entries must necessarily be searched more precisely than one that largely includes books but that addresses a small fraction of this number of entries. The second is that a journal search is different from that of the computerized library catalog in that it allows for one important intervening step. As examples in chapter 6 show, you search the electronic library catalog by defining and then combining sets that are made up of some combination of subject and keyword entries. The computer screen yields just the final result of this thoughtful but essentially numerative process. It pulls from its innards the net consequence of the search and usually presents the most recently published ones on a screen and in a printout.[16]

The search of the computerized journal provides the important service of identifying the number of citations *in each constituent set* as these are created. You can then decide just how to combine sets so as to maximize the output. For example, if you want to combine your particular interest with a more general phenomenon, such as a specific methodology, you can at least try this in the following way: Let us suppose that you wish, for some reason, to find life-cycle accounts of government employees that have been constructed using the technique of oral history, and that you start out with the database *Sociofile* (the computerized form of *Sociological Abstracts*). Figure 11 shows the evolution of this search.

Set 6 shows the results of a command to display the number of entries, or "hits," found under the subject headings "Bureaucracy," "Bureaucrats," or "Civil Service" (there is no heading for "Civil Servants," so this phrase has been searched free-text.[17] The result is a respectable 761 hits. In set 9 we are told that a search of the subject heading "Oral History" only yields 42 entries. This tells you a number of important things. If "Oral History" is indeed the correct and

Figure 11
Searching by Set Number

```
SilverPlatter 2.00          sociofile (1/74 - 1/91)      F10=Commands F1=Help
______________________________________________________________________________

  No.       Records  Request

  #1:           204  BUREAUCRATS
  #2:          1297  BUREAUCRACY
  #3:            72  CIVIL-SERVICE
  #4:          2912  CIVIL
  #5:           335  SERVANTS
  #6:           761  (BUREAUCRATS in DE) or (BUREAUCRACY in DE) or
                     (CIVIL SERVICE in DE) or (CIVIL SERVANTS)
  #7:           709  ORAL
  #8:         24333  HISTORY
  #9:            42  (ORAL HISTORY) in DE
  #10:            0  #6 and #9

______________________________________________________________________________

FIND:

Type a search then press Enter (DY). Use the INDEX (F5) to pick terms.
```

only appropriate descriptor (it is), then we cannot expect a great deal from this database. Either the method sought is little used and rarely cited (wrong) or *Sociofile* was a poor first choice as a database (probably right.)[18]

It is obvious that we cannot expect a large number of hits in combining a large set with a small one. Combination of sets 6 and 9 ("Find: #6 and #9") yields an unsurprising zero. The point here is that the system has given us a good idea of why the search was unsuccessful: This was because the database is apparently deficient in the method variable, not the substance variable. In subsequent searches of other databases, one would do well to keep an eye on the relative sizes of sets 6 and 9 or their equivalents. If either is low (unless one of the variables truly reflects a rare perspective), the chances are that the database is not the most appropriate.

In searches of computerized sources (like the library catalog) that provide only the end product of a search and not those of its constituent steps, you learn nothing about the system's limitations. The ability of a system to present results step by step is therefore important in helping users assess the value of it to their particular combinations of interests. Computerized databases of journal articles generally have this ability.

A further important aspect of these computerized services is that they can be searched *free-text*, that is, in the abstract as well as the subject and title fields. Searching crucial words or phrases in the abstract field is much more likely to yield results than searching them in titles. This is because abstracts are generally much longer than titles and therefore offer increased chances that the terms searched will be found. Second, abstracts are explicitly descriptive in a way that titles often are not. The purpose of abstracts is to summarize and inform. In recent years it has become fashionable among social scientists to give titles to their published works that seem to be eye-catching rather than descriptive. These may give a backhanded and provocative reference to their subject-matter, but not in a way anyone engaged in a literature search could predict.[19]

Keyword searching is especially valuable when one is working with those databases in which subject access is inadequate. The importance of dissertations and theses to the researcher has already been emphasized. *Dissertation Abstracts Online* provides citations and abstracts for a high proportion of dissertations accepted for doctoral degrees in North America, as well as some from elsewhere. Unfortunately, the subject headings provided are very general and mostly reflect the discipline in which the degree was awarded. Keyword searching in both titles and in the lengthy abstracts online is the only way to exploit this database effectively.

There are, in addition, a number of databases that appear to be supported by efficient systems of subject headings, but experience shows these headings to be assigned inconsistently and even capriciously. A subject access system is, of course, only as good as the effort put into creating it and assigning headings to individual entries. A few databases and printed indexes have systems of subject access that are unreliable. As only those who are professional searchers are in a position to determine just which databases these are, occasional users should always combine keyword searching with the formal subject approach.

Two databases, *SciSearch* and *Social SciSearch*, warrant special attention due to the unique and important search techniques that can be applied to them. Both are databases of tremendous importance to readers of this book. *SciSearch* includes over 10 million entries, and although its focus is the pure and applied sciences, it includes a very large number of items addressing management, administration, policy, and the behavioral sciences. *Social SciSearch* is of more obvious relevance to this discussion and presently includes over 2 million records. Neither resource can be searched by subject category, and neither includes abstracts. The subject approach is generally made through keywords or phrases in titles.

The distinctive feature of these two databases is that they can be searched by *cited reference*. Suppose that a preliminary review of the outstanding literature on your topic shows, as it generally does, that three or four key books and articles serve as general reference points for discussion, and most serious works in the area cite, discuss, and perhaps criticize them. Search these databases by asking them which articles in their holdings have *cited* any of these benchmark works in their bibliographies. This will result in a very comprehensive bibliography of all works that have contributed to debates surrounding the topic. In many ways this is the superior method of subject access. The researcher here relies on personal knowledge of the bibliography that defines a topic and not on the presumed ability of an indexer to assign the most appropriate headings. A well-thought-out approach of this kind will fail only if your personal knowledge is deficient (in which case you are not yet ready for a citation search), or if the topic is discussed in some context that ignores the classic literature. This last is unlikely, as even those who take untraditional approaches to their topics generally take care to at least acknowledge this literature. A citation search will be worthless if it is ill conceived. In this setting, this would probably be so if the search was too general. It must be remembered that the two databases in question at present together include over 12 million entries (plus the attendant bibliography of each)—and they are being updated weekly. Someone rash enough to search, for example, Max Weber's classic essay on bureaucracy would certainly generate a printout long enough to paper the walls of a mansion. A search of a topic related to the theory of bureaucracy can be done, but, like the topic itself, it must be qualified enough to be manageable.

Let us say that you are interested in stress among schoolteachers but particularly in the organizational climate as a stress-inducing factor, rather than stress caused by the pressures of the job itself. Your thesis or research question might suggest that it is the demands of dysfunctional bureaucracies that are the greatest inducers of job-related stress. In preparing your citation search you would draw up two short groups of references: those that relate to theories of bureaucracy (or other organizational theories you hope to apply) and those that relate to job stress specifically. Then instruct the system to seek out those entries with bibliographies that include one or more items in group A and in group B. (Other citation searches could be designed later to search out other combinations of interest, such as stress in the classroom.) If the citation search cannot be made manageable in this way, then neither can the proposed research project.

Clearly a computerized literature search requires a great deal of planning, and there is no magic formula, other than that provided by the application of informed thought, that ensures its success. Levels of success here are measured by the numbers of useful citations identified, and not by the numbers of the worthless ones. The latter will always be found. Use of title and abstract keywords will produce them because the same words and phrases can almost always be used in more than one context. Citation searches will always produce them because authors cite secondary sources for all kinds of strange reasons. As long as the printout appears to include valuable material (and as long as it is not lengthy enough to cause distress to whoever is paying for it), the search has done the job.[20] Other databases that permit citation searches are generally specialized ones in the field of law.[21] *SciSearch* and *Social SciSearch* with their immense combined coverage meet the needs of most social and policy scientists.

In many, though not all, databases there is yet one other way to search. This is by *code*. Codes are numeric or alphanumeric designations for hierarchical broad subject categories within the database. By designating a code, the searcher can in effect create a subfile within the database and apply only the entered keyword and/or subject terms to it. In a large database this technique might be applied to limit the output, excluding entries in which the topic is referred to incidentally or in which the keywords searched have meaning in other contexts.

Figure 12 shows the structure of one of the 99 category codes used in COSATI (the code system of the Committee on Scientific and Technical Information).[22] A subfile can be created from the entire category 5 ("Behavioral and Social Sciences") or from any combination of its constituent subcategories.[23] As COSATI is generally used in databases with a primarily scientific or technological bias, this technique can exclude extraneous material. Use of code systems, when these are available, is most helpful when searching large databases that either focus on subject areas apart from yours or that address a broad range of areas; the more foreign to you the subject matter in the database is the more likely it is that keywords and key phrases will emerge in unexpected contexts.

Code systems are not standardized to any great extent. A few, like COSATI, are used in a number of databases. If a database is organized according to codes, the system used will be described in its thesaurus.

Figure 12
Searching by Code: The Cosati System

5. *Behavioral and Social Sciences*
    - A. Administration and Management
    - B. Documentation and Information Technology
    - C. Economics
    - D. History, Law, and Political Science
    - E. Human Factors Engineering
    - F. Humanities
    - G. Linguistics
    - H. Man-made Machines
    - I. Personnel Selection, Training, and Evaluation
    - J. Psychology (Individual and Group Behavior)
    - K. Sociology
    - GE. General

The schema outlined above is that for one of ninety-nine code categories included in the classification system created by the Committee on Scientific and Technical Information and used extensively in databases supported by the US federal government.

3. DIRECTORIES OF DATABASES

At an early point, consult the directories of the three principal database vendors (BRS and CompuServe, DIALOG, and ORBIT), after determining those to which your institution subscribes. The other directories cited here list all databases covered by the three vendors, together with the many hundreds developed by governmental agencies, corporations, associations, research units, and even private individuals. All directories cited provide subject indexes to the sources included and detailed descriptions of them. Descriptions do not usually indicate the hourly cost of searching. This significant omission is generally because subscription arrangements to them can be complicated. The reader should be aware that databases in some fields are expensive and beyond the reach of many academic institutions. Items listed below should be used to supplement those documenting the broader area of machine-readable data archives in chapter 12.

Books and Periodicals Online: A Guide to Publication Contents of Business and Legal Databases. (1987–). New York: Books and Periodicals Online. Annual.

Lists over 10,000 serials whose contents are indexed by over 1,400 databases and CD-ROMs.

BRS Database Catalog. (1976–). McLean, VA: BRS Information Technologies. Annual.

System includes about 150 databases. Updated by the bimonthly *BRS Bulletin*.

CompuServe Database Catalog. (1979–). Columbus, OH: CompuServe Information Service. Annual.

Includes about 1,400 databases. Updated by the monthly *CompuServe Magazine*.

Daniells, Lorna M. (1985). *Business Information Sources* (rev. ed.). Berkeley, CA: University of California Press. 673 p.

Databases are discussed in the context of the bibliography of individual subject areas.

Data Base Directory. (1984–). White Plains, NY: Knowledge Industry Publications. Semiannual.

Updated by the monthly *Data Base Alert*. Also available online. Sponsored by the American Society for Information Science.

Database: The Magazine of Database Reference and Review. (1978–). Weston, CT: Online. Bimonthly.

Reviews and describes new products, including new database files available online or on CD-ROM.

Datapro Directory of On-Line Services. (1982–). Delran, NJ: Datapro Research. Monthly.
A loose-leaf service that includes descriptions of new bibliographic databases as well as other online products and services.

DIALOG Database Catalog. (1965-). Palo Alto, CA: DIALOG Information Services. Annual.
Includes about 370 databases. Updated by a number of publications including the monthly *CHRONOLOG.*

Directory of Online Databases. (1979–). New York: Cuadra/Elsevier. Semiannual, with an update to each issue.
Itself also available online as the *Cuadra Directory of Databases.* Documented by a separately published user's guide *Online Database Selection.*

Directory of Periodicals Online: Indexed, Abstracted and Full-Text. (1985–). Washington, DC: Federal Document Retrieval. Annual.
Particularly concerned with documenting full-text online newspapers and newsletters and other materials in the field of law.

Freed, Melvyn N., Diodato, Virgil P., & Rouse, David A. (1991). *Business Information Desk Reference: Where to Find Answers to Business Questions.* New York: Macmillan. 513 p.
Online databases are addressed as a group in three separate chapters.

Fulltext Sources Online/BiblioData. (1989–). Needham, MA: BiblioData. Semiannual.
Lists only databases that provide the full texts of journals, magazines, newspapers, and other periodicals.

Information Industry Directory. (1971–). Detroit: Gale. Annual.
The most comprehensive directory of its kind. Provides detailed descriptions of vendors, systems, archives, and machine-readable data files as well as databases. Early volumes entitled *Encyclopedia of Information Systems and Services.*

Marcaccio, Kathleen Y. (Ed.). (1990). *Computer-Readable Databases: A Directory and Data Sourcebook* (6th ed.). Detroit: Gale. 1,379 p.

Online Databases in the Securities and Financial Markets. (1987). New York: Cuadra/Elsevier. 322 p.

A subset of the *Directory of Online Databases* (see above).

ORBIT Search Service Databases. (1973–). McLean, VA: ORBIT Search Service. Annual.

Includes about 100 databases, mainly in the fields of science and technology. Updated by *ORBIT Searchlight* (monthly) and *Databases at a Glance.*

Scanlan, Jean M., de Stricker, Ulla, & Fernald, Anne C. (1989). *Business Online: The Professional's Guide to Electronic Information Sources.* New York: Wiley. 368 p.

Williams, Martha E. (Ed.). (1979–). *Computer-Readable Data Bases: A Directory and Data Sourcebook.* Washington, DC: American Society for Information Science. Biennial.

Like most directories of its kind, now includes a variety of nonbibliographic databases. A version of this directory is also available in database form.

4. DESCRIPTIONS OF DATABASES

The few databases described below are all bibliographic and, in keeping with the subject of this chapter, focus primarily on the journal literature. Those presented are exemplary in that they are chosen to illustrate the range of such resources and not the limits of its universe. Databases that emphasize forms of published material other than journals are discussed elsewhere. Those that have print equivalents are distinguished in the annotations by an asterisk (*).[24] Those that were also available on CD-ROM at the time of writing are indicated by an ampersand (**&**). Annotations also indicate the year the database was established and the approximate number of entries held at the beginning of 1992. Unless otherwise indicated, all include abstracts as well as bibliographic citations.

ABI/Inform. (1971–). Louisville, KY: UMI/Data Courier. 516,000 records. Updated weekly. (**&**).

Emphasizes management, industry, and other topics of primary interest to those in the private sector. Also covers a number of journals in public administration and related areas.

America: History and Life. (1964–). Santa Barbara, CA: ABC–Clio. 270,000 records. Updated quarterly. (*).

Covers all aspects of North American history, including interdisciplinary approaches to it. Subject headings are those used in the printed version. Unfortunately not easily searched by historical period. Imaginative searching techniques are usually needed to yield successful results.

Canadian Business and Current Affairs. (1980–). Toronto: Micromedia. 1,465,000 records. Updated monthly. (* **&**).

Indexes a large range of Canadian journals, magazines, and newspapers of interest to business and management operations of both private and public organizations. Citations only.

Child Abuse and Neglect. (1965–). Washington, DC: U.S. National Center on Child Abuse and Neglect. 12,000 records. Updated semiannually. (*).

Includes articles, descriptions of funded projects, court decisions, and other materials arranged within five subfiles.

Criminal Justice Abstracts. (1968–). St. Paul, MN: West. Updated quarterly.(*).

The online version of the printed abstracting service of the same title (formerly *Crime and Delinquency Literature*). Includes review essays as well as abstracts and citations.

Criminal Justice Periodical Index. (1975–). Ann Arbor, MI: University Microfilms International. 170,000 records. Updated monthly. (*).

Covers over 100 journals and newsletters, most of which address professional and managerial rather than scholarly concerns. Citations only.

Current Contents. (Current six months only). Philadelphia: Institute for Scientific Information. 642,000 records. Updated weekly. (* **&**).

Reproduces and indexes the tables of contents of leading journals in all fields of scholarly endeavor. The seven constituent subfiles cover clinical medicine; life sciences; engineering, technology, and applied sciences; agriculture, biology, and environmental sciences; physical, chemical, and earth sciences; social and behavioral sciences; and arts and humanities. Citations only.

Economic Literature Index. (1969–). Pittsburgh, PA: American Economic Association. 202,000 records. Updated quarterly. (* **&**).

Covers scholarly journal articles and books. Since 1984 provides abstracts as well as citations. The print forms are represented by the index section of the *Journal of Economic Literature* and the annual *Index of Economic Articles.*

Environmental Bibliography. (1973–). Santa Barbara: Environmental Studies Institute. 400,000 records. Updated bimonthly. (* **&**).

Indexes journal articles dealing with all aspects of the subject, managerial and political as well as legal and technical.

ERIC. (1966–). Washington, DC: U.S. Educational Resources Information Center. 720,000 records. Updated monthly. (* **&**).

Covers the contents of over 700 journals as well as other materials, including research reports and papers prepared under federal or other funding. A limited version of ERIC is provided by two printed indexes: *Resources in Education* and *Current Index to Journals in Education.*

Family Resources. (1970–). St. Paul, MN: National Council on Family Relations. 118,000 records. Updated bimonthly.

Includes summaries of books, articles, and other published forms that primarily address therapeutic and other psychosocial aspects of family relationships.

FRANCIS. (1972–). Paris: Centre National de la Recherche Scientifique, Institut de l'Information Scientifique et Technique. 1,300,000 records. Updated quarterly. (* **&**).

The computerized version of the CNRS printed *Bulletin Signalétiques.* Organized within 22 subfiles, a number of which are relevant to the study of public administration and its related fields and are cited in chapter 8.

Harvard Business Review. (1971–). New York: Wiley. 2,700 records. Updated bimonthly. (*).

Includes the full text of the *HBR* from 1976 onward, and abstracts of it and other journals from 1871 to 1975.

Health Planning and Administration. (1975–). Bethesda, MD: U.S. National Library of Medicine. 518,000 records. Updated monthly. (**&**).

A subset of the immense medical database *MEDLINE*, which also includes the contents of the printed *Hospital Literature Index.*

Historical Abstracts. (1973–). Santa Barbara, CA: ABC–Clio. 326,000 records. Updated bimonthly. (*).

Addresses world history (excluding North America) from 1450 onward. Primarily a source for European history.

HRIN Daily Developments Database. (1982–). Indianapolis: Executive Telecom System International. Updated daily.

Provides the full texts of current articles documenting legal and other developments of relevance to human resource management. Supplements the more extensive *HRIN Special Reports Library.*

Institute of Management International Databases. (1992–). London: Bowker-Saur. Updated quarterly. (**&**).

A collection of six files indexing and abstracting journals, books, "company practice," short courses, audio-visual material, and training exercises.

Legal Resource Index. (1980–). Foster City, CA: Information Access. 427,000 records. Updated monthly. (* **&**).

Indexes all the 750 or more major law reviews in the English-speaking world. The computerized version of the printed *Current Law Index.* Citations only.

Linguistics and Language Behavior Abstracts. (1973–). San Diego, CA: Sociological Abstracts. 120,000 records. Updated quarterly. (*).

Interprets its subject matter very broadly and should be used as a complementary file to other databases in the social and behavioral sciences. Covers over 1,000 journals.

Management Contents. (1974–). Foster City, CA: Information Access. 284,000 records. Updated monthly.

One of the two (with *ABI/Inform,* see above) principal databases addressing the literature of all aspects of management. Particularly valuable for its coverage of nonjournal materials, such as conference proceedings and government documents. Regularly abstracts the contents of over 120 journals.

Mental Health Abstracts. (1969–). Alexandria, VA: IFI/Plenum Data. 481,000 records. Updated monthly.

Reflects the holdings of the National Clearinghouse for Mental Health Information of the U.S. National Institute for Mental Health. Covers over 1,200 journals. A very important database for those with behavioral concerns because it addresses a large group of medical journals not covered by *PsycINFO* (see below).

NCJRS. (1972–). Rockville, MD: US National Criminal Justice Reference Service. 106,000 records. Updated monthly. (* **&**).

The only database devoted exclusively to criminal justice and its many managerial and policy-related aspects. Very good for its inclusion of technical reports and other products of the federal funding that has traditionally strongly influenced research in this area. Attention is drawn to the availability of this file on CD-ROM, as its printed version is extremely difficult to use.

Occupational Safety and Health (NIOSH). (1973–). Cincinnati: U.S. National Institute for Occupational Safety and Health Technical Information Center. 163,000 records. Updated quarterly.

Very important for its coverage of technical reports and legal materials. Also covers several hundred journals.

PAIS International. (1972–). New York: Public Affairs Information Service. 337,000 records. Updated monthly. (* &).

Indexes several hundred journals in major Western languages that include all major sources in public administration and many in political science. Perhaps the most important database for students of public administration and the policy sciences.

Philosopher's Index. (1940–). Bowling Green, OH: Bowling Green State University. Philosophy Documentation Center. 156,000 records. Updated quarterly. (*).

Covers over 270 journals in philosophy and related fields. Very useful for its inclusion of published discussions relating to the nature of methodology in various social sciences.

Politique et Société. (1981–). Paris: Documentation Française. 180,000 records. Irregular updates. (&).

Provides broad coverage of French-language social science literature. On CD only.

PsycINFO. (1967–). Washington, DC: American Psychological Association. 754,000 records. Updated monthly. (* &).

Like its printed counterpart, a source of major importance to students of the social and policy sciences, as well as behavioral scientists. This is because its coverage goes far beyond its stated concerns. A much larger database than *Sociological Abstracts*, and a necessary complement to it. Includes books published since 1987.

SciSearch. (1974–). Philadelphia: Institute for Scientific Information. 10,000,000 records. Updated weekly. (* &).

A huge database of major concern to those concerned with any aspect of behavior or management. Important for its amenability to searches by cited reference (see section 2). Use in conjunction with *Social SciSearch* (below). This database has a printed form, use of which is emphatically not recommended.

Social SciSearch. (1972–). Philadelphia: Institute for Scientific Information. 2,200,000 records. Updated weekly. (* &).

See also *SciSearch.* These databases should always be used in conjunction because, despite their titles, distinctions between the two in terms of subject matter are difficult to make.

Sociofile. (1963–). San Diego, CA: Sociological Abstracts. 306,000 records. Updated five times a year. (* &).

The computerized version of *Sociological Abstracts* and of obvious importance to readers of this book. Covers more than 1,600 journals. This database is much smaller than *PsycINFO* and does not overlap much with *Linguistics and Language Behavior Abstracts*. Those concerned with the social and policy sciences should ignore the titles of these three databases and treat them as resources of equal importance.

Westlaw. (Dates of coverage vary). St. Paul, MN: West. Updates from daily to quarterly.

This is the generic name for a system of over 70 separate databases, each of which addresses some aspect of the law of the United States or one of a few other countries. These constituent databases are typically massive. They include bibliographic data, but their main content provides the full texts of statutes, court decisions, regulations with the force of law, and other legal materials of a primary nature.

Many of these databases are quite specialized. The *Westlaw Federal and Multistate Criminal Justice Database*, for example, "contains full text of case law and other documents related to US state and federal law covering criminal acts and the investigation, prosecution, and punishment of crimes. Covers searches and seizures, bail, habeas corpus, parole, prisons, probation, and the Racketeer Influenced and Corrupt Organizations Act (RICO). Includes cases from the Supreme Court since 1789, Courts of Appeals since 1891, District Courts since 1789," and all relevant statutory and regulatary law.

The Westlaw system (which is only one of several large legal database systems currently available) is mentioned here in part to counter the emphasis of chapter 12 on primary sources of a statistical nature available through computer systems.

Wilson Business Abstracts. (1986–). Bronx, NY: H. W. Wilson. Updated twice a week. (* &).

Provides abstracts of articles cited in the *Business Periodicals Index* (chapter 8) since 1986.

5. DATABASES ON CD-ROM

One important factor inhibiting computerized searching has traditionally been the cost involved. Nonprofit institutions, such as academic libraries, are understandably reluctant to support unlimited searches, but in most circumstances this need not have a serious effect. A narrow and clearly focused search will usually not consume inordinate amounts of computer time or retrieve an unmanageable number of entries. (If it does either, then the chances are that the search has been badly planned).

However, there are situations in which a productive search requires considerable time online and the generation of a great many citations. Many important databases cannot be searched effectively using descriptors. This may be because the topic addressed does not fit easily within existing subject definitions, or because subject indexing is inadequate (as in *Dissertation Abstracts*) or nonexistent (*SciSearch* and *Social SciSearch*). In these cases searching by keyword or phrase is appropriate. Although keyword searching is frequently very rewarding, it is often a hit-or-miss affair, as it relies on the searcher's ability to second-guess the content of likely titles or abstracts. As this ability also depends on the cooperation of authors and abstracters in themselves using predictable terms, the results of this approach can be haphazard indeed.[25]

Matters are even more complicated with databases (like *Dissertation Abstracts*) that have long abstracts. These provide a greater mass at which to aim keyword searching and are therefore correspondingly more likely to yield greater numbers of hits. On the other hand, searching of lengthy entries in this way will pull up a larger proportion of items in which the keywords are used in quite different contexts. In other words, keyword searching of databases with lengthy abstracts tends to produce a larger volume of entries, a higher proportion of which are useless. Searching in this kind of scenario therefore demands a great deal of time and effort.

Effort of this kind is often well rewarded, as the databases that must be searched in this way include some of those, such as the ones noted earlier in this section, that are of great importance to the social and policy researcher. "Fishing expeditions" in them may be justified because of their importance, and because there is often no other way to search them effectively. It is, however, doubtful if many librarians or other salaried computer searchers will be agreeable to such extensive investment of time and money. It is, moreover, unreasonable to expect such persons to have the knowledge or informed intuition that this activity requires. Searching of this particular nature needs to be done, or at least planned, by the user of the end product.

Until recently, there was every incentive for institutions to require all searching to be done by librarian intermediaries. Only in this way could they control the length, and therefore financial costs, of searches. This usually discouraged general, free-ranging excursions that some topics and some databases require. All this has changed dramatically with the emergence of the database accessible through the physical form of the CD-ROM (computer disk, read-only memory). With its immense memory, a CD usually has sufficient capacity to store the contents of databases with hundreds of thousands of citations.[26] A database in this form can be searched directly, without having to enter the online system of a commercial vendor. For our purposes, the most important thing about the CD in this context is its pricing. Because no computer time is used, nothing can be charged. The library typically pays a flat monthly rental for the disk and can allow unlimited searching of it by patrons while incurring no further costs. The advantages of this are obvious. Complicated and discursive searches can be done at will, and the institution has no financial interest in curbing their nature or volume.

Researchers at the appropriate stage in their literature-searching should always make an effort to identify which of the databases they need are available on CD and should then plan and execute their own searches, with the help of a librarian, if this is necessary. The principal sources for identification are listed below. In so doing, a couple of important points should be borne in mind. First, the position of the CD-ROM in the world of bibliographic searching is gaining at a very rapid rate, with new files becoming available in this form all the time. An indicator of the speed of this development is that the 1990 edition of the major directory listing files on CD (see below) included about 600; the 1992 edition listed almost 3,000. Second, databases on CD are not always the same versions as those available through online systems. The user should be aware whether taking this option carries the cost of using an abridged file.

Searching requires some technical expertise, the nature of which, unfortunately, varies somewhat from database to database. This can be acquired fairly quickly, but acquired it must be. It is a fact that most amateur searchers do not bother to learn these skills. This need not be disastrous for them, as not everyone needs to exploit a database to its full potential. For those seeking to explore important databases in imaginative ways, learning the necessary skills is imperative.[27] Otherwise the enterprise will result only in a waste of time and computer paper.

CD-ROM Databases. (1987–). Boston: Worldwide Videotext. Updated daily.

A directory in database form that includes databases on CD-ROM that are currently being marketed. Full ordering information given, but no descriptions.

CD-ROMs in Print: An International Guide. (1987–). Westport, CT: Meckler. Annual.

Descriptions given mainly refer to the kinds of hardware and operating systems with which particular CDs are compatible. (This is because use of CDs in this context is so new that little in the way of format standardization has developed.)

For descriptions of the contents of the files, the directories cited in section 3 should be used. Entries are arranged by title and are accessible through a subject index.

CD-ROM Librarian. (1985–). Westport, CT: Meckler. Monthly.

Updates *CD-Roms in Print* with a section in each issue entitled "Supplement to CD-ROMs IN PRINT." Also reviews new CD products, including related hardware and software.

Ensor, Pat. (1991). *CD-ROM Research Collections: An Evaluative Guide to Bibliographic and Full-Text CD-ROM Databases.* Westport, CT: Meckler. 302 p.

6. JOURNAL INDEXES IN LIBRARY NETWORKS

A recent development is for library catalogs and large library systems to provide access to databases which include citations to journal articles. As this arrangement is intended for end-user searching, these databases have all the advantages of CD-ROMs. Most are general in nature but are large enough to be of interest to the specialized researcher. OCLC's *Article 1st* database, for example, now includes about one million citations (with some abstracts) from issues of about 12,000 journals published since the beginning of 1990. Journals covered are primarily, but not exclusively, scholarly, and represent all fields of inquiry.

Individual library systems have in many cases customized these systems for the greater convenience of their patrons. Columbia University's *UnCover* database, for example, provides all the advantages of *Article 1st* but also allows users to order desired articles online. Entering an acceptable credit card number permits the researcher to obtain the wanted materials by mail or fax within 24 hours.

As this development is convenient for libraries worried about the soaring costs of journal subscriptions, one would expect it to expand. It is clear, however, that the convenience it offers to researchers may be offset by considerable financial cost.

7. FUTURE DEVELOPMENTS

In an area characterized by change that has been as fast as it has been dramatic, long-term developments are hard to predict. The beginnings of the immediate future are, however, with us now, and these suggest two developments that are imminent.

The first is the expansion of the CD-ROM to include databases that are numeric or otherwise nonbibliographic. As has happened with online databases, new CD products are increasingly addressing consumer information needs for very current statistical data. In addition, libraries are increasingly developing their CD holdings through cooperation in local networks that allow the negotiation of more favorable subscription rates with vendors.

The second, as noted above, is the linkage of groups of databases to library catalogs. The user can use the same terminal to search any of these resources, either separately or in tandem. The practical effect of this is to greatly expand the scope of the computerized catalog. Valuable though this obviously is, it requires the successful user to conduct narrower and better-constructed searches.

At the moment, the bulk of the quantitative data files accessible through both online and CD databases are closely related to the interests of business and industry. Given the history of the computerized bibliographic database and the size and buying power of the business sector, this is not surprising. There is, on the other hand, every reason to expect that the database industry will also come to serve the needs of the academic researcher more effectively. Modern technology continues to increase the capacity and reduce the cost of the CD. This trend will soon allow a single disk to incorporate greater volumes of data. A time may soon be reached where disks can hold the packaged programs necessary for data manipulation, as well as the data themselves. At this point, the tasks of locating primary data and orchestrating their analysis will be greatly eased.

Chapter 12, section 6, documents these developments further and offers more descriptions of some of the numeric files of primary data presently available on CD-ROM. We can have every expectation that these will soon increase in number, size, and ease of use. Further developments in electronic communication have even greater potential significance for the near future. The proliferation of electronic bulletin boards will certainly bring increased access to a variety of library systems, including the kinds of bibliographic databases discussed here. To appreciate the strength of these developments, the reader should consult section 9 of chapter 15.

NOTES

1. Many, though by no means all, indexes and abstracts can be searched by author and title as well as subject. A number substitute *keywords* appearing in title entries for subject entries. This in itself is, of course, a hierarchical arrangement.

2. Because of the lack of insularity in modern social research, alluded to elsewhere, exposure to such related material is often a greater stimulus than the researcher ever imagines.

3. The particular example in the figure is drawn from the Library of Congress guide to subject headings. The principle, however, is the same in printed indexes.

4. None of us doubts the ability of the computer to generate masses of data. Simpson's first rule of thumb on computerized searching is that anyone who walks away from a computer search with a printout more than one-quarter of an inch thick is either working on a topic that is poorly focused or has been on a computerized fishing expedition. In either case, the person would be well advised to dump the catch and start planning all over again.

5. *America: History and Life* and *Historical Abstracts*.

6. Attempts can be made in this way to search references to a topic associated with particular methods or theoretical approaches. These are not, however, always successful, as such associations often come up in settings or contexts not immediately apparent in subject or title entries.

7. The user can, of course, also use the standard technique of searching titles of known value and seeing from the entry retrieved which subject headings have been assigned to them.

8. Bibliographic Retrieval Services (BRS), Lockheed Information Services (DIALOG), and ORBIT Search Services (ORBIT). CompuServe is a subsystem of BRS.

9. Most academic institutions subscribe to one or more of these four systems. The contents of them overlap to a large extent. The one most favorable to social and policy scientists is DIALOG.

10. See chapter 12, section 6.

11. Searching one of the databases in education costs, at the moment of writing, around $20 an hour. Searching the sophisticated legal databases, predictably enough, costs a great deal more than this.

12. Some of these systems do indeed offer services to individuals. BRS's After Dark program offers cut-rate searching in a limited number of BRS files to individuals providing this is conducted in the evenings and on weekends. The costs of this, however, are still prohibitive to those not in possession of federal grants or distinguished professorships.

13. The exception here is obviously those scientists and other lucky individuals who have money for computer searching built into their research grants.

14. "What's been written on fiscal policy in Marin County, California?"

15. Title words and subject headings are known in the world of database searching as "descriptors" or "identifiers."

16. Or rather the items most recently entered in the database, which usually comes to the same thing.

17. Lower set numbers simply document the progress of the system in conducting the search. It first searches each individual word free-text, and only in set 6 displays the cumulative results of searching the words and phrases in their appropriate fields.

18. One or another of the historical databases would probably have been a better bet.

19. Many of these catchy titles are qualified by subtitles that are more informative. A number are not. It would be hard to design a keyword search that recognized that an

article entitled "Enmeshment in the American Family" refers to the tendency of parents to gain self-esteem from the success of their children.

20. This yields Simpson's second rule of thumb in this area. If 25 percent or more of the citations produced are on target, the search has been a good one.

21. *Shepard's Citations* allows a user to search any reported (that is, published) law case in the United States to determine which later reported cases have discussed or otherwise cited it. This is an important route for determining whether a case is still "good law," and how it relates to other cases addressing the same legal issues.

22. This system is used in a number of databases maintained by the federal government, for example *NTIS*, one of the databases of the U.S. National Technical Information Service.

23. The particular command here would be "SH=5," "SH" being the search command for "Section Heading."

24. As observed in chapter 8, when printed indexes and abstracts metamorphosize into bibliographic databases, they frequently acquire new names. Users should therefore search the subject indexes of the directories cited in section 3 for suitable objects of attention. They should not rely on the possibility that printed and computerized versions of the same source share the same name.

25. Some help in this area is available. A recent dictionary of a novel sort is invaluable in listing words and phrases associated with particular social science concepts. This guide is even more helpful than it sounds because it endeavors to recognize the fact that such concepts are often expressed in rather different words in the various social and behavioral sciences. Sara Knapp's book is therefore important for introducing planners of searches to the vocabularies of unfamiliar territories: *The Contemporary Thesaurus of Social Science Terms and Synonyms: A Guide for Natural Language and Computer Searching*. (1992). Phoenix, AZ: Oryx. This source should, of course, be used in conjunction with the thesauri which document the descriptors used in individual databases.

26. A single CD can store more than 250,000 pages of text; enough, as has been pointed out, to store the entire contents of the white pages of every telephone exchange in the United States. This is not always sufficient. *SciSearch*, for example, currently occupies at least five disks.

27. For example, combining cited references and title keywords in *Social SciSearch*.

10

PUBLISHED BIBLIOGRAPHIES

Anyone undertaking a research project is obviously more concerned with the end product of the effort than with the techniques used to achieve it. In the preparation of a bibliography, the worker's main concern will be that the sources consulted have been adequate and that the appropriate among them have been consulted. There is no virtue to be gained from the information-gathering process itself. Its value lies only in the results it produces. Any legitimate shortcut is of considerable value in reducing the time and effort expended on this stage of the research enterprise. One possible shortcut is through the use of published bibliographies. If someone else has gone to the trouble of preparing and publishing a bibliography of interest, the researcher's intent should be to identify and use it, and not to replicate it. It is rare that use of such bibliographies will relieve the need to search other bibliographic tools. There are several reasons why this should necessarily be so. One's own topic is frequently a customized entity that may make unusual connections between research setting and theory. It may well be that no one else has searched the literature with such connections in mind and has aggregated relevant literature in suitable way. Furthermore, a bibliography, like any other publication, is dated from the day it is issued. Even the most relevant bibliography will need to be updated through indexes and other sources in print and online form. Third, a great deficiency of many bibliographies, even those that appear to be among the most thorough, is that they do not identify which published materials they cover. If there is no way of determining whether, for example, a journal of particular promise has been covered in a given bibliography, the researcher may decide that a separate search of an index covering this journal is justified.

The obvious line of approach is to identify and examine published bibliographies of potential value and, on the basis of this evaluation, to make a decision about which other bibliographic tools should also be searched, and over what time period. This is clearly the way to proceed in seeking research studies directly related to the substance of one's topic. For other types of search, bibliographies alone may serve the purpose. A search for interesting theoretical models and methods to be applied in the research project will probably not, as has been noted, require an intensive search of the literature. When the purpose is a search that is selective in its focus, a good and up-to-date bibliography will often suffice.

The remainder of this chapter is devoted to a classified listing of published bibliographies of potential value to readers of this book. It should be used to supplement those specialized bibliographies discussed in other chapters. This bibliography of bibliographies is presented in section 2, and comments on how it was compiled and what it represents are given there. There are standard techniques for identifying these sources. As these techniques are implicit in the discussions of earlier chapters, they are described in section 1 in a concise fashion.

1. SOURCES OF PUBLISHED BIBLIOGRAPHIES

1.1. Published Discussions

The way that most of us have learned to develop a topical bibliography is, of course, to use the bibliographies provided in published discussions, whether journal articles, books, or other forms, known to be relevant. There is absolutely nothing wrong with this traditional method of approach provided its limitations are recognized. The first of these is that users are initially limited by their knowledge of works that provide the starting point. The second is that bibliographies published in this (or any other) way are necessarily restricted by their dates of publication. If bibliographies in known works are supplemented by those created using indexes and abstracts and through other more systematic means, their value is increased.

In this context attention is drawn once again to the importance of dissertations as sources of bibliography. As noted elsewhere, writers of dissertations are required to justify their choices of subject matter through exhaustive reviews of the existing literature. If a dissertation is up to standard, it will include an excellent bibliography, limited, of course, by its date of completion and its precise definition of its topic. A good dissertation in a field can be the best of all sources of a working bibliography. Other sources important in this respect are review articles in annual reviews, specialized encyclopedias, and other sources of this kind.

The "invisible college," mentioned in chapter 1, is another wonderful approach to bibliography. Those of us in the social sciences who have the advantage of calling upon colleagues knowledgeable in areas related to our interests are very aware of how valuable their bibliographic insights can be. An approach that lacks a formal structure should not automatically be denigrated. Results are what count. Style often triumphs over structure. The point here is that formal mechanisms for information-finding should be seen as complementing, not replacing, other ways of doing things. Social science researchers, unlike librarians, are, naturally enough, concerned with the end product, rather than the means of its achievement.

1.2. Library Catalogs and Computerized Databases

Too much should not be made of the limitations noted in section 1.1 of using bibliographies in published discussions of known value. As one finds and reads new materials, one's knowledge of the literature expands. Furthermore, a good bibliography, even if dated, is always a good point of embarkation. With the marvels of computerized searching, a good bibliography can easily be updated. The reader is reminded, for example, that the database *Social SciSearch* can be directed to produce all items in it that cite a particular work in their bibliographies (see chapter 9). This technique is, of course, limited in only yielding citations to works that refer to a given body of literature. It does not produce those that address a topic in other contexts.

Databases can be searched in other ways for this purpose. Many include "Bibliography" as a standard subheading. A fairly broad subject can be qualified with this heading to isolate works dealing only with bibliographic aspects of it. Using such qualification is a means of surveying an extensive subject category without creating a search product of unmanageable size. A further characteristic of a number of databases is that they can be searched by *form* of published material. If this is categorized as a literature review or bibliography, a set can be created that includes these forms. This can then be combined with other sets reflecting a subject approach. Although this approach is valuable, it is subject to practical qualification. Printed and computerized indexes are generally sparing in identifying the articles and other materials they include in this way. Indexes emphasizing published forms other than books will usually not yield many items in the "bibliography" category.

Library catalogs, whether in computerized or card form, can be searched in comparable, but more effective, ways. "Bibliography" is a standard subdivision in all catalogs using the LC system. In database catalogs a subject approach can easily be combined with one geared to producing only those works with this subdivision. The same thing can also be done when the catalog is in card form, but this requires looking through a variety of entries a ddressing geographic and other aspects of the subject before coming to the "Bibliography" subdivision.[1]

Of particular value here are the several union catalogs, usually in database form, that document works acquired or cataloged by member institutions of research library systems. These are discussed in chapters 5 and 6. Searches of these systems can be assumed to represent thorough searches of recent books commercially published in English, as well as more selective investigations of other forms of separately published material.

A number of publishers specialize in issuing series of bibliographies relevant to the subject areas considered here. Garland, for example, issues a number of important bibliographies in its "Public Affairs and Administration Series." In a computerized library catalog these can easily be identified by searching a subject heading in combination with a key phrase associated with a series.[2] Of particular importance in this regard are bibliographies issued by two specialized publishing houses: Vance Bibliographies in Monticello, Illinois, and the Council of Planning Librarians (otherwise known as CPL Bibliographies) in Chicago. Each produces a large number—many dozens each year—of specialized bibliographies, of varying length and value, but always on topics of direct interest to the student of public administration or the policy sciences. These are singled out here for particular mention because they can be such valuable resources and because their number makes impractical the inclusion of more than a small fraction of them in section 2. They can, however, be identified readily enough, either by subject or key-phrase searching of a large library catalog, or through bibliographies of the publications issued by each of these houses and revised regularly (see the entries under Coatsworth, Ravenhall, and Hecimovich and Vance in section 1.4 for the latest editions of these).

1.3. Review Essays

Scholarly journals frequently include articles reviewing literature on a given topic in extended book reviews or review articles. Abstracting services frequently include such bibliographic essays and, when they do so, usually address areas that have recently come to attract the attention of social researchers.[3] Annual reviews (appendix 1) have the explicit function of reviewing and evaluating current research in a given area. There are also a few journals that regularly report recent bibliographic developments[4] Review essays can easily be identified in those databases which recognize them as a distinct form. Other databases and most indexes and abstracting services categorize them as bibliographies.

1.4. Bibliographies of Bibliographies

Printed and database indexes and abstracts make some attempt to distinguish bibliographies through a standard subdivision of the relevant subject headings. The most useful sources in this regard are indexes that cover materials other than journal articles. The *PAIS International* and the U.S. Government Printing Office *Monthly Catalog*, for example, are both excellent for their inclusion of bibliographies published in monograph form. In addition, there are a number of standard serial and other works that specialize in identifying various types of bibliographies. The most important of these are cited below.

American History: A Bibliographic Review. (1985–). Westport, CT: Meckler. Annual.

Reviews bibliographies, guides to archives and collections, and other reference sources.

American Reference Books Annual. (1970–). Englewood, CO: Libraries Unlimited.

Provides excellent, though selective, coverage of recent major reference works, including bibliographies.

Ballou, Patricia K. (1986). *Women: A Bibliography of Bibliographies* (2nd ed.). Boston: G. K. Hall. 268 p.

Beers, Henry P. (1982). *Bibliographies in American History, 1942–1978: Guide to Materials for Research.* Woodbridge, CT: Research Publications. 2 vols.

Berndt, Judy. (1986). *Rural Sociology: A Bibliography of Bibliographies.* Metuchen, NJ: Scarecrow. 177 p.

Besterman, Theodore. (1971). *Education: A Bibliography of Bibliographies.* Totowa, NJ: Rowman & Littlefield. 306 p.

Besterman, Theodore. (1972). *History and Geography: A Bibliography of Bibliographies.* Totowa, NJ: Rowman & Littlefield. 4 vols.

Besterman, Theodore. (Comp.). (1965–66). *A World Bibliography of Bibliographies and Bibliographical Catalogues, Calendars, Abstracts, Digests, Indexes, and the Like* (4th ed.). Lausanne: Societas Bibliographica. 5 vols.

A truly massive listing of bibliographies unrestricted by subject or language of publication. Updated to some extent by Toomey (below) and by the other works by Besterman cited here.

Bibliographic Index. (1937–). Bronx, NY: H. W. Wilson. Three issues a year, including annual cumulation. A very extensive subject listing of substantial bibliographies published separately or as addenda to books, essays, and journal articles. International in coverage. Addresses both the humanities and the social sciences.

Boehm, Eric H. (Ed.). (1988). *Bibliographies in History: An Index to Bibliographies in History Journals and Dissertations Covering the U.S. and Canada.* Santa Barbara, CA: ABC-Clio. 2 vols.
Based on the contents of *America: History and Life.*

Boehm, Eric H. (Ed.). (1965). *Bibliographies on International Relations and World Affairs: An Annotated Directory.* Santa Barbara, CA: Clio. 33 p.

Brock, Clifton. (1969). *The Literature of Political Science: A Guide for Students, Librarians, and Teachers.* New York: Bowker. 232 p.
One of the two parts includes listings of published bibliographies and other reference works in the area. Public administration is strongly represented in these.

Burchfield, Laverne. (1935). *Student's Guide to Materials in Political Science.* New York: Holt. 426 p.
Strong in its citations of published bibliographies in fields that include public administration. Very valuable for its coverage of older sources frequently omitted in recent guides.

Coatsworth, Patricia A., Ravenhall, Mary, & Hecimovich, James. (1989). *An Annotated Bibliography and Index Covering CPL Bibliographies 1–253, January 1979–December 1989.* Chicago: Council of Planning Librarians. 51 p.

Coulter, Edith M., & Gerstenfeld, Melanie. (1935). *Historical Bibliographies: A Systematic and Annotated Guide.* Berkeley: University of California Press. 206 p.

Davis, Bruce L. (Comp.). (1978). *Criminological Bibliographies: Uniform Citations to Bibliographies, Indexes, and Review Articles of the Literature of Crime Study in the United States.* Westport, CT: Greenwood. 182 p.

Drazan, Joseph G. (Comp.). (1982). *An Annotated Bibliography of ERIC Bibliographies, 1966–1980.* Westport, CT: Greenwood. 520 p.
Covers materials acquired by the major clearinghouse of educational literature.

Friend, William L. (1944). *Anglo-American Legal Bibliographies: An Annotated Guide*. Washington, DC: GPO. 166 p.
Identifies about 300 sources.

Government Reference Books: A Biennial Guide to U. S. Government Publications. (1968/69–). Englewood, CO: Libraries Unlimited. Biennial.
Summarizes a large number of bibliographies, as well as other reference works. Since 1988, has had a companion entitled *Government Reference Serials.*

Gray, Richard A., & Villmow, Dorothy. (1969). *Serial Bibliographies in the Humanities and Social Sciences*. Ann Arbor, MI: Pierian. 345 p.
Subject identification of bibliographies either published separately or as regular features of established journals.

Gropp, Arthur E. (1968). *A Bibliography of Latin American Bibliographies.* Metuchen, NJ: Scarecrow. 515 p.
Updated by a series of supplements, each of which has the same title, but different authors, issued every four or five years. See also McNeil and Volk (below).

Guerry, Herbert (Ed.). (1977). *A Bibliography of Philosophical Bibliographies.* Westport, CT: Greenwood. 332 p.

Harmon, Robert B. (Comp.). (1973–1976). *Political Science Bibliographies.* Metuchen, NJ: Scarecrow. 2 vols.
Entries arranged by Library of Congress subject headings.

Henige, David P. (Comp.). (1986). *Serial Bibliographies and Abstracts in History: An Annotated Guide.* Westport, CT: Greenwood. 220 p.

Kanely, Edna M. (Comp.). (1976). *Cumulative Subject Guide to U.S. Government Bibliographies, 1924–1973*. Arlington, VA: Carrollton. 7 vols.
A thorough guide to the many social science and other bibliographies published by all arms of the federal government. Use in conjunction with Scull (below).

Klein, Carol, Horton, David M., & Kravitz, Marjorie (Comps.). (1980). *Bibliographies in Criminal Justice*. Washington, DC: GPO. 47 p.

Legal Bibliography Index. (1978–). Shreveport: Louisiana State University. Annual.

McNeil, Robert A., & Valk, Barbara G. (Eds.). (1990). *Latin American Studies: A Basic Guide to Sources* (2nd ed.). Metuchen, NJ: Scarecrow. 458 p.
To some extent replaces Gropp (above) and its supplements.

Prucha, Francis P. (1987). *Handbook for Research in American History: A Guide to Bibliographies and Other Reference Works.* Lincoln, NE: University of Nebraska Press. 289 p.

Scull, Roberta A. (1974). *A Bibliography of United States Government Bibliographies, 1968–1973.* Ann Arbor, MI: Pierian. 353 p.
Updated by a supplement covering 1974–76 and published in 1979. Use in conjunction with Kanely and Government Reference Books (above).

Simpson, Antony E. (1976). *Guide to Library Research in Public Administration.* New York: John Jay College of Criminal Justice. Center for Productive Public Management. 210 p.
The work on which the present volume was based. One chapter includes a listing of general bibliographies in public administration, mainly those published in English in the 1960s and early 1970s.

Smith, Margo L., & Damien, Yvonne M. (Comps.). (1981). *Anthropological Bibliographies: A Selected Guide.* South Salem, NY: Redgrave. 307 p.
Arranged by geographical area. Includes bibliographies in books and journals as well as those separately published.

Toomey, Alice F. (1977). *A World Bibliography of Bibliographies, 1964–1974: A List of Works Represented by Library of Congress Printed Catalog Cards, A Decennial Supplement to Theodore Besterman, A World Bibliography of Bibliographies.* Totowa, NJ: Rowman & Littlefield. 2 vols.
Not nearly as comprehensive or easy to use as the work it purports to update.

Universal Reference System. (1967–69). *Bibliography of Bibliographies in Political Science, Government, and Public Policy.* Princeton, NJ: Princeton Research Publishing. 927 p.
One of 10 basic volumes updated by a supplement now entitled *Political Science Abstracts.* This is limited to its listings of published bibliographies. Others are specialized bibliographies in themselves and address administrative management; public policy; comparative government; international affairs; law and jurisprudence; public opinion and political psychology; the legislative process; current events and social problems; and economic regulation.

Vance Bibliographies. (1986). *Subject Index to Public Administration Series: Bibliography No. P 1001 to P 2000 (July 1982–September 1986).* Monticello, IL: Vance. 60 p.

Weiner, Neil A. (Comp.). (1984). *Bibliography of Bibliographies on Criminal Violence.* Philadelphia: University of Pennsylvania. Center for Studies in Criminology and Criminal Law. 26 p.

Weintraub, Irwin. (1986). *Selected Guide to Abstracting and Indexing Sources and Bibliographies Related to Planning.* Chicago: Council of Planning Librarians. 22 p.

Williamson, Jane. (1979). *New Feminist Scholarship: A Guide to Bibliographies.* Old Westbury, NY: Feminist Press.

2. PUBLISHED BIBLIOGRAPHIES

The previous section covers the sources of published bibliographies; this section deals with bibliographies themselves. Any such list must necessarily be very selective. In the research conducted for this, the universe was initially limited to bibliographies in monograph form (the many prepared as journal articles being excluded) published in English (or French or Spanish, if issued in North America) since 1980 on public administration or in fields relevant to it. Even so, the number of entries found was in the thousands, and therefore unmanageable for inclusion within one short chapter.[5]

No such list of bibliographies could ever be created. Apart from anything else, the diverse interests of those undertaking research in the name of public administration ensure that definitions of subject matter are usually personalized and can make important connections to many other fields of study. Existing bibliographies can certainly be valuable in saving research time. When they serve this function well, it is usually because they are quite narrow and specialized in focus. No list of bibliographies likely to be of potential value to all readers of this book could therefore be presented here. Instead, a selection of outstanding bibliographies of a more general nature is given.

Citations are arranged within four broad groups. The first includes major noncurrent bibliographies in the social sciences as a whole considered of greatest potential interest to users of this book. The second includes those in general administration and management. Category three includes major bibliographies in public administration and the policy sciences. The final group includes bibliographies that are rather more specialized but address major currents within public administration and the policy sciences in some direct fashion. Although the listings emphasize sources published from the 1980s onward, some of the most valuable earlier bibliographies have also been included. A selective list of bibliographies addressing methodological issues is included in chapter 14. More specialized bibliographies may be located using the sources and techniques mentioned in section 1. Literature found in this way can be updated using the many sources of current bibliography discussed at various points in this account.

The criteria for inclusion used here are to some extent idiosyncratic, and the resultant lists suffer from a common deficiency identified in earlier discussion: the reader has no way of knowing what has been included and what excluded. This list includes mainly those bibliographies published in the last decade that are substantive, germane to the area of interest, and not otherwise easily identifiable. Due to space considerations, most of the bibliographies published by Vance and CPL have been omitted. The lists that follow are therefore illustrative, not definitive.

2.1. General Social Sciences

The ABS Guide to Recent Publications in the Social and Behavioral Sciences. (1965). New York: American Behavioral Scientist. 781 p.

A compilation of listings of recent books and articles a ppearing in the *American Behavioral Scientist*, a major journal in its area. Between 1965 and 1975 updated by the annual *Recent Publications in the Social and Behavioral Sciences: The ABS Supplement.*

Abstracts of Popular Culture: A Quarterly Publication of International Popular Phenomena. (1976-82). Bowling Green, OH: Bowling Green State University Popular Press.

When current, covered an area somewhat vaguely defined, but of growing scholarly interest, especially to anthropologists and social historians. Useful in indexing journals and other materials not generally addressed elsewhere.

Aldcroft, Derek H., & Rodger, Richard (Comps.). (1984). *Bibliography of European Economic and Social History.* Manchester, UK: Manchester University Press. 243 p.

Cited here as one of a number of excellent bibliographies documenting the emergence of the Western world, including its political and administrative institutions.

C.R.I.S.: The Combined Retrospective Index Set to Journals in History, 1838–1974. (1977–78). Washington, DC: Carrollton. 11 vols.

With its two companion sets (below), the major point of access to the classical journal literature. These are keyword indexes that are not always easy to use, but perseverance is invariably rewarded. Over half of the citations in this set address American history.

C.R.I.S.: The Combined Retrospective Index Set to Journals in Political Science, 1886-1974. (1977–78). Washington, DC: Carrollton. 8 vols.

Four volumes address *Public Administration*; one, *International Affairs and Organizations*; and one, *General Studies and Methodology*. The remaining two are author indexes.

C.R.I.S.: The Combined Retrospective Index Set to Journals in Sociology, 1895-1974. (1978). Washington, DC: Carrollton. 6 vols.

One volume covers social and cultural anthropology. Others focus strongly on private and public institutions and their social contexts.

Cumulative Index to Sociology Journals, 1971–1985 . (1987). Washington, DC: American Sociological Association. 763 p.

Fundaburk, Emma L. (1973). *The History of Economic Thought and Analysis: A Selective International Bibliography.* Metuchen, NJ: Scarecrow. 6 vols.

Fundaburk, Emma L. (1971). *Reference Materials and Periodicals in Economics: An International List in Five Volumes.* Metuchen, NJ: Scarecrow. 5 vols.

Gottsegen, Gloria B. (Ed.). (1979). *Group Behavior: A Guide to Information Sources.* Detroit: Gale. 219 p.

Harmon, Robert B. (1965). *Political Science: A Bibliographic Guide to the Literature.* New York: Scarecrow. 388 p.

Updated by supplements published in 1968, 1972, and 1974.

Kemper, Robert V., & Phinney, John F. S. (1977). *The History of Anthropology: A Research Bibliography.* New York: Garland. 212 p.

Key to Economic Science and Managerial Sciences. (1953–87). The Hague: Netherlands Economic Information Service. Semimonthly.

Abstracted journal articles, books, and other materials in the language of original publication. Early volumes entitled *Economic Abstracts.*

Recently Published Articles. (1976–90). Washington, DC: American Historical Association. Three issues a year.

Presents classified lists of articles in over 4,000 journals on all aspects of world history. Related articles elsewhere in the social sciences are also included. No cumulations and no indexes.

2.2. General Administration and Management

Andrade, Kerry M., & Ontiveros, Suzanne R. (Eds.). (1986). *Organizational Behavior: Contemporary Viewpoints.* Santa Barbara, CA: ABC-Clio. 250 p.

Bakewell, K. G. B. (Ed.). (1977). *Management Principles and Practice: A Guide to Information Sources.* Detroit: Gale. 519 p.

Chaffee, Ellen., & De Alba, Renee. (1983). *Strategic Management: A Comprehensive Bibliography.* Boulder, CO: National Center for Higher Education Management Systems. 32 p.

Dunphy, Dexter C., & Stening, Bruce W. (1984). *Japanese Organization Behaviour and Management: An Annotated Bibliography.* Hong Kong: Asian Research Service. 214 p.

Foster, Eloise C. (1985). *Current Management Resources.* Chicago: American Hospital Association. 58 p.

Franklin, Jerome L. (Ed.) (1978). *Human Resource Development in the Organization: A Guide to Information Sources.* Detroit: Gale. 175 p.

Harvard University. Graduate School of Business Administration. Baker Library. (1970–). *Core Collection: An Author and Subject Guide.* Boston. Revised annually.

Harvard University. Graduate School of Business Administration. Division of Research. (1981). *Organizational Behavior; Including Cases in Human Resources Management.* Boston. 240 p.

Jreisat, Jamil E., & Ghosheh, Zaki R. (1986). *Administration and Development in the Arab World: An Annotated Bibliography.* New York: Garland. 259 p.

Leavitt, Judith A. (1988). *Women in Administration and Management: An Information Sourcebook.* Phoenix, AZ: Oryx. 228 p.

Pondy, Louis R., Fitzgibbons, Dale E. & Wagner, John A. III. (1980). *Organizational Power and Conflict: A Bibliography.* Monticello, IL: Vance. 19 p.

Rogers, Donald P. (1982). *Organizational Communication: A Selected, Annotated Bibliography* (rev. ed.). Washington, DC: U.S. Educational Resources Information Center. 1 vol., unpaged.

Saulniers, Alfred H. (Comp.). (1985). *Public Enterprise: An International Bibliography.* Austin, TX: University of Texas. Institute of Latin American Studies. 469 p.

Soltow, Martha J., & Sokker, Jo Ann S. (1979). *Industrial Relations and Personnel Management: Selected Information Sources.* Metuchen, NJ: Scarecrow. 286 p.

Stout, Russell. (1980). *Organizations, Management, and Control: An Annotated Bibliography.* Bloomington: Indiana University Press. 189 p.

U.S. Department of Labor. Library. (1980). *The Practice of Management: Selected Recent References.* Washington, DC: GPO. 101 p.

U.S. Department of the Army. Library. (1979). *Management and the Executive: Philosophy, Problems, and Practices.* Washington, DC. 254 p.

Whetten, David A. (1981). *Beyond the Organization: Organization-Environment Relations.* Monticello, IL: Vance. 22 p.

Woy, James. (Ed.). (1990). *Encyclopedia of Business Information Sources: A Bibliographic Guide to Approximately 20,000 Citations Covering About 1,000 Subjects of Interest to Business Personnel* (7th ed.). Detroit: Gale. 896 p.

2.3. Public Administration and Policy Sciences

Alexander, Ernest R., Catanese, Anthony J., & Sawicki, David S. (Eds.). (1979). *Urban Planning: A Guide to Information Sources.* Detroit: Gale. 165 p.

Armstead, Karen D. (Comp.). (1985). *Health Care Administration and Planning: A Guide to Sources of Information.* Bethesda, MD: U.S. National Library of Medicine. 35 p.

Ashford, Douglas E., Katzenstein, Peter J. & Pempel, T. J. (Eds.). (1978). *Comparative Public Policy: A Cross-National Bibliography.* Beverly Hills, CA: Sage. 272 p.

Bamford, H. M., Campbell, B. A., & Rogers, S. J. (1985). *An Initial Bibliography of Australian Public Sector Organisations.* Townsville, Australia: James Cook University. Organisation Studies Unit. 359 p.

Casper, Dale E. (1987). *Current Issues in Public Administration, 1980–1986.* Monticello, IL: Vance. 13 p.

Casper, Dale E. (1988). *Public Policy and Decision-Making: Journal Articles, 1983–1987.* Monticello, IL: Vance. 8 p.

Coleman, James R., & Dugan, Robert E. (1990). *Public Administration Deskbook.* Newton, MA: Government Research Publications. 270 p.

Includes selective lists of works, as well as guides to information sources in the field.

Coppa & Avery Consultants. (1980). *Public Administration and Public Policy: A Bibliographical Overview.* Monticello, IL: Vance. 12 p.

Drucker, Mark L. (Ed.). (1981). *Urban Decision Making: A Guide to Information Sources.* Detroit: Gale. 187 p.

Englefield, Dermot, & Drewry, Gavin (Eds.). (1984). *Information Sources in Politics and Political Science: A Survey Worldwide.* London: Butterworths. 509 p.

One of the 24 chapters specifically addresses public administration. Others address it tangentially. Emphasis is on both British and U.S. materials.

Goehlert, Robert U., & Martin, Fenton S. (1985). *Policy Analysis and Management: A Bibliography.* Santa Barbara, CA: ABC–Clio. 398 p.

Grasham, W. E., & Julien, Germain (Comps.). (1972). *Canadian Public Administration: Bibliography. Administration Publique Canadienne: Bibliographie.* Toronto: Institute of Public Administration of Canada. 261 p.

Updated by supplements published about every three years (the latest is the fifth and covers 1983–85). Abstracts are included and written in English or French.

Great Britain. Ministry of Overseas Development. Library. (1980). *Public Administration: A Select Bibliography* (7th ed.). London. 14 p.
Between editions, supplements are issued every three or four years.

Grossman, Jorge (Comp.). (1954). *Bibliography on Public Administration in Latin America.* Washington, DC: Pan American Union. Department of Cultural Affairs. 115 p.

Henderson, Keith M. (1984). *Public Administration: The Last Twenty-Five Years.* Monticello, IL: Vance. 18 p.

Hills, William G., et al. (1975). *Administration and Management: A Selected and Annotated Bibliography.* Norman, OK: University of Oklahoma Press. 182 p.
Despite its title, focuses on the public sector.

Holler, Frederick L. (1986). *Information Sources of Political Science* (4th ed.). Santa Barbara, CA: ABC-Clio. 417 p.
One chapter is devoted exclusively to public administration.

Honadle, Beth W. (1983). *Public Administration in Rural Areas and Small Jurisdictions: A Guide to the Literature.* New York: Garland. 146 p.

Index to U.S. Government Periodicals. (1974–87). Chicago: Infordata International. Quarterly, with annual cumulation.
When current, indexed articles in 180 or so journals published by agencies of the U.S. federal government. A high proportion of these addressed issues related to governance and to the economy and its management.

Lacson, Zenaida C., Bataclan, Francisca C., & Arbarquez, Rosario H. (1980–). *Philippine Public Administration: An Annotated Bibliography.* Manila: University of the Philippines. College of Public Administration. Irregular; last volume published covers 1969–1977.

Lake, Gashaw W. (1989). *African Public Administration: A Bibliography.* Monticello, IL: Vance. 192 p.

Lovrich, Nicholas P., & Neiman, Max. (1984). *Public Choice Theory in Public Administration: An Annotated Bibliography.* New York: Garland. 122 p.

McCaffery, Jerry, & Mikesell, John L. (Eds.). (1980). *Urban Finance and Administration: A Guide to Information Sources.* Detroit: Gale. 225 p.

Martin, Daniel W. (1989). *The Guide to the Foundations of Public Administration.* New York: Dekker. 454 p.

Maurice, Nelson R., & Miller, Richard U. (1975). *The Management of Public Enterprise: A Bibliography.* Madison, WI: University of Wisconsin. School of Business. 166 p.

Munro, Jim L., & Chaney, Waldo. (1966). *Administrative Behavior: An Annotated Bibliography with Emphasis on Public Administration.* Columbia, MD: University of Missouri. 596 p.

Murin, William J., Greenfield, Gerald M., & Buenker, John D. (Eds.). (1981). *Public Policy: A Guide to Information Sources.* Detroit: Gale. 283 p.

Murphy, Thomas P. (Ed.). (1980). *Urban Indicators: A Guide to Information Sources.* Detroit: Gale. 234 p.

Murphy, Thomas P. (Ed.). (1980). *Urban Law: A Guide to Information Sources.* Detroit: Gale. 320 p.

Murphy, Thomas P. (Ed.). (1978). *Urban Politics: A Guide to Information Sources.* Detroit: Gale. 248 p.

Nagel, Stuart S. (1984). *Basic Literature in Policy Studies: A Comprehensive Bibliography.* Greenwich, CT: JAI Press. 453 p.

Namazi, Mohammed, & Crum, Robert P. (1984). *A Comprehensive Compilation of Multi-Objective Techniques and Applications in Public Policy Decision Making.* Monticello, IL: Vance. 88 p.

Oman, Ray C., & Ayers, Tyrone B. (1988). *Management Analysis in Public Organizations: An Annotated Bibliography.* Monticello, IL: Vance. 26 p.

Pan American Union. Department of Economic Affairs. (1965). *La Administración Pública como Instrumento del Desarrollo.* Washington, DC. 7 parts.

Pan American Union. Department of Economic Affairs. (1965). *Administración Pública en América Latina.* Washington, DC. 43 p.

Robey, John S. (Comp.). (1984). *The Analysis of Public Policy: A Bibliography of Dissertations, 1977–1982.* Westport, CT: Greenwood. 225 p.

Robey, John S. (1984). *Public Policy Analysis: An Annotated Bibliography.* New York: Garland. 195 p.

Ross, Bernard H. (Ed.). (1979). *Urban Management: A Guide to Information Sources.* Detroit: Gale. 288 p.

Santora, Joseph C., & FitzSimmons, Diane. (1983). *Public Administration: Decision-Making in the Public Sector: A Selected Bibliography.* Monticello, IL: Vance. 23 p.

Seckler-Hudson, Catheryn. (1953). *Bibliography on Public Administration, Annotated* (4th ed.). Washington, DC: American University Press. 131 p.

Steiner, Michael, & Mondale, Clarence. (1988). *Region and Regionalism in the United States: A Source Book for the Humanities and Social Sciences.* New York: Garland. 495 p.

Stevenson, Hugh A. (Comp.). (1980). *Public Policy and Futures Bibliography: A Select List of Canadian, American, and other Book-Length Materials, 1970 to 1980, Including Highly Selected Works Published between 1949 and 1969.* Toronto: Ontario Ministry of Education. 413 p.

Suljak, Nedjelko. (1970). *Administration in a World of Change.* Davis, CA: University of California. Institute of Governmental Affairs. 135 p.

Tompkins, Dorothy C. (Comp.). (1971). *Research and Service: A Fifty Year Record.* Berkeley, CA: University of California. Institute of Governmental Studies. 154 p.

Cites reports and studies produced by the Institute's Bureau of Public Administration over a 50-year period.

Vance, Mary. (1982). *Policy Science: A Bibliography.* Monticello, IL: Vance. 24 p.

Vance, Mary. (1987). *Policy Sciences: Monographs.* Monticello, IL: Vance. 53 p.

2.4. Specialized Areas

Adams, John S. (Ed.). (1976). *Contemporary Metropolitan America.* Cambridge, MA: Ballinger. 4 vols.

Adams, John S. (Ed.). (1976). *Urban Policymaking and Metropolitan Dynamics: A Comparative Geographical Analysis.* Cambridge, MA: Ballinger. 576 p.

Aldcroft, Derek H., & Rodger, Richard (Eds.). (1992). *European Ecomonic and Social History* (2nd ed.). Manchester, UK: Manchester University Press. 192 p. An annotated bibliography.

Arrowsmith, David (Comp.). (1982). *Productivity Trends: Bibliography with Selected Annotations.* Kingston, Ont.: Queen's University. Industrial Relations Centre. 16 p.

Balachandran, Sarojini. (1987). *Decision Making: An Information Sourcebook.* Phoenix, AZ: Oryx. 208 p.

Baldwin, J. Norman. (1985). *Differences and Similarities between the Public and Private Sectors: A Bibliography.* Monticello, IL: Vance. 16 p.

Banister, David, & Pickup, Laurie. (1989). *Urban Transport and Planning: A Bibliography with Abstracts.* London: Mansell. 354 p.

Beauregard, Christian, Dufour, Jean-Marie, & Vaillancourt, François. (1980). *An Annotated Bibliography of Canadian Public Finance (Revenue Side), 1946–1979: A First Round.* Montreal: Université de Montreal. 222 p.

Beauregard, Christian, Dufour, Jean-Marie, & Vaillancourt, François. (1981). *An Annotated Bibliography of Canadian Public Finance (Revenue Side), 1946–1979: Extension and Update.* Montréal: Université de Montréal. 43 p.

Beirne, Piers, & Hill, Joan (Comps.). (1991). *Comparative Criminology: An Annotated Bibliography.* Westport, CT: Greenwood. 144 p.

Entries arranged by author within three broad areas: meaning and measurement; cross-national crime rates; social control and criminal justice. Five hundred entires include publications in English since 1960. An important source in an area difficult to search in conventional ways.

Bell, Gwen, Randall, Edwina, & Roeder, Judith E. R. (Eds.). (1973). *Urban Environments and Human Behavior: An Annotated Bibliography.* Stroudsburg, PA: Dowden, Hutchinson, & Ross. 271 p.

Bibliography on Productivity Measurement and Analysis. (1981). Tokyo: Asian Productivity Organization. 75 p.

Bick, Patricia A.. (1988). *Business Ethics and Responsibility: An Information Sourcebook.* Phoenix, AZ: Oryx. 204 p.

Bowman, James S., Elliston, Frederick A., & Lockhart, Paula (Eds.). (1984). *Professional Dissent: An Annotated Bibliography and Resource Guide.* New York: Garland. 322 p.

Bowman, Sarah Y., & Shafritz, Jay M. *Public Personnel Administration: An Annotated Bibliography.* New York: Garland. 209 p.

Brand, Horst, & Belitsky, Harvey A. (Comps.). (1980). *Productivity: A Selected Bibliography, 1976–78.* Washington, DC: GPO. 166 p.

Brealey, Richard, & Edwards, Helen. (1991). *A Bibliography of Finance.* Cambridge, MA: MIT Press. 822 p.

Brown, J. Cudd. (1980). *A Selective Bibliography and Specific Bibliographies Relevant to Management Improvement and Productivity Enhancement in the United States Government in Compliance with the Civil Service Reform Act of 1978.* Washington, DC: U.S. Office of Personnel Management. 54 p.

Buenker, John D., Greenfield, Gerald M., & Murin, William J. (1981). *Urban History: A Guide to Information Sources.* Detroit: Gale. 448 p.

Cannon, Joan B., & Smith, Ed (Eds.). (1982). *Resources for Affirmative Action: An Annotated Directory of Books, Periodicals, Films, Training Aids, and Consultants on Equal Opportunity.* Garrett Park, MD: Garrett Park Press. 190 p.

Casper, Dale E. (1988). *Politics and Public Administration of State Affairs: A Historical Perspective, Journal Articles, 1982–1987.* Monticello, IL: Vance. 10 p.

Cayer, N. Joseph, & Dickerson, Sherry S. (Comps.). (1984). *Labor Management Relations in the Public Sector: An Annotated Bibliography.* New York: Garland. 395 p.

Cheshire, P. C., Hay, Dennis, & Carbonaro, Gianni (Comps.). (1986). *Regional Policy and Urban Decline: The Community's Role in Tackling Urban Decline and Problems of Urban Growth. Urban Problems in Europe: A Review and Synthesis of Recent Literature.* Washington, DC: European Community Information Service. 74 p.

Childs, Jeff. (1985). *Select Bibliography of Works Relating to the Civil Service Including the Welsh Office.* London: Great Britain. Welsh Office. 14 p.

Collester, J. Bryan. (1979). *The European Communities: A Guide to Information Sources.* Detroit: Gale. 265 p.

Crimando, William T., & Riggar, T. F. (1990). *Staff Training: An Annotated Review of the Literature.* New York: Garland. 341 p.

Cummings, L. S. (1982). *Improving Human Resource Effectiveness: An Annotated Bibliography.* Berea, OH: ASPA Foundation. 335 p.

Daniells, Lorna M. (Comp.). (1982). *Business Intelligence and Strategic Planning: A Selected Bibliography* (rev. ed.). Boston: Harvard Business School. Baker Library. 46 p.

Dillman, David L. (1987). *Civil Service Reform: An Annotated Bibliography.* New York: Garland. 239 p.

Dworaczek, Marian. (1991). *Job Evaluation: A Bibliography.* Monticello, IL: Vance. 62 p.

Ensign, Marie S., & Adler, Laurie N. (Eds.). (1985). *Strategic Planning: Contemporary Viewpoints.* Santa Barbara, CA: ABC-Clio. 231 p.

Ferre, John P., & Willihnganz, Shirley C. (1991). *Public Relations and Ethics: A Bibliography.* Boston: G. K. Hall. 127 p.

Frankel, Mark S. (Ed.). (1987). *Values and Ethics in Organization and Human Systems Development: An Annotated Bibliography.* Washington, DC: American Association for the Advancement of Science. 104 p.

Gauthier, Martine, & Pelchat, Denise. (1988). *Répertoire des Recherches, des Etudes, et des Enquêtes en Matière de Gestion des Ressources Humaines à la Fonction Publique du Québec.* Québec: Office des Ressources Humaines. 2 vols.

Gellen, Martin. (1983). *History of Urban Planning in the United States: An Annotated Bibliography.* Chicago: CPL Bibliographies. 23 p.

Ghorayshi, Parvin. (1990). *The Sociology of Work: A Critical Annotated Bibliography.* New York: Garland. 214 p.

Ghosh, Pradip K. (Ed.). (1984). *Urban Development in the Third World.* Westport, CT: Greenwood. 546 p.

Goehlert, Robert. (1981). *Political Decision Making.* Monticello, IL: Vance. 13 p.

Gunn, Elizabeth M. (1980). *Ethics and the Public Service: An Annotated Bibliography and Overview Essay.* Norman, OK: University of Oklahoma. Bureau of Government Research. 47 p.

Halasz, D. (Comp.). (1967). *Metropolis: A Select Bibliography of Administrative and Other Problems in Metropolitan Areas throughout the World* (2nd ed.). The Hague: Nijhoff. 267 p.

International Labour Office. (1991). *Labour Information: A Guide to Selected Sources.* Geneva. 231 p.

Kemp, Donna R. (1989). *Employee Assistance Programs: An Annotated Bibliography.* New York: Garland. 264 p.

Klosterman, Richard E. (1982). *Methods of Planning Analysis: A Bibliography and Reference Guide.* Chicago: CPL. 30 p.

Krismann, Carol. (1990). *Quality Control: An Annotated Bibliography through 1988.* White Plains, NY: Quality Resources/Kraus International. 482 p.

Lake, Gashaw W. (1991). *International Public Personnel Administration: A Bibliography.* Monticello, IL: Vance. 36 p.

Leistritz, F. Larry, & Ekstrom, Brenda L. (1986). *Social Impact Assessment and Management An Annotated Bibliography.* New York: Garland. 343 p.

Marme, Jay. (1988). *Leadership Styles in the Public and Private Sectors: A Selective Bibliography.* Monticello, IL: Vance. 12 p.

Marquette, R. Penny, & Forrest, Pat (Eds.). (1986). *An Annotated Bibliography of Articles—Government Accounting, Auditing, and Municipal Finance, 1971–1985.* Sarasota, FL: American Accounting Association. 129 p.

Marshall, Marion B. (1987). *Public Finance: An Information Sourcebook.* Phoenix, AZ: Oryx. 287 p.

Matty, Paul. (1981). *Planning Publications: An Annotated Bibliography and Reference Guide.* Chicago: CPL Bibliographies. 100 p.

Midgley, James, & Piachaud, David (Eds.). (1984). *The Fields and Methods of Social Planning.* New York: St. Martin's. 215 p.

Murin, William F., & Pryor, Judith. (1988). *Delivering Government Services: An Annotated Bibliography.* New York: Garland. 315 p.

Murrell, Kenneth L., & Duffield, Robert H. (1985). *Management Infrastructure for the Developing World: A Bibliographic Sourcebook.* New York: Kumarian. 118 p.

Neufeld, Maurice F., Leab, Daniel J., & Swanson, Dorothy. (1983). *American Working Class History: A Representative Bibliography.* New York: Bowker. 356 p.

Newson, Tony. (1986). *Housing Policy: An International Bibliography.* London: Mansell. 398 p.

Olsen, Shirley A. (1981). *Research, Theory, and Methods Pertaining to Team Problem Solving, Planning, and Policy Making.* Monticello, IL: Vance. 54 p.

Oman, Ray C. (1989). *Organization Productivity at the Crossroads: A Partially Annotated Bibliography.* Monticello, IL: Vance. 54 p.

Palumbo, Dennis J., & Taylor, George A. (1979). *Urban Policy: A Guide to Information Sources.* Detroit: Gale. 198 p.

Parish, David W. (Ed.). (1980). *Changes in American Society, 1960–1978: An Annotated Bibliography of Official Government Publications.* Metuchen, NJ: Scarecrow. 438 p.

Rabin, Jack. (1991). *Public Budgeting and Financial Management: An Annotated Bibliography.* New York: Garland. 160 p.
Includes no references later than 1986.

Roess, Anne C. (1991). *Public Utilities: An Annotated Guide to Information Sources.* Metuchen, NJ: Scarecrow. 393 p.

Sangl, Judith A., & Lizanec, Patricia M. (1980). *Health Planning: An Annotated Bibliography.* Hyattsville, MD: U.S. Health Resources Administration. 743 p.

Santora, Joseph C. (1987). *Planning: A Selected Guide to Periodical Literature, 1975–1985.* Monticello, IL: Vance. 28 p.

Schaad, Evelyn (Comp.). (1991). *Rural Development: An Annotated Bibliography of ILO Publications and Documents, 1983–1990.* Geneva: International Labour Office. 338 p.

Shearer, Barbara S., & Shearer, Benjamin F. (Comps.). (1983). *Periodical Literature on United States Cities: A Bibliography and Subject Guide.* Westport, CT: Greenwood. 574 p.

Siddiqui, Akhtar H. (1982). *Project Planning, Management, Implementation, and Appraisal: A Select Bibliography.* Islamabad: Pakistan Institute of Development Economics. 83 p.

Singh, Mohinder, & Sharma, Rajendra N. (1981). *Civil Service and Personnel Administration: An Annotated Bibliography.* New Delhi: Indian Institute of Public Administration. 406 p.

Sutcliffe, Anthony. (1981). *The History of Urban and Regional Planning: A Annotated Bibliography.* London: Mansell. 284 p.

Thompson, Chris, & Offord, John. (1984). *Local Government in the United Kingdom: A Select Bibliography.* Chicago: CPL Bibliographies. 23 p.

U.S. Bureau of Labor Statistics. (1990). *Productivity: A Selected, Annotated Bibliography, 1983–87.* Washington, DC: GPO. 160 p.
The latest edition of a bibliography that is revised regularly.

U.S. National Transportation Research Board. (1980). *Bibliography on Project Evaluation and Priority Programming Criteria.* Washington, DC: National Academy of Sciences. 35 p.

U.S. Office of Personnel Management. Library. (1980). *The Federal Civil Service: History, Organization, and Activities.* Washington, DC: GPO. 24 p.

U.S. Office of Personnel Management. Library. (1981). *Labor-Management Relations in the Public Service.* Washington, DC. 18 p.

U.S. Office of Personnel Management. Library. (1981). *The Personnel Management Function.* Washington, DC. 72 p.

U.S. Office of Policy Development and Research. (1980). *Fiscal Impact Analysis for State and Local Government.* Washington, DC. 28 p.

U.S. Office of Policy Development and Research. (1981). *Productivity Improvement for State and Local Government.* Washington, DC: GPO. 108 p.

Vance, Mary. (1986). *Productivity in Public Administration: A Bibliography.* Monticello, IL: Vance. 21 p.

Weintraub, Irwin. (1987). *Reference Sources in Urban and Regional Planning: An Annotated Bibliography.* Chicago: CPL Bibliographies. 38 p.

Wertheim, Arthur F. (Ed.). (1984). *American Popular Culture: A Historical Bibliography.* Santa Barbara, CA: ABC-Clio. 246 p.

West, Jonathan P. (1983). *Career Planning, Development, and Management: An Annotated Bibliography.* New York: Garland. 306 p.

White, Anthony G. (1989). *Administrative Rituals, Rites, and Ceremonies: A Selected Bibliography.* Monticello, IL: Vance. 6 p.

White, Anthony G. (1986). *Strategic Management: A Selected Bibliography.* Monticello, IL: Vance. 7 p.

White, Paul M. (1980). *Soviet Urban and Regional Planning: A Bibliography with Abstracts.* New York: St. Martin's. 276 p.

Wolfgart, Ludger, Polinski, Katja, & Staeck-Freytag, Sabine. (1986). *New Technology in the Public Service: A Bibliographical Study.* Luxembourg: Office for Official Publications of the European Communities. 301 p.

Yeh, Anthony G. (1987). *Urban Development and Planning in Hong Kong: A Research Guide.* Hong Kong: University of Hong Kong. Centre of Asian Studies. 162 p.

NOTES

1. "Organizational Behavior—Albania—Bibliography," "Organizational Behavior—Arkansas—Bibliography,"; and so forth.

2. Other important publishers' series of this kind include Greenwood's "Bibliographies and Indexes in World History"; Clio's "Bibliography and Reference Series"; Dekker's

"Public Administration and Public Policy" series; Gale's "American Government and History Information Guides"; the "Personnel Bibliography Series of the U.S. Office of Personnel Management"; Lexington's "Policy Studies Organization Series"; and another series issued by Garland: "Reference Library of Social Science." "Works in Social Theory: A Bibliographic Series," published by the Reference and Research Services Press, specialize in extensive bibliographies on individual theorists. Recent titles address the scholarship of Antonio Gramsci and Michel Foucault. Other series of interest can be identified through Bowker's *Books in Series in the United States*, the latest (1985) edition of which covers series initiated between 1950 and 1984.

3. Each issue of *Criminal Justice Abstracts*, for example, includes an essay of this kind.

4. *The Behavioral and Social Sciences Librarian*, published quarterly since 1979, is a major journal serving this function.

5. Computerized databases searched included *LC Marc* (covering books published commercially in English), *GPO Monthly Catalog* (federal documents), and *PAIS* (materials in a variety of forms).

11

PUBLISHED STATISTICS

1. USES OF STATISTICS

Anyone engaged in a serious study of a social phenomenon has a clear obligation to identify and interpret all data, quantitative or qualitative, relevant to the situation under study. The key word here is "relevant" and the data so defined will depend on the nature of the approach taken in the study, as well as on the substance of the phenomenon addressed. A person examining, for example, the influence of bureaucratic structure on deviant behavior among its members might take an ethnographic or other qualitative approach in observing the nature of internal agency interactions and their consequences.[1] This researcher would seek, by direct observation, to relate these processes to the forms of organizational culture and their influence at different levels within the hierarchy. Such an approach would probably involve use of some quantitative data, perhaps as these related to the size and complexity of the organization and its internal transactions. Statistics used in this scenario would largely be *descriptive* and, although important, would primarily serve to underpin qualitative forms of analysis.

On the other hand, a researcher who was concerned with phenomena that are intrinsically measurable would obviously deal with quantitative sources more carefully and at greater length. Answers to questions relating to important recent phenomena, such as the relation between public-sector growth and the ability of fiscal mechanisms to sustain it, must clearly have some strong quantitative and theoretical basis.[2]

The point is that statistical data are rarely irrelevant to the interests of any social researcher. Use of such data, and the amount of attention paid to them in their collection and analysis, will vary greatly according to the researcher's particular concerns. At an early point in the enterprise, it is necessary to decide, first, how important statistical analysis is to the project, and, second, how much attention should be allotted to the creation of sets of original data.

There is a widespread misconception among beginning researchers, especially those preparing doctoral dissertations, that the extraction of quantitative data from archival or other primary data is an act worthy of reward in itself. Before governments assumed their now-massive burdens of data collection and dissemination, this position may have made some sense. Given the tremendous availability of raw data in a variety of accessible forms, its virtue is tenuous today.

Statistics may be used *descriptively* or *analytically*. A given set of statistics can be used in either way. To document the growing importance of the criminal justice process in 19th-century Nuevo Albion, prepare an annual count of cases heard in the various courts. This use is descriptive, as the figures simply document the activities of the courts. To draw more significance from these statistics, analyze them according to the gender of the accused, offense charged, outcome, or any other variable provided by the data that has significance for the hypothesis or research question. You could also integrate court data with another data set. For example, to show that felony prosecutions in this state increased in relative, as well as in absolute, terms, use population data to present prosecutions per unit of population. You would then be using statistics analytically.

In this or any other example, it is not necessary to go to archival sources for relevant statistics unless they are not otherwise available. Chances are quite high that someone has already collected them (or estimated them), and all you must do is locate them. Your claim to fame would lie in how you analyzed or extracted meaning from the data, and not in the pedestrian, though important, contribution of data collection. The focus of social or policy research can never be the collection of data, no matter how arduous an activity this may be. This is because the fruits of such research lie in data analysis.

Data collection is only important as a precursor of data analysis. As a stage in the research process, data-collection activity can be limited if the scholar takes the trouble to become familiar with the means of locating relevant data that have already been collected.

Existing statistical data may be published or unpublished; from the research point of view, it does not matter which. Two things do, however, matter very much. The meaning and provenance of the data must be properly appreciated. If the data are drawn from official sources, definitions of categories must be understood in detail. In the example of the 19th-century court records, you must know answers to the following, among other things: Which offenses did this court cover? Are its records an indicator of all prosecutions, or of felonies only? Was this the only state court in Nuevo Albion that heard felonies? How active were federal courts at this time? Did definitions of individual felonies (or of court jurisdictions) change over the century, and would this make a difference to the comparability of the statistics over time? If data are drawn from other sources, you must understand, again in detail, just how they were calculated and what they represent. To follow the same example, there are many modern assessments of state population levels at different points in the past. Evaluation of them can be quite difficult because they variously emphasize factors such as contemporary estimates, records of taxation, births, deaths, inward and outward migration, apprenticeship figures, parish membership, census returns, and the like. The better you understand the sources and origins of your figures, the better you can analyze them meaningfully.

A search for existing statistical data should begin with an investigation of published data because published sources can be surveyed more easily and the characteristics of the data evaluated more readily. Machine readable and other forms of unpublished data in many ways have greater potential for analysis (see the following chapter), but their investigation requires a greater investment of time and effort. Published figures are often quite suitable, especially if your purpose is descriptive in nature. They may be suitable also for analytical research, either on their own or, as is more likely, in combination with other quantitative variables. If the object of the research has a focus other than the analysis of primary sources in some original fashion, use of published statistics should always suffice.[3]

The works cited include guides to statistical sources and collections of statistics. (In fact, there is often considerable overlap between the two since the better collections include information on the sources from which data were drawn or, more usually, abstracted.) In this arrangement bibliographic guides precede collections, and sources covering similar areas are grouped together.

2. SOURCES

Sources of statistics are as varied as the literature of the social and policy sciences. Statistics collected by others and published in books and articles provide valid data provided their significance is properly understood and proper recognition of the compiler of the data is given. There is nothing wrong with reanalyzing data collected by someone else, as long as the results have meaning and the origins of the data are viewed with a critical eye. However, note that data presented in published works are often encapsulated and may reflect only a fraction of the data actually available in their original form, so that reanalysis that has significance is difficult.[4]

The bibliographic sources cited here are arranged within seven broad groups. The first three emphasize the United States in general with particular attention to federal, state, and local sources. Category 4 covers census material, primarily that generated in English-speaking countries. Category 5 includes works relating to Great Britain, Canada, some other Anglophone countries, and a selection of the outstanding sources related to Latin America and Europe. Readers with other geographical interests are advised to begin their inquiries with standard guides to national bibliographies or government publications of the country under study. The sixth group addresses associations and some other generators of specialized statistics. Lastly, election statistics, surveys, and opinion polls are considered.

Only those bibliographic sources with a particular and expressed concern for identifying statistics are listed here. The reader should recognize that many other bibliographic tools index statistical material in an incidental fashion. Of particular interest are general guides to governmental publications of various kinds (see chapter 13, especially those sections dealing with state and local documents), and indexing and abstracting services covering particular disciplines related to government and to the social and policy sciences (see chapter 8).

2.1. General Sources of U.S. Statistics

Balachandran, M. (1988). *A Guide to Statistical Sources in Money, Banking, and Finance.* Phoenix, AZ: Oryx. 119 p.

Covers a variety of sources but provides little detail on any of them. Of interest because of its references to labor and public finance.

Black Americans: A Statistical Sourcebook. (1990–). Boulder, CO: Numbers & Concepts. Annual.

Most of the data derive from the Bureau of the Census, but some from nonfederal sources are also included. See also *Hispanic Americans*; Horton and Smith; McFate (below).

Findex: The Directory of Market Research Reports, Studies, and Surveys. (1979–). New York: Find/SVP Clearinghouse. Annual.

The principal guide to identifying market surveys. (Others are included in databases such as *Management Contents* and *ABI/Inform*, described in chapter 9.) It should be noted that the surveys themselves are very expensive, and are rarely accessible through academic libraries.

Gilmartin, Kevin J., et al. (1979). *Social Indicators: An Annotated Bibliography of Current Literature.* New York: Garland. 123 p.

Annotated listings of articles and other materials concerned with the nature and use of social indicators. A supplement to Wilcox, Brooks, Beal, and Klonglan (see below).

Goehlert, Robert U. (1986). *Statistical Data Sources.* Monticello, IL: Vance. 14 p.
A modest list of sources that concentrates on those covering the United States. No annotations.

Hispanic Americans: A Statistical Sourcebook. (1990–). Boulder, CO: Numbers & Concepts. Annual.
Similar to *Black Americans* (above) in form and sources used. See also Schick and Schick (below).

Horton, Carrell P., & Smith, Jessie C. (Eds). (1990). *Statistical Record of Black America.* Detroit: Gale. 707 p.
Especially valuable for the range of its data sources which include state agencies and other non-federal sources. Entries arranged within 19 broad categories. Use in conjunction with McFate and *Black Americans.*

McFate, Katherine (Ed.). (1988). *The Metropolitan Area Fact Book: A Statistical Portrait of Black and Whites in Urban America.* Washington, DC: Joint Center for Political Studies. 109 p.
Uses data primarily from federal sources to document economic and social patterns in 48 metropolitan areas with black populations exceeding 100,000. Information based largely on 1980 census data. A useful supplement to Horton and Smith and *Black Americans.*

Merwin, Donna J. (1976). *The Quality of Life: A Bibliography of Objective and Perceptual Social Indicators.* Monticello, IL: Council of Planning Librarians. 13 p.

Predicasts Forecasts. (1960–). Cleveland: Predicasts. Quarterly.
Covers economic forecasts and market surveys relating to the United States appearing in over 500 newspapers and magazines published worldwide. Indexes over 50,000 sources each year.

Schick, Frank L., & Schick, Renee (Comps.). (1991). *Statistical Handbook on U.S. Hispanics.* Phoenix, AZ: Oryx. 255 p.
Convenient as a compilation of data originally published elsewhere. As most are generated by federal sources, the data reflect problems in classifying those of this ethnic and cultural group. See also *Hispanic Americans* (above).

Schmittroth, Linda (Ed.). (1991). *Statistical Record of Women Worldwide.* Detroit: Gale. 763 p.

A compilation of tables drawn from about 20 sources, including a number of opinion polls. See also Taeuber (below).

Statistical Reference Index: A Selected Guide to American Statistical Publications from Sources Other Than the U.S. Government. (1980–). Washington, DC: Congressional Information Service. Monthly, with quarterly and annual cumulations.

Popularly known as the *SRI.* One of the best guides to statistics originating outside the public sector, although publications of state governments are included. Abstracts are detailed and well indexed. Like its parallel collections, the *Index to International Statistics* (section 2.5) and the *American Statistics Index* (section 2.2), backed by a microfiche collection that includes full texts of a large proportion of the materials indexed. The three complementary collections are also combined in a single CD-ROM, the *Statistical MasterFile* (see section 7 of chapter 12).

Stratford, Juri, & Stratford, Jean S. (1987). *Guide to Statistical Materials Produced by Governments and Associations in the United States.* Alexandria, VA: Chadwyck-Healey. 279 p.

An annotated bibliography whose three parts cover statistical publications of federal and state governments and associations. Annotations are clear and analytical. Includes title and subject indexes.

Surveys, Polls, Censuses, and Forecasts Directory: A Guide to Sources of Statistical Studies. (1983–). Detroit: Gale. Frequency unknown.

Covers data generated in the main from private sources. Very brief descriptions are given, but these indicate availability of data. By no means comprehensive, but an important source of its kind. Intended to be published three times a year, but no issues have appeared for several years.

Taeuber, Cynthia (Ed.). (1991). *Statistical Handbook on Women in America.* Phoenix, AZ: Oryx. 385 p.

Primarily a compilation of statistical tables generated by the federal government between 1985 and 1990. Useful for its discussions of statistical definitions and categories used and of sources for further research. See also Schmittroth (above).

Terleckyj, Nestor E., & Coleman, Charles D. (1991). *Regional Economic Growth in the United States: Projections for 1991–2010.* Washington, DC: NPA Data Services. 3 vols.

Presents detailed projections at the national, state, regional, and local levels and is intended as a major resource for planning in the public and private sectors. Intended to be revised annually.

Vance, Mary A. *Quality of Life: A Bibliography*. Monticello, IL: Vance. 18 p.

Wilcox, Leslie D., Brooks, Ralph M., Beal, George M., & Klonglan, Gerald E. (1973). *Social Indicators and Societal Monitoring: An Annotated Bibliography*. New York: Elsevier. 464 p.
Supplemented by Gilmartin, (see above).

2.2. Statistics Produced by the Federal Government

American Statistics Index. (1973–). Washington, DC: Congressional Information Service. Basic set updated by monthly and annual supplements.

Presents substantial abstracts of all federal publications that include statistics, whether serial or monograph. (Statistical publications from Congress are also included in the *CIS Index*; see chapter 13). Abstracts are arranged by agency of origin. Very detailed indexes provide excellent access. A version of this index exists in computerized form. The publishers of *ASI* also issue the documents indexed in a separate microfiche collection, to which most large libraries subscribe. Documents in this are arranged according to the numbering system used in the *ASI Index*. Updates a retrospective set for the years 1960–73. Further observations on this important source are given in the annotation to its companion set, the *SRI* (section 2.1).

Andriot, John L. (Ed.). (1973–). *Guide to U.S. Government Statistics*. McLean, VA: Documents Index. Annual in 2 vols.

Lists and describes mainly serial statistical publications arranged by agency of origin. Has several indexes, including those by title and subject. Has nowhere near the detail of the *ASI* but is for this reason more useful as an overview of publications of individual agencies.

County and City Extra: Annual Metro, City and County Data Book. (1992–). Lanham, MD: Bernan.

An amalgamated and updated version of the Bureau of the Census's *County and City Data Book* and *State and Metropolitan Area Data Book*. Planned as an annual to keep it more informed by current census data than either of these two official publications. Available on CD as *Counties* and *Cities Plus* (chapter 12).

Evinger, William R. (1991). *Federal Statistical Source: Where to Find Agency Experts and Personnel.* (28th ed.). Phoenix, AZ: Oryx. 161 p.

This work does provide some insight into federal data collection efforts. Its great virtue, however, lies in its identification of the names, telephone numbers, and responsibilities of 4,000 or so of the employees engaged in them. This information can be invaluable in wending one's way through the labyrinth that is the federal information network. Revised every couple of years. Earlier editions entitled *Federal Statistical Directory.*

Hoel, Arline A., Clarkson, Kenneth W., & Miller, Roger L. (1983). *Economics Sourcebook of Government Statistics.* Lexington, MA: Lexington Books. 271 p.

Provides critical descriptions of over 50 common economic indicators generated by the federal government. Includes information on their sources, historical range, frequency of issue, and limitations of use.

O'Hara, Frederick M., & Sicignano, Robert. (1985). *Handbook of United States Economic and Financial Indicators.* Westport, CT: Greenwood. 224 p.

Covers over 200 standard indicators. Descriptions include characteristics and frequency of publication.

Rowe, Judith S., & Anderson, Susan. (1983). Keeping Up with Federal Statistics. *Behavioral and Social Sciences Librarian, 3*, 11–18.

Discusses the changing nature of federal statistics occasioned by a reduction in governmental data–collection activities. Identifies privately generated sources that can be used to take up some of the slack.

Sears, Jean L., & Moody, Marilyn. (1985–86). *Using Government Publications.* Phoenix, AZ: Oryx. 2 vols.

Volume 1 is entitled *Searching by Subject and Agencies*; volume 2 is *Finding Statistics and Using Special Techniques.* Refers to federal documents only.

Sy, Karen J. & Robbin, Alice. (1990). Federal Statistical Policies and Programs: How Good Are the Numbers? *Annual Review of Information Science and Technology, 25*, 3–54.

A critical examination of federal efforts in this area which documents changing governmental policies affecting the quality of data collected and the ways these are disseminated.

U.S. Bureau of Justice Statistics. (1973–). *Sourcebook of Criminal Justice Statistics.* Washington, DC: GPO. Annual.

A subject-oriented statistical abstract. Very useful for its inclusion of nonfederal data and of crime survey data (for example, victimization studies), often compared to arrest rates and other official measures of the incidence of crime.

U.S. Bureau of the Census. (1985–). *Census Catalog and Guide.* Washington, DC: GPO. Annual.

Describes the bureau's activities and cites all bureau publications in print. This is especially valuable for its inclusion of machine-readable data (see chapter 12) in a variety of forms, together with software needed to use it. Updated by the *Monthly Product Announcement, Census and You* (formerly the *Data User News*). The annual and periodicals together replace the Bureau's *Catalog*, published monthly, with annual cumulations, between 1947 and 1984.

U.S. Bureau of the Census. (1984). *Business Statistics Data Finder.* Washington, DC. 19 p.

A short but useful guide to the Bureau's efforts in this area.

U.S. Bureau of the Census. (1967). *Directory of Federal Statistics for States: A Guide to Sources, 1967.* Washington, DC: GPO. 372 p.

Provides tables of federal statistics relating to state matters published between 1960 and 1966. Like many Bureau publications, including most of those listed in this section, provides the source of each table presented. An appendix includes a list of other sources. Still valuable, as many of the tables given are drawn from annuals or other serials that are still being published.

U.S. Bureau of the Census. (1978). *Directory of Federal Statistics for Local Areas: A Guide to Sources, 1976.* Washington, GPO. 359 p.

U.S. Bureau of the Census. (1979). *Directory of Federal Statistics for Local Areas: A Guide to Sources, Urban Update, 1977–1978.* Washington, DC: GPO. 490 p.

Between them, these two guides cover federal statistical interest in governmental structures below the state level up to the 1970s. Useful appendixes include one citing nonfederal sources of local government statistics.

U.S. Bureau of the Census. (1970). *Directory of Non-Federal Statistics for States and Local Areas: A Guide to Sources, 1969.* Washington, DC: GPO. 677 p.

Of great value in its coverage of the publications of a variety of organizations, private and academic as well as governmental. Includes an appendix of other relevant sources. As with its companion volumes, its usefulness is undoubtedly limited by its age.

U.S. Bureau of the Census. (1950–). *Economic Indicators.* Washington, DC: GPO. Monthly.

Probably the major source for indicators of this nature. Primarily domestic in its concerns, but some international indicators are included.

U.S. Bureau of the Census. (1985). *Economic Surveys Data Finder.* Washington, DC. 15 p.

Covers surveys in print and nonprint forms.

U.S. Bureau of the Census. (1973–). *Social Indicators: Selected Data on Social Conditions and Trends in the United States.* Washington, DC. Triennial.

A massive compendium of raw statistics addressing economic and other "quality-of-life" indicators measured by agencies of the federal government.

U.S. Bureau of the Census. (1958–). *Census of Governments.* Washington, DC: GPO. Irregular.

Reports the latest of the special censuses that have been held every five years since 1957. Considerable detail on all aspects of the business of local and state government is presented, including finance, public employment, and organizational structure.

U.S. Bureau of the Census. (1949–). *County and City Data Book.* Washington, DC: GPO. Irregular; about every five years.

Reports detailed statistics by subject and by state and county. An appendix lists and describes sources for each table given. Also available on diskette in a form suitable for manipulation by spreadsheet.

U.S. Bureau of the Census. (1975). *Historical Statistics of the United States, Colonial Times to 1970.* Washington, DC: GPO. 2 vols.

The standard historical compilation relating to the United States, this work includes series, usually on an annual basis, going back as far as 1610. Many of the older series are generated by nonfederal sources.

U.S. Bureau of the Census. (1980). *Social Indicators III: Selected Data on Social Conditions and Trends in the United States.* Washington, DC: GPO. 585 p.

The latest edition of a collection of largely noneconomic data taken from federal government and other sources, published and unpublished.

U.S. Bureau of the Census. (1979–). *State and Metropolitan Area Data Book.* Washington, DC: GPO. Annual.

Similar to the *County and City Data Book* (above) in organization and detail of coverage. Both sources are based on the most recent Census of Population data. The two differ only in the level of social unit covered. A supplement to the *Statistical Abstract* (below). Now available on disk in a form amenable to manipulation through standard spreadsheet programs and statistical packages.

U.S. Bureau of the Census. (1878–). *Statistical Abstract of the United States.* Washington, DC: GPO. Annual.

The standard and most detailed compilation since the late 19th century. An important feature is that, like *Historical Statistics,* it not only summarizes the relevant data, but also provides citations at the end of each table indicating where more complete data can be found. In addition, each section includes a discussion of other statistical data sources, whether or not these are generated by the federal government.

U.S. National Center for Health Statistics. (1937–). *Vital Statistics of the United States.* Washington, DC: GPO. Annual.

A multivolume series providing data on all aspects of births and deaths. Updates a series covering the period 1900-37.

U.S. Office of Management and Budget, Statistical Policy Division. (1975). *Statistical Services of the United States Government* (rev. ed.). Washington, DC: GPO. 234 p.

Although rather old, this remains the standard guide to federal efforts in this area. It discusses individual published series and their contents, but its chief value lies in its descriptions of how and why these series are generated and its discussions of data-collection activities that do not necessarily result in publications. Updated by U.S. Congress. House. Committee on Government Operations. (1984). *The Federal Statistical System, 1980 to 1985.* Washington, DC: GPO. 284 p.

2.3. Other Statistics Relating to State and Local Governments

Balachandran, M., & Balachandran, S. (Eds.). (1990). *State and Local Statistics Sources: A Subject Guide to Statistical Data on States, Cities, and Locales.* Detroit: Gale. 1,124 p.

Entries are arranged by state and within this by topic. Appendixes provide annotated lists of nonprint sources and of sources used in compilation of the directory. Very useful for its coverage of a wide variety of data produced by governmental and unofficial sources.

Eichholz, Alice (Ed.). (1989). *Ancestry's Red Book: American State, County, and Town Sources.* Salt Lake City: Ancestry. 758 p.

A guide to official records generated by state and local governments and to library and archival collections supporting research in these records. Intended for the genealogist, but valuable to all involved in research of this nature. Entries arranged by state and subdivided by type of record.

The Government Directory of Addresses and Telephone Numbers: Your Comprehensive Guide to Federal, State, County, and Local Government Offices in the United States. (1992). Detroit: Omnigraphics. 1,290 p.

Use to supplement Evinger (section 2.2) for local government sources.

Index to Current Urban Documents. (1972–). Westport, CT: Greenwood. Quarterly, with annual and biennial cumulations.

Indexes the publications of about 200 of the larger cities and counties in the United States and Canada. Most have a strong statistical bias. The documents themselves, which are usually very hard to obtain outside of their jurisdictions, are for the most part published separately, and in their entirety, in Greenwood's *Urban Documents Microfiche Collection.*

Lainhart, Ann S. (1992). *State Census Records.* Baltimore: Genealogical Publishing. 116 p.

Lists and describes data sources including those supplementing official state records. Also documents libraries and archives supporting research with census materials at this level.

Municipal Finance Officers Association of the United States and Canada. (1982–). *State and Local Government Fiscal Almanac.* Chicago. Annual.

Primarily a membership directory of the MFOA, but also includes financial data.

The Municipal Yearbook. (1934–). Washington, DC: International City Management Association.

Includes articles, usually with a strong statistical bias, on topics of current concern to municipal government. Also frequently includes subject bibliographies and guides to sources in specific areas. Important for its inclusion of statistical data, collected by the ICMA, relating to U.S. municipalities with populations in excess of 10,000.

New York State. Office of Statistical Coordination. (1968–). *New York State Statistical Yearbook.* Albany, NY.

Includes many tables that are prepared by state agencies for publication in this work, and that do not appear in any other source. Appears irregularly, despite the title. Cited here as but one example of the kind of statistical annual published by most states in the United States.

Parish, David W. (1981). *State Government Reference Publications: An Annotated Bibliography* (2nd ed.). Littleton, CO: Libraries Unlimited. 355 p.
Includes a chapter on statistical publications.

2.4. Censuses of Population and Housing

Censuses regularly conducted by nations as part of their regular business of government are now very complicated and politicized operations. Definitions of variables and categories often change between censuses, and this can create problems of interpretation and comparison. The decennial U.S. Census of Population, for example, is used, among other things, as a basis for regional revenue sharing of federal funds. For this reason, if no other, its methodology attracts a great deal of attention.

The conclusion here is that detailed analysis of census data should not be undertaken without considerable preparation. Below are cited introductory guides to the structure of these census operations in the United States and some other countries. Potential users should also be aware that in the United States and many other countries, individual guides to each individual census are published regularly.

Anderson, Margo J. (1988). *The American Census: A Social History.* New Haven, CT: Yale University Press. 257 p.

Bohme, Frederick G. (1989). *200 Years of U.S. Census Taking: Population and Housing Questions, 1790–1990.* Washington, DC: GPO. 109 p.
Together these two books present an overview of census operations. They discuss their structure and objectives in their social and political contexts. Reviews are also given of the bibliography documenting them.

Dubester, Henry J. (1950). *Catalog of United States Census Publications, 1790–1945.* Washington, DC: GPO. 320 p.
The classic guide to census data collection and publication. Covers special censuses as well as those of population and housing.

Schulze, Suzanne. (1983). *Population Information in Nineteenth Century Census Volumes.* Phoenix, AZ: Oryx. 446 p.

Complements Dubester by providing more detailed indexing. Covers the period 1790 through 1890.

Schulze, Suzanne. (1988). *Population Information in Twentieth Century Census Volumes, 1950–1980.* Tucson, AZ: Oryx. 317 p.

An update of Dubester. A parallel (1985) volume covers the period 1900–1940 and supplements Dubester.

U.S. Bureau of the Census. (1970). *1970 Census Users' Guide.* Washington, DC: GPO. 2 vols.

An example of the detail of documentation provided to the often-complicated technical aspects of each census.

U.S. Library of Congress. (1974). *Catalog of United States Census Publications, 1790–1972.* Washington, DC: GPO. 591 p.

Largely based on the Library's holdings and does not reflect the entire range of publications generated by the bureau. Update using the Census Bureau's *Census Catalog and Guide* (see section 2.2).

Gerhan, David R., & Wells, Robert V. (Comps.). (1989). *A Retrospective Bibliography of American Demographic History from Colonial Times to 1983.* Westport, CT: Greenwood. 474 p.

A companion volume is planned to cover studies focusing on historical change.

Goyer, Doreen S., & Eliane Domschke. (1983). *The Handbook of National Population Censuses: Latin America, the Caribbean, North America, and Oceania.* Westport, CT: Greenwood. 711 p.

Most useful for its coverage of countries other than the United States. Describes the history, structure, and documentation of the census in each country and provides short profiles of population changes since 1945. Parallel volumes cover Africa and Asia (1984) and Europe (1992).

Great Britain. Office of Population Censuses and Surveys. (1977). *Guide to Census Reports: Great Britain, 1801–1966.* London: HMSO. 279 p.

A very detailed guide to the scope and content of the census series of this country.

Simoneau, Karin. (1990). *South American Population Censuses since Independence: An Annotated Bibliography of Secondary Sources.* Madison, WI: University of Wisconsin, Madison. Library. 75 p.

Addresses the structure, content, and methodology of censuses in 12 South American countries. No primary materials are cited or discussed directly.

Travis, Carole (Ed.). (1990). *A Guide to Latin American and Caribbean Census Material: A Bibliography and Union List.* Boston: G. K. Hall. 739 p.
Most valuable as a guide to the structure and documentation of census activities in the countries addressed. Less useful as a finding tool, as locations of materials are limited to those in about 30 British collections.

2.5. Foreign and International Statistics

Ball, Joyce (Ed.). (1967). *Foreign Statistical Documents: A Bibliography of General, International Trade, and Agriculture Statistics.* Stanford, CA: Hoover Institution. 173 p.
A country listing of sources published in Western languages. Based on the extensive holdings of the Stanford University Library.

Current National Statistical Compendiums. (1974–). Washington, DC: Congressional Information Service.
A microfiche collection of the official statistical yearbooks of a wide range of countries. Continuously updated. Probably the best single source of detailed comparative statistical data.

Index to International Statistics: A Guide to Statistical Publications of International Intergovernmental Organizations. (1983–). Washington, DC: Congressional Information Service. Monthly, with quarterly and annual cumulations.
Includes primarily documents in English published by around 100 organizations, including the UN and its satellites, the OAS, and the EC. One of the better sources in an area poorly served in this regard. For important comments on this collection, see the description of its companion the *SRI* (section 2.1).

International Marketing Data and Statistics. (1975–). London: Euromonitor. Annual.
Presents detailed information on consumer markets throughout the world (except Europe). Socioeconomic trend data for the previous 10 years are usually presented in a form that permits cross-national comparison. Extensive bibliographies document further sources.

Kurian, George T. (1985). *Sourcebook of Global Statistics.* New York: Facts on File. 413 p.
A bibliography of statistical sourcebooks published throughout the world and by both private and governmental bodies. The information given on each source is good. The work is limited mainly by the rather small number of sources covered.

Manheim, Jarol B., & Ondrasik, Allison. (1983–). *Data Map 1989: Index of Published Tables of Statistical Data.* Phoenix, AZ: Oryx. Annual.

Valuable, as far as it goes, as it provides detailed indexing of a number of sources of great interest to social researchers. Limited by the narrow range of works covered.

Moore, Geoffrey H., & Moore, Melita H. (1985). *International Economic Indicators: A Sourcebook.* Westport, CT: Greenwood. 373 p.

Provides detailed information on the major indicators used to measure and compare economic activity in seven major Western countries.

Muller, Georg P., & Bornschier, Volker. (1988). *Comparative World Data: A Statistical Handbook for Social Science.* Baltimore: Johns Hopkins University Press. 496 p.

Presents data for between 30 and 50 variables documenting 128 countries. These data are primarily social indicators and focus on measures with international breadth (for example, "national prestige"). Covers only the 1970s.

Pieper, F. C. (Comp.). (1978). *SISCIS: Subject Index to Sources of Comparative International Statistics.* Beckenham, UK: CBD Research. 745 p.

Probably the best guide to sources of its kind, as it covers a very extensive range of statistical publications. Limited to sources published since the mid-1960s.

Population Index. (1935–). Princeton, NJ: Princeton University. Office of Population Research. Quarterly, with annual index and regular cumulations.

"A comprehensive annotated bibliographic journal of world literature on population and demography." Covers over 300 journals. Formerly *Population Literature.*

Taylor, Charles L., & Jodice, David A. (1983). *World Handbook of Political and Social Indicators* (3rd ed). New Haven, CT: Yale University Press. 2 vols.

A series of indicators collected and constructed by the Yale Political Data Program and now available in machine-readable form through the Inter-University Consortium for Political and Social Research (ICPSR; see chapter 12). A very widely used source. Volume 1 is subtitled *Cross-National Attributes and Rates of Change*; volume 2, *Political Protest and Government Change.*

United Nations. Statistical Office. (1982). *Directory of International Statistics.* New York. 274 p.

A guide to the structures, policies, and publications of the UN and some of its affiliates as these relate to the collection of statistical data. Includes a section with quite lengthy descriptions of machine-readable data files. This work is listed as "volume 1." It is planned that the second volume (cited as "in progress") will include material drawn from agencies other than the UN.

U.S. Library of Congress. Census Library Project. (1953). *Statistical Yearbooks; An Annotated Bibliography of the General Statistical Yearbooks of Major Political Subdivisions of the World.* Washington, DC: GPO. 123 p.
A descriptive and comprehensive guide covering over 200 countries. Its age makes it most useful to those seeking sources of historical data. Supplement using Westfall (see below).

Westfall, Gloria. (1986). *Bibliography of Official Statistical Yearbooks and Bulletins.* Alexandria, VA: Chadwyck-Healey. 247 p.
The most up-to-date list of sources of this kind.

Whitaker's Almanack. (1869–). London: Whitaker. Annual.
Among other things, provides digests of statistical data from countries throughout the world. Valuable for the long runs of its data. Best for its coverage of countries in Europe and the British Commonwealth.

World Almanac and Book of Facts. (1868–). New York: Pharos Books. Annual.
Complements Whitaker (above). Cited here as the oldest of the almanacs published in the United States, and therefore the one with the longest series of historical data.

The Europa World Year Book. (1959–). London: Europa. Annual.
Probably the most comprehensive of the several annuals that present profiles, descriptive and statistical, of the world's nations. Includes guides to sources. Also documents the activities of international organizations.

Future Survey Annual: A Guide to the Recent Literature of Trends, Forecasts, and Policy Proposals. (1979–). Bethesda, MD: World Future Society. Annual.
Presents detailed abstracts of "trends, forecasts, and policy proposals" reported in books, articles, documents, and other published forms.

Liesner, Thelma. (1989). *One Hundred Years of Economic Statistics.* New York: Facts on File. 344 p.
Most useful as a source of time-series data on a group of advanced Western economies. Data generally span 100 years.

United Nations. Statistical Office. (1948–). *Statistical Yearbook.* New York. Annual.

The principal international compendium of statistics covering a broad range of economic and social data. Statistics presented are largely those collected by the UN, but bibliographies included in the *Yearbook* and its occasional supplements document sources published by the nations represented. Abstracted every few years in the *Compendium of Social Statistics* (last published in 1980). Continues the *Statistical Yearbook of the League of Nations*, published between 1926 and 1944. Updated and supplemented by the *Monthly Bulletin of Statistics*, published since 1947.

United Nations. Statistical Office. (1948–). *Demographic Yearbook.* New York.

Compiles statistics on all aspects of demography, including divorce, collected by individual nations. This and the UNESCO publication cited below are the two major statistical serials of the UN that focus on noneconomic data.

United Nations Educational, Scientific, and Cultural Organization. (1964–). *Statistical Yearbook.* Paris.

Presents data on a wide range of cultural attributes (including literacy and educational levels) of populations throughout the world. Data are reported by UNESCO from information submitted by individual nations.

United Nations Educational, Scientific, and Cultural Organization. Social and Human Sciences Documentation Centre. (1988). *Selective Inventory of Social Science Information and Documentation Services* (3rd ed.). New York: St. Martin's. 680 p.

Describes information centers throughout the world in the business of producing and disseminating information of a social nature. All centers listed provide assistance to those other than their immediate constituents.

World Index of Economic Forecasts: Including Industry Tendency Surveys and Development Plans (3rd ed.). (1988). New York: Stockton. 563 p.

Probably the most comprehensive single source documenting forecasts of economic performance in a large number of countries.

Harvey, Joan M. (1980). *Statistics America: Sources for Market Research (North, Central, and South America)* (2nd ed.). Beckenham, UK: CBD Research. 385 p.

A bibliographic guide to sources of statistics and an excellent starting point for research. Similar guides by the same author cover countries in Africa, Asia, and Australasia, and Europe.

America en Cifras. (1960–1977). Washington, DC: Organization of American States. Annual.

The latest edition of the most comprehensive statistical compendium dealing with the Americas as a whole. Data are presented with an indication of their sources. A condensed version entitled *Statistical Compendium of the Americas* is published irregularly. Updated and supplemented by the *Statistical Bulletin of the OAS*, published monthly since 1979.

Latin America and Caribbean Contemporary Record. (1982–). New York: Holmes & Meier. Annual.

A guide, by country, to recent developments in the region. Includes statistical tables and bibliography. One of a number of works of its kind, but probably the best in its statistical detail.

United Nations Economic Commission for Latin America and the Caribbean. (1973–). *Statistical Yearbook for Latin America and the Caribbean.* Santiago, Chile.

Tables presented are primarily economic. Figures documenting the activities of intergovernmental associations as well as countries are presented. Text in Spanish and English.

University of California at Los Angeles Latin American Center. (1955–). *Statistical Abstract of Latin America.* Los Angeles. Annual.

Overlaps with the previous items to some extent; they should be used in tandem. Recent editions are supplemented by issues addressing particular topics in some detail, for example, U.S.-Mexico border statistics since 1900.

United Nations Economic Commission for Asia and the Pacific. (1969–). *Statistical Yearbook for Asia and the Pacific/Annuaire Statistique pour l'Asie et le Pacifique.* Bangkok, Thailand.

Earlier: *Statistical Yearbook for Asia and the Far East/Annuaire Statistique pour l'Asie et l'Extreme Orient.*

Shoup, Paul S. (1981). *The East European and Soviet Data Handbook: Political, Social, and Developmental Indicators, 1945–1975.* New York: Columbia University Press. 482 p.

A parallel source to Mitchell (below) providing data on countries within the former Soviet bloc, Albania, and Yugoslavia.

Vienna Institute for Comparative Economic Studies. (1979–). *Comecon Data.* Westport, CT: Greenwood. Biennial.

Presents trend data of major social and economic indicators for former member countries of the Soviet Union and others in Eastern Europe. Published alternately with *COMECON Foreign Trade Data.*

Blauvelt, Euan, & Durlacher, Jennifer (Eds.). (1983). *Sources of European Economic Information* (4th ed.). Cambridge, MA: Ballinger. 642 p.

Presents extensive discussions of statistical series published by the European Community and its member countries.

The Book of European Forecasts. (1992). London: Euromonitor. 311 p.

Includes three types of forecast data: those from government and private agencies, private industry, and Euromonitor's own surveys. Important for a final section citing sources of forecasting information. One of many guides to sources of forecasts issued by this publisher.

European Communities. Statistical Office. (1958–). *Basic Statistics of the Community.* Brussels. Annual.

Covers the growing number of EC countries and presents some comparisons with other Western nations.

European Directory of Non-official Statistical Sources. (1988). London: Euromonitor. 281 p.

Listings are arranged by name of source and cover financial institutions, trade associations, research institutes, and others.

European Marketing Data and Statistics (1962–). London: Euromonitor. Annual.

Similar in objective and depth of coverage to *International Marketing Data and Statistics* (above). Title occasionally given as *EMDAS.*

Eurostatistics: Data for Short-Term Economic Analysis. (1979–). Brussels: European Communities. Statistical Office. Monthly.

Documents trends of up to five years in member nations, Japan, and the United States.

Guide to European Market Information: EC Countries. (1991). London: London Business School Information Service. 120 p.

Most useful as a guide to current sources documenting particular national consumer markets. Only basic statistical data on member countries are presented.

Mitchell, Brian R. (Ed.). (1992). *International Historical Statistics: Europe, 1950–1988* (3rd ed.). London: Macmillan. 942 p.

Presents data on all Western European countries, arranged within 11 broad categories. Most address economic indicators, but a number of social and other issues (climate, population, education, and labor force) are also covered. Includes a subject index and a list of sources.

Ramsay, Anne (Comp.). (1983). *EUROSTAT Index: A Detailed Keyword Subject Index to the Statistical Series Published by the Statistical Office of the European Communities, with Notes on the Series.* (2nd ed.). Edinburgh, Scotland: Capital Planning Information. 184 p.

Annuaire de Statistique Internationale de Grand Villes. (1961–). The Hague: International Statistical Institute. Biennial.

Provides detailed information on European cities with populations in excess of 100,000. Also includes data on cities outside of Europe with populations of 750,000 or more.

The Annual Register of World Events. (1758–). London: Longmans, Green.

Now in its third century of continuous publication and provides tremendous runs of statistical data. (The further these go back, the less reliable they of course are.) Founded and for many years edited by the philosopher and stateman Edmund Burke.

Great Britain. Central Statistical Office. (1840–). *Annual Abstract of Statistics.* London: HMSO.

Updated by the *Monthly Digest of Statistics.*

Great Britain. Central Statistical Office. (1990). *Guide to Official Statistics* (2nd ed.). London: HMSO. 191 p.

A very detailed guide most profitably used by those with some knowledge of British governmental structure.

Index to Business Reports. (1982–). Harrogate, UK: Quarry Press. Bimonthly.

Indexes forecasts, market surveys, and other economic surveys published in British newspapers and magazines.

Mitchell, Brian R. (1988). *British Historical Statistics.* Cambridge, UK: Cambridge University Press. 885 p.

Statistics are presented within 16 broad chapters, each introduced by an essay discussing and evaluating the sources of information used. This is most valuable for earlier data based, at least in part, on private sources and informed estimates.

Mort, David (Comp.). (1990). *Sources of Unofficial UK Statistics* (2nd ed.). Brookfield, VT: Gower. 413 p.

Complements the official guide just cited above. The nature and availability of the data are discussed.

Reviews of United Kingdom Statistical Sources. (1970–). Oxford, UK: Pergamon. Irregular.

Each of the 26 or so volumes in this publisher's series provides detailed consideration of the sources, current and historical, documenting one defined area of concern. Recent titles include "Crime," "Health Survey," and "Wages and Earnings."

Canada. Bureau of Statistics. (1905–). *Canada Year Book: Official Annual.* Ottawa: Statistics Canada.

Leacy, F. H. (1983). *Historical Statistics of Canada* (2nd ed). Ottawa: Statistics Canada. 900 p.

In form and structure, based on its counterpart for the United States. Very few entries for the period before the 1860s.

Statistics Canada. (1982). *A Bibliography of Federal Data Sources Excluding Statistics Canada.* Ottawa: Statistics Canada. 189 p.

2.6. Other Sources: Associations and Agency Annual Reports

Nongovernmental organizations not primarily in the business of publishing can be of great importance as generators of statistical information. Trade and professional associations and other nongovernmental bodies are worthy of particular notice in this regard. These organizations, however, do not generally market their publications or other data resources through government printing offices or through the scholarly or commercial publishing channels. Identifying promising sources of this origin can be quite a task in itself, although one that can definitely be worthwhile.

A number of the bibliographic guides cited earlier in this chapter, as has been noted, do help the user in this regard by the incidental indexing of such material. The first work cited below is probably the single most useful tool for this purpose, as it serves as an extensive guide to the associations in the United States by area of interest. It should be noted that many other Western nations are covered by directories with a similar purpose.

Encyclopedia of Associations. (1961–). Detroit: Gale Research. Annual, now in 5 vols. Updated between editions by *New Associations.*

The most comprehensive listing of trade, professional, and other associations in the United States. Lengthy annotations indicate the size of the organization, the kinds of materials it publishes, and if it maintains a library or information center. Very useful as a source for locating organizations that are not primarily in the business of publishing, but frequently collect and disseminate statistical data. Arranged by broad category, with detailed subject and other indexes. Other directories serving related purposes are cited in section 4 of chapter 15.

Statistics Sources. (1962–). Detroit: Gale. Annual.
Valuable for the attention paid to statistical publications of associations and other private organizations not usually considered as important in generating statistics. Annotations are minimal, but the volume and range of sources covered is impressive. International in scope, but best for its coverage of the United States.

Accident Facts. (1927–). Chicago: National Safety Council. Annual.
A detailed compilation of raw data drawn from a variety of sources, including insurance companies and other organizations concerned with the collection of primary information in this area. Cited here as an example of the value of nontrade and nongovernmental generators of quantitative data.

Source Book of Health Insurance Data. (1959–). New York: Health Insurance Institute. Annual.
Presents actuarial data and vital statistics drawn from insurance companies, government agencies, medical associations, and other sources.

Spomer, Cynthia R. (Ed.). (1992). *American Directory of Organized Labor: Unions, Locals, Agreements, and Employers.* Detroit: Gale. 1,638 p.
A guide to organizational and financial data on over 230 unions.

Trzyna, Thaddeus C., & Childers, Roberta (Eds.). (1992). *World Directory of Environmental Organizations: A Handbook of National and International Organizations and Programs—Governmental and Nongovernmental—Concerned With Protecting the Earth's Resources* (4th ed.). Sacramento: California Institute of Public Affairs. 231 p.
Also lists directories, databases, and other sources of information.

For researchers concerned with the activities of the public sector, a resource of great importance may be the annual reports of public agencies at the national, state, or local level. Most public agencies are required by law to issue periodic, usually annual, reports, and because these document the routine functions carried out by agencies in their normal course of business, they conform to the most stringent definition of a primary source (see chapter 16). In a world that tends to measure and judge productivity in quantitative terms, it is not surprising that the content of such reports is often heavily statistical. Agency annual reports usually have the additional advantage of having been in existence for a considerable period of time and therefore of offering long runs of data.

To identify and locate interesting sources of this kind, the user should first go to the latest edition of the appropriate manual of governmental structure.[5] These manuals will serve to identify clearly the agencies responsible for a particular function and their position in the governmental hierarchy. Once the agencies have been identified, their annual reports, or those of the larger structures of which they are a part, can be located, either through an appropriate depository library or by other means. They may also be traced through the *ASI*, the *SRI*, or other sources documenting statistical publications of governmental agencies.

The official guide to the structure of U.S. federal bureaucracies is discussed below and should be used in conjunction with Whitnah. Manuals to government agencies at the state and other levels can be identified through sources discussed in section 2.3 and in chapter 13.

United States Government Manual. (1935–). Washington, DC: GPO. Annual.

Documents agencies and their history, legal authority, internal organization, and place in the structure of government. For many years entitled the *United States Government Organization Manual.*

Whitnah, Donald R. (Ed.). (1983). *Greenwood Encyclopedia of American Institutions: Government Agencies*. Westport, CT: Greenwood. 683 p.

Detailed discussions of over 100 agencies, past and present. Essays document their problems, tasks, successes and failures, and organizational development. Critical bibliographies are included.

Periodicals associated with a particular trade, industry, or other specialization frequently collect and disseminate statistical data of interest to their readers. The directory by Uhlan, cited below, identifies special issues of a large number (almost 1,400) of periodicals of this kind published in the United States and Canada. A substantial proportion of these special issues include data of a statistical nature. It must be said that most of the journals listed and described by Uhlan are of greatest interest to the private sector. Nonetheless, a number of sources relating to public-sector activities are included.

Uhlan, Miriam (Ed.). (1985). *Guide to Special Issues and Indexes of Periodicals* (3rd ed.). New York: Special Libraries Association. 160 p.

2.7. Election Statistics, Surveys, and Opinion Polls

Election statistics, survey results, and opinion polls have been the meat of much social and political research for several generations, and the protocols of their uses are now well established. Guides to their methodologies are discussed in chapter 14. Consideration is limited here to sources of the raw data themselves.

2.7.1. Elections

American voting statistics from presidential, other national, and gubernatorial elections are generally well documented. The principal sources relating to them are cited below. Many of these statistics have been extensively analyzed by political scientists and are now available in some machine-readable form for secondary analysis (see chapter 12).

America Votes: A Handbook of Contemporary American Election Statistics. (1956–). Washington, DC: Congressional Quarterly. Biennial.

Documents national and gubernatorial elections held since 1948. The best single source of recent national voting patterns. Data presented by state and county.

Burnham, W. Dean. (1955). *Presidential Ballots, 1836–1892.* Baltimore: Johns Hopkins Press. 956 p.

Figures are detailed at the county level. With works by Petersen, Robinson, Runyon, and Scammon (cited below), the major source of historical presidential election statistics.

Congressional Quarterly's Guide to U.S. Elections (2nd ed.). (1985). Washington, DC. 1,308 p.

Sections cover political parties, presidential, congressional, and gubernatorial elections, primaries, and popular vote. Updated by several serial publications, the most current of which is the *Congressional Quarterly Weekly Report.* Based on an archive accessible through the ICPSR (see chapter 12) that includes data back to 1824.

Crewe, Ivor, Day, Neil, & Fox, Anthony. (1991). *The British Electorate, 1963–1987: A Compendium of Data from the British Election Studies.* Cambridge, UK: Cambridge University Press. 500 p.

Notable for its inclusion of a variety of social and demographic data suitable for comparison with patterns of election returns. Also cites and summarizes a wealth of data from opinion polls.

Glashan, Roy R. (Comp.). (1979). *American Governors and Gubernatorial Elections, 1775–1978.* Westport, CT: Meckler. 370 p.
Election results by state, with some other data on candidates.

Gorvin, Ian (Ed.). (1989). *Elections since 1945: A Worldwide Reference Compendium.* Chicago: St. James Press. 420 p.
A statistical abstract in that it gives some documentation of the sources of the data summarized.

Mackie, Thomas T., & Rose, Richard. (1991). *The International Almanac of Electoral History* (3rd ed.). Washington, DC: Congressional Quarterly. 511 p.
Provides current and historical statistics for national elections held in about 25 advanced industrial democracies. Sources of data are provided. The latest edition of a standard source. Similar to Gorvin (above), but provides a greater range of historical data.

Maisel, L. Sandy, & Bassett, Charles (Eds.). (1991). *Political Parties and Elections in the United States: An Encyclopedia.* New York: Garland. 2 vols.
Discussions are largely historical and analytical, but sources of electoral and other statistics are noted in context.

Miller, Warren E., and Traugott, Santa A. (1989). *American National Election Studies Data Sourcebook, 1952–1986.* Cambridge, MA: Harvard University Press. 374 p.
The latest edition of a work that summarizes the results of an extensive series of polls related to election issues and broken down by occupation, political affiliation, and other characteristics of respondents. Original data are available in machine-readable form through the ICPSR (see chapter 12).

Petersen, Svend. (1981). *A Statistical History of the American Presidential Elections, with Supplementary Tables Covering 1968–1980.* Westport, CT: Greenwood. 250 p.
Tables go back to 1789 and provide data on the state level only.

Robinson, Edgar E. (1934). *The Presidential Vote, 1896-1932.* Stanford, CA: Stanford University Press. 403 p.

Robinson, Edgar E. (1947). *They Voted for Roosevelt: The Presidential Vote, 1932–1944.* Stanford, CA: Stanford University Press. 207 p.

Runyon, John H., Verdini, Jennefer, & Runyon, Sally S. (Comps.). (1971). *Sourcebook of American Presidential and Election Statistics, 1948–1968.* New York: Ungar. 380 p.

Distinguished by its inclusion of a variety of relevant data, such as campaign costs and opinion polls.

Scammon, Richard M. (Comp.). (1965). *America at the Polls: A Handbook of American Presidential Election Statistics, 1920–1964.* Pittsburgh, PA: University of Pittsburgh Press. 521 p.

Scammon, Richard M., & McGillivray, Alice V. (Eds.). (1988). *America at the Polls 2: A Handbook of American Presidential Election Statistics, 1968–1984.* Washington, DC: Congressional Quarterly. 594 p.

Schlesinger, Arthur M. (Ed.). (1971). *History of American Presidential Elections, 1789–1968.* New York: Chelsea House. 4 vols. Supplementary volume (1986) covers 1972–1984.

Includes some statistics, but mainly provides context and background necessary for the analysis of election data, including debates and campaign and election speeches.

Stanley, Harold W., & Niemi, Richard G. (1992). *Vital Statistics on American Politics* (3rd ed.). Washington, DC: CQ Press. 465 p.

A compendium of current and historical statistics drawn from published sources. Most useful for its inclusion of privately-generated data and for an extensive concluding chapter discussing the sources of electoral statistics.

Voting statistics for state and local elections, particularly elections held before World War II, are much less accessible. They must be tracked down through a number of sources, including state statistical yearbooks and blue books, newspapers, and local agencies and archives. The work by Maurer is of some help in this regard, although its focus is elections and political behavior at the national level. The other two sources listed are bibliographies, each of which includes sections citing secondary sources that have used such records.

The American Electorate: A Historical Bibliography. (1983). Santa Barbara, CA: ABC-Clio. 388 p.

Includes relevant citations and articles taken from the abstracting service *America: History and Life* between 1973 and 1982.

Freidel, Frank B. (Ed.). (1974). *Harvard Guide to American History* (rev. ed.). Cambridge, MA: Belknap Press. 2 vols.

Sections or chapters include those entitled "Suffrage and Voting Behavior," "Urban History," and "Regional, State, and Local Histories." Works in these address both primary and secondary sources.

Maurer, David J. (1978). *U.S. Politics and Elections: A Guide to Information Sources*. Detroit: Gale. 213 p.

2.7.2. Surveys and Opinion Polls

The existence and content of many surveys and opinion polls are identified by sources noted earlier. Many have been preserved in their original machine-readable format and are covered by the works noted in the following chapter. Works listed here are, first, those that provide either information about the existence of surveys and polls or techniques for their use, and second, those that present the findings of such surveys, whether or not these are available in some more extensive format. The reader is also reminded that a number of periodical indexes and other sources of current bibliography, whether these are in printed or computerized form, are also valuable in identifying collections of survey data and instances of their analysis (see chapters 8 and 9). Sources listed here should be considered as supplementing those cited at various points in chapter 12.

Almasy, Elina, Anne Balandier, and Jeanine Delatte. (1976). *Comparative Survey Analysis: An Annotated Bibliography, 1967–1973*. Beverly Hills, CA: Sage. 93 p.

Emphasizes cross-national surveys.

American Public Opinion Index. (1981–). Boston, MA: Opinion Research Service. Annual.

Each volume indexes and describes a hundred or so polls taken in North America. Indexed by subject. The value of this source is greatly enhanced by the existence of a microfiche set, *American Public Opinion Data*, which includes most or all of the polls indexed.

Cantril, Hadley. *Public Opinion, 1935–1946*. (1951). Princeton, NJ: Princeton University Press. 1,191 p.

Indexes more than 12,000 polls conducted throughout the world. Indicates the source for each and provides a summary of the results.

Caplow, Theodore, Bahr, Howard M., Modell, John, & Chadwick, Bruce A. (1991). *Recent Social Trends in the United States, 1960-1990.* Frankfurt am Main: Campus Verlag. 590 p.
Summarizes trends in such a way as to allow for cross-national comparisons; (future volumes are planned for France, Germany, Quebec, and Spain). Based on both official and private data. A guide to sources as well as trends.

Converse, Philip E., Dotson, Jean D., Hoag, Wendy J., & McGee, William H. (1980). *American Social Attitudes Data Sourcebook, 1947–1978.* Cambridge, MA: Harvard University Press. 441 p.
Summarizes data collected by the Survey Research Center of the University of Michigan. Best used as a guide to the machine-readable archives of this center, rather than as a source of data in itself.

Dodd, Sue A. (1984). Characteristics and Sources of Public Opinion Polls in the United States. In Ching-Chih Chen & Peter Hernon (Eds.)., *Numeric Databases* (pp. 105–24). Norwood, NJ: Ablex.
Of major interest for its detailed list of major polling organizations and their major products.

Eaton, Allen. (1930). *A Bibliography of Social Surveys: Reports of Fact-finding Studies Made as a Basis for Social Action.* New York: Russell Sage Foundation. 467 p.

Gallup, George H. (1971). *The Gallup Poll: Public Opinion, 1935–1971.* New York: Random House. 3 vols.
Gives descriptions and findings of Gallup polls published in the United States. Updated by a 1978 supplement covering 1972–1977, by an annual with the same title published since 1978, and by the *Gallup Poll Monthly*, published as the *Gallup Report* or with other variant titles, since 1965.

Gallup, George H. (1976). *The Gallup International Public Opinion Polls: France, 1939, 1944–1975.* New York: Random House. 1,257 p.
A parallel work, with a variant subtitle, covers Britain from 1937 to 1975.

The Harris Survey Yearbook of Public Opinion: A Compendium of Current American Attitudes. (1970–76). New York: Louis Harris & Associates. 4 vols.
Extensive descriptions of polls conducted by this organization. Updated by the two-volume *ABC News–Harris Survey*, published in 1980, and by the semi-weekly *Harris Survey*, published since 1981.

Index to International Public Opinion. (1978/79–). Westport, CT: Greenwood. Annual.

Provides detailed descriptions of polls taken in over 150 countries. Selective in reporting only data from "polling organizations which, in the judgement of the editors, are engaged in research of the highest scientific quality." In many cases data are available in computerized sets, in SPSS format, and with codebooks available from the publishers.

Lasswell, Harold D., Casey, Ralph D., & Smith, Bruce L. (1935). *Propaganda and Promotional Activities: An Annotated Bibliography.* Minneapolis: University of Minnesota Press. 450 p.

The classic bibliography in this area. Updated to some extent by Smith, Lasswell, and Casey. (see below).

Noelle, Elisabeth, & Neumann, Erich P. (Eds.). (1981). *The Germans: Public Opinion Polls, 1947–1966.* Westport, CT: Greenwood. 630 p.

Originally published in German in 1967. Presents the findings of a large number of polls published in West Germany. Supplemented by a volume covering the years 1967–1980.

Opinions: Extracts from Public Opinion Surveys and Polls. (1990–). Detroit: Gale. Three issues a year, with annual cumulation.

Excerpts, on a very selective basis, the results of polls reported in a large number of newspapers and magazines published in the United States. Useful in indexing polls not otherwise easily identified, but the objectives of many are trivial and unsuitable for social analysis.

Public Opinion Quarterly. (1937–). New York: Columbia University Press.

Regularly includes reviews of polling activities throughout the world. Indexed by a number of sources, including the PAIS *Bulletin* (see chapter 8). The retrospective *Public Opinion Quarterly Index* (1984) provides access to the contents of the *Quarterly* for the years 1937 through 1982.

Roper Reports. (1981–). New York: Roper Organization. Ten issues a year.

Indexes and describes the activities of one of the major polling organizations in the country.

Smith, Bruce L., Lasswell, Harold D., & Casey, Ralph D. (1946). *Propaganda, Communication, and Public Opinion: A Comprehensive Reference Guide.* Princeton, NJ: Princeton University Press. 435 p.

Primarily a bibliography of books and articles in the field, but includes a number of classic discussions of early approaches to the field.

Smith, Bruce L., & Smith, Chitra M. (1956). *International Communication and Political Opinion: A Guide to the Literature.* Princeton, NJ: Princeton University Press. 325 p.

An update of Smith, Lasswell, and Casey. Despite its title, maintains the focus on propaganda as a means of influencing foreign opinion.

Walden, Graham R. (1988). Public Opinion Polls: A Guide to Accessing the Literature. *RSR: Reference Services Review, 16*, 65–74.

Essentially a guide to locating published data resulting mainly from recent polling organizations but also from some historical ones. Publications of all major organizations are discussed and identified. Also includes a bibliography of works dealing with the critical use of such data.

Walden, Graham R. (1990). *Public Opinion Polls and Survey Research: A Selective Annotated Bibliography of U.S. Guides and Studies from the 1980s.* New York: Garland. 306 p.

Best used as a reliable and up-to-date guide to works dealing with methods and approaches, but also covers data sources themselves.

Published statistics now represent only a fraction of the quantitative data now fairly easily available. Statistical data maintained in some computerized form are discussed in the chapter that follows.

NOTES

1. Allan Kornblum, for example, studied police deviance from this perspective and concluded that much of such behavior stemmed from individual officers' inability to meet the unrealistic demands of a punitive organizational structure: (1976). *The Moral Hazards; Police Strategies for Honesty and Ethical Behavior.* Lexington, MA: Lexington Books.

2. Such as that presented by James O'Connor: (1973). *The Fiscal Crisis of the State.* New York: St. Martin's.

3. This would prbably be the case for a term paper or master's thesis.

4. Reanalysis can, however, be done to great effect. I am familiar with one person who wrote a very good dissertation reanalyzing the data included in some traditional works in sociology using more sophisticated quantitative methods. His findings were rather different from those presented in the original studies. His contribution to the field was methodological, not theoretical, in nature, but was none the worse for that.

5. These may be identified through Vladimir M. Palic. (1975). *Government Organization Manuals: A Bibliography.* Washington, DC: U.S. Library of Congress.; and Richard I. Korman. (1982). *Checklist of Government Directories, Lists, and Rosters.* Westport, CT: Meckler; and Westfall (cited in section 2.5).

12

MACHINE-READABLE DATA FILES

Data collection of any kind is an arduous and time-consuming business. This is especially the case when primary data are sought. This activity is, moreover, only a prelude to the process of analysis, which, if it is statistical, today usually involves the application of techniques and use of packaged statistical programs that are quite sophisticated. It is generally recognized that for those with limited research time at their disposal, excessive effort spent on data collection results in correspondingly limited time for data analysis. Appreciation of this reality has been encouraged by developments in technology and the associated availability of data sets in machine-readable form (MRDFs) and packaged programs necessary to analyze them. It has also been encouraged by trends within the various fields of social and public policy research that have, rightly or wrongly, come to encourage large-scale statistical analysis and to reward those who acquire the skills to undertake it.

This is not to deny that data collection can constitute a major part of the research process. Those of us who delve into dusty, noncomputerized archives of organizations that flourished in other centuries believe that our activities are necessary and important, even though the data sets we create are not always amenable to processing in the maw of the computer. What is important is that the researcher determine (1) if collection of original data is absolutely necessary to the investigation planned, and (2) if better results might not be achieved by using a data set that is already in existence.

It is important in this determination that the needs of the project be given pride of place, and not the methodological interests or phobias of the researcher. Someone interested, for example, in fear of crime among citizens as a function of police effectiveness could certainly proceed by constructing an original measure of the dependent variable, at least. A questionnaire designed to assess feelings of vulnerability could be constructed and administered to scientifically selected samples of appropriate populations. The results could then be coded and analyzed against measures of effectiveness (arrest, clearance, and victimization rates) drawn from police and other official sources. Such an approach would conceivably be quite respectable and could result in profitable findings. It might not, however, be cost-effective. Survey research can be very time-consuming, and if the project is a one-person operation, the data yielded are often limited in scope and value. There is certainly nothing *wrong* with undertaking research of this kind. However, researchers should determine first if this collection of original data is absolutely *necessary*.

In the example given in the preceding paragraph, those using the sources cited in this chapter will quickly determine the existence and availability of relevant data sets that have already been collected, coded, and translated into computerized form. In many cases they are accompanied by codebooks and computer programs, standardized or otherwise, created to facilitate their use. One such data set is the machine-readable version of the *Uniform Crime Reports*, which allows data on law-enforcement agencies to be analyzed according to size, geographic area, and other variables. Others represent computerized versions of a variety of crime surveys, including those addressing fear of crime, victimization, and other measures of public opinion on crime-related issues. It is often possible to combine data sets, provided their electronic forms and the populations represented are compatible. In this way new data sets can be created and analyzed in new ways. It is very likely that someone working on the topic mentioned above will, with a little effort, find relevant primary data that have already been collected and coded and that are otherwise suitable for analysis. Attention can therefore be focused on the difficult, but ultimately more rewarding process of analysis, rather than on the lengthy and often-stultifying process of data collection.

This is not to suggest that use of MRDFs is an easy or a casual process. Potential users must first identify data sets relevant to the topic of interest and to its broader theoretical perspective. They must then access the data to determine whether they are amenable to the kind of reanalysis planned, with or without being combined with other data sets. Access is not usually a problem. Academic institutions usually maintain a data archive center, based in the library or the computer center, with the primary function of obtaining particular MRDFs and their supporting codebooks or other documentation needed by potential users.

Using individual data sets may be problematic because some can only be manipulated using software especially designed for them. Others come with inadequate coding information or with other deficiencies. However, these obstacles should not be overemphasized. An ever larger number of publicly accessible MRDFs are being generated, suggesting a greater variety of subject content and an accordingly greater potential value to creative researchers. Those generated are prepared increasingly for analysis with SPSS, SAS, or other standardized statistical packages used by social and policy researchers. This makes it easier to combine two or more data sets. It also provides the side benefit of requiring the user to develop the valuable and marketable skill of being able to apply at least one of these statistical packages in a sophisticated way. Most data files include far more data than could ever be collected by a single individual working without external support. This fact negates many of the difficulties encountered by dissertation students who try to extract meaning from findings based on small numbers. Furthermore, these data files are increasingly PC-compatible.[1] This is especially attractive since it makes the physical research setting as close as one's own home or office.

There will always be situations in which MRDFs relevant to the project at hand cannot be found. In such a case, redefinition of the entire enterprise is the only alternative to engaging in the process of data collection in any of its many forms. It is important that the researcher's choices in this regard be informed ones. All decisions about research should ideally be based on hard knowledge about what information is available and what can be done with it. Whatever the decision about the level of effort to be put into data collection, it must be based on an awareness of alternatives. Knowledge of what computerized data sets are available and how they have been used can provide researchers with new insights and methods as well as information about alternative data resources.

1. SOURCES OF MRDFs

The traditional and still-popular way to identify interesting collections of MRDFs is through personal contacts with mentors and colleagues. Most graduate students and faculty who follow this data route have learned to do so through mentors who have taught them to explore the characteristics of individual files in great detail and through the use of a particular statistical package. As long as it works, there is nothing wrong with this approach; no researcher will ever argue against success, regardless of how it is achieved.

However, this informal way of selecting a data set is less than satisfactory. In the first place, most researchers tend to stick with what they know and what serves them well. They have little interest in becoming experts on the availability of data. Second, the world of computerized data is now too large to allow thorough access by casual means. A tremendous volume of such data is currently being generated by governmental agencies alone. A well-informed choice requires a systematic examination of the bibliographic sources that document them.

Finally, it should be understood that the selection of raw data for analysis is not usually a mechanical exercise. It would be nice to think that one figures out the objectives and theoretical implications of the project and then searches for the ideal data set or sets as a proving ground. The research activity rarely works in this way. The characteristics of the data determine the nature of the analysis that can be applied to them. Preliminary findings constantly modify the researcher's objectives and perspectives. In this sense, data selection is an integral part of the research process.[2] An awareness of just what data resources are available will inevitably color the form and nature of the analysis. The more heightened the awareness, the better, one would assume, is the choice of approach as well as of data.

By the same token, a knowledge of how other researchers have used the data sets under consideration cannot help but be informative about the potential, as well as the characteristics, of the data. Some of the catalogs described below (that of the ICPSR, for example), provide annotations to the data sets they include that cite publications that have resulted from their use. As commitment to a data set as the lynchpin of a research enterprise is no small thing, anyone contemplating its use is well advised to get all the information possible regarding strengths and limitations. Reading studies emerging from its use by other scholars is an obvious and important way to do this.

Unfortunately, most guides and catalogs do not provide such annotations. However, there is one further way to obtain this information. A chapter in this book is devoted to searching the literature by computer (see chapter 9). Many of the bibliographic databases discussed there include abstracts of, as well as citations to, journal articles or other published forms. If a particular data set has provided the basis for the analysis presented, this set is likely to be mentioned by name in the abstract. Accordingly, a search for the data set by a phrase including this name in appropriate data bases is in order.

The databases searched in this way will, of course, depend on the nature of the data set and on the subject disciplines in which it is most likely to have been applied. (One would not, for example, search for uses of the *Uniform Crime Reports* in the database covering European history.) *Dissertation Abstracts*, which provides citations and lengthy abstracts for most dissertations accepted for doctoral degrees in North America, could also be very worthwhile. Another bibliographic database of tremendous potential in this regard is *Social SciSearch*. As noted in chapter 9, one can also search this database by a *cited reference*, that is, any item that has been cited in a footnote or bibliography of any article indexed in the database. Such references are not always to published materials. Scholars who have used a particular data set as the basis for their analyses will most certainly cite it in any published article. Other scholars can retrieve the article, and others like it, by conducting a cited-reference search for the data set.

Unfortunately, the cited-reference search is less than foolproof in this context. Rules of bibliographic citation are strict when applied to published materials; they can be vague when imposed upon primary sources. Primary data are often cited in many different ways, making retrieval of references to them usually problematic. There is a way around this dilemma that preserves the value of this application of the citation search. If you know at least one *secondary* work that refers to the primary collection in point, this work can be searched as a cited reference in the hope that others using the same data set have cited it. A series of citation searches of this kind will, if you are lucky, identify most or all other users of the data. A commitment to a particular data set is a serious matter. It can take quite a while to learn the data set's potential. If it is computerized, knowledge of its structure and the statistical packages needed to manipulate it can involve a commitment of some considerable effort. Legwork expended on the identification and examination of its previous uses is effort well spent.

The bibliographic sources of primary data described in this chapter include only those data sets that are known to be publicly available. Those produced by governmental agencies may not reflect the full detail of the data originally collected. The Bureau of the Census, for example, which maintains data archives containing information relating to *individuals*, will only release recent population data files after they have been programmed to suppress demands for information in units smaller than the city block. Requests for information regarding population characteristics (family size, income, age, race, and so on) will be given for city blocks within a given area, but the characteristics of households within these blocks will not be released.

A further important characteristic of "class 1" data sets is that the codebooks for them are published and are acquired as a matter of routine by institutions subscribing to the ICPSR network. Library holdings of codebooks of this kind can provide considerable sustenance for the numerate student anxious to determine just what MRDFs are available and how easily they can be used to address specific research questions. Every summer the consortium offers a series of workshops in Ann Arbor, each lasting between one and four weeks, on different aspects of quantitative analysis using ICPSR data.[3] Stipends funded by the federal government are often available to participants. These workshops are intensive and demanding and provide a first-rate preparation for informed beginners in this area.

The National Opinion Research Center (NORC), associated with the University of Chicago, is slightly different; it is not a clearinghouse for data from other sources, but actually generates data files from its own surveys. These go back to 1941 and represent what is probably the largest single body of data in the world dealing with public opinion. As the surveys were produced by the same source, they exhibit a level of standardization that makes comparative analysis relatively easy. Like the ICPSR, NORC publicizes its holdings and research efforts through the regular publication of catalogs and bibliographies.

Organizations of this kind are, above all, user-oriented. This is also reflected in the ease with which data files can be obtained from them. Costs of acquiring them are modest and, together with costs of computer time required in their analysis, are almost always borne by the college or university with which the researcher is affiliated.

The bibliographic sources noted in this chapter are the principal ones covering organizations that are in some way active in encouraging the use of their holdings by social scientists. Other data files and collections are noted in some of the works listed in directories covering computerized databases of a primarily bibliographic nature (chapter 9). Data sets, which can either be in computerized or printed forms (for example, opinion polls), are discussed in chapter 11.

There is an almost infinite variety of data files maintained by public agencies and private organizations, and many are of great potential interest to the researcher. Few are listed in any standard bibliographic source. Access can be limited by legal restrictions, organizational policy, and, above all, by the unwillingness of bureaucracies to expose themselves to outside scrutiny. Researchers who are fortunate enough to gain access to such data usually do so through contacts of a personal or institutional nature.

Resources of this kind can be a tremendous boon to the scholar, if only because most represent data never before tapped for purposes of social or policy analysis. In using them, the researcher should be careful to understand them in their organizational context. It is also of great importance to determine beforehand whether the data can be assigned social or policy significance and whether they are in a form amenable to manipulation through quantitative analysis.

Literature providing access to this kind of primary material can be conveniently divided into three groups: works that describe how one sets about the secondary analysis of such data and only incidentally address particular data sources; bibliographies of studies based on specific groups of files; and directories of files and archives. Listings that follow are arranged within these categories. Directories are further grouped according to whether their archival focus is governmental or not.

2. GUIDES TO SECONDARY ANALYSIS

Most handbooks on survey research and related fields pay some attention to secondary analysis. The guides listed below include only those that specifically address the use and/or location of computerized data sets for this purpose.

Bowering, David J. (Ed.). (1984). *Secondary Analysis of Available Data Bases.* San Francisco: Jossey-Bass. 115 p.

A short collection of essays that primarily address the needs of those undertaking evaluation research. Includes one chapter discussing identification and location of sources.

Dale, Angela, Arber, Sara, & Procter, Michael. (1988). *Doing Secondary Analysis.* London: Allen & Unwin. 241 p.

Outstanding for its discussions of the selection and use of particular data files. Particularly good for its account of the data files of the Economic and Social Research Council, the principal British data archive. Not as good in its coverage of North American sources.

Hakim, Catherine. (1982). *Secondary Analysis in Social Research: A Guide to Data Sources and Methods with Examples.* London: Allen & Unwin. 202 p.

Excellent for its illustrative examples. Its sections on sources are valuable, but only to those concerned with British sources.

Hyman, Herbert H. (1972). *Secondary Analysis of Sample Surveys.* New York: Wiley. 353 p.

Excellent for its detailed examples. Now quite old, and the narrative does not reflect the electronic and other advances of recent years.

Kiecolt, K. Jill, & Nathan, Laura. (1985). *Secondary Analysis of Survey Data.* Beverly Hills, CA: Sage. 88 p.

Clear and concise, although its brevity is at the cost of providing illustrative examples. Like Hyman (above), includes a modest discussion of the principles of data-file selection and a very selective list of the major data archives.

Stewart, David W. (1984). *Secondary Research: Information Sources and Methods.* Beverly Hills, CA: Sage. 135 p.

The most valuable work of its kind. Discusses, with practical examples, the location and selection of raw data as part of the process of research design. Selection of the data sources discussed seems to be idiosyncratic; there is an entire chapter on census data, but very little on opinion polls.

3. GUIDES TO RELATED METHODS

In addition to guides of the kind noted in section 2 and directly concerned with secondary analysis of MRDFs, there are many others that address related aspects of data analysis. These are generally addressed in chapter 14.

4. BIBLIOGRAPHIES OF SECONDARY STUDIES

Bibliographies of this kind are frequently issued by the larger data archives. They usually include citations to published works based on analysis of their data files, and details of the publications, products, and services of the archive. Most archives include bibliographic information in their directories of data holdings (see sections 5 and 6). The National Opinion Research Center is an exception, and its bibliographies are cited below. This section should be consulted in conjunction with chapter 11, which addresses statistics published in conventional form.

Allswang, John M., & Bova, Patrick (Eds.). (1964). *NORC Social Research, 1941–1964: An Inventory of Studies and Publications in Social Research.* Chicago: National Opinion Research Center. 80 p.

Includes annotations. Updated by a supplement covering the years 1961 through 1982 (one for 1983 through 1987 is in preparation), by Smith and Ward, and by the *NORC Report* (below).

Bloomfield, Valerie. (1976). *Commonwealth Elections, 1945–1970: A Bibliography*. London: Mansell. 306 p.

Covers governmental and other primary sources as well as secondary studies. One of a number of bibliographies reflecting the interest of social scientists in the social progress of former colonies.

Communication Abstracts. (1978–). Newbury Park, CA: Sage. Bimonthly.

Interprets its subject matter broadly to include mass communication, public opinion, and political attitudes. Abstracts books and articles.

Frey, Frederick W., Stephenson, Peter, & Smith, Katherine A. (Eds.) (1969). *Survey Research on Comparative Social Change: A Bibliography*. Cambridge, MA: MIT Press. 77 p.

One of a number of bibliographies published during the 1960s that documented change in then newly independent nations.

Gitter, A. George, & Grunin, Robert. (1980). *Communication: A Guide to Information Sources*. Detroit: Gale. 157 p.

An annotated bibliography on this broad field. Extensive listings for matters concerning social attitudes and the communication process.

Gordon, Thomas F., & Verna, Mary E. (1973). *Mass Media and Socialization: A Selected Bibliography*. Philadelphia: Temple University. 47 p.

Entries, without annotations, of articles, dissertations, and other materials concerned with media influences on social values and beliefs. Updated and extended by Gordon and Verna 1978.

Gordon, Thomas F., & Verna, Mary E. (1978). *Mass Communication Effects and Processes: A Comprehensive Bibliography, 1950–1975*. Beverly Hills, CA: Sage. 229 p.

Hansen, Donald A., & Parsons, J. Herschel (Comps.). (1968). *Mass Communication: A Research Bibliography*. Santa Barbara, CA: Glendessary Press. 144 p.

A major bibliography updated by supplements appearing regularly in *Journalism Quarterly*.

Mowlana, Hamid. (1971). *International Communications*. Dubuque, IA: Kendall/Hunt. 130 p.

Extensive, but with no annotations. Emphasizes studies outside of the United States.

NORC Report. (1987–). Chicago. Biennial.

Reviews NORC activities over the previous two years, including new data sets generated, and secondary publications by NORC researchers or based on NORC data.

Shearer, Benjamin F., & Huxford, Marilyn (Comps.). (1983). *Communications and Society: A Bibliography on Communications Technologies and Their Social Impact*. Westport, CT: Greenwood. 242 p.

The best recent bibliography of its kind. Covers dissertations as well as articles and other forms. No annotations.

Smith, Tom W., & Arnold, Bradley J. (1990). *Annotated Bibliography of Papers Using the General Social Surveys* (8th ed.). Chicago: National Opinion Research Center. 697 p.

Documents the largest of the data sets maintained by NORC. This is the General Social Survey, a massive attitudinal survey conducted each year since 1972. Revised regularly. An example of the special subject bibliographies issued periodically by this organization. (See also Niemi, Mueller, and Smith in section 6).

Universal Reference System. (1969). *Public Opinion, Mass Behavior, and Political Psychology*. Princeton, NJ: Princeton Research Publishing. Annual.

A very extensive bibliography. Organized within a somewhat cumbersome subject classification that is not easy to use. Well worth persevering with.

Updated by an annual supplement, and more lately by *Political Science Abstracts*.

5. DIRECTORIES OF GOVERNMENTAL DATA ARCHIVES

Publicly accessible data files held by public agencies are usually cited in their publication catalogs and in directories covering statistical sources in printed form. For this reason, the sources noted below should be supplemented by publications such as the Bureau of the Census *Catalog and Guide* and by other works discussed elsewhere in this chapter.

There is no single directory that lists all data files available even within the federal government. All the guides cited below overlap with one another to some extent and should be used in conjunction with each other. Many directories listed in the following section include data from both public and private sources. In many cases these are preferable as sources of governmental data, as they list files that have been combined to increase their richness or otherwise modified for greater ease of use.

Electronic bulletin boards (section 9 of chapter 15) are becoming increasingly important as sources for locating archival materials of all types. Collections so located often have the great advantage of being instantly and electronically accessible.

APDU Newsletter. (1976–). Princeton, NJ: Association of Public Data Users. Monthly.

Reviews newly available public data sets and related services. Also addresses a variety of issues bearing upon the accessibility and use of data generated by public agencies.

Carroll, Stephen J. (1980). *City Data: A Catalog of Data Sources for Small Cities.* Santa Monica, CA: Rand. 354 p.

A collection listing almost 300 data sets (a high proportion of which are machine-readable) documenting "quality-of-life" indicators for municipalities. Most, but not all, of the sources cited are produced by governmental agencies. Only includes series published or updated on a regular basis.

Chen, Ching-Chih, & Hernon, Peter (Eds.). (1984). *Numeric Databases.* Norwood, NJ: Ablex. 332 p.

Most of the 16 essays address the concerns of those in the pure and applied sciences. A few, however, are of direct relevance to social and policy disciplines and are cited individually at various points in this chapter. The general bibliography is most useful for its citations of guides to secondary analysis and directories of sources.

Declassified Documents Catalog. (1975–). Woodbridge, CT: Research Publications. Bimonthly, with annual subject index.

Tracks federal materials (including data sets) as these become publicly accessible.

Dukakis, Arthur G., & Cohen, Judith W. (1984). Data Available from the U. S. Bureau of the Census. In Ching-Chih Chen & Peter Hernon (Eds.), *Numeric Databases* (pp. 125–52). Norwood, NJ: Ablex.

Documents the changing structure and content of major Bureau of the Census files. Related discussion of points of access is important as very current developments are not addressed.

Evinger, William R. (Ed.). (1988). *Federal Statistical Data Bases: A Comprehensive Catalog of Current Machine-Readable and Online Files.* Phoenix, AZ: Oryx. 670 p.

Like Lesko (1990 below), includes some bibliographic databases, but is primarily devoted to identifying and describing MRDFs. If it is revised regularly, this will be a major work in this area.

Heim, Kathleen M. (1984). Government-Produced Statistical Data for Social Science Inquiry: Scope, Problems, and Strategies for Access. In Ching-Chih Chen & Peter Hernon (Eds.), *Numeric Databases* (pp. 105–24). Norwood, NJ: Ablex.

Discusses patterns of data collection and dissemination, including the decline of some efforts in this area. Notes access sources provided by individual agencies.

Lesko, Matthew. (1990). *The Federal Data Base Finder: A Directory of Free and Fee-based Data Bases and Files Available from the Federal Government* (3rd ed.). Kensington, MD: Information USA. 571 p.

Arranged by agency with a detailed subject index. Descriptions are thorough and include the names and telephone numbers of contact persons. Updated by a monthly, *Data Informer.*

Lesko, Matthew. (1989). *State Data and Database Finder.* Chevy Chase, MD: Information USA. 536 p.

The only source of its kind and a guide to data files that are otherwise extremely difficult to identify. Also updated by *Data Informer.*

United Nations. Advisory Committee for the Coordination of Information Services. (1984–). *Directory of United Nations Databases and Information Services.* New York. Irregular.

Covers sources in a wide variety of formats, some computerized, some not. All sources listed appear to be generally accessible. The last edition was published in 1990. Early editions were entitled *Directory of United Nations Information Systems.*

U.S. Bureau of the Census. (1979). *Directory of Data Files.* Washington, DC: GPO. 119 p.

The directory of perhaps the most prolific generator of data sets in the federal government. Updated by the bureau's annual *Census Catalog and Guide* and its *Monthly Product Announcements.*

U.S. National Archive of Computerized Data on Aging. (1987–). *Data Collections from the National Archive of Computerized Data on Aging.* Ann Arbor, MI: ICPSR. Biennial.

U.S. National Archives and Records Service. (1977). *Catalog of Machine-Readable Records in the National Archives of the United States.* Washington, DC. 37 p.

A limited listing of MRDFs generated throughout the federal government. Update using Lesko (1990) and Evinger (see above).

U.S. National Center for Health Statistics. (1988). *Catalog of Public Use Data Tapes from the National Center for Health Statistics.* Hyattsville, MD. 69 p.

U.S. National Institute of Justice. (1992). *Data Resources of the National Institute of Justice* (5th ed.). Washington, DC. 228 p.

Describes all available data sets resulting from NIJ-sponsored research. Most are available, with supporting documentation, through the Inter-University Consortium for Political and Social Research (see section 6).

U.S. National Technical Information Service. (1982–). *A Directory of Computerized Data Files: A Guide to U.S. Government Information in Machine-Readable Form.* Springfield, VA. Biennial.

Includes data generated by private contractors under federal funding, as well as those produced by federal agencies. The current (1991) edition documents over 2,500 files originating in over 100 agencies.

U.S. Office of Educational Research and Improvement. (1987–). *OERI Directory of Computer Tapes.* Washington, DC. Annual.

U.S. Office of Federal Statistical Policy and Standards. (1981–). *Directory of Federal Statistical Data Files.* Washington, DC. Annual.

Should be used with Evinger (1988) and Lasko (1990) (above); the three works are the most comprehensive directories in this area.

6. DIRECTORIES OF NONGOVERNMENTAL ARCHIVES

American Enterprise. (1978–). Washington, DC: American Enterprise Institute. Bimonthly.

Each issue includes a listing of recent polls. This is selective and the product of a strongly conservative think tank and research organization. Formed from the merger of three journals: *Public Opinion, Regulation,* and *AEI Economist.*

American Public Opinion Index. (1983–). Louisville, KY: Opinion Research Service. Annual.

Identifies major opinion polls in both archival and published form. The major source of its kind.

Current Opinion. (1973–). Williamstown, MA: Roper Center. Monthly.

Reports recent activities of more than 100 polling organizations. "A digest of the public's views on contemporary issues."

Directory of Online Databases. (1979–). New York: Cuadra/Elsevier. Semiannual.

Includes only those databases that are "electronically published," that is, accessible to subscribers to major computer networks. International in coverage. Most sources listed are bibliographic, but numeric databases are also included.

ESRC Data Archive Catalogue. (1986). Cambridge, UK: Chadwyck-Healey. 2 vols.

Describes the holdings of Britain's principal data archive, the Economic and Social Research Council, which includes both private and governmental data files. Updated by the *Data Archive Bulletin,* published three times a year since 1985.

Information Industry Directory (1971–). Detroit: Gale. 2 vols. Now annual in 2 vols.

"A comprehensive international descriptive guide to more than 4,500 organizations, systems, and services involved in the production and distribution of information in electronic form." A very worthwhile source that gives full descriptions of bodies generating data files (not of the files themselves) and thus helps identify promising sources. Earlier entitled *Encyclopedia of Information Systems and Services.*

Inter-University Consortium for Political and Social Research. *Guide to Resources and Services.* (1976–). Ann Arbor, MI. Annual.

The catalog of the most important clearinghouse for archival data in the United States. Full descriptions of data are accompanied by remarks on technical access and, when applicable, by citations to published analyses of the data. Updated by the quarterly *ICPSR Bulletin*, which describes recent acquisitions and also highlights new methods of approach. Now available in database form as ICPSR *Guide-on-Line.*

Inter-University Consortium for Political Social Research. (1979–). *Data Collections Available from the National Archive of Criminal Justice Data.* Ann Arbor, MI. Annual.

Documents the resources of the archive (formerly known as the Criminal Justice Archive and Information Network, CJAIN), a subsystem of the ICPSR.

Bibliographic Citations for All Released ICPSR Data Collections (3rd ed.). (1992). Ann Arbor: University of Michigan, Inter-University Consortium for Political and Social Research.

The latest edition of a CD-ROM database which includes citations documenting the use of data sets listed in the *ICPSR Bulletin.*

Marcaccio, Kathleen Y. (Ed.). (1990). *Computer-Readable Databases: A Directory and Data Sourcebook* (6th ed.). Detroit: Gale. 1,379 p.

Lists and describes almost 5,000 databases of all kinds: governmental and private, American and foreign, bibliographic and numeric.

Nasatir, David. (1973). *Data Archives for the Social Sciences: Purposes, Operations and Problems.* Paris: UNESCO. 126 p.

Includes a directory of archives. Although quite old, this is valuable for identifying the many collections that are now long-established.

Niemi, Richard G., Mueller, John, & Smith, Tom W. (1989). *Trends in Public Opinion: A Compendium of Survey Data.* Westport, CT: Greenwood. 344 p.

A compilation cf indicators of political behavior drawn from numerous sources, but chiefly the General Social Survey (GSS) conducted annually by the National Opinion Research Center since 1972. Provides a short but valuable "Additional Sources of Over-Time Survey Data." Included in this section because of its value as a digest and a guide to the availability of data in more detailed and manipulable form. (See also Wood, below.)

Davis, James A. (1992). *The NORC General Social Survey: A User's Guide.* Newbury Park, CA: Sage. 95 p.

An essential starting-point for anyone using, or contemplating the use of, the GSS.

Roper Center for Public Opinion Research. (1982). *A Guide to Roper Center Resources for the Study of American Race Relations.* Storrs, CT. 706 p.

Roper Reports. (1981–). New York: Roper Organization. Ten issues a year.

Documents data sets that reflect an annual attitudinal poll of about 2,000 American adults on a variety of social and political subjects.

Survey Research. (1969–). Urbana, IL: University of Illinois, Urbana. Survey Research Laboratory. Quarterly.

A newsletter reviewing the recent activities and products of the major centers of survey and public opinion research in the United States. Documents data collections and projects completed and in progress. Best for its coverage of nongovernmental bodies.

Wood, Floris W. (Ed.). (1990). *An American Profile: Opinions and Behavior, 1972–1989.* Detroit: Gale. 1,065 p.

Like Niemi, Mueller, and Smith (above), abstracts selected results from the GSS and is best used as a guide to the contents of this data set.

Young, Copeland H., Savola, Kristen L., & Phelps, Erin. (1991). *Inventory of Longitudinal Studies in the Social Sciences.* Newbury Park, CA: Sage. 567 p.

Cites and describes over 200 studies, a number of which are held in the archives of the Murray Research Center of Radcliffe College. Annotations indicate references to secondary works, sample characteristics, instrumentation, and constructs measured.

There are many avenues to the use of existing collections of primary data. These are discussed in some detail in chapter 16. Other approaches are suggested in the materials included in chapter 14.

7. STATISTICS IN READ-ONLY DATABASES

Although primarily bibliographic in nature, many database systems discussed in chapter 9 now include a number of files that are exclusively concerned with presenting statistics and other forms of primary data. This is a relatively new trend, but one that is likely to accelerate in the immediate future. At the present time these files are remarkable principally for their convenience and the timeliness of their contents. The data in them can for the most part only be read and cannot be manipulated online. This is, however, an area that has recently experienced tremendous change, and the possibility that most of these files will one day be susceptible to more sophisticated analysis is a strong one. Some have already made this transition.

Some of these files are discussed below. Others can be located using the directories cited in chapter 9 (this chapter also addresses their access). Annotations include the date the file was established (or the earliest date of its coverage), the frequency with which it is updated, and the approximate size of its holdings as of the beginning of 1991, when this is known. The examples given here exclude the many that exist exclusively to provide statistical data relating to companies, industries, and the financial and other markets.

Many databases that include primary data of one sort or another are becoming available on compact disk at a rapid rate. A discussion of this development, which includes consideration of its great importance, is also given in chapter 9.

Arthur D. Little/Online. (1977–). Burlington, MA: Arthur D. Little Decision Resources. Bimonthly. 2,000 records.

Includes a large number of published forecasts, market surveys, and opinion polls. Most address projected industrial demand and production. Some of the data are presented full-text; others are summarized.

CENDATA. (Current year). Washington, DC: U.S. Bureau of the Census. Updated daily. 52,000 records.

Mainly includes selected statistical series from the population censuses of 1980 and 1990 (as these become available) and those from over 200 foreign countries. The qualifier here is "selected," as this file cannot be relied upon to provide exhaustive coverage in any area. Also includes press releases and Census Bureau product information.

Centrally Planned Economies Databank. (1960–). Bala Cynwyd, PA: WEFA Group. Updated semiannually. 9,000 records.

Mainly time-series data documenting macroeconomic trends in Eastern Europe. Also includes short- (five-year) and long-term forecasts.

ClusterPLUS. (1980–). Stamford, CT: Donnelley Marketing Information Services. Updated annually.

Includes population census data from 1980 onward grouped according to "clusters," that is, households grouped within some 47 categories according to income, life-style, and other demographic criteria.

Consumer Price Index. (1913–). Washington, DC: U.S. Bureau of Labor Statistics. Updated monthly.

Includes constituent time series data for the CPI broken down by region, consumer group, a range of aggregates of goods and services.

Counties and Cities Plus. (1992–). Washington, DC: Slater Hall. Updated annually.

The CD equivalent of *County and City Extra* (chapter 11) and a database capable of some limited manipulation on disk. As noted in the previous chapter, other Bureau of the Census statistical directories are now available in this way.

Country Report Services. (Current year). Syracuse, NY: Political Risk Services. Updated monthly.

Includes basic economic and political data on 131 countries. Also includes 18-month and 5-year forecasts of political developments and "risk ratings" assessing probabilities of political and economic change and their likely effects.

CRindex (Cambridge Reports Consumer and Public Opinion Database). (1974–). Cambridge, MA: Cambridge Reports. Updated quarterly.

Includes the full texts and responses of a series of attitudinal surveys of 1,500 adults chosen as a sample of the U.S. population.

Cronos. (1955). Luxembourg: Commission of the European Communities. Statistical Office. 900,000 records.

Time series, some of which go back to 1955, address economic data for EC countries in the areas of national accounts and finance, industry and services, agriculture, forestry and fishing, and foreign trade.

Current Economic Indicators. (1989–). Paris: Organisation for Economic Cooperation and Development. Updated daily (for the U.S. and Canada) and weekly for other nations.

Includes time series data for selected economic indicators for Canada, France, Germany, Italy, Japan, the United Kingdom, and the United States.

D & B—Donnelley Demographics. (Current year). Stamford, CT: Donnelley Marketing Services. Replaced annually. 62,000 records.

Includes more detailed population census data than *ClusterPLUS* (above) broken down regionally. The next (1991) reload will include preliminary results of the 1990 census.

Dati Elettorali. (1976 and 1979). Rome: Camera dei Deputati. Servizio per la Documentázione Automatica.

Documents two of Italy's national elections and cited here as an example of one of a growing number of primary data files maintained outside of the English-speaking world.

DRI Asian Forecasts. (1970s–). Washington, DC: DRI/McGraw-Hill. Updated quarterly.

One of a series of files produced by this vendor and documenting economies in various parts of the world with time-series and historical data. Most series go back to the 1970s. Ten-year forecasts are included.

Econbase: Time Series and Forecasts. (1948–). Bala Cynwyd, PA: WEFA Group. Updated monthly. 12,000 records.

Includes extensive econometric time-series data that generally focus on income and business and industrial conditions in the US. Some data from other countries are included.

Hospital Admissions Records—Canada. (1982–). Ottawa: Health and Welfare Canada. Updated irregularly.

Includes medical and demographic data on about 70% of all admissions to Canadian hospitals in the last ten years. Cited here as an example of the range of data collected by public agencies now available in machine-readable form.

HOTLINE. (1988–). Falls Church, VA: American Political Network. Updated daily.

A full-text database providing information on U.S. national, state, and local election campaigns. Data on opinion polls and forecasts are included.

International Financial Statistics. (1948–). Washington, DC: International Monetary Fund. Updated monthly. 23,000 records.

Presents monthly, quarterly, and annual time series of economic and financial data on about 150 countries. Some series go back to 1948.

Long–Term Forecast Data Base. (Coverage varies). Bala Cynwyd, PA: WEFA Group. Updating varies by file.

Comprises two constituent files, one presenting baseline forecasts and the other extended forecasts. Each includes about 3,300 time series and forecasts for 20- or 25-five-year periods.

PTS International Forecasts. (1971–). Cleveland: Predicasts. Updated monthly. 900,000 records.

Abstracts forecasts from countries throughout the world, excluding the United States. Most are economic and are based on published information from official and nongovernmental sectors. Also includes historical data.

PTS U.S. Forecasts. (1971–). Cleveland: Predicasts. Updated monthly. 600,000 records.

Parallels the previous item in including only economic forecasts covering the United States.

PTS U.S. Time Series. (1965–). Cleveland: Predicasts. Updated quarterly. 31,000 records.

Records go back between 10 and 25 years and generally address economic issues.

Public Opinion Online (POLLS). (1960–). Storrs, CT: Roper Center for Public Opinion Research. Updated monthly.

A database that includes the full text of the results of more than 130,000 polls conducted by major polling organizations throughout the country and collected by the Roper Center.

Statistical MasterFile. (1980–). Washington, DC: Congressional Information Service. Updated quarterly.

An electronic compilation of three indexes discussed in chapter 11; (the *American Statistics Index*, the *Index to International Statistics*, and the *Statistical Reference Index*). Excellent for its coverage of U.S. federal and state sources. Less extensive in its coverage of statistics generated by the private sector and by international organizations.

U.N. Demographics. (1950–). New York: United Nations. Department of International Economic and Social Affairs. Updated annually.

Contains about 9,200 time series for over 150 countries. These extend from 1950 to 2025, in five-year intervals. Only demographic data are included.

U.S. ECON Plus. (1947–). New York: ADP Data Services. Updated daily.

About 25,000 time series address a range of economic data that are mainly financial. Most data go back to 1947.

U.S. Economic Statistics. (1901–). New York: Haver Analytics. Updating varies by series.

Almost 6,000 time series address the U.S. economy, in some cases back to 1901. Series emphasize economic activity other than the financial markets.

The Urban Underclass Database. (1960–). New York: Social Science Research Council. Updated with availability of new data.

A collection of existing data drawn primarily from federal government sources documenting 5,800 indicators for metropolitan areas between 1960 and 1990. Variables are drawn from 28 institutional sources and were selected as suitable key indicators over time of "changes in labor market opportunities, patterns of residential segregation, household composition, degree of poverty concentration, health status, crime, and homelessness."

It is a common misapprehension among graduate students in the areas addressed by this book that original research of consequence necessarily has a quantitative focus. This belief is perhaps most strongly impressed upon students by the fact that most social science methods courses undeniably have a statistical bent. However, it is a mistake to equate training with the range of practice. Statistical methods are emphasized in graduate programs because they are vital tools of one's trade. The world of research, on the other hand, comprehends a variety of means of approach, many of which do not involve the manipulation of raw numeric data and may not use quantitative approaches at all. Few would deny that these are of equal validity with quantitative research.[4] The competent researcher selects his or her data sources and the methods used to analyze them, whether these be quantitative or qualitative, according to the questions being asked, and not according to the researcher's particular methodological expertise.

Statistical data, published or machine-readable, are but one type of archival material. Other archival forms that are susceptible to various kinds of analysis, and that may or may not be attractive to the appetite of the calculator or computer, are considered in chapter 14.

NOTES

1. Even if the data files are not PC-compatible, their associated statistical packages now are and can be applied to data files located on mainframe systems and accessible elsewhere via a PC-connected modem.

2. Robert Merton described the research process as involving just such an interaction between theoretical perspective and empirical findings. He characterized the process as a dynamic one, with the findings exerting a constant modifying influence on the interpretive framework (see chapter 3 of his [1949]. *Social Theory and Social Structure.* Glencoe, IL: Free Press). Later writers, such as Barney Glaser and Anselm Strauss, place even greater emphasis on the role of data in generating the schema of interpretation (see [1967]. *The Discovery of Grounded Theory: Strategies for Qualitative Research.* Chicago: Aldine).

3. Offerings in the summer of 1992 included Quantitative Analysis of Crime and Criminal Justice; Game Theory and Rational Choice; Regression Analysis; Dimensional

Analysis; Time Series; Causal Models; ANOVA (Analysis of Variance); LISREL Type Models; Categorical Analysis; Dynamic Modeling; Historical Analysis; Electoral Behavior; Latino Research Issues; Survey of Income and Program Participation; 1990 Census; Intergenerational Studies; Logit and Log-Linear Models; Regression Diagnostics and Data Analysis; Network Analysis; and General Structural Equation Models.

4. Many go even further. Scholars such as Robert Nisbet suggest that theoretical breakthroughs in the social sciences are rarely achieved through quantitative analysis, but are largely the products of imagination and theoretical sensitivity; see Robert Nisbet. (1976). *Sociology as an Art Form* New York: Oxford University Press.

13

GOVERNMENT DOCUMENTS

Documents, specifically defined in the bibliographic world as publications of governmental agencies, are of great relevance to most fields of study. They may be primary sources that document the business of an agency and in this sense qualify as the raw data of original research. Such research may be quantitative, as in the case of someone using figures tabulated in a series of agency annual reports or other sources of the kind discussed in chapter 11. It may be qualitative, as in the case of someone using legislative documents to assess the intent of Congress in enacting a bill into law. It may be some combination of the two. Published documents may be used to supplement other archival sources for this purpose and may even be an adequate substitute for them.[1]

Aside from their primary value, documents have great potential as sources of secondary information. Governments generate, collect, analyze, and publish vast amounts of information. The U.S. Government Printing Office (GPO), for example, is probably the most prolific publisher in the world, and its publications, although geared toward the activities and interests of the government's branches, cover a broad spectrum of topics. There can be few students of the social and policy sciences who have not at some time used documents originating from a federal agency. GPO publications are well documented, and it is easy to identify those in an area of interest through the sources noted here.

Poore, Benjamin P. (1885). *A Descriptive Catalogue of the Government Publications of the United States, September 5, 1774–March 4, 1881.* Washington, DC: GPO. 1,392 p.

Documents are listed by date of publication and no annotations are given. A subject index is included. The standard bibliography for the materials and period covered.

Ames, John G. (1905). *Comprehensive Index to the Publications of the United States Government, 1881–1893.* Washington, DC: GPO. 2 vols.

Updates Poore and is principally a listing of congressional publications, as few documents were issued by other branches of the federal government in this period.

U.S. Superintendent of Documents. (1896–1945). *Catalog of the Public Documents of Congress and of All the Departments of the Government of the United States for the Period March 4, 1893–December 31, 1940.* Washington, DC: GPO. 25 vols.

Essentially a duplication of the contents of the *Monthly Catalog* (below) for this period, but much better indexed and more comprehensive in its coverage in that it includes many documents published by federal agencies other than the GPO.

U.S. Superintendent of Documents. (1978). *Checklist of United States Public Documents, 1789–1976.* Washington, DC: U.S. Historical Documents Institute. 5 vols.

Indexes the contents of the microfilm collection of the federal Public Documents Library in Washington. Includes documents formerly classified and those published by agencies other than the GPO. The most complete collection for the period covered, although not the easiest to use. Supplemented by the 16-volume *Cumulative Title Index.*

U.S. Superintendent of Documents. (1895–). *Monthly Catalog of United States Government Publications.* Washington, DC: GPO.

Arranged by agency. Detailed indexes in each issue cumulate annually. Cumulated subject indexes cover the periods 1895—1900 and 1900—1971. Full ordering information is given for each item cited. Since 1976 this has been available in computerized form (and now also on CD-ROM) as the *GPO Monthly Catalog.*

Andriot, John L. (Ed.). (1962–). *Guide to U.S. Government Publications.* McLean, VA: Documents Index. Annual.

Issued in two volumes, one of which covers current periodicals and other current serials, and the other, noncurrent items. The former is revised every five years. Parallels Andriot's *Guide to U.S. Government Statistics*, noted in chapter 11. Invaluable as a guide to the many works in series published by the GPO.

1. THE EXECUTIVE BRANCH

Comprehensive though the works just cited appear to be, they are not in themselves sufficient to exhaust the published resources of even the executive branch of government. One problem is that the GPO has never, monopolized federal publishing activities. Individual agencies have always run their own publishing operations. This trend of agency publication has recently strengthened as limited resources in the last few years have made the GPO more selective about its choice of works for publication. Nonetheless, the *Monthly Catalog* is still a valuable source for identifying publications of agencies, as these are often distributed by the Superintendent of Documents and are therefore included in this catalog.

Some agencies are prolific-enough publishers to support their own publications catalogs. These can be important sources, especially as they now usually include statistical series and machine-readable files (of the kind noted in chapter 12). The massive and often highly quantitative products of the Bureau of the Census are a case in point. Catalogs of this nature are well covered in Andriot (above) and in the works noted in this section (see especially Zink 1988 and *Government Reference Books*). A reader who expects to be closely involved with federal publications in general (as either primary or secondary sources) or with those of a particular agency is well advised to become familiar with at least some of these sources.

Bibliographic Guide to Government Publications--U.S. (1975–). Boston: G. K. Hall. Annual.

Updates the New York Public Library catalog (see below). Much easier to use than its parent because of its use of standard LC subject headings, and its identification of works by series. Includes state and local as well as federal documents.

Boyd, Anne M., & Rips, Rae E. (1949). *United States Government Publications* (3rd ed.). New York: H. W. Wilson. 627 p.

With Schmeckebier and Easton (below), one of the two standard guides for those undertaking historical work with federal documents.

Government Reference Books: A Biennial Guide to U.S. Government Publications. (1968/69–). Englewood, CO: Libraries Unlimited.

A classified, annotated list that is strong in bibliographies, statistical compilations, document catalogs, and other materials of concern. This can be updated using *U.S. Government Books*, an annotated list of new reference works published quarterly since 1982 by the GPO.

Morehead, Joe, & Fetzer, Mary. (1992). *Introduction to United States Public Documents* (4th ed.). Littleton, CO: Libraries Unlimited. 450 p.

Cited here because it is recent enough to address important trends in computerized and other nontraditional forms of publication and information dissemination.

New York Public Library. Research Libraries. (1972). *Catalog of Government Publications in the Research Libraries.* Boston: G. K. Hall. 40 vols.

Arranged by country and then by agency. A strong source for identifying state, local, and foreign documents. Updated by a supplement published in 1976 and by the *Bibliographic Guide to Government Publications* noted above.

O'Hara, Frederic J. (1979). *A Guide to Publications of the Executive Branch.* Ann Arbor, MI: Pierian. 287 p.

A guide to agency structure as well as major series and patterns of publication.

Robinson, Judith S. (1985). *Subject Guide to U.S. Government Reference Sources.* Littleton, CO: Libraries Unlimited. 333 p.

Excellent for its coverage of bibliographies. There is one general chapter on these, together with sections in subject-oriented chapters.

Schmeckebier, Laurence F., & Eastin, Roy B. (1969). *Government Publications and Their Use* (2nd ed.). Washington, DC: Brookings Institution. 502 p.

Use with Boyd and Rips (above) as a starting-point for any historical approach to legislative or executive functions of the federal government.

Sears, Jean L., & Moody, Marilyn. (1985–86). *Using Government Publications.* Phoenix, AZ: Oryx. 2 vols.

A major recent work discussing strategies for federal information-finding as well as the appropriate bibliographic sources. The second volume is particularly useful as a guide to locating statistical data.

Williams, Wiley J. (1987). *Subject Guide to Major United States Government Publications* (2nd ed.). Chicago: American Library Association. 257 p.

Important for its inclusion of appendixes documenting the many *Subject Bibliographies* published by the Library of Congress, and the bibliographic guides to the literature of the operations of the government of the United States.

Zink, Steven D. (1988). *United States Government Publications Catalogs* (2nd ed.). Washington, DC: Special Libraries Association. 292 p.

Publications catalogs (not all of which are published by the Superintendent of Documents) are listed by agency. Most are serial in their nature.

Another reason why social or policy researchers should have a particular interest in publications of executive agencies concerns the importance of these agencies in the area of research funding. Most federal money supporting scholarly research is distributed through federal agencies such as the Department of Justice or through independent but federally supported organizations such as the National Endowment for the Humanities. Only a small proportion of the products of this research is published in a conventional sense. The remainder are circulated in a more limited fashion as *technical reports*.

These reports are important for a number of reasons. In the first place, they often reflect research findings that are published in no other form. Second, even if these findings are later reflected in the substance of articles, books, or other forms, it can be a year or even several years before this occurs. Technical reports can be the only source for locating the fruits of most federally funded research and the most timely source for the remainder. On the face of it, access to these materials is relatively easy. The National Technical Information Service (NTIS), an arm of the U.S. Department of Commerce, collects and disseminates these reports as they are generated throughout the government. It markets them through a series of publications and services that provide the user with subject access, abstracts, and ordering information for the documents themselves. *GRA and I: Government Reports Announcements and Index* has been published biweekly, under various titles, since 1946. Citations and abstracts are arranged according to the COSATI classification system (see figure 12). An annual cumulated index to this is published in the form of the *Government Reports Annual Index*. In addition, *Abstract Newsletters* are issued weekly in each of 26 constituent subject areas, thus allowing individual subscribers to focus only on limited sections of NTIS holdings.

Selected Research in Microfiche (SRIM) further allows a subscriber to construct a personal interest profile and have the full text, on microfiche, of new acquisitions sent on a biweekly basis. Finally, the computerized database *NTIS* (now also available on CD-ROM) includes citations and abstracts for all reports acquired since the early 1960s. Before the days of widespread computer searching in libraries, the agency conducted most of the searches for its patrons. Over 1,000 of these are marketed as *Published Searches* and constitute useful and ready-made bibliographies. These are indexed by the *Published Search Master Catalog* published annually by NTIS since 1986.

This system of information access is clearly an impressive one. However, it is not always as valuable as it might sound. The focus of NTIS holdings, like the focus of federal research funding, is on the pure and applied sciences. Social and behavioral science research is represented, but it reflects only a fraction of the one million or so reports in the NTIS database. Second, the access system described is first-rate, but only for retrieving items already in the system. NTIS has the mandate to acquire reports submitted under grants from any and all federal agencies. However, as all who are concerned with the operations of large bureaucracies know, the wish is not always the same as its fulfillment. There is no doubt that many technical reports of this nature escape the NTIS net and must be found through other sources.

Computerized databases are often the best starting point since a number have some governmental sponsorship. *NCJRS: National Criminal Justice Reference Service*, for example, is supported by the Department of Justice; *Mental Health Abstracts*, by the National Institute for Mental Health. Failing this, and if it is considered worthwhile, reports of funded projects are usually listed and described in the annual reports of agencies.

2. THE LEGISLATIVE BRANCH

The lawmaking, regulatory, investigative, and other activities of the House of Representatives, the Senate, and the Office of the President are, as one might imagine, extremely well documented. This is necessary not just to satisfy the democratic needs of scholars and the citizenry at large but to ensure the proper functioning of the governmental process. For example, one of the several functions of the courts in the United States is to interpret and apply legislation in specific instances. This is done by courts at the federal, state, and local levels. To do so, courts must have some understanding of the *intent* of a legislature in enacting a statute as well as the substance of the law itself. Courts gain such understanding through examination of the *legislative history* of the statutes in point. A legislative history includes the paper trail generated by a bill in its journey toward enactment into law.

A bill is introduced in a legislature and examined in committee in open session or in private hearings. Appropriate committees listen to (or at least hear from) interested parties and, after deliberating, issue reports to the legislatures they represent. Unsuccessful bills usually die in committee. Those destined to be enacted as statutes are at some point debated in the houses of the legislature as a whole and voted upon in existing or revised form. Once approved, the bill is submitted, with its supporting documentation, to the president or the state governor, who may, depending on the rules that apply, reject it, delay it, or sign it into law. This documentation constitutes the bill's legislative history. Examination of it provides the courts with insight as to what the legislative branch of government hoped to achieve when it enacted the bill into law.

Most of the publications surrounding the important activities outlined that are published and are identifiable through standard sources such as the *Monthly Catalog* and other bibliographic tools adverted to in the previous section. No informed person, however, would search for them in this way. The reasons for this are twofold. First, not all elements of the legislative history are in fact published. Committee hearings on a bill are often published; more often they are not. Decisions regarding this are not always obvious to even the best-informed parties and probably relate more to the impulses of the Superintendent of Documents than to the politics of the process. There are ways of locating the texts of committee hearings in manuscript form, but these are not achieved through the *Monthly Catalog* or its satellites. Second, the law is a very important matter and is consequently documented much better than most other institutions one grapples with in life. There are many focused bibliographic and other aids that enable researchers to explore the resources through which one learns to appreciate and examine the legislative process, whether for legal or academic purposes.[2]

There are easy ways to identify the status of a bill, the existence and whereabouts of hearings (published or unpublished), similar bills that were earlier or later rejected or amended beyond their original purpose, and the status of an act and how it has been subsequently amended and interpreted by appellate courts. Such information can be found fairly easily, but not through the services of the Superintendent of Documents or his or her state counterparts. There are particular ways to obtain this information, and there are published guides that inform their readers as to how they can be fully exploited. Some of those addressing the single issue of legislative intent are cited in this section. Other aspects of the documentation surrounding the business of legislatures at all levels of government are described in the various guides to research in the social sciences (political science in particular) in chapter 4 and in the guides to legal research cited in section 3 of this chapter.

Billtext. (Current session only). Washington, DC: U.S. Government Printing Office. Updated daily.

Provides the complete texts of all bills introduced in the current session of Congress together with information on current status, supporting documentation, and texts of revised versions. A retrospective version of this service, the *Billcast Archive*, provides similar information on bills introduced from 1985 to the Congressional session preceding the current session.

Carter, Robert A. (1981). *Sources of Legislative Intent in New York State: Materials, Cases, and Annotated Bibliography.* Albany, NY: New York State Library. Legislative and Governmental Services. 57 p.

Cited here as one of the many guides addressing the use and sources of legislative history in a particular state.

CIS Index to Publications of the United States Congress. (1970–). Washington, DC: Congressional Information Service. Loose-leaf. Cumulates as the *CIS Annual.*

Its major use is to identify the current status of pending legislation but also identifies related bills, committee hearings and reports, and other elements of legislative history. Sometimes entitled *Index to Publications of the United States Congress*. Can be updated on a daily basis through the electronic *Congressional Legislative Reporting Service*.

CIS Index to Unpublished US House of Representatives Committee Hearings 1833–1936. (1988). Bethesda, MD: Congressional Information Service. 2 vols.

As with other indexes published by CIS, the index is supported by a microfiche set providing the full texts of the documents themselves. Supplemented by a (1990) set covering 1937–46. The two represent but an illustration of many important efforts of CIS to make accessible document collections from all branches of the federal government. The wise researcher will make an early attempt to identify any such efforts.

Congressional Masterfile 1. (1989). Bethesda, MD: Congressional Information Service.

Congressional Masterfile 2. (1989–). Bethesda, MD: Congressional Information Service. Updated quarterly.

Between them, these two CD-ROM files attempt to index and abstract all Congressional publications (including hearings, reports, and prints) published between 1789 and the present. Full texts of the documents themselves are available in the several microfiche collections issued by the same publisher.

Fisher, Mary L. (1985–). *Guide to State Legislative Materials* (3rd ed.). Littleton, CO: Rothman. Loose-leaf.

For each state, provides brief (6- or 7-page) summaries of what legislative materials (including those dealing with intent) are available, how they are organized, and how they can be obtained.

Goehlert, Robert U., & Martin, Fenton S. (1989). *Congress and Law-Making: Researching the Legislative Process* (2nd ed.). Santa Barbara, CA: ABC-Clio. 306 p.

A very practical guide that emphasizes the mechanics of the research process in this area, even to the point of presenting sample pages of relevant sources. Limited in that its useful bibliographies include no recognition of the legislative process at the state level.

How Federal Laws are Made. (2nd ed.). (1985). Washington, DC: WANT. 135 p.

Good for its discussions of process, but does not give detailed attention to sources.

Legislative Retrieval System. (1976–). Albany, NY: Legislative Retrieval System. Updated daily.

Provides extensive documentation of the activities of the New York State legislature. Noted here as an example of a computerized access system to historical legal materials at the state level.

Loewenberg, Gerhard, Patterson, Samuel C., & Jewell, Malcolm E. (Eds.). (1985). *Handbook of Legislative Research.* Cambridge, MA: Harvard University Press. 810 p.

Includes 16 essays, each reviewing the products of academic research in some aspect of the area. Emphasizes findings, not sources.

Nabors, Eugene. (1982). *Legislative Reference Checklist: The Key to Legislative Histories from 1789–1903.* Littleton, CO: Rothman. 440 p.

One of a number of guides to histories that have already been collected. More recent histories are covered by *Sources of Compiled Legislative Histories* (below).

NAMNET: The Public Policy Electronic Network. (Current Congress). Philadelphia: National Association of Manufacturers. Updated daily.

Includes a subfile, *Public Policy Research,* which provides either abstracts or the full texts of newsletter articles, position papers, and other materials relating to current issues. Most discussion addresses current or proposed legislation.

Sources of Compiled Legislative Histories: A Bibliography of Government Documents, Periodical Articles, and Books. (1979–). Littleton, CO: Rothman. One loose-leaf volume.

Cites both primary and secondary sources. Use in conjunction with works such as Nabors (above).

U.S. Department of Justice. Office of Legal Policy. (1989). *Using and Misusing Legislative History: A Re-Evaluation of the Status of Legislative History in Statutory Interpretation.* Washington, DC. 123 p.

One of a number of recent official discussions of the changing influence of evidence of legislative intent on the interpretation of statutes by the courts.

Zwirn, Jerrold. (1983). *Congressional Publications: A Research Guide to Legislation, Budgets, and Treaties.* Littleton, CO: Libraries Unlimited. 195 p.

Generally, not as good as Goehlert and Martin (above), but important for its attention to matters beyond the immediate legislative process (for example, international treaties and the budgetary process).

3. THE JUDICIARY

Legal research is an activity unto itself. The reason for this is that its objectives are not primarily bibliographic and are therefore completely different from those of the traditional researcher. Legal researchers are usually not interested in preparing bibliographies. They seek to determine *primary authority*. If the immediate object of attention is a statute, the researcher must determine if it has subsequently been amended or even repealed, how its substance relates to other legislation and to the regulatory activities of executive agencies, what the intent of the legislative body was, and how it has been interpreted by the courts, especially the appellate courts. Those whose interest in the law goes beyond the instrumental and into the social and political correlates of legal behavior have an additional concern. Recognizing the tremendous discretion of those institutions charged with enforcing the law, they seek to identify patterns in how it has been implemented through criminal prosecutions or civil actions.

A unique characteristic of the common-law system, used in most English-speaking societies and some others, is the paramount importance ascribed to case law. In translating statutory language into policy in specific instances, the courts have a function that is in no sense mechanical but is part of the process of law creation. The meaning of a statute cannot be understood properly unless the reader is familiar with the principal cases that have interpreted it. Statute and case law are part and parcel of the same body of legal substance. Furthermore, courts are, expected to defer to the findings of higher courts.

When the object of interest is a court case, the researcher must first determine whether or not the finding was overturned by a higher court. Even if it was not, an effort must be made to determine how the case fits into the larger body of case law (much of which may be later in origin) on the legal points addressed. Has the court's finding or reasoning been criticized or otherwise made redundant by later case law? Is the case still a "leading case" (if it ever was) in the issues it addresses, or has it been superseded? How has it been cited or discussed in the years since it was heard? All these and other questions must be answered if the importance of the case is to be appreciated.

Usually, cases and statutes are addressed in the context of some subject-oriented approach. If the subject is at all controversial or in the midst of legal change, the primary sources for it will probably be in case law. Researchers will then also search for legal documentation that is not *binding*, but that is nonetheless *persuasive*.[3] Such documentation is used by jurists as well as by scholars for assistance in understanding the legal issues raised, and how these have been analyzed in similar legal contexts. Persuasive authority includes legal encyclopedias, law review articles, treatises, and cases from other jurisdictions; these days it can also include the research findings of social and behavioral scientists. It is clear from all this that legal research is a very specialized business. It should also be clear that the common-law system briefly described can only function in a complex society if it is supported by a highly sophisticated system of bibliographic access. Legal reasoning applied in the hundreds of thousands of cases heard by the appellate courts in the United States each year would have little effect on the substance of the law if it could not be identified readily.[4]

The many published guides to legal research are generally excellent. Those noted below include some of the standard texts used in the mandatory courses in legal bibliography given in law schools. Most are general in nature and address both federal and state sources of law. Allen is cited as an example addressing the law relating to a particular state; other guides of this nature are listed in Foster and Boast and in Parish 1981 (cited in section 4). Mashaw and Merrill is mentioned because of its concern for administrative law—that is, the body of law relating to the activities of governmental agencies empowered to promulgate regulations that carry the force of statutes.

One area of the law not well documented is that generated by governments at the local levels. Discussion of this is sometimes included in those guides covering the states in which the localities of concern are located.

Discussion in section 4 of chapter 16 shows that common law jurisdictions in the United States and some other English-speaking countries have historically shared certain principles. They have even relied at times on the same body of legal documentation. For this reason, the standard guides to legal research of some of these countries are cited here.

Allen, Cameron. (1984). *A Guide to New Jersey Legal Bibliography and Legal History.* Littleton, CO: Rothman. 636 p.

Banks, Margaret A. (1985). *Using a Law Library: A Guide for Students and Lawyers in the Common Law Provinces of Canada* (4th ed.). Toronto: Carswell. 249 p.

Bradney, Anthony. (1991). *How to Study Law* (2nd ed.). London: Sweet & Maxwell. 277 p.

Corbin, John. (1989). *Find the Law in the Library: A Guide to Legal Research.* Chicago: American Library Association. 327 p.

Foster, Lynn, & Boast, Carol. (1981). *Subject Compilations of State Laws: Research Guide and Annotated Bibliography*. Westport, CT: Greenwood. 473 p.

An annotated bibliography of both primary and secondary sources. Updated regularly by supplements with the same primary title but different authors published every two or three years.

Jacobstein, J. Myron, & Mersky, Roy M. (1990). *Fundamentals of Legal Research* (5th ed.). Westbury, NY: Foundation Press. 734 p.

JUSTIS. (1952–). London: Context. Updated weekly.

A linked group databases (*European Update, Info 92* and *Spearhead*) which together document legal developments affecting the European Community. Also includes a file covering U.K. domestic law.

Logan, R. G. (Ed.). (1986). *Information Sources in Law*. London: Butterworths. 370 p.

Includes some discussion of legal sources in other common-law jurisdictions and also in the European Community.

Mashaw, Jerry L., & Merrill, Richard A. (1985). *Administrative Law, the American Public Law System: Cases and Materials* (2nd ed.). St. Paul, MN: West. 976 p.

One of the few guides to focus on the functioning of regulatory agencies whose regulations have the force of law.

Price, Miles O., Bitner, Harry, & Bysiewicz, Shirley R. (1979). *Effective Legal Research* (4th ed.). Boston: Little, Brown. 643 p.

Rombauer, Marjorie D. (1983). *Legal Problem Solving: Analysis, Research, and Writing* (4th ed.). St. Paul, MN: West. 424 p.

State Legislative Sourcebook. (1986–). Topeka, KA: Government Research Service. Annual.

"A resource guide to legislative information in the fifty states" and remarkable as one of the very few sources providing comparative information on legislation at the state level.

Primary legal materials are used extensively by historians and other social scientists as powerful indicators of the beliefs and practices of the societies that produced them. Observations on the uses of the law in this way are presented in section 4 of chapter 16. This section also cites some of the important sources of legal history.

4. STATE GOVERNMENT DOCUMENTS

At the state level, bibliographic control of official publications varies considerably between jurisdictions. No fully satisfactory guide to the use of state documents exists, although some of the works cited earlier give passing attention to documents other than those of the federal government. Wilcox's book is excellent as far as it goes, but is too old to be of interest to those whose concerns are other than historical. The book by Adrian is useful; although it is intended as a textbook rather than a guide to sources, it does serve this latter function. It is, however, now also quite old. Parish's two books (see below) are as close as one can come to anything approaching a useful introduction to this area of publication. The first (1985) lists current as well as retrospective sources of state documents. The second (1981) lists the many sources documenting organizational structure, activities, and processes of governments at this level. Information in these two books can be supplemented by the works of Lane.

As far as it goes, the U.S. Library of Congress's *Monthly Checklist Of State Publications* is a good source. However, it only includes items received by the Library of Congress, and cooperation with this system varies considerably from state to state. Usually, the best way to search for documents of this nature is to identify (using one of the books by Parish or through other sources) appropriate bibliographic sources at the individual state level. To illustrate the kinds of sources that exist, several are cited below that document the publications of the state of New York.

Adrian, Charles R. (1976). *State and Local Governments* (4th ed.). New York: McGraw-Hill. 416 p.

Butch, Dorothy. (1987). *New York State Documents: An Introductory Manual.* Albany, NY: New York State Library. 138 p.

City & State. (1992–). Chicago: Crain. Updated semimonthly.

A database providing the full texts of articles drawn from a limited number of newsletters and newspapers concerned with major developments in state and local government.

Council of State Governments. (1959–). *State Government Research Checklist.* Lexington, KY. Bimonthly.

Formerly the *Legislative Research Checklist.* Documents cited are available from the council in microform.

Dow, Susan L. (1990). *State Document Checklists: A Historical Bibliography.* Buffalo, NY: William S. Hein. 224 p.
An annotated guide to "all state document checklists for each of the fifty states," whether current or retrospective. Excluded are lists documenting individual agencies. Also discusses major sources for identifying state publications.

Hellebust, Lynn (Ed.). (1990). *State Blue Books, Legislative Manuals, and Reference Publications: A Selective Bibliography.* Topeka, KA: Government Research Service. 142 p.
Best for its coverage of current serial titles. Particularly valuable as a guide to sources of statistical information.

Hernon, Peter (Ed.). (1981). *Microforms and Government Information.* Westport, CT: Microform Review. 287 p.
One chapter is entitled "State Government Publications in Microform."

Koslofsky, Regis (Comp.). (1972). *Selected Bibliography on State Government, 1959–1972.* Lexington, KY: Council of State Governments. 237 p.
Updated by a 1979 supplement.

Lane, Margaret T. (1987). *Selecting and Organizing State Government Publications.* Chicago: American Library Association. 254 p.
Includes lengthy sections on bibliographies and other sources.

Lane, Margaret T. (1981). *State Publications and Depository Libraries: A Reference Handbook.* Westport, CT: Greenwood. 573 p.
Part 2 includes discussion of the bibliography of state documents. A chapter reviewing sources is followed by others surveying the bibliography of individual states.

Lopez, Manuel D. (1980). *New York, A Guide to Information and Reference Sources.* Metuchen, NJ: Scarecrow. 372 p. A 1987 supplement covers the years 1979–1986.

New York State Library. (1947–). *A Checklist of Official Publications of the State of New York.* Albany, NY. Monthly, with annual cumulations.

New York State Library. (1973–). *Dictionary Catalog of Official Publications of the State of New York.* Albany, NY. Now quarterly, with annual and five-year cumulations.
This includes fewer items than the *Checklist* (above) and is not therefore a substitute for it.

Parish, David W. (1985). *A Bibliography of State Bibliographies, 1970-1982.* Littleton, CO: Libraries Unlimited. 267 p.

Parish, David W. (1981). *State Government Reference Publications: An Annotated Bibliography* (2nd ed.). Littleton, CO: Libraries Unlimited. 355 p.

Pross, Catherine A. (1983). *Guide to the Identification and Acquisition of Canadian Government Publications: Provinces and Territories* (2nd ed.). Halifax, NS: Dalhousie University. School of Library Science. 103 p.

State Education Documents: A State-by-State Directory for their Acquisition and Use. (1989). Chicago: Association of College and Research Libraries. 45 p.

Sulzer, Jack, & Palen, Roberta (Comps.). (1986). *Guide to the Publications of Interstate Agencies and Authorities.* Chicago: American Library Association. 48 p.

Tompkins, Dorothy C. (1954). *State Government and Administration: A Bibliography.* Berkeley, CA: University of California. Bureau of Public Administration. 269 p.

U.S. Library of Congress. Exchange and Gift Division. (1910–). *Monthly Checklist of State Publications.* Washington, DC. Index published annually.

Wilcox, Jerome K. (1940). *Manual on the Use of State Publications.* Chicago: American Library Association. 342 p.

5. CITY, COUNTY, AND OTHER LOCAL GOVERNMENTS

If bibliographic control of state publications is inferior to that of the federal system, control of documents issued by governments below these levels is worse yet. It is notoriously difficult to search for documents produced at the local levels of government in any kind of systematic fashion. Some modest efforts have been made to facilitate searches for documents in the United States in general. The products of these efforts are noted below. Outstanding among them are the two current indexing services, *FYI* and the *Index to Current Urban Documents*. The second of these is of particular interest in that a large proportion of the documents indexed are available in microform in a backup collection produced by the same publisher. One chapter in Hernon 1981 (cited in the previous section) is entitled "Local Documents in Microform." A number of other printed and computerized indexes also provide limited coverage of local documents.[5] Several of the most important of these are cited below, together with other useful sources.

As with state documents, the best approach to local publications is often strictly at the local level. If the researcher is fortunate, the city or county will provide some documentation of its publication efforts. As an example of this, some of the works documenting materials published by New York City are cited here.

Bollens, John C., Bayes, John R., & Utter, Kathryn L. (1969). *American County Government, with an Annotated Bibliography.* Beverly Hills, CA: Sage. 433 p.

FYI: Resources on Local Government. (1983–). Washington, DC: International City Management Association. Annual.

"A compilation of the most important publications pertaining to local government."

Government Affairs Foundation. (1957). *Metropolitan Communities: A Bibliography, with Special Emphasis upon Government and Politics.* Chicago: Public Administration Service. 392 p. Supplements cover 1955–70.

Halasz, D. (Comp.). (1967). *Metropolis: A Select Bibliography of Administrative and Other Problems in Metropolitan Areas throughout the World* (2nd ed.). The Hague: Nijhoff. 267 p.

Hernon, Peter, et al. (Eds.). (1978). *Municipal Government Reference Sources: Publications and Collections.* New York: Bowker. 341 p.

Represents the only major effort to identify bibliographic sources in this area. Covers the larger municipalities only.

Hodgson, James G. (Comp.). (1937). *The Official Publications of American Counties, a Union List, with an Introduction on the Collecting of County Publications.* Fort Collins, CO: Author. 594 p.

Index to Current Urban Documents. (1972–). Westport, CT: Greenwood. Quarterly, with annual and biennial cumulations.

Indexes several thousand documents each year, but only those of the largest cities and counties in Canada and the United States. Many of the documents themselves are published on microfiche by Greenwood in its *Urban Documents Microfiche Collection.*

International Union of Local Authorities. (1963–). *Bibliographia: New Publications in the Library of the I.U.L.A.* The Hague. Bimonthly.

Jackson, Kathryn E. (1981). *Local Government Bibliography with Emphasis on New York State.* Monticello, IL: Vance. 154 p.

Koehler, Cortus T. (1977). *Selected County Government Bibliography with Annotations.* Monticello, IL: Council of Planning Librarians. 87 p.

Kronman, Barbara. (1984). *Guide to NYC Public Records* (3rd ed.). New York: Public Interest Clearinghouse. 100 p.

A guide to archives that includes discussion of legal and other materials and their location and use.

LOGA: Local Government Annotations Service. (1966–). London: Havering Public Libraries. Monthly.

Emphasizes British sources.

The Municipal Year Book. (1934–). Washington, DC: International City Management Association.

Each volume includes two chapters listing and describing relevant reference works published by governmental and private sources.

Murphy, Thomas P. (Ed.). (1978). *Urban Politics: A Guide to Information Sources.* Detroit: Gale. 248 p.

New York City. Municipal Reference and Research Center. (1914–). *Notes.* New York. Monthly.

Provides good coverage of New York City organizational structure and its documentation.

Recent Publications on Governmental Problems. (1932–). Chicago: Merriam Center. Library. Semimonthly.

Some limited coverage of documents at the state and local levels. Has no indexes and is therefore hard to use.

Ross, Bernard H. (Ed.). (1979). *Urban Management: A Guide to Information Sources.* Detroit: Gale. 288 p.

Sage Urban Studies Abstracts. (1973–). Newbury Park, CA: Sage. Quarterly, with annual indexes.
Mainly a source of periodical literature, but does cover some local documents.

White, Anthony G. (1975). *Reforming Metropolitan Governments: A Bibliography.* New York: Garland. 116 p.

6. UNPUBLISHED SOURCES AND "FREEDOM OF INFORMATION"

The Freedom of Information Act of 1966 was a consequence of sustained efforts to prevent federal agencies from abusing their discretionary powers by unnecessarily withholding information about their activities. Later interest in it has also been motivated by a public desire to understand the kinds of data collected by these agencies and how their collection policies were justified. Many information-gathering activities of agencies are, of course, exempt from disclosure under FOI. These are generally in situations in which harm to identifiable public or private interests is perceived as a likely outcome.

The FOI statute has been amended many times since its original enactment. Policies on disclosure differ between agencies, as do procedures for requesting and obtaining data. These policies also vary over time, and, when state and local governments are concerned, they vary between jurisdictions. Prizing unpublished records from governmental agencies can be a very difficult matter. Obstacles encountered may relate to bureaucratic incompetence, indifference, or downright hostility and have no necessary connection to legal interpretations of rights under FOI. Nonetheless, researchers seeking information of this kind should, for their own protection, be aware of which of their requests are entitled to reasonable accommodation under law. For these reasons, knowledge of rights under FOI is important to the researcher in this situation. These rights cannot be understood without expert guidance of the kind provided in the works cited in this section.

Not all the works noted here address FOI explicitly. Some focus on the very important skills of identifying unpublished sources within governments and developing personal strategies for accessing them. This aspect of mining governmental agencies for data involves its own considerable skills. A sustained effort to obtain specific data from an agency will only be productive if the agency addressed is the appropriate one and is approached in an appropriate fashion.

FOI is a concept that has little meaning in many countries. The sources given here generally consider its application only in the United States.

APDU Newsletter. (1976–). Princeton, NJ: Association of Public Data Users. Monthly.

Mainly concerned with access to machine-readable data sets, but does address issues related to information access in general.

D'Aleo, Richard J. (1986). *FEDfind: Your Key to Finding Federal Government Information: A Directory of Information Sources, Products, and Services* (2nd ed.). Springfield, VA: ICUC Press. 480 p.

Addresses both printed and unpublished sources. Not intended primarily for the scholar but useful to anyone needing to negotiate the federal maze in search of information. One of the best of many guides of this kind.

Declassified Documents Catalog. (1975–). Woodbridge, CT: Research Publications. Bimonthly, with annual subject index.

Devoted to the description and documentation of materials and collections as these are declassified.

FOIA Update. (1979–). Washington, DC: U.S. Department of Justice. Quarterly.

Reports new legal requirements and how these are translated into agency policies and procedures.

Hernon, Peter, & McClure, Charles R. (1988). *Public Access to Government Information: Issues, Trends, and Strategies* (2nd ed.). Norwood, NJ: Ablex. 524 p.

One of the most extensive works of its kind. Discusses published and unpublished sources. Includes chapters discussing state and local documents and those of intergovernmental organizations.

How to Find Business Intelligence in Washington (10th ed.). (1990). Washington, DC: Washington Researchers. 470 p.

Similar in structure to D'Aleo (above) but addresses a narrower constituency. Has considerable value beyond its market.

Ullmann, John, & Honeyman, Steve (Eds.). (1983). *The Reporter's Handbook: An Investigator's Guide to Documents and Techniques.* New York: St. Martin's. 504 p.

One of several valuable guides developed for the rather different, but related, needs of the investigative reporter.

U.S. Department of the Interior. (1991–). *Freedom of Information Act Handbook.* Washington, DC. 1 loose-leaf vol., with updates.

The best and most current guide to rights of agencies and citizens under the Act.

The ability to exploit government data resources is an essential component of the skills of the archival researcher. Guides to the location and use of archives in general are discussed in chapters 14 and 16.

7. FOREIGN GOVERNMENTS

Bibliographic control of government publications of other countries varies considerably. For European and other Western countries, these publications are often much better documented than those of the United States. The obvious reason for this is that most of these countries have more extensive federal systems. Government publication, like governmental control, tends to be centralized, and publication patterns reflect the underlying structures of the political and administrative systems that they document. Anyone researching any aspect of a foreign political system has a clear obligation to understand both the structure of the system and the way it is documented.

Published guides to the use of government documents exist for most democratic countries. These generally also address the nature of the political system that generates them. Lists of these works are included in the general reference sources in the social sciences cited in chapters 3 and 4. General sources of foreign government documents also include those listed immediately below.

American Library Association. Government Documents Round Table. (1990). *Guide to Official Publications of Foreign Countries.* Washington, DC: Congressional Information Service. 359 p.

Lists and describes the major bibliographic sources of the documents of 157 countries. In cases where an official source of a particular type does not exist (for example, an annual statistical abstract) privately-generated sources are cited, when possible. See also Horn (below).

Bibliographic Guide to Government Publications—Foreign. (1975–). Boston: G. K. Hall. Annual.

Updates New York Public Library's *Catalog of Government Publications* (see section 1). The best single source for identifying current foreign documents.

Cherns, J. J. (1979). *Official Publishing, An Overview: An International Survey and Review of the Role, Organisation, and Principles of Official Publishing.* Oxford, UK: Pergamon. 527 p.

Eastern Europe: A directory and Sourcebook. (1992). London: Euromonitor. 436 p.

Intended to present overviews of interest to potential investors, but also valuable for its discussions and listings of information sources, private and public.

The European Communities Encyclopedia and Directory 1992. (1991). London: Europa. 390 p.

Primarily a sourcebook and a directory, but also includes statistical data and some narrative discussion. Valuable only as long as it remains current.

Howell, John B. (1978). *Kenya: Subject Guide to Official Publications.* Washington, DC: U.S. Library of Congress. 423 p.

Cited here as an example of an extensive series of country-based guides to official documents published by the Library of Congress. Most of these address Third World countries.

Horn, Judy (Ed.). (1991). *Directory of Government Document Collections and Librarians* (6th ed.). Bethesda, MD: Congressional Information Service. 650 p.

Identifies document collections of all kinds: federal, state, local, foreign, and international.

McGonagle, John J. (Ed.). (1991). *The Arthur Andersen European Community Sourcebook: The Most Comprehensive, Authoritative Reference Guide Ever Assembled on the European Market.* Chicago: Triumph. 499 p.

A comprehensive work which almost lives up to its ambitious title.

Myers, Robert A. (Comp.). (1991). *Ghana.* Santa Barbara, CA: ABC–Clio. 436 p.

An example of Clio's extensive "World Bibliographical Series" introducing the reader to a country through its bibliographic resources. In this (and many other) instances, considerable discussion of the country's system of official publication is given. Many of the world's less-publicized countries are covered in this series.

Palic, Vladimir M. (Comp.). (1977). *Government Publications: A Guide to Bibliographic Tools, Incorporating Government Organization Manuals.* New York: Pergamon. 553 p.

Addresses U.S. federal, state, and local documents as well as those of foreign countries.

Rolland, Denis. (1983). *Guide des Organisations Internationales et de Leurs Publications: Amérique Latine.* Paris: Publications Sorbonne. 221 p.

Turner, Carol A. (Comp.). (1985). *Directory of Foreign Document Collections.* New York: Unipub. 149 p.

Westfall, Gloria (Ed.). (1990). *Guide to Official Publications of Foreign Countries.* Bethesda, MD: Congressional Information Service. 359 p.

The guides cited below include only those covering official publications of individual countries that are the immediate neighbors of the United States by virtue of geography or language. For countries that have no such guides, the works by Palic and Westfall (above) are of value in providing discussions of at least the basic sources for government documents published by a wide range of countries. In the listing below, guides are presented in alphabetical order of the countries covered.

Borchardt, Dietrich H. (Ed.). (1979). *Australian Official Publications.* Melbourne: Longman Cheshire. 365 p.

Harrington, Michael. (1990). *The Guide to Government Publications in Australia.* Canberra: Australian Government Publishing Service. 164 p.
An essential supplement to Borchardt.

Bishop, Olga B. (1981). *Canadian Official Publications.* New York: Pergamon. 297 p.

Higgins, Marion V. (1935). *Canadian Government Publications: A Manual for Librarians.* Chicago: American Library Association. 582 p.

Jordan, Alma. (1984). *The English-speaking Caribbean: A Bibliography of Bibliographies.* Boston: G. K. Hall. 411 p.

Patchett, Keith, & Jenkins, Valerie. (1973). *A Bibliographical Guide to Law in the Commonwealth Caribbean.* Mona, Jamaica: University of the West Indies. Institute of Social and Economic Research. 80 p.

U.S. Library of Congress. (1945–49). *A Guide to the Official Publications of the Other American Republics.* Washington, DC: GPO. 19 vols.

The 19 countries covered include several in the Caribbean and Central America.

Ford, Percy, & Ford, Grace. (1972). *A Guide to Parliamentary Papers: What They Are, How to Find Them, and How to Use Them* (3rd ed.). Shannon, Ireland: Irish University Press. 87 p.

Pemberton, John E. (1973). *British Official Publications* (2nd ed.). New York: Pergamon. 328 p.

Richard, Stephen (Comp.). (1981). *Directory of British Official Publications: A Guide to Sources* (2nd ed.). London: Mansell. 431 p.

Rodgers, Frank. (1980). *A Guide to British Government Publications.* New York: H. W. Wilson. 750 p.

Maltby, Arthur, & McKenna, Brian. (1980). *Irish Official Publications: A Guide to Republic of Ireland Papers, with a Breviate of Reports, 1922–1972.* New York: Pergamon. 377 p.

Fernandez Esquivel, Rosa M. (1967). *Las Publicaciónes Oficiales de México: Guía de Publicaciónes Periódicas y Seriadas, 1937–1967.* Mexico City: Universidad Nacional Autónoma de México. 269 p.

Ker, Anita M. (1940). *Mexican Government Publications.* Washington, DC: GPO. 333 p.

Carpenter, C. L. (Comp.). (1980). *Guide to New Zealand Information Sources: Official Publications.* Palmerston North, NZ: Massey University. Library. 41 p.

8. INTERNATIONAL GOVERNMENTS

The importance of international governments as vehicles for international cooperation and policy-making of course varies over time, according to the world political climate and the economic relationships this reflects. The United Nations has varied considerably in its role as catalyst of voluntary cooperation and in its ability to exert global influence since its founding after World War II. A very different kind of organization, the European Community, is emerging as a truly international government representing the economic and political union of a very powerful section of the Western world.

Documents of governments and organizations of this nature are generally included in some of the sources, such as the *Bibliographic Guide to Government Publications—Foreign*, identified earlier. Other generalized sources of these documents and guides to their use are cited below.

Atherton, Alexine L. (1976). *International Organizations: A Guide to Information Sources*. Detroit: Gale. 350 p.

Baer, George W. (1991). *International Organizations, 1918–1945: A Guide to Research and Research Materials* (rev. ed.). Wilmington, DE: Scholarly Resources. 212 p.

Best for its coverage of the League of Nations and the early records of the United Nations, but the documents of many League affiliates are also discussed.

Dimitrov, Theodore D. (Comp.). (1981). *World Bibliography of International Documentation.* Pleasantville, NY: UNIFO. 2 vols.

Encyclopedia of Associations. (1961–). Detroit: Gale. Annual, now in five vols. Updated between editions by *New Associations.*

One volume addresses international associations, private as well as governmental.

Fraser, Robert (Ed.). (1992). *Western European Economic Organizations: A Comprehensive Guide*. London: Longman. 448 p.

Discusses national and international organizations whose activities influence economic policies. Gives some limited attention to their bibliography.

Haas, Michael. (1971). *International Organization: An Interdisciplinary Bibliography.* Stanford, CA: Hoover Institution Press. 944 p.

Hajnal, Peter I. (Comp.). (1991). *Directory of United Nations Documentary and Archival Sources.* Milkwood, NY: Kraus International. 106 p.

Most valuable for its discussions of unpublished records and other archival data.

International Bibliography: Publications of Intergovernmental Organizations. (1973–). New Ycrk: Unipub. Quarterly.

Strongest in documentation of agencies affiliated with the UN. Earlier titled *International Bibliography, Information, Documentation.*

Johnson, Harold S., & Singh, Baljit. (1969). *International Organization: A Classified Bibliography.* East Lansing, MI: Michigan State University. Asian Studies Center. 261 p.

Speeckaert, Georges P. (1965). *Select Bibliography on International Organization, 1885–1964.* Brussels: Union of International Associations. 150 p.

Yearbook of International Organizations. (1948–). Brussels: Union of International Associations.

Describes activities and cites publications. Updated by the monthly *International Associations.*

Guides to the publications of some particular organizations are noted below. These are listed in the following order of the institutions they represent: the European Community, the League of Nations, the Organization of American States, and the United Nations.

EC Index (European Communities Index). (1984–). Maastricht, The Netherlands: Europe Data. Monthly, with quarterly and annual cumulations.

Indexes and abstracts all documents published by community institutions. The texts of all publicly accessible documents are published in a microfiche set, *COM Documents.*

Jeffries, John. (1981). *A Guide to the Official Publications of the European Communities* (2nd ed.). London: Mansell. 318 p.

Lodge, Juliet (Ed.). (1983). *The European Community: Bibliographical Excursions.* Phoenix, AZ: Oryx. 259 p.

Palmer, Doris M. (Ed.). (1979). *Sources of Information on the European Communities.* London: Mansell. 230 p.

Aufricht, Hans. (1951). *Guide to League of Nations Publications: A Bibliographical Survey of the Work of the League, 1920–1947.* New York: Columbia University Press. 682 p.

Birchfield, Mary E. (1976). *Consolidated Catalog of League of Nations Publications Offered for Sale.* Dobbs Ferry, NY: Oceana. 477 p.

Reno, Edward A. (Ed.). (1973–75). *League of Nations Documents, 1919–1946: A Descriptive Guide and Key to the Microfilm Collection.* New Haven, CT: Research Publications. 3 vols.

Organization of American States. Department of Public Information. (1977). *Organization of American States, A Handbook.* Washington, DC. 36 p.

Welch, Thomas L., & Gutierrez, René L. (1990). *The Organization of American States: A Bibliography.* Washington, DC: Organization of American States. 87 p.

Birchfield, Mary E. (1982). *The Complete Reference Guide to United Nations Sales Publications, 1946-1978.* Pleasantville, NY: UNIFO. 2 vols.

Hajnal, Peter I. (1983). *Guide to UNESCO.* London: Oceana. 578 p.

UNDOC: Current Index: United Nations Documents Index. (1979–). New York: United Nations. Ten issues a year, with annual cumulations.
Indexes documents of the UN and its satellites. Continues a series going back to 1946.

United Nations Publications in Print. (1973–). New York: Unipub. Annual.

United Nations. Staff of Permanent Missions. (1981). *United Nations Documentation: A Brief Guide.* New York. 51 p.

Winton, Harry N. M. (Comp.). (1972). *Publications of the United Nations System: A Reference Guide.* New York: Bowker. 202 p.
Updated by listings in the quarterly *International Bibliography.*

Each country has its own system of bibliographic and statistical documentation. Some sources for the latter are addressed in chapter 11. Those particularly interested in the concerns of other countries will be better off using this chapter as a starting point for thought and not as a basis for sustained action.

NOTES

1. For a discussion of archival sources, see chapter 16.

2. Joseph Gusfield's (1963) *Symbolic Crusade* (Urbana, IL: University of Illinois Press) is an exciting examination of the enactment of Prohibition and is a classic example of how academics have analyzed legislative processes to shed light on the broader social and political strains that they represent. Gusfield, like other scholars concerned with the sociology or political economy of law, interprets "legislative history" to include biographical data and institutional records of individuals and organizations lobbying for or against the Volstead Act, as well as a wide range of other materials.

3. That is, a court is not obliged to follow its reasoning or apply it to the case in point, but may be persuaded to do so by the cogency of its argument and the strength of the legal precedent it quotes.

4. The common-law system is considered to have become a modern one sometime in the early 19th century. Legal scholars generally consider the development of a well-developed system of case reporting as a crucial element in this shift to modernization.

5. The *NCJRS* database, for example (see chapter 9), includes many documents produced by state and local criminal justice agencies.

14

SOURCES OF METHODOLOGY AND RESEARCH INSTRUMENTS

Methodological approaches in the social and policy sciences are quite stylized, in that the mechanics of such things as questionnaire and poll design, sampling, coding, and other structural features of the survey must conform to established rules. Explanations of these rules and of the processes of survey analysis and other approaches to research are not hard to come by. Perhaps the easiest way to locate them is by browsing through the several areas of the library stacks dealing with research design. In academic libraries, which universally use the Library of Congress classification system, the crucial areas would be the "H" and "HA" call-number schedules. These address research design in general. Works dealing generally with quantitative aspects of the research process are found under the call number "QA 76." The limitations of this technique are evidenced by the fact that methodological works addressing particular disciplines are not as accessible because they are assigned call numbers associated with their disciplinary focuses.[1] Browsing is a good way of looking for methodology. It is an informal approach; it is not a foolproof one.

The search for an appropriate methodology is as important as any other activity related to the project in hand. There is, however, a strong difference between a search on a topic and one for the method used to address it. The former is comprehensive and the latter quite selective. A search for a methodology, like a search for a data source (and the two often go together), is for something appropriate, and this is all. There is no sense in which an investigation for a suitable methodology should be exhaustive. Nor is the chosen methodology necessarily the only suitable one for its purpose. It is simply one that can do the job and has for this reason become the researcher's object of choice.

The process of searching for methods or instruments is free-ranging but not entirely unstructured. It is thoughtful and expansive but not just wishful or uncontrolled. It is not on a par with looking for a needle in a haystack or Elvis Presley in a shopping mall. There are some formal techniques for identifying appropriate methodologies. Library catalogs, indexes, abstracts, and databases can provide such information, but they do so tangentially. Subject access is their focus. These resources can be of great help if they are used with some subtlety. Chapters 6 and 9 vaunt the advantages of the keyword search and suggest how this searching can help obviate the natural bias of these systems against methodological interest (section 4 of chapter 6 addresses this problem explicitly). Information systems are subject-oriented; they do not relate to methodological issues. These must be massaged from them through keyword associations that combine knowledge and imagination.

In chapter 6 reference was made to keyword searching of computerized library catalogs to identify individual titles in book series. This technique is of some concern here as a number of publishers who regularly bring out works in series devoted to methodological series. Noteworthy here are the Sage series entitled "Advanced Quantitative Techniques in the Social Sciences," "Measurement Methods for the Social Sciences," "Guides to Major Social Science Data Bases," "Applied Social Research Methods," and the "Sage Library of Social Research." A number of the works cited in this chapter are from these series.

The principle behind every literature search recognizes that the successful researcher builds on the work of others and does not operate in an intellectual vacuum. Questionnaires, tests, and other instruments may be borrowed in original or modified forms and applied in new settings. It is just as acceptable to do so as it is to use theories or secondary data developed by the work of other people. Appropriate acknowledgments are, of course, mandatory when this is done.

Some structured help is available in the form of the many excellent guides to social research. The best provide overviews of the many approaches to research and include bibliographies of exemplary and otherwise illuminating material. A selection of these guides is presented below: first, those concentrating on research design; next, those that address particular aspects of quantitative research. Section 3 includes important works concerned with qualitative techniques. Current sources are discussed in section 4. Following this, the distinctive techniques of archival and other historical research, whether qualitative or quantitative, are discussed. The final categories include the self-contained area of psychological tests and the unique resources that constitute the Human Relations Area Files. Excluded are guides to secondary analysis of machine-readable data. These are considered in chapter 12. Sources of statistical data are discussed in chapters 11 and 12. Chapters 13, 15, and 16 include discussion of printed primary sources of a nonquantitative nature.

Annotations are given only for those works listed here whose titles do not indicate their obvious value. Citations are grouped according to form of approach; disciplinary attachments are ignored.

1. RESEARCH DESIGN

Adams, Gerald R., & Schvaneveldt, Jay D. (1991). *Understanding Research Methods* (2nd ed.). New York: Longman. 405 p.

Alreck, Pamela L., & Settle, Robert. (1985). *The Survey Research Handbook.* Homewood, IL: Richard D. Irwin. 429 p.

Bausell, R. Barker. (1991). *Advanced Research Methodology: An Annotated Guide to Sources.* Metuchen, NJ: Scarecrow. 903 p.

A very important bibliography on research design and its quantitative applications. Entries are grouped within 48 broad subject categories (causal modeling, reliability theory, and so on).

Belson, William A., & Thompson, Beryl-Anne. (1973). *Bibliography on Methods of Social and Business Research.* New York: Wiley. 300 p.

Indexes studies published between 1930 and 1970 by subject and also by methodological issues addressed.

Berry, William D., & Lewis-Beck, Michael S. (Eds.). (1986). *New Tools for Social Scientists: Advances and Applications in Research Methods.* Beverly Hills, CA: Sage. 288 p.

Blum, Milton L., & Foos, Paul W. (1985). *Data Gathering: Experimental Methods Plus.* New York: Harper & Row. 324 p.

Bositis, David A. (1990). *Research Designs for Political Science: Contrivance and Demonstration in Theory and Practice.* Carbondale: Southern Illinois University Press. 167 p.

Bracken, Ian. (1981). *Urban Planning Methods: Research and Policy Analysis.* New York: Methuen. 400 p.

Brewer, John, & Hunter, Albert. (1989). *Multimethod Research: A Synthesis of Styles.* Newbury Park, CA: Sage. 209 p.

Brinberg, David, & McGrath, Joseph. (1985). *Validity and the Research Process.* Beverly Hills, CA: Sage. 175 p.

Caplovitz, David. (1983). *The Stages of Social Research.* New York: Wiley. 434 p.

Chadwick, Bruce A., Bahr, Howard M., & Albrecht, Stan L. (1984). *Social Science Research Methods.* Englewood Cliffs, NJ: Prentice-Hall. 454 p.

Clark, Charles L. (Ed.). (1982). *A Guide to Theories of Economic Development: Cross-National Tests.* New Haven, CT: HRAF Press. 321 p.

Cozby, Paul C. (1989). *Methods in Behavioral Research* (4th ed.). Mountain View, CA: Mayfield. 302 p.

Das, T. K. (Comp.). (1990). *The Time Dimension: An Interdisciplinary Guide.* New York: Praeger. 344 p.

A unique source addressing the literature of temporal research and unrestricted by discipline and perspective. Entries are arranged within 21 subject categories. No annotations.

Denzin, Norman K. (1989). *The Research Act: A Theoretical Introduction to Sociological Methods* (3rd ed.). Englewood Cliffs, NJ: Prentice Hall. 306 p.

Hagan, Frank E. (1982). *Research Methods in Criminal Justice and Criminology.* New York: Macmillan. 461 p.

Useful as a guide to quantitative methods that includes many illustrations from actual studies. Also describes various sources of crime data and cites studies that have analyzed them. Among the best of several similar handbooks.

Hakim, Catherine. (1986). *Research Design: Strategies and Choices in the Design of Social Research.* London: Allen & Unwin. 211 p.

Johnson, Glenn L. (1986). *Research Methodology for Economists: Philosophy and Practice.* New York: Macmillan. 252 p.

Johnson, Janet B., & Joslyn, Richard A. (1991). *Political Science Research Methods* (2nd ed.). Washington, DC: CQ Press. 407 p.

Mann, Peter H. (1985). *Methods of Social Investigation* (2nd ed.). Oxford, UK: Blackwell. 222 p.

McInnis, Raymond G., & Scott, James W. (1984). *Social Science Research Handbook.* New York: Garland. 436 p.

Important for its consideration of approaches taken throughout the social sciences and including cross-cultural research. Rather limited in value now as it is an unrevised reprint of a 1975 work.

Miller, Connie, & Treitel, Corinna. (1991). *Feminist Research Methods: An Annotated Bibliography*. Westport, CT: Greenwood. 279 p.

Entries address the question of whether feminist researchers do bring new methods, as well as new perceptions, to social issues. Arranged by subject.

Miller, Delbert C. (1991). *Handbook of Research Design and Social Measurement* (5th ed.). Newbury Park, CA: Sage. 704 p.

One of several works providing practical discussions of the construction and implementation of research projects, together with some consideration of primary sources.

O'Sullivan, Elizabethann, & Rassel, Gary R. (1989). *Research Methods for Public Administrators.* New York: Longman. 450p.

A well-reviewed work designed as a teaching text. Valuable for its critical coverage of the secondary use of machine-readable data files, in particular its interesting observations on the use of 1990 census data.

Oyen, Else (Ed.). (1990). *Comparative Methodology: Theory and Practice in International Social Research.* Newbury Park, CA: Sage. 227 p.

Perry, James L., & Kraemer, Kenneth L. (1986). Research Methodology in the *Public Administration Review*, 1975-1984. *Public Administration Review, 46*, 215-26.

Assesses all research studies published in the *PAR* in this period from the point of view of the methodologies used. Concludes that such methodologies were often flawed in their application, and that research objectives were primarily problem-directed.

Plano, Jack C., Riggs, Robert E., & Robin, Helenan S. (Eds.). (1982). *The Dictionary of Political Analysis* (2nd ed.). Santa Barbara, CA: ABC-Clio. 197 p.

A very specialized dictionary addressing the terminology of methods. Theoretical constructs are only mentioned in the context of their application. (See, for example, the clear explanation of the prisoner's dilemma game.) The major source of its kind. Recommended for browsing into social science thinking about methods of approach.

Redman, Deborah A. (1989). *Economic Methodology: A Bibliography with References to Works in the Philosophy of Science, 1860–1988.* Westport, CT: Greenwood. 285 p.

Rossi, Peter, Wright, James, & Anderson, Andy (Eds.). (1983). *Handbook of Survey Research.* New York: Academic Press. 755 p.

A detailed guide to the major issues and problems involved in the design and analysis of sampling surveys. Subjects include theoretical as well as technical discussions of sampling and measurement methods, questionnaire construction, data collection, analysis of qualitatative data, and assessment of surveys as social indicators.

Selltiz, Claire, Wrightsman, Lawrence S., & Cook, Stuart W. (1980). *Research Methods in Social Relations* (4th ed.). New York: Holt, Rinehart & Winston. 483 p.

A useful and popular general guide, but limited by its relative neglect of research designs incorporating the use of existing data.

Shennan, W. M. (1984). *Towards New Methodological Realms in Urban and Regional Planning.* Chicago: Council of Planning Librarians. 10 p.

Smith, Robert B., & Manning, Peter K. (Eds.). (1983–). *Handbook of Social Science Methods.* Cambridge, MA: Ballinger.

An unusual work for several reasons. It gives considerable attention to theoretical and other problems raised by the techniques of social research described, and it pays a great deal of attention to qualitative methods. Three volumes published so far.

Weiss, Carol (Ed.). (1977). *Using Social Research in Public Policy-Making.* Lexington, MA: Lexington Books. 256 p.

Case studies included address policy evaluation as well as creation.

Wenger, G. Clare (Ed.). (1987). *The Research Relationship: Practice and Politics in Social Policy Research.* London: Allen & Unwin. 228 p.

2. QUANTITATIVE METHODS

2.1. General

Arrow, Kenneth J., & Intriligator, Michael (Eds.) (1981–91). *Handbook of Mathematical Economics.* Amsterdam: Elsevier. 4 vols.

An important source that presents long essays. Each includes extensive bibliographies.

Brodsky, Stanley L., & Smitherman, H. O'Neal. (1983). *Handbook of Scales for Research in Crime and Delinquency.* New York: Plenum. 615 p.

One of a number of specialized guides of its kind. Very useful for its inclusion of sample research instruments and references for further reading.

Griliches, Zvi, & Intriligator, Michael (Eds.). (1983–86). *Handbook of Econometrics.* New York: Elsevier. 3 vols.

A comprehensive guide to this area. Articles are quantitative and intended for the expert. The best guide in this area for informed persons.

Hovik, Nils. (1987). *Indicators of Social Change, Measures of the Quality of Life, Economic Sociology, Complex Organizations, and Futures Methodology: An Annotated Bibliography.* Monticello, IL: Vance. 47 p.

Kotz, Samuel, & Johnson, Norman L. (Eds.). (1982–89). *Encyclopedia of Statistical Sciences.* New York: Wiley. 10 vols.

An extremely ambitious and comprehensive work. Purports to be a resource for both the novice and the advanced researcher. In fact, discussions are sophisticated and generally pay most attention to advanced concepts.

Kruskal, William H., & Tanur, Judith M. (Eds.) (1978). *International Encyclopedia of Statistics.* New York: Free Press. 2 vols.

A compilation of all articles of a quantitative nature originally published in the *International Encyclopedia of the Social Sciences* (see chapter 3). Original articles have been revised, and some new ones have been added. A companion to Ross (see below).

McCloskey, Donald N., & Hersh, George K. (1990). *A Bibliography of Historical Economics to 1980.* New York: Cambridge University Press. 505 p.

Documents the multidisciplinary efforts of those who have applied a variety of economic techniques and models to historical circumstances. Entries are arranged within 17 subject categories.

Meier, Kenneth J., & Brudney, Jeffrey L. (1987). *Applied Statistics for Public Administration* (rev. ed.). Monterey, CA: Brooks/Cole. 460 p.

Nesselroade, John R., & Cattell, Raymond B. (Eds.). (1988). *Handbook of Multivariate Experimental Psychology* (2nd ed.). New York: Plenum. 966 p.

Price, James L., & Mueller, Charles W. (1986). *Handbook of Organizational Measurement.* Marshfield, MA: Pitman. 293 p.

Each of the 32 chapters addresses some aspect of the work setting and discusses concepts of measurement in it. Research in each field is reviewed, but these reviews are selective and not always useful as guides to further reading.

Ross, John A. (Ed.). (1982). *International Encyclopedia of Population.* New York: Free Press. 2 vols.

Like Kruskal and Tanur (above), largely a compilation of articles originally published in the *International Encyclopedia of the Social Sciences*, although some new material is included. Many references to sources and statistical compilations.

Vito, Gennaro F., & Latessa, Edward J. (1989). *Statistical Applications in Criminal Justice.* Newbury Park, CA: Sage. 120 p.

Wall, Francis J. (1986). *Statistical Data Analysis Handbook.* New York: McGraw-Hill. 285 p.

Highly recommended for the researcher with some statistical background and seeking reviews of specific ideas and concepts. Not a substitute for statistical training and not recommended to those without it.

Welch, Susan, & Comer, John. (1988). *Quantitative Methods for Public Administration: Techniques and Applications* (2nd ed.). Chicago: Dorsey Press. 377 p.

2.2. Polls and Questionnaires

Beed, Terence W., & Stimson, Robert J. (Eds.). (1985). *Survey Interviewing: Theory and Techniques.* Boston: Allen & Unwin. 224 p.

Berdie, Douglas R., Anderson, John F., & Niebuhr, Marsha A. (1986). *Questionnaires: Design and Use* (2nd ed.). Metuchen, NJ: Scarecrow. 330 p.

An important annotated bibliography that addresses both sources and methods.

Bourgeois, Donald J. (1985). *Annotated Bibliography, Public Opinion and Social Policy*. Ottawa: Canada. Ministry of the Solicitor General. 56 p.

Excellent for its citations (some with annotations) of the creative uses of this data. Does not address their sources.

Dickinson, John R. (1990). *The Bibliography of Marketing Research Methods* (3rd ed.). Lexington, MA: Lexington Books. 1,025 p.

A comprehensive annotated guide to a literature that addresses the philosophy and techniques of many forms of polling and survey analysis.

Fairweather, George W., and Tornatzky, Louis G. (1977). *Experimental Methods for Social Policy Research.* New York: Pergamon. 420 p.

Reviews findings in this area. Can also be used as a guide to method.

Fowler, Floyd J. (1988). *Survey Research Methods* (rev. ed.). Beverly Hills, CA: Sage. 159 p.

Hennessy, Bernard C. (1985). *Public Opinion* (5th ed.). Monterey, CA: Brooks/Cole. 366 p.

The standard work used in courses addressing this area.

Hyman, Herbert H. (1991). *Taking Society's Measure: A Personal History of Survey Research.* New York: Russell Sage Foundation. 257 p.

Unique as a personalized guide to the stages of the research process from which novices can profit.

Jenkins, Thomas H., & Seufert, Robert. (1975). *Theory, Research, Policy, and Action: A Bibliography on Planning and Social Analysis.* Monticello, IL: Council of Planning Librarians. 29 p.

Kalton, Graham. *Introduction to Survey Sampling.* Beverly Hills, CA: Sage, 1983. 96 p.

An example of one of many excellent short guides to method published by Sage, primarily in its Quantitative Applications in the Social Sciences series.

Lake, Lucinda C. (1987). *Public Opinion Polling.* Washington, DC: Island Press. 166 p.

Moore, David W. (1992). *The Superpollsters: How They Measure and Manipulate Public Opinion in America.* New York: Four Walls Eight Windows. 384 p.

A cautionary discussion of the potential influence of polls and the pollster on the substance of the data collected.

Nieburg, Harold L. (1984). *Public Opinion, Tracking and Targeting.* New York: Praeger. 287 p.

Sonquist, John A., & Dunkelberg, William C. (1977). *Survey and Opinion Research: Procedures for Processing and Analysis.* Englewood Cliffs, NJ: Prentice-Hall. 502 p.

Walden, Graham R. (1990). *Public Opinion Polls and Survey Research: A Selective Annotated Bibliography of U.S. Guides and Studies from the 1980s.* New York: Garland. 306 p.

Young, Michael L. (Ed.). (1992). *Dictionary of Polling: The Language of Contemporary Opinion Research.* Westport, CT: Greenwood. 266 p.
Definitions are lengthy and taken from identified sources. Extremely valuable as an introduction to the techniques and concepts of opinion research.

2.3. Electoral Behavior

Clubb, Jerome M., Flanigan, William H., & Zingale, Nancy H. (Eds.). (1981). *Analyzing Electoral History: A Guide to the Study of American Voter Behavior.* Beverly Hills, CA: Sage. 310 p.
The best guide of its kind and one that addresses data sources as well as method. One chapter is devoted to discussion of sources of machine-readable data.

Electoral Studies. (1982–). Guildford, UK: Butterworths. Quarterly.
Important for its regular discussions of new methodological developments.

Flanigan, William H., & Zingale, Nancy H. (1991). *Political Behavior of the American Electorate* (7th ed.). Washington, DC: CQ Press. 204 p.
A compilation of recent data which is revised regularly.

Goehlert, Robert. (1981). *Voting Research and Modeling: A Bibliography.* Monticello, IL: Vance. 49 p.

Ordeshook, Peter C. (Ed.). (1989). *Models of Strategic Choice in Politics.* Ann Arbor, MI: University of Michigan Press. 379 p.
Discusses the application of mathematical models to voting and other political behaviors.

Shaffer, William R. (1972). *Computer Simulations of Voting Behavior.* New York: Oxford University Press. 164 p.

2.4. Evaluation Research

Dworaczek, Marian. (1989). *Program Evaluation: A Bibliography.* Monticello, IL: Vance. 26 p.

Updates a much longer bibliography with the same author and title published in 1983.

Dynes, Patrick S., & Marvel, Mary K. (1987). *Program Evaluation: An Annotated Bibliography.* New York: Garland. 241 p.

Over 400 entries, all with long annotations. The first chapter (63 entries) presents "Overviews of Program Evaluation."

Klein, Malcolm W., & Teilmann, Katherine S. (Eds.). (1980). *Handbook of Criminal Justice Evaluation.* Beverly Hills, CA: Sage. 693 p.

Has the twin objectives of presenting standard techniques in the particular context addressed and discussing those techniques and concepts unique to evaluation in criminal justice settings. All essays are by prominent scholars.

Kosecoff, Jacqueline B., & Fink, Arlene. (1982). *Evaluation Basics: A Practitioner's Manual.* Beverly Hills, CA: Sage. 247 p.

Presents the mechanics of the process very well, but is little concerned with its contexts.

Leistritz, F. Larry, & Ekstrom, Brenda L. (1986). *Social Impact Assessment and Management: An Annotated Bibliography.* New York: Garland. 343 p.

Pollard, William E. (1986). *Bayesian Statistics for Evaluation Research: An Introduction.* Beverly Hills, CA: Sage. 256 p.

Discusses applications of these standard mathematical techniques to evaluation processes.

Rossi, Peter H., & Freeman, Howard E. (1989). *Evaluation: A Systematic Approach* (4th ed.). Newbury Park, CA: Sage. 384 p.

A collection of essays compiled by one of the experts in this area. Now rather dated, but still expressive of major dilemmas in this approach.

Struening, Elmer L., & Guttentag, Marcia (Eds.). (1975). *Handbook of Evaluation Research.* Beverly Hills, CA: Sage. 2 vols.

Concentrates on the methods of this type of analysis, but also includes essays addressing its political and social contexts. One section includes several illustrative essays on aspects of its approach to one area: mental health services. A major resource in its field.

3. QUALITATIVE METHODS

Berg, David N., & Smith, Kenwyn K. (Eds.). (1985). *Exploring Clinical Methods for Social Research.* Beverly Hills, CA: Sage. 400 p.

Bernard, H. Russell. (1988). *Research Methods in Cultural Anthropology.* Newbury Park, CA: Sage. 520 p.

Brenner, Michael, Brown, Jennifer, & Canter, David (Eds.). (1985). *The Research Interview: Uses and Approaches.* London: Academic Press. 276 p.

Fetterman, David M. (1989). *Ethnography: Step by Step.* Newbury Park, CA: Sage. 156 p.

Glazier, Jack D., & Powell, Ronald B. (1992). *Qualitative Research in Information Management.* Englewood, CO: Libraries Unlimited. 200 p.

Gravel, Pierre B., & Ridinger, Robert B. (1988). *Anthropological Fieldwork: An Annotated Bibliography.* New York: Garland. 241 p.

Gummesson, Evert. (1991). *Qualitative Methods in Management Research.* Newbury Park, CA: Sage. 224 p.

A detailed explication of the ways in which the anthropological field technique of participant observation can profitably be applied in the study of organizations.

Jorgensen, Danny L. (1989). *Participant Observation: A Methodology for Human Studies.* Newbury Park, CA: Sage. 133 p.

Kirk, Jerome, & Miller, Marc L. (1986). *Reliability and Validity in Qualitative Research.* Beverly Hills, CA: Sage. 87 p.

Marshall, Catherine, & Rossman, Gretchen B. (1989). *Designing Qualitative Research.* Newbury Park, CA: Sage. 175 p.

Naroll, Raoul, & Cohen, Ronald (Eds.). (1970). *A Handbook of Method in Cultural Anthropology.* Garden City, NY: Natural History Press. 1,017 p.

Although now quite old, still the standard overview of this area. Presents discussion within 49 chapters that collectively provide an approach to methods integrated with consideration of research design.

Schein, Edgar H. (1987). *The Clinical Perspective in Fieldwork.* Newbury Park, CA: Sage. 72 p.

Shaffir, William B., & Stebbins, Robert A. (Eds.). (1991). *Experiencing Fieldwork: An Inside View of Qualitative Research.* Newbury Park, CA: Sage. 274 p.

Stewart, David, & Mickunas, Algis. (1990). *Exploring Phenomenology: A Guide to the Field and Its Literature* (2nd ed.). Columbus: Ohio State University Press. 181 p.

A guide to an area encompassing its own qualitative methodological concerns as well as its own theoretical perspective. Rather dated, as this edition varies only slightly from that published in 1975.

Strauss, Anselm, & Corbin, Juliet. (1990). *Basics of Qualitative Research: Grounded Theory Procedures and Techniques.* Newbury Park, CA: Sage. 272 p.

A primer on translating a particular conceptual approach to research design (see chapter 2) into a detailed research plan.

Taylor, Steven J., and Bogdan, Robert. (1984). *Introduction to Qualitative Research Methods* (2nd ed.). New York: Wiley. 302 p.

Whyte, William F. (1984) *Learning from the Field: A Guide from Experience.* Beverly Hills, CA: Sage. 295 p.

A guide to methods of fieldwork, such as participant observation, pioneered in anthropology, but now used widely in organizational studies by other social scientists.

4. CURRENT SOURCES

Most of the annual reviews discussed in appendix 1 pay some attention to methodological issues. Those in section 11 of this appendix address methodological issues exclusively. They should be used to supplement the specialized indexing services discussed here.

Applied Science and Technology Index. (1913–). Bronx, NY: H. W. Wilson. Monthly, with quarterly and annual cumulations.

An important and long-established index in this field. Cited here for its variety of coverage of journals in the social and behavioral sciences with a quantitative focus. Former title: *Industrial Arts Index.*

Computer Directory. (Current year). New York: Ziff Communications. Updated monthly.

An electronic catalog of over 60,000 computer-related products currently being marketed. Includes many software packages, such as tests and other instruments, of potential interest to the social and behavioral researcher. one of a number of databases of this kind.

Current Index to Statistics: Applications—Methods—Theory. (1975–). Alexandria, VA: American Statistical Association. Annual.

Cosponsored by the Institute for Mathematical Statistics. Covers about 100 journals.

Historical Methods: A Journal of Quantitative and Interdisciplinary History. (1967–). Washington, DC: Heldref. Quarterly.

The oldest of the substantial group of journals devoted to quantitative approaches in historical methodology.

International Abstracts in Operations Research. (1961–). Amsterdam: North-Holland. Bimonthly.

Abstracts are in English and are grouped within four broad categories. A subject index is included in each issue. Sponsored by the International Federation of Operational Research Societies. Covers over 200 journals.

ICPSR Variables. (1948–). Ann Arbor: University of Michigan, Inter-University Consortium for Political and Social Research. Updated quarterly.

A database that includes the full texts of questionnaires and response patterns from about 150 of the most-used ICPSR public opinion data sets.

Journal Contents in Quantitative Methods. (1979–). Manchester, UK: University of Manchester. School of Management. Monthly.

Each issue reproduces the contents pages of about 150 journals in operations research, statistics, and other areas with a quantitative emphasis.

Journal of Economic and Social Measurement. (1972–). New York: North-Holland. Quarterly.

Addresses "the production, distribution, and use of statistical data . . . the methodology of economic and social measurements, the application of these data to research problems, the development and use of software tools, and the technical as well as legal problems associated with these measurement activities." Formerly *Review of Public Data Use*.

Operations Research/Management Science. (1961–). Whippany, NJ: Executive Sciences Institute. Monthly.

A loose-leaf service presenting summaries in English of articles from journals published throughout the world. Entries are arranged in classified order. Covers about 150 journals.

Qualitative Sociology. (1978–). New York: Human Sciences Press. Quarterly.

"Dedicated to the qualitative interpretation and analysis of social life." "Qualitative" is interpreted to include "research methods such as interviewing, participant observation, ethnography historical analysis, content analysis, and others which do not rely primarily on numerical data."

Quality Control and Applied Statistics Yearbook. (1956–). Whippany, NJ: Executive Sciences Institute.

International in coverage and with abstracts in English. Articles covered are very technical in their focus. This service is very much geared to the needs of the scholar, not the practitioner.

Social Research and Methodology Abstracts. (1979–). Rotterdam: Erasmus University. SRM-Documentation Centre. Annual.

Abstracts articles dealing with empirical methods published in over 100 journals. In a separate section relevant articles abstracted elsewhere are presented. Some volumes are entitled *SRM Abstracts*. Updated by the quarterly *Social Research and Methodology Bibliography*.

Statistical Theory and Method Abstracts. (1959–). Voorburg, Netherlands: International Statistical Institute. Quarterly.

Provides international coverage of a large number of articles purporting to present new approaches in this area. Abstracts are in English. Covers proceedings and conference papers as well as journals. Articles are grouped within 12 main categories.

Survey Methodology Information System. (1960–). Ann Arbor: University of Michigan, Institute for Political and Social Research. 7,800 records. Updated irregularly.

Provides citations with abstracts, of articles and other publications dealing with sampling, data analysis, and other aspects of research design. Otherwise known as *SMISS*. In database form only.

Survey Methodology Journal. (1974–). Ottawa: Statistics Canada. Semiannual.
Articles address problems of data collection and project design encountered by this governmental agency.

5. HISTORICAL METHODS AND ARCHIVAL RESEARCH

There are a number of published guides intended to introduce the academic novice to the world of archival research. A high proportion of them are now quite old. However, this happens to be one area of scholarly endeavor in which the currency of the approach (although not in the identification of sources) is not always consequential unless it is quantitative analysis that is planned. Not surprisingly, most of the guides that do exist are written for the archivist or historian and do not address the needs and interests of other social scientists. This is perhaps not a great disadvantage, as the discipline of history has had many generations to address its own problems of method and verifiability of data. Courses in historiography are required in doctoral programs in this discipline and generally emphasize problems of data acquisition and interpretation.

Many of the guides cited below include some discussion of the process of finding archival collections suitable for analysis. As this process is of such major importance to the historical researcher (even more so than for other social researchers, if this is possible), these discussions cannot be fully relied upon for this purpose. Careful use of the sources noted in chapter 16 is also advised. Rights of researchers to unpublished data held by government agencies are discussed in section 6 of chapter 13.

Brooks, Philip C. (1969). *Research in Archives: The Use of Unpublished Primary Sources.* Chicago: University of Chicago Press. 127 p.
The best general guide to archival research. Intended for the researcher and not the professional archivist and is particularly useful to the graduate student beginning work in this area. A well-written and well-organized text.

Brundage, Anthony. (1989). *Going to the Sources: A Guide to Historical Research and Writing.* Arlington Heights, IL: Harlan Davidson. 79 p.
A brief introductory guide to the processes of historical research and their relation to archival sources. For more advanced discussion, see works such as those of Handlin and Tilly (below).

Emmison, Frederick G. (1974). *Archives and Local History* (2nd ed.). Chichester, UK: Phillimore. 112 p.
One of the many guides that takes as its focus the interest of the local historian. Materials discussed relate to Great Britain only. (See also Parker and Josephson below.)

Evans, Frank B. (Comp.). (1971). *The Administration of Modern Archives: A Select Bibliographic Guide.* Washington, DC: U.S. Office of the National Archives. 213 p.
The outstanding guide to the older literature in the area. Primarily addresses archive administration, but also includes several chapters of interest to the researcher. Such chapters deal with federal, state, and local government, business, and labor union archives.

Evans, Frank B., & Pinkett, Harold T. (Eds.). (1975). *Research in the Administration of Public Policy.* Washington, DC: Howard University Press. 229 p.
Includes the text of the proceedings of a conference organized by the National Archives and Records Service in 1970 and designed to make scholars more aware of the potential of government archives as primary material for research in areas related to public administration. Papers emphasize the scope and volume of federal archives and provide excellent introductions to their use. One of the five sections concentrates on research techniques and the writing of histories of governmental agencies.

Handlin, Oscar. (1979). *Truth in History.* Cambridge, MA: Belknap Press. 437 p.
A thorough discussion of the objectives and methods of historical research by one of the major social historians of our age.

Hays, Samuel P. (1980). *American Political History as Social Analysis: Essays.* Knoxville: University of Tennessee Press. 459 p.
Uses examples taken from electoral data to illustrate their potential in addressing broader social questions. This is also a good introduction to the application of quantitative techniques to archival sources.

Hoy, Suellen M., & Robinson, Michael C. (Eds.). (1982). *Public Works History in the United States: A Guide to the Literature.* Nashville, TN: American Association for State and Local History. 477 p.
A valuable collection of essays dealing with the methods and accomplishments of scholars working in this increasingly popular area.

Iredale, David. (1973). *Enjoying Archives: What They Are, Where to Find Them, How to Use Them.* Newton Abbot, UK: David and Charles. 264 p.

A very clear and readable discussion of archival methods and of resources in England and Wales. Chapters are devoted to particular types of repository (for example, national archives, cathedral and parish records). Outstanding guides and sources are discussed in the text.

Jarausch, Konrad H., & Hardy, Kenneth A. (1991). *Quantitative Methods for Historians: A Guide to Research, Data, and Statistics.* Chapel Hill: University of North Carolina Press. 247p.

A comprehensive review of the appliciation of standard social science methodology to archival sources. Intended for both social scientists unfamiliar with archival research and historians unfamiliar with more general social science techniques.

Larsen, John C. (Ed.). (1988). *Researcher's Guide to Archives and Regional History Sources.* Hamden, CT: Shoestring Press. 167 p.

Modest, but the fourteen essays included are useful for the current nature of their discussions of methods and sources. Intended for the social scientist unfamiliar with the historical approach.

Mawdsley, Evan, & Munck, Thomas. (1993). *Computing for Historians: An Introductory Guide.* Manchester, UK: Manchester University Press. 200 p.

An introduction to microcomputer systems using spreadsheets, database, and statistical softward. Valuable for its use of 19th century census data in illustrating how historical data can be entered, stored, and analyzed. Most useful for the beginner.

Monkkonen, Eric H. (Ed.). (1992). *Theory and Methods in Criminal Justice History.* Westport, CT: Meckler. 550 p.

Essays survey the findings as well as the methodology of this rapidly growing field. In keeping with the editor's interests, several of the discussions address quantitative approaches.

Parker, Donald D., & Josephson, Bertha E. (1944). *Local History: How to Gather It, Write It, and Publish It.* New York: Social Science Research Council. 186 p.

Addresses both techniques and sources of local records in the United States. (see also Emmison above).

Parker, Lee D., & Graves, O. Findley (Eds.). (1989). *Methodology and Method in History: A Bibliography.* New York: Garland. 246 p.

The major bibliography of its kind and one that provides selective guidance to the literature of various qualitative and quantitative approaches to historical research.

Pitt, David C. (1972). *Using Historical Sources in Anthropology and Sociology.* New York: Holt, Rinehart & Winston. 88 p.
A modest introduction to the use of archives by nonhistorians. Most of the illustrative situations addressed come from anthropological research.

Pók, Attila (Ed.). (1992). *A Selected Bibliography of Modern Historiography.* Westport, CT: Greenwood. 284 p.
A guide to an area defined to address the nature and objectives of historical research. Entries are world-wide in coverage and occasionally include short annotations.

Preston, Jean. (1965). Problems in the Use of Manuscripts, *The American Archivist, 28*, 367–79.
Discusses problems in archival research resulting from copyright clearance, restriction of access, and other difficulties. Problems considered here are those that relate to private papers and not to classified material in government agencies.

Rubincam, Milton (Ed.). (1980). *Genealogical Research: Methods and Research* (rev. ed.). Washington, DC: American Society of Genealogists. 579 p.
A guide from the very flourishing field of genealogy that emphasizes both the sources themselves and the techniques used for their interpretation.

Rundell, Walter. (1970). *In Pursuit of American History: Research and Training in the United States.* Norman: University of Oklahoma Press. 445 p.
Primarily an overview of how graduate students in history departments are prepared for the research process. The last section includes a practical discussion of the problems involved in locating and using archival materials.

Saffady, William. (1974). Manuscripts and Psychohistory, *American Archivist, 37*, 551–64.
Essentially a bibliographic essay discussing how archives of various kinds have been used to support research in this quite specialized field. Included here as an example of the varied ways in which archives can be used in research.

Shafer, Robert J. (1980). *A Guide to Historical Method* (3rd ed.). Homewood, IL: Dorsey. 272 p.

Discusses social science methodologies in the context of the particular difficulties of those working with historical records. Addresses quantitative as well as qualitative analysis.

Skocpol, Theda (Ed.). (1984). *Vision and Method in Historical Sociology.* Cambridge, UK: Cambridge University Press. 410 p.
A collection of essays by experts in their fields on the use of historical materials by social analysts.

Tilly, Charles. (1981). *As Sociology Meets History.* New York: Academic Press. 237 p.
An important discussion of the use of archival sources to address theoretical questions of larger social concern.

Trask, David F., & Pomeroy, Robert W. (Eds.). (1983). *The Craft of Public History: An Annotated Select Bibliography.* Westport, CT: Greenwood. 481 p.
Works cited emphasize approaches to a rapidly growing field of historical inquiry that is based on the use of archives of public agencies.

Winks, Robin W. (Ed.). (1969). *The Historian as Detective: Essays on Evidence.* New York: Harper & Row. 543 p.
An important collection of essays addressing the nature of fallacy in historical interpretation and the nature of acceptable levels of proof. Each essay discusses these questions in specific contexts.

A number of scholarly journals regularly include articles dealing with methodological aspects of archival and other kinds of historical research. These include *Historical Methods* (1967–), *Political Methodology* (1974–85), *Public Historian* (1978–), and, most important of all, the *American Archivist* (1938–). The last-named of these includes an annual bibliography entitled "Writings on Archives, Historical Records, and Current Records."

6. PSYCHOLOGICAL TESTS AND RELATED MEASURES

Use of mental tests is characteristic of much research done in the disciplines of psychology and education. Because of the modern world's growing concern for the skills and abilities of its workers and students and their reactions to their places of work and study, use of tests of individual characteristics of various kinds has become widespread. Many are standardized and published commercially with guides to their interpretation and use. For these reasons, mental tests are much easier to identify and locate than other kinds of research instruments. Bibliographic control is excellent. Some sources noted here cover tests that are unpublished, that is, developed by researchers for their own use and not marketed commercially. Other unpublished tests can be found through the less systematic method of imaginative keyword searches in appropriate databases.

Advances in Experimental Social Psychology. (1964–). New York: Academic Press. Irregular (usually annual).

Most annual reviews pay some attention to methodological developments in their fields. This is one of the many to address areas heavily influenced by testing research.

Advances in Psychological Assessment. (1968–). San Francisco: Jossey-Bass. Annual.

Reviews new tests, techniques, and trends in assessment. Also provides literature reviews showing how, where, and by whom the measures have been used.

Beere, Carol A. (1990). *Gender Roles: A Handbook of Tests and Measures.* Westport, CT: Greenwood. 575 p.

Beere, Carol A. (1990). *Sex and Gender Issues: A Handbook of Tests and Measures.* Westport, CT: Greenwood. 605 p.

Between them these two works discuss the characteristics, use, and historical applications of several hundred tests, both social and psychological, in a gender-related context. Chapters are arranged by setting: heterosocial relations; family violence. The two titles constitute a revision of the author's 1979 one-volume *Women and Women's Issues: A Handbook of Tests and Measures.*

Buros, Oscar K. (Ed.). (1938–). *Mental Measurements Yearbook.* Highland Park, NJ: Gryphon. Irregular (latest is 1989), with occasional supplements.

Describes separately published tests marketed commercially. Cites and summarizes works reviewing tests and those that discuss their validation and use. Arranged by subject. The major source of its kind. Popularly known as the *MMY.*

Fabiano, Emily. (1989). *Index to Tests Used in Educational Dissertations.* Phoenix, AZ: Oryx. 371 p.

The only source devoted to the identification of the many tests (of greatly varying quality) in doctoral dissertations.

Goldman, Bert A., & Saunders, J. L. (Eds.). (1974–). *Directory of Unpublished Experimental Mental Measures.* New York: Human Sciences Press. Irregular.

A current source (the latest volume was published in 1990) that has coverage similar to that of Ki-Taek, Cobb, and French (below) and can be used to update it.

Groth-Marnat, Gary. (1990). *Handbook of Psychological Assessment* (2nd ed.). New York: Wiley. 594 p.

An important guide to the critical use of a limited number of tests, most of which were developed for clinical purposes. No discussion of test sources is included.

Journal of Personality Assessment. (1936–). Burbank, CA: Society for Personality Assessment. Quarterly.

Former titles include *Journal of Projective Techniques* and *Rorschach Research Exchange and Journal of Projective Techniques.* One of a number of journals in the behavioral sciences that regularly review new research instruments, most of which are psychological tests. Others include *Applied Psychological Measurement* (1977–), *Educational and Psychological Measurement* (1941–), *JEM, Journal of Educational Measurement* (1964–), *Journal of Psychoeducational Assessment* (1983–), *Measurement and Evaluation in Counseling and Development* (1967–), and *Psychological Assessment* (1989–).

Keeves, John P. (Ed.). (1988). *Educational Research, Methodology, and Measurement: An International Handbook.* New York: Pergamon. 832 p.

Similar in methodological focus, although not in broad subject matter, to Touliatos, Perlmutter, and Straus (below).

Ki-Taek, Chun, Cobb, Sidney, & French, John R. P. (Eds.). (1975). *Measures for Psychological Assessment: A Guide to 3,000 Original Sources and Their Applications.* Ann Arbor, MI: University of Michigan. Survey Research Center. 664 p.

A bibliography of tests not commercially published, but developed by researchers for their own purposes. Included are references to use of such tests by their originators and by others in articles in sociology and psychology journals published during the decade 1960–70.

Linn, Robert L. (Ed.). (1989). *Educational Measurement* (3rd ed.). New York: Macmillan. 620 p.

Includes 18 chapters, each addressing some aspect of the selection, construction, development, administration of tests and other educational measures.

Attention is given to the relationship of theoretical perspective to the concept and nature of measurement in this context.

McGiverin, Rolland H. (1990). *Educational and Psychological Tests in the Academic Library.* New York: Haworth. 94 p.

A succinct, but comprehensive, guide to bibliographic sources for identifying tests, whether published or unpublished.

Mitchell, James V. (Ed.). (1983). *Tests in Print III: An Index to Tests, Test Reviews, and the Literature on Specific Tests.* Lincoln, NE: University of Nebraska. Buros Institute of Mental Measurements. 714 p.

Supplements the *MMY* by citing and discussing only tests included in this source which are still available from their publishers. Earlier editions of this (*TIP I* and *TIP II*) were published in 1961 and 1974.

NT: News on Tests. (1969–). Princeton, NJ: Educational Testing Service. Ten issues a year.

Like other ETS products, emphasizes materials concerned with educational assessment. Formerly entitled *Test Collection Bulletin.*

O'Brien, Nancy P. (Comp.). (1988). *Test Construction: A Bibliography of Selected Resources.* Westport, CT: Greenwood. 299 p.

Almost 3,000 references refer to the subject in general and to the uses of specific tests (published or unpublished).

PSYTKOM. (1945–). Regensburg, Germany: Universitat Regensburg. 2,100 records. Updated five times a year.

This database includes abstracts of published and unpublished psychological and educational tests and other instruments. All sources are in the German language.

Sweetland, Richard C., & Keyser, Daniel J. (Eds.). (1986). *Tests: A Comprehensive Reference for Assessments in Psychology, Education, and Business* (2nd ed.). Kansas City, MO: Test Corporation of America. 1,122 p.

Cites, but does not evaluate, over 3,100 tests. (See *Test Critiques*, cited immediately below).

Test Critiques. (1984–). Kansas City, MO: Test Corporation of America. Annual.

Reviews published tests and assesses them for reliability and ease of use. Updates Sweetland and Keyser (above) and supplements it by providing the critiques lacking in this work.

Tests in Microfiche. (1975–). Princeton, NJ: Educational Testing Service. Updated regularly.

A microform collection of the tests themselves, most of which reflect some concern relevant to education. Extremely valuable, as this collection is widely available in libraries. Contents are accessible through the *Annotated Index* and *The ETS Test Collection Catalog*, published annually since 1986. Access is also available through a database, *ETS Test Collection*, maintained by BRS.

Touliatos, John, Perlmutter, Barry F., & Straus, Murray A. (1990). *Handbook of Family Measurement Techniques.* Newbury Park, CA: Sage. 797 p.

One of many guides to research in areas where the use of mental tests of some sort is dominant. Includes extensive discussions of how the tests have been used, as well as of their structure and interpretation.

Testing, whether for the academic purpose of research or the usually pragmatic one of assessment, has become an important feature of American life. It is, of course, testing for the latter purpose that has come to dominate, perhaps even obsess, many aspects of the educational process. Because of this, there are many bibliographies devoted exclusively to those tests that are widely used. An illustrative example is given below. Other bibliographies devoted to individual tests may be located by searching computerized catalogs of large libraries by keyword, combining the name of the test with such headings as "Bibliography," "Abstracts," "Methodology," and "Research." (The reader will by now, one hopes, have come to appreciate the benefits of keyword searching when these are obtained through an amalgam of subject knowledge, searching skill, and imagination.)

Taulbee, Earl S., Wright, H. Wilkes, & Stenmark, David E. (1977). *The Minnesota Multiphasic Personality Inventory (MMPI): A Comprehensive Annotated Bibliography (1940–1965).* Troy, NY: Whitston. 603 p.

"Beginning with 1967, the Psychological Abstracts Information Services . . . retrieve MMPI references appearing in *Psychological Abstracts* (and on its CD-ROM equivalent *PsycINFO*)."

7. THE HUMAN RELATIONS AREA FILE

Recent decades have seen the use of collections originally thought of as comprising secondary materials in new ways. The Human Relations Area Files (HRAF), for example, were developed as a collection of descriptions (published or in manuscript) of pretechnological cultures throughout the world. The collection was initiated in 1949 as a cooperative venture, based at Yale

University, of ethnographers and cultural anthropologists and now serves as a clearinghouse and archive for papers and monographs submitted by social scientists from over 250 academic institutions located worldwide. It is now huge and includes secondary data relating to over 300 cultural groups. These data are published on microfiche, and the collection is available in many large research libraries. In this sense HRAF functions as an important collection of secondary material in its area, and a number of current bibliographies and other reference works in anthropology rely heavily on its contents. In recent years HRAF has included machine-readable data in its holdings and is to this extent a repository of primary material.

However, this collection has a further singularly important use, and this is a consequence of the detailed system of indexing of it that has been created. As the contents of these files grew, an elaborate system of subject access was formulated to enable anthropologists and other interested parties to test propositions and hypotheses against a broad range of information. HRAF's records are now (in part) computerized. They can be searched by subject and also according to theoretical concepts and the means used to test them. In this way HRAF has become an important source for the theoretician as well as the area specialist. It is of interest here because, unlike most other bibliographic resources, detailed access is possible by *method*, *population*, and *concept* tested. Researchers may conduct searches of the collection to obtain descriptive data against which to test particular theoretical propositions.

Use of HRAF in this way as a *primary* resource (see chapter 16) is permitted only by its careful and unusual system of indexing. It follows that understanding of the structure of HRAF and the means of subject access to it are of extraordinary importance. The principal works concerned with this are cited below. Those considering using the archive for original purposes should take full advantage of this extensive bibliography associated with it, only a sampling of which is presented here.

Behavior Science Research. (1966–). New Haven, CT: Human Relations Area Files. Quarterly.

Publishes articles that document the results of cross-cultural research, particularly that using HRAF data. Formerly *Behavior Science Notes* and *HRAF Journal of Comparative Studies.*

Ember, Carol, & Ember, Melvin. (1988). *Guide to Cross-Cultural Research Using the HRAF Archive.* New Haven, CT: HRAF Press. 24 p.

The most detailed guide to the system, its organization, and its potential for exploitation. Also provides discussion of the many bibliographic aids to the collection not cited here. Use with Levinson 1988 (below).

HRAF Data Archive. (1989–). New Haven, CT: Human Relations Area Files. Updated regularly.

A full-text computerized version of the HRAF collection that as yet includes only a small proportion of the available material. When complete, this database will greatly ease the problem of customized access to the archive. This database is available through online vendors and on CD-ROM. When in the latter form, known as the *Cross-Cultural CD Computer File.*

HRAF Electronic Databases. (1992–). New Haven, CT: Human Relations Area Files. Annual.

Lists and describes individual data sets available in computerized form.

HRAF Source Bibliography. (1954—). New Haven, CT: Human Relations Area Files. Loose-leaf, with irregular updates.

Documents the bibliographic sources accessible through the *Index* and the *Data Archive.* Arranged by *OWC* code (see Murdock 1983 below), indicative of cultural category.

Index to the Human Relations Area Files. (1972). New Haven, CT. 8 vols., with 1979 and 1987 supplements.

Arranged by *OCM* category (see Murdock 1982 below). Update using the *HRAF Data Archive.* Should be used in conjunction with the *HRAF Source Bibliography* and the various sales catalogs issued regularly by the organization.

Lagacé, Robert O. (Ed.). (1977). *Sixty Cultures: A Guide to the HRAF Probability Sample Files.* New Haven, CT: Human Relations Area Files. 507 p.

A guide to the group of 60 files, each representing one cultural unit. Essays discuss problems and potential for comparison and cross-cultural analysis and cite important secondary literature. Intended as a serial, but only one volume seems ever to have been published.

Levinson, David. (1977). *Guide to Social Theory: Worldwide Cross-Cultural Tests.* New Haven, CT: HRAF Press. 5 vols.

Provides an inventory of theories and hypotheses that have been tested using HRAF data.

Levinson, David. (1988). *Instructor's and Librarian's Guide to the HRAF Archive.* New Haven, CT: Human Relations Area Files. 23 p.

Use to supplement Ember and Ember (above).

Murdock, George P. (1982). *Outline of Cultural Materials* (5th ed.). New Haven, CT: Human Relations Area Files. 247 p.

Lists and defines the *subject* categories (with their many subdivisions) used in HRAF and the codes associated with them. (This constitutes the *OCM* category.) This and the following work constitute the HRAF *thesaurus*.

Murdock, George P. (1983). *Outline of World Cultures* (6th ed.). New Haven, CT: Human Relations Area Files. 259 p.

Details the system under which human *cultures* are classified and indicates codes used within the system to represent them (*OWC* codes).

Naroll, Raoul, Michik, Gary L., & Naroll, Frada. (1976). *Worldwide Theory Testing*. New Haven, CT: Human Relations Area Files. 138 p.

Discusses the mechanics and cross-cultural applications of the archive using examples taken from the HRAF Probability Sample.

NOTE

1. The work by Hagan, for example (section 1), is given a call number ("HV") that reflects its intended disciplinary object, not its style of approach.

15

OTHER SOURCES OF INFORMATION

Earlier discussion relating to secondary sources has concentrated on information published in conventional ways, that is, in books, journal articles, and government documents. However, as the chapters dealing with statistics and other primary sources have indicated, much information of potential value is not accessible in these forms. Many important information resources are available through organizations that are not primarily in the business of publishing material for consumption by the scholarly community. Access to this information can often be achieved through indexes, abstracts, library catalogs, and other standard bibliographic resources. The coverage of these resources, however, is usually spotty, and specialized bibliographic tools must be used for systematic exploitation of materials in published forms that do not fall within the framework of conventional academic publication.

Sources providing coverage of these various forms are discussed in this chapter. Their relative importance to the research enterprise will, of course, depend on the nature of the project. Someone examining popular perceptions of the legal process, for example, would probably rely heavily on reports of trials and investigations published in the media. Someone else might be more than usually concerned with identifying research that is too recent to be published. In this case, papers presented at conferences would probably be of particular value. As with all stages in the research effort, decisions about which sources are to be examined, and what priority they are to be given, will result from the researcher's own informed assessment of how the topic is likely to be documented.

1. THESES AND DISSERTATIONS

At various points in this book the importance of dissertations has been emphasized.[1] Their potential value goes far beyond the findings they report. They can be invaluable as sources of method, theoretical perspective, primary data, and bibliography. A search for relevant dissertations is important whatever the topic of study. *Dissertation Abstracts*, published monthly in hard copy and also available online and on compact disk, provides extensive coverage of almost all dissertations accepted for higher degrees in the United States since the 1860s. For a number of years its coverage has been expanding steadily, and its universe now incorporates the academic products of a large number of other countries. Most dissertations identified through this source can be purchased from University Microfilms, which publishes this abstracting service. Others can usually be borrowed from their home institutions on interlibrary loan.

The lengthy abstracts provided by this service allow for imaginative searching of keywords and phrases when using one of its computerized versions. These abstracts also provide clear indications of a dissertation's potential value to the user and a means of culling the definitely relevant from the merely promising. Unfortunately, this important resource cannot be searched effectively by subject. Subject-headings are assigned to entries in it, but they confuse more than they help because they are driven by the nature of the academic department in which the degree was awarded. Keyword searching is often an effective substitute for formal subject access, but due to the size of the database and the length of the abstracts, it can be productive only when carefully planned.

For a number of reasons, it is important for the researcher to know of dissertations that are not directly related to the topic of concern, but have some other relevance to it. A study of the development of governmental regulatory power in one jurisdiction, for example, would probably be informed by studies of the same phenomenon in others. Studies of this kind are not easily found by database searching. The various title indexes to the contents of *Dissertation Abstracts* provide a more effective approach, and catalogs of dissertation titles in broad subject areas are published by UMI (University Microfilms International). UMI currently publishes *Dissertation Subject Catalogs* in more than 20 areas.[2] These catalogs are revised regularly and are updated by subject listings appearing in UMI's semiannual *Research Update*. Libraries rarely subscribe to these important sources, but personal subscriptions to them can be obtained at no cost by calling UMI's toll-free number (in the United States, 1-800-521-0600).

The listings given below include the most important indexes of this nature. Other works cited include current bibliographies of dissertations from countries not well represented in *Dissertation Abstracts*. Sources of dissertations from countries not addressed here are discussed in the guides by Allen and Deubert,

Borchardt and Thawley, and Reynolds. Other specialized bibliographies of dissertations are represented below by the works of Fox and Howard, Gilbert, and Robey.

Scholarly journals frequently include lists of dissertations recently accepted or in progress. These include the *Accounting Review*, the *American Economic Review*, *Business Horizons*, *Current Anthropology*, the *Industrial and Labor Relations Review*, the *Journal of Business*, the *Journal of Creative Behavior*, the *Journal of Economic History*, the *Journal of Finance*, *Omega*, and *P.S.* These can be informative, but the reader is warned that those in the first category are invariably picked up by the standard sources and those in the second are often red herrings in that they never result in acceptable products. Furthermore, sources of this kind are usually more limited than their titles suggest. *Doctoral Dissertations in History*, for example, includes only dissertations in this academic discipline and ignores the considerable historical work undertaken by students in other academic departments.

The various social science literature guides cited in chapters 3 and 4 include a much broader variety of sources for locating dissertations than those noted here. Only the most comprehensive sources are cited below.

Allen, G. G., & Deubert, K. (1984). *Guide to the Availability of Theses: II, Non-University Institutions.* New York: K. G. Saur. 124 p.

A supplement to Borchardt and Thawley (below).

American Doctoral Dissertations. (1956–). Ann Arbor, MI: University Microfilms. Annual.

More comprehensive than *Dissertation Abstracts* in that it includes references to dissertations from universities in the United States that are held in the University Microfilms collection. Continues a series, *Doctoral Dissertations Accepted by American Universities*, published annually between 1933 and 1955. Previously titled *Index to American Doctoral Dissertations.*

Bilboul, Roger R. (Ed.). (1975–77). *Retrospective Index to Theses of Great Britain and Ireland, 1716–1950.* Santa Barbara, CA: ABC-Clio. 5 vols.

Subject arrangement. Updated by *Index to Theses* (below). One of several examples of national bibliographies of dissertations cited here. (In common with the situation in many countries outside of the United States, this work makes no distinction between theses and dissertations and includes both.)

Borchardt, Dietrich H., & Thawley, J. D. (1981). *Guide to the Availability of Theses.* New York: K.G. Saur. 443 p.

The BRITS Index: An Index to British Theses Collections (1971–1987) Held at the British Library Document Supply Centre and London University. (1989). Godstone, UK: British Theses Service. 3 vols.

Covers about 68,000 theses and dissertations. Listing by author, title, and subject. No abstracts are provided.

Canadian Graduate Theses in the Humanities and Social Sciences, 1921-1946. (1951). Ottawa: Cloutier. 194 p.

A supplementary volume covers the period 1947-60.

Canadian Theses. Thèses Canadiennes. (1947–). Ottawa: National Library of Canada. Annual.

Comprehensive Dissertation Index, 1861–1972. (1973). Ann Arbor, MI: University Microfilms. 37 vols.

Arranged within broad, and not always helpful, subject categories. Updated by a supplement covering 1973–82 and by an annual published since 1974. Also online and on CD-ROM.

Dissertation Abstracts International. (1938–). Ann Arbor, MI: University Microfilms International. Monthly, with indexes that cumulate annually.

Published in three parts: sciences and engineering, the humanities and social sciences, and European dissertations. The last of these is published quarterly. Early volumes entitled *Microfilm Abstracts*. The cumulated volumes since 1986 are now available on CD-ROM and are best searches in this form.

Doctoral Dissertations in History. (1909–). Washington, DC: American Historical Association. Semiannual.

Since 1958 has included works in progress and those completed. Before this, covered only those in progress. Early volumes carry variant titles. Preceded by the *List of Doctoral Dissertations in Progress* published between 1901 and 1909.

Fox, Milden J., & Howard, Patsy C. (1983). *Labor Relations and Collective Bargaining: A Bibliographic Guide to Doctoral Research.* Metuchen, NJ: Scarecrow. 281 p.

Gilbert, Victor F. (Comp.). (1982). *Labour and Social History Theses: American, British, and Irish University Theses and Dissertations in the Field of British and Irish Labour History, Presented between 1900 and 1978.* London: Mansell. 194 p.

Greenwood Annual Abstract of Legal Dissertations and Theses. (1988–). Westport, CT: Greenwood.

The first volume covers 1985 through 1987 but only cites materials accepted at four law schools in the United States. No further volume has yet been published.

Index to Theses with Abstracts Accepted for Higher Degrees by the Universities of Great Britain and Ireland and the Council for National Academic Awards. (1953–). London: Aslib. Annual.

Updates Bilboul (above).

Kuehl, Warren F. (1965). *Dissertations in History: An Index to Dissertations Completed in History Departments of United States and Canadian Universities, 1873–1960.* Lexington: University of Kentucky Press. 249 p.

Supplements, by the same author and published in 1972 and 1985, cover the period 1960–70 and 1970–80.

Masters Abstracts International. (1962–). Ann Arbor, MI: University Microfilms International. Monthly, with cumulative indexes.

A highly selective source that reflects only a fraction of the theses accepted in North America and elsewhere. Formerly *Masters Abstracts.*

Master's Theses Directories. (1976–). Cedar Falls, IA: Research Publications. Annual.

Also quite selective. Lists bibliographies published commercially and directories of the products of individual academic institutions.

Reynolds, Michael M. (1985). *Guide to Theses and Dissertations: An International Bibliography of Bibliographies* (rev. ed.). Phoenix, AZ: Oryx. 263 p.

Includes lists published by individual institutions, as well as those in particular subject areas.

Robey, John S. (Comp.). (1984). *The Analysis of Public Policy: A Bibliography of Dissertations, 1977–1982.* Westport, CT: Greenwood. 225 p.

Robitaille, Denis, & Waiser, Joan. (1986). *Theses in Canada: A Bibliographic Guide. Thèses au Canada: Guide Bibliographique.* Ottawa: National Library of Canada. 72 p.

Includes theses in preparation.

Theses Accepted for Higher Degrees. (1963–). Mona, Jamaica: University of the West Indies. Annual.

Includes dissertations and theses.

U.S. Civil Service Commission. Library. (1957–). *Dissertations and Theses Relating to Personnel Administration Accepted by American Colleges and Universities.* Washington, DC. Irregular.

Most useful for its listings of master's theses. No volumes appear to have been published since 1968.

Young, Arthur P. (Comp.). (1989). *Cities and Towns in American History: A Bibliography of Doctoral Dissertations.* Westport, CT: Greenwood. 438 p.

2. NEWSPAPERS

Students undertaking term papers are usually discouraged from citing the popular press, but in certain situations this material serves a unique function. Documentation of a public event may require extensive use of media sources, including television news footage as well as printed media forms. Most court trials, for example, are not well documented by official sources. Transcripts of them are not usually made unless the verdict is appealed. Most trials that attract public attention are reported in greatest detail by the media, and it is the products of this reporting that are most important for the scholar. This is especially true for earlier times when reports of court cases attracted even more media attention than today and when court records were even more terse. Use of these materials must be made with a critical eye. They must be evaluated for internal consistency and after comparison with all other available sources. Media reports are used to *amplify* official records and are only *substitutes* for them when these records do not exist or provide inadequate detail.

When newspapers and magazines are used in this way, they are being analyzed as *primary* sources. A newspaper reports (or fails to report) events as they occur and in the normal course of its business. In doing so, it presents at least one perspective upon them. One can use media reports as primary evidence provided they are truly contemporary perceptions. I could, for example, use reporting in the *New York Times* for April 1865 as primary data on the assassination of Abraham Lincoln. Articles in this newspaper on the hundredth anniversary of Lincoln's death could also be used, but only as *secondary* sources. This is because the 1965 articles only give us a modern view of this event; they provide no reliable indicators as to how it was perceived and reported at the time.

There are many newspaper indexes, collections, union lists, and sources for locating titles. The outstanding ones are cited below. Traditionally, many of these were unpublished and maintained in manuscript form by individual newspapers for their own reference. The best formal way to identify them is through Milner (below). With the advance of computerization, many of these indexes, and even the full texts of newspapers, are becoming available online.[3] Older newspaper indexes, which in one case go back to the late eighteenth century, are a mixed blessing because, generally speaking, the older they are, the less are they reliable.

Bjørner, Susan N. (Ed.). (1992). *Newspapers Online: A Directory to North American Daily Newspapers Whose Articles Are Online in Full Text.* Needham Heights, MA: Biblio Data. 179 p.

Lists about 130 sources. Most useful for those seeking raw news material for analysis by techniques such as content analysis.

Brigham, Clarence S. (1962). *History and Bibliography of American Newspapers, 1690-1820* (rev. ed.). Hamden, CT: Archon. 2 vols.

Based on the holdings of the American Antiquarian Society and a guide to the holdings of the microform collection *Early American Newspapers.* Supplement with Kellerman and Wilson to identify sources in microform not in the AAA collection.

Canadian Literature Index: A Guide to Periodicals and Newspapers. (1987–). Markham, Ont.: Butterworths Canada. Annual.

Indexes over 100 newspapers, newsletters, and literary journals.

Early American Newspapers. (1983–). New York: Readex.

A microfilm collection which now includes over 2,000 newspapers published between the 17th and the early 19th centuries. Initially based on the massive holdings of the American Antiquarian Society but now reflects the holdings of a great many more institutions. Documented by Kellerman and Wilson (below).

Editor and Publisher International Year Book. (1920–). New York: Editor & Publisher.

Lists newspapers published throughout the world by geographic location. Annotations indicate circulation, political focus, and type.

Gale Directory of Publications and Broadcast Media. (1880–). Detroit: Gale. Annual. now in 3 vols.

Lists newspapers and popular magazines published in the United States, Canada, and some other countries. For most of its life published as the *Ayer Directory of Publications.*

Kellerman, Lydia S., & Wilson, Rebecca A. (Comps). (1990). *Index to [the] Readex Microfilm Collection of Early American Newspapers.* New Canaan, CT: Readex. 1 vol.; various pagings.

Primarily a source-list for the collection cited above.

McLeod, William R., & McLeod, V. B. (1982). *A Graphical Directory of English Newspapers and Periodicals, 1702–1714.* Morgantown, WV: West Virginia University. School of Journalism. 320 p.

Continues Nelson and Seccombe (below). An example of the many comprehensive aids for identifying newspapers and periodicals.

Milner, Anita C. (1977–1982). *Newspaper Indexes: A Location and Subject Guide for Researchers.* Metuchen, NJ: Scarecrow. 3 vols.

Lists U.S. newspapers by state and county. Annotations address published indexes and repositories maintaining indexes in manuscript form. Also includes some foreign sources.

The Morning Call (Allentown, PA). (1984–). Philadelphia: VU/TEXT. Updated daily.

Included here as one of several dozen local newspapers whose contents are now available electronically in full text and going back over a number of years.

National Newspaper Index. (1979–). Menlo Park, CA: Information Access. Monthly.

One of a number of sources that index groups of newspapers, in this case five, including the *Christian Science Monitor*, the *Los Angeles Times*, the *New York Times*, the *Wall Street Journal*, and the *Washington Post.* Available in both microfilm and database versions.

Nelson, Carolyn, & Seccombe, Matthew (Comps.). (1987). *British Newspapers and Periodicals, 1641–1700: A Short-Title Catalogue of Serials Printed in England, Scotland, Ireland, and British America.* New York: Modern Language Association. 724 p.

An appendix takes coverage to 1702, the starting point for McLeod and McLeod (above).

New York Times Index. (1851–). New York: New York Times. Semimonthly, with annual cumulations.

Cited here as an example of a printed index to a single newspaper. Like its British counterpart (below), valuable for its policy of summarizing, as well as indexing, the contents of the newspaper.

Newspaper and Periodical Abstracts. (1984–). Louisville, KY: UMI/Data Courier. 800,000 records. A database updated daily.

Indexes and abstracts the contents of about 25 major newspapers and 450 magazines. An earlier version entitled *Newspaper Abstracts.*

NEXIS. (1975–). Dayton, OH: Mead Data Central. Updated daily.

A database that includes the full texts of numbers of newspapers, magazines, wire-service products, radio broadcasts, and government regulations and other legal materials. The most extensive database of its kind.

Palmer's Index to the Times Newspaper. (1868–1943). London: Samuel Palmer. 162 vols.

A quarterly that indexed the London *Times* from 1790. Updated by the monthly *Times Index* and by a supplementary volume covering the period 1786–89.

Schwarzlose, Richard A. (1987). *Newspapers, A Reference Guide.* Westport, CT: Greenwood. 417 p.

Primarily an historical and bibliographic review of journalism and newspaper publishing but also includes important chapters dealing with newspaper collections, sources, and indexes.

U.S. Library of Congress. Catalog Publication Division. (1984). *Newspapers in Microform: Foreign Countries, 1948–1983.* Washington, DC. 504 p.

U.S. Library of Congress. Catalog Publication Division. (1984). *Newspapers in Microform: United States, 1948–1983.* Washington, DC. 2 vols.

Two union lists of more than 100,000 newspapers held in libraries in the United States and elsewhere. Listings are geographic, and annotations indicate libraries and their range of holdings. Each is updated by annual and quarterly supplements.

3. POPULAR MAGAZINES

These sources can be used in exactly the same ways as newspapers. They should be used warily, if at all, as secondary sources, but they can, if used properly, serve as unique documentation of a circumstance or event, or of contemporary perceptions of it. For the scholar, the importance of both newspapers and magazines lies in their strong potential as primary sources, rather than their dubious authority as secondary works.

Magazines are accessible in just the same way as newspapers. There are indexes, collections, and excellent union lists and other finding aids for them. In fact, they are easier for researchers to use than newspapers because there are fewer of them and a much higher proportion are indexed. Some magazines, like newspapers, have their own indexes. The contents of others are accessible through sources such as the *Readers' Guide*. For those using them as primary sources, the absence of an index to a particular magazine is usually of no great moment. Indexes to other magazines, or even newspapers, can be used to identify the time period during which the event of interest was in the public eye. The magazine of concern can then be searched page by page for that period.

As with many other current indexes noted at various points in this book, a number of the sources cited below are now available in electronic form, whether online or on CD-ROM.

Access: The Supplementary Index to Periodicals. (1975–). Evanston, IL: Burke. Three issues a year; one is the annual cumulation.

Indexes about 300 magazines not covered by the *Readers' Guide*. See also the *Magazine Index*.

Alternative Press Index. (1969–). Baltimore: Alternative Press Centre. Quarterly.

Indexes 200 or so serial publications—mostly magazines, but also some newspapers—with a radical or otherwise "alternative" flavor. Valuable for its coverage of serials not indexed elsewhere.

American Periodicals, 1741–1900. (1946–77). Ann Arbor, MI: UMI. Over 3,000 microfilm reels in three separate series: 1741–1800; 1800–1850; 1850–1900. Indexed by Hoornstra and Heath (below).

Noted here as one of several major collections of its kind. Sources of others are discussed in chapter 16.

Hoornstra, Jean, & Heath, Trudy (Eds.). (1979). *American Periodicals, 1741–1900: An Index to the Microfilm Collections—American Periodicals, 18th Century, American Periodicals, 1800–1850, American Periodicals, 1850–1900, Civil War and Reconstruction.* Ann Arbor, MI: UMI. 341 p.

Magazine Index. (1959–). Menlo Park, CA: Information Access. Updated monthly and cumulated every five years.

The complement of the *National Newspaper Index* and published in the same ways. Indexes about 400 popular magazines. One of several indexes providing access to popular magazines not addressed by the *Readers' Guide*.

Nineteenth Century Readers' Guide to Periodical Literature, 1890-1899, with Supplemental Indexing 1900–1922. (1944). New York: H. W. Wilson. 2 vols.
Indexes 50 magazines published between 1890 and 1922.

Poole, William F. (1963). *Poole's Index to Periodical Literature.* Gloucester, MA: P. Smith. 6 vols.
Indexes British and U.S. magazines published between 1802 and 1907.

Readers' Guide Abstracts. (1988–). New York: H. W. Wilson. Ten issues a year, with semiannual cumulations.
Abstracts the articles cited in the *Readers' Guide to Periodical Literature.*

Readers' Guide to Periodical Literature. (1900/04–). New York: H. W. Wilson. Biweekly, with monthly and annual cumulations.
Indexes almost 200 magazines and most valuable for its historical range.

Ulrich's International Periodicals Directory. (1932–). New York: Bowker. Annual.
Includes sections listing magazines and newspapers, and indexes to them, currently being published.

Union List of Serials in Libraries of the United States and Canada (3rd ed.). (1965). New York: H. W. Wilson. 5 vols.
Updated by various series of *New Serial Titles.* The best source for identifying and locating noncurrent magazines and other serials, wherever these were published. (For listings of current publications, see *Ulrich's*, above.)

4. CONFERENCE PROCEEDINGS

Papers presented at scholarly meetings are frequently the first public reports of research findings. Scholars will often present preliminary results of ongoing research, with the understanding that their papers will not be subject to the same critical scrutiny given to published studies. Scholarly conferences are in fact the major forum in which tentative findings can be presented and discussed with the understanding that they may be revised in the light of peer commentary and later research.

Many factors assure a considerable time lag between the submission of a manuscript to a publisher and its appearance in the form of a journal article or book. Usually some version of a research report appears in conference-paper form a year or two before its formal publication (if it ever is published). Conference papers therefore perform the important function of informing scholars just what is going on in the way of current research and giving them some idea of what the products of it are likely to be.

General themes and trends reflected in the proceedings of conferences in a discipline are good indicators of the current direction of the discipline. Annual meetings of many scholarly associations now frequently serve as platforms for the presentation of several hundred papers grouped around themes that, again, generally reflect the immediate scholarly concerns of association members. It has become fairly common practice for associations to publish their conference proceedings in microform, but these collections rarely include all papers presented. The most thorough way of identifying papers of interest is to search the conference guides (available from the sponsoring agencies and rarely through libraries), which usually include quite lengthy abstracts of all papers presented. Authors' affiliations are always given, and the authors themselves may be approached directly for copies. They are almost always eager to oblige.

The sources noted below also include directories that list and describe academic and other associations with some interest in the public sector. These usually describe the structure and function of each association and frequently note its publications and the dates and venues of its forthcoming conventions.

Association Meeting Directory. (1987–). Washington, DC: Association Meeting Directory. Annual.

Bibliographic Guide to Conference Proceedings. (1974–). Boston: G. K. Hall. Annual.

An author, title, and subject index to materials acquired by the Research Libraries of New York Public Library. Usually cites over 25,000 papers and other materials each year.

Conference of Social Science Councils and Analogous Bodies. (1978–). *International Directory of Social Science Organizations.* New York: K. G. Saur. Irregular.

Conference Proceedings Index. (1980–). Boston Spa, UK: British Library. Monthly updates.

A computerized database covering over 250,000 conferences going back to the 19th century. About 25,000 records are added each year.

Directory of Associations in Canada. (1973–). Toronto: Micromedia. Biennial.

Directory of British Associations and Associations in Ireland. (1965–). Beckenham, UK: CBD Research. Biennial.

Directory of European Industrial and Trade Associations. (1971–). Beckenham, UK: CBD Research. Irregular.
Formerly the *Directory of European Associations.* Latest edition is 1986.

Directory of Historical Organizations in the United States and Canada. (1956–). Nashville, TN: AASLH Press. Biennial.

Encyclopedia of Associations. (1961–). Detroit: Gale. Annual, now in 5 vols. Updated between editions by a supplement *New Associations.*

Nagel, Stuart S., & Burkholder, Kathleen (Eds.). (1980). *Policy Publishers and Associations Directory: A Directory Describing Policy-Relevant Scholarly Associations, Journals, Book Publishers, and Interest Groups.* Urbana, IL: Policy Studies Organization. 153 p.

Policy Research Centers Directory. (1978–). Urbana, IL: Policy Studies Organization. Irregular.
Describes "university and non-university centers, institutes, or organizations that conduct policy studies research."

Research Centers Directory. (1960–). Detroit: Gale. Biennial.
Describes the activities of nonprofit and primarily nongovernmental, centers. Updated by the quarterly *New Research Centers.*

U.S. Labor Management Services Administration. (1974). *A Directory of Public Management Organizations: A Guide to National Organizations of State and Local Governments and Associations of Public Officials with an Interest in Public Employee-Management Relations.* Washington, DC: GPO. 51 p.

World Index of Social Science Institutions. (1970–). Paris: UNESCO. Loose-leaf.

World Meetings: Social and Behavioral Sciences, Human Services, and Management. (1971–). New York: Macmillan. Quarterly.

More direct access to papers presented at conferences can be obtained through abstracting services in printed and computerized form, as discussed in chapters 8 and 9. Some of the more general of these regularly include abstracts of papers given at major conferences. *Psychological Abstracts* (*PsycINFO* in database form), *Sociological Abstracts* (*Sociofile*), and *ERIC* are of particular value in this regard. There are, in addition, several indexes and abstracts devoted exclusively to this type of material. These are cited below. The reader is warned that they often provide coverage in a piecemeal and haphazard fashion. An intensive search for these papers is usually necessary only in uncommon circumstances—for example, when the topic of interest is currently a dynamic and popular one among researchers. When a search of this nature is deemed appropriate, the best way to conduct it is by identifying promising associations and obtaining their conference guides in the fashion outlined earlier.

Conference Papers Index. (1973–). Palo Alto, CA: DIALOG. Updated every two months.

A database with over 1.5 million records, the great majority of which refer to papers in the pure and applied sciences.

Conference Proceedings Index. (1964–). London: British Library. Updated monthly.

Like the previous source, primarily scientific in its focus. Gives good coverage of European materials. Includes over 300,000 records.

Directory of Published Proceedings: Series SSH—Social Sciences/Humanities. (1968–). White Plains, NY: Interdok. Quarterly.

Index to Social Sciences and Humanities Proceedings. (1979–). Philadelphia: Institute for Scientific Information. Quarterly, with annual cumulations.

Proceedings in Print. (1964–). Arlington, MA: Proceedings in Print. Bimonthly.

Yearbook of International Congress Proceedings: Bibliography of Reports Arising out of Meetings Held by International Organizations. (1969–70). Brussels: Union of International Associations. 2 vols.

The only two issues published document papers presented at these specialized conferences between 1960 and 1969.

5. TECHNICAL REPORTS

Technical reports are usually the first written products of research conducted under grant or contract, and because they are prepared for narrow audiences, they can be difficult to identify and locate. As with conference papers (many of which are technical reports in another guise), their potential value lies in their timeliness in documenting current research in rapidly developing fields. As discussed in chapter 13, section 1, reports generated by federal funding are reasonably well documented. Those produced by state and local governments are much less so. Others are frequently picked up by those subject-oriented bibliographic services and databases that are not restricted by form.

There is in fact not much one can do to search in a systematic way for technical reports in a field generated outside of the public sector. However, many dissertations and conference papers result from privately funded research, and, as has been shown, these forms are searchable in productive ways. Moreover, most concerns for reports generated by private sources are target-driven and are fairly easily satisfied. Someone applying for a grant from a foundation will naturally be interested in the funding patterns of that institution and the reports these have produced. A search of recent annual reports of the foundation will quickly produce the information needed.

The few sources documenting technical reports and the organizations likely to produce them are cited below. They are included here for the sake of completeness and will not be at the top of any researcher's list of reference sources, unless for quite specific reasons. The only current bibliographic guide intended to discuss sources of technical reports and similar materials exclusively is by Auger and is cited immediately below. This work is mostly concerned with the technical report as a source of information in the pure and applied sciences, but it also includes a chapter on the use of this medium in business and economics. Its focus is the United Kingdom, but its coverage of U.S. sources is extensive.

Auger, C. P. (1989). *Information Sources in Grey Literature* (2nd ed.). New York: Bowker-Saur. 175 p.

Defines "grey literature" to include technical reports, technical notes, specifications, proceedings, translations, trade literature, and other "difficult-to-define publications not usually available through normal bookselling channels."

Hernon, Peter, & McClure, Charles R. (1988). *Public Access to Government Information: Issues, Trends, and Strategies* (2nd ed.). Norwood, NJ: Ablex. 524 p.

Includes a chapter entitled "Technical Report Literature" (pages 207–28), but this is largely concerned with reports generated within the U.S. federal system.

Holloway, A. H. (1976). *Information Work with Unpublished Reports.* London: Deutsch. 302 p.

The two sections address sources in public and private information centers. Discussion is dated and primarily concerned with the United Kingdom.

MICROLOG: Canadian Research Index. Index de Recherche du Canada. (1979–). Toronto: Micromedia. Monthly, with annual cumulations.

Covers research sponsored by the provincial as well as national governments and is therefore broader in its jurisdiction scope than the publications of the U.S. National Technical Information Service.

Rand Corporation. (1963–). *Selected Rand Abstracts.* Santa Monica, CA. Quarterly.

Covers only reports of this important research institute. Updates its *Index of Selected Publications, 1946–1962.*

System for Information on Grey Literature in Europe. (1981–). The Hague: European Association for Grey Literature Exploitation. 240,000 records. Updated monthly.

A database covering technical reports and other non-trade literature generated within the public and private sectors of the European Community.

U.S. National Technical Information Service.

The extensive services and publications of the NTIS are discussed in some detail in section 1 of chapter 13.

University Research in Business and Economics. (1950–). Morgantown, WV: West Virginia University. Bureau of Business Research. Annual.

Lists working papers and other materials written by faculty of member institutions of the Association for University Business and Economic Research.

6. OTHER RESEARCH IN PROGRESS

Dissertations, conference papers, and technical reports can all be considered as interim reports of research in progress, in the sense that they represent work that is ongoing and likely to be later published in some more sophisticated form. A search that uncovers relevant materials of these kinds is also one that has gone a good way toward identifying at least those ongoing projects that are well advanced. There are additional sources that attempt to identify research activities planned or under way, whether or not preliminary reports of them have been issued. Many journals and other sources regularly include lists or discussions of current projects, and information included in these will certainly be of interest.

It is not, however, recommended that much effort be put into examining these lists. First of all, many are dominated by citations of dissertations approved or dissertation proposals accepted. As noted earlier, those in the former group can be identified more completely through other sources, and those in the second are often never completed. Second, projects that are well advanced are likely to be reported in conference papers, which, as shown, are fairly accessible. Many projects, even those funded by governmental or other grants, are phantoms that never result in interesting products.

The sources mentioned here are worthy of some attention, but their examination should be cursory and should emphasize current projects. Research enterprises rarely allow the luxury of searches for the findings of research activities that may or may not be fruitful.

One interesting recent development is illustrated by the database *RIPD* (below). As discussed in chapter 9, large library networks are increasingly inclined toward including periodical indexes in their access points. *RIPD* (a subset of RLIN) is the latest twist on this. It presently includes pre-publication information for a small group of journals, mainly in the humanities. One can expect in the near future that it will include a much larger universe.

Abstracts of Working Papers in Economics. (1983–). Cambridge, UK: Cambridge University Press. Eight issues a year.

Includes research activities in business, finance, and econometrics conducted in almost 100 institutions worldwide.

American Review of Public Administration. (1967–). Parkville, MO: Midwest Review of Public Administration. Quarterly.

Includes a regular section, "Current Public Administration Research." This kind of listing is a standard feature of a number of journals in public administration and in other fields.

Business Horizons. (1958–). Bloomington: Indiana University. Graduate School of Business. Bimonthly.

Each issue features a "Research Clearinghouse."

Current Research in Britain: Social Sciences. (1951–). Boston Spa, UK: British Library. Annual.

Arranged by broad subject; one is "Politics (Including International Relations and Public Administration)." Close to comprehensive in its coverage of British institutions. In its early years combined with a serial variously titled *Research in British Universities, Polytechnics, and Colleges* and *Scientific Research in British Universities and Colleges.*

Economics Working Papers Bibliography. (1973–). Dobbs Ferry, NY: Trans-Media. Semiannual.

The text of most of the papers indexed is available in a microfilm collection *Economics Working Papers*, produced by the same publisher.

ECRS Directory of Unpublished Research: Business and Economics: Base Volume. (1987). New York: Economic Consulting & Research Systems. 1,776 p.

A computer-generated bibliography of papers arranged by broad subject category. Updated by annual supplements.

Federal Research in Progress. (Current year). Springfield, VA: US National Technical Information Service. 120,000 records. Updated monthly.

Documents current research funded by agencies of the federal government.

Local Government Information Network. (1979–). St. Paul MN: Login Services. 35,000 records. Updated daily.

A database that includes short descriptions of innovative techniques and projects designed to improve governmental efficiency. Most are derived from research centers and local agencies themselves and are not published elsewhere.

P.S. (1968–). Washington, DC: American Political Science Association. Quarterly.

Like other journals of its kind (see section 1), lists dissertations in progress as well as those recently completed.

Revista Interamericana de Bibliografica/Inter-American Review of Bibliography. (1930–). Washington, DC: Organization of American States. Quarterly.

Most useful to the social scientist for its regular listings of "Research in Progress," "Recent Articles," and "Recent Dissertations."

RIPD. (Current). Mountain View, CA: Research Libraries Information Network. Updated monthly.

A database that now includes pre-publication information for about 50 journals in the humanities. Also includes grants and other information related to funding bodies. Also known as *Research in Progress Database.*

Science and Technology: Research in Progress. (1973–). Orange, NJ: Academic Media. 12 vols. Biennial, updated by supplements issued every other year.

Primarily a directory of current research funded by the federal government, but includes many nonfederal projects. Volumes 11 and 12 are entitled *Behavioral Sciences* and *Social Sciences.* Easily the most comprehensive work of its kind.

SSIE (Current Research). (1977–). Washington, DC: Smithsonian Science Information Exchange.

The computerized version of *Science and Technology* (above). Only includes projects registered with the SSIE.

U.S. Department of Labor. Manpower Administration. (1963–). *Manpower Research and Development.* Washington, DC. Annual.

An example of a register of grants and contracts sponsored by a particular federal agency. Lists are usually either published separately or included in the agency's annual report. Published under several slightly variant titles.

Urban History Yearbook. (1974–). Leicester, UK: Leicester University Press.
Regularly features a "Register of Research in Urban History." Cited here as an example of one of many yearbooks that include listings of this type.

7. CASE STUDIES

The case-study form of analysis is generally considered to be peculiar to the fields of public administration and business administration. It is truer to say that this form often characterizes the *teaching* of these subjects. Case studies do not represent any unique research genre. They simply report findings of intense research efforts conducted in a variety of ways and directed at a single institution or group of institutions. Case studies can therefore reflect a variety of perspectives and methods; they reflect no single and identifiable approach. They are, moreover, frequently problem-oriented and conducted with the intent of offering solutions to problems that are local and immediate. Many are not intended as explorations of any theoretical concern.

Materials in this form can nonetheless have extraordinary value. Someone researching a particular type of organization will clearly profit from the findings of those with a similar, although perhaps less theoretical, interest. Examination of groups of related case studies can reveal patterns and trends with larger implications. Microscopic in focus though many such studies may be, examination of groups of them can yield insights of broader generalization. This is not the only life situation in which the whole can be much greater than the sum of its parts.

Furthermore, many case studies have made distinguished contributions to organizational theory. The work of Peter Blau is worthy of attention in this respect for its contributions to the understanding of the mechanics of communication within bureaucracies and the extent to which structures of this kind may deviate from familiar ideal types.[4]

Identification of these materials can be difficult. On the face of it, library catalogs allow for searches of materials of this nature as well as one could expect. The Library of Congress system of subject headings includes "Case Studies" as a standard subdivision. Subject keyword searches can therefore easily be constructed that will identify all monographs in one's library network that relate this subdivision to the broader topic of interest. Unfortunately, this approach is quite limited. Case studies are usually published, but they are not generally well publicized or marketed extensively.

The sources noted below reflect the activities of those clearinghouses that publish case studies, but do not attempt to disseminate them beyond a universe limited to their subscribers and other constituents. Conventional library techniques should certainly be used to find case studies. Sources mentioned here are an important supplement to these important techniques. It must be said that studies abstracted in these sources often reflect their suitability as teaching materials rather than scholarly contributions to organizational theory.

Cases in Public Policy and Management: Intercollegiate Bibliography. (1978–). Boston: Intercollegiate Case Clearing House. Annual.

Each issue abstracts 500 or more cases published by the ICCH and available from it.

Directory of Management Cases. (1983–). Boston: Harvard Business School. Division of Research. Annual.

Lists case studies published or otherwise available from Harvard or elsewhere.

Feagin, Joe R., Orum, Anthony M., & Sjoberg, Gideon. (1991). *A Case for the Case Study.* Chapel Hill: University of North Carolina Press. 290 p.

Essays address the many uses of the case study and are not limited to consideration of organizations as the only settings for its application. No attention is paid to sources.

Guide to Management Improvement Projects in Local Government. (1977–). Washington, DC: International City Management Association. Management Information Service. Quarterly.

An interesting source that summarizes applied experiments undertaken primarily at the local level of government. Information is given on the organizations, and even the names, of those conducting these case studies.

HBR Case Study. (1922–). *Harvard Business Review.* Boston: Harvard University. Graduate School of Business Administration. Bimonthly.

Each issue of the *HBR* includes an essay addressing problematic instances of "real companies and their executives." Associated articles discuss the substance of the particular situation considered.

Inter-University Case Program. (1971). *Index and Summary of Case Studies of the Inter-University Case Program.* Syracuse, NY. 1 vol., unpaged.

Between 1951 and 1970 the IUCP published rather more than 100 case studies in the area of public-sector management. These are identifiable in a library system by searching "Cases in Public Administration and Policy Formation" as a phrase or added entry.

Sanders, Ralph, & Timbers, Edwin. (1983). *Guide to the Analysis of Management Cases.* Washington, DC: National Defense University. 47 p.

Addresses analysis of management cases in the classroom setting.

Stillman, Richard J. (Ed.). (1988). *Public Administration: Concepts and Cases* (4th ed.). Boston: Houghton Mifflin. 514 p.
An example of the many casebooks of this kind. Access to them is easily obtained through standard library approaches.

White, Anthony G. (1984). *Case Method in Public Administration Instruction: A Selected Bibliography.* Monticello, IL: Vance. 5 p.
A limited bibliography primarily concerned with the case study as an integral part of a distinctive approach to teaching.

8. RESEARCH GRANTS

The dream of anyone undertaking a research project is to obtain a research grant that will fund the costs of the enterprise and the salary of the investigator. Many people get such grants. Those who do have generally adhered to the several iron laws of research funding:

1. Spend a great deal of time on the preparation of the proposal, in the understanding that grantsmanship is now a professional activity. He who submits an application in a cavalier fashion is doomed to disappointment.
2. Form is sometimes superior to substance. Having a good idea is a necessary, but not sufficient, characteristic of the successful proposal. The idea must be justified and expressed well. Certain parts of the proposal, such as the budget, should be prepared with the assistance of the university grants officer or some other expert person.
3. Submissions must be prepared well in advance. One should typically apply for a grant a year or so before the project is due to start. It can take this long for applications to be processed and decisions made. Many scholars, especially graduate students, shoot themselves in the foot by looking for grant money a month or two before they intend to start work on thc project.
4. The proposal must be clearly focused and *precise* in the sense that it tells the reader exactly how the research goal is to be accomplished. Ideas, of course, inform research strategy. Those who dish out money for research certainly seek to fund the thoughtful, but they also wish to reserve their support for projects whose tactics, as well as strategy, are clearly articulated.[5] They do so for the simple reason that they prefer to give their money to those they deem likely to produce a finished product.

5. The researcher must decide how much time to allot to the search for funding. Grantsmanship can be a very time-consuming business. Universities now typically employ numbers of people to undertake it as a full-time job. Individuals should certainly investigate grant possibilities but should not allow this activity to dominate their professional lives. Two or three weeks full-time, or their equivalent, should be the maximum that a researcher without institutional support spends on this activity.
6. The proposal should be tailored to fit the interests of a small group of targeted foundations. To know which these foundations are, the investigator must look at the profiles and annual reports of likely candidates to determine which among them should be favored with a submission. The game plan here should be accommodation to the documented interests of a few foundations. Shotgun approaches aimed at the general interests of the many are rarely, if ever, productive.

If these rules have any strength, then many of the sources documented in this section are of limited value. The several publications of the Foundation Center, among others, give tremendous amounts of information about the tens of thousands of foundations in the United States that award many millions of dollars each year. However, unless one commands a research team of professional grants privateers, most of this information is less than useful. What individual, as opposed to institutional, academic researchers usually need is a selective guide to those two or three foundations likely to be most receptive. A university grants officer can often act as such a guide. The Foundation Center, a nonprofit corporation with offices in major cities across the United States, can also be helpful in this respect. The works cited here help in culling out those foundations that are possible from those that are unlikely. Some provide forms and texts of successful proposals.

Most directories listed here are well indexed and provide easy access by name of foundation, purpose, subject matter addressed, geographical location and restriction, and names of principal officers or functionaries. Two sources cited are also available for searching online. This capability is useless to the reader of this book. All that even the most finely tuned computerized search of a grants database can produce is an unmanageable listing of vaguely promising sources. This is the last thing individual researchers need. Computerized searches serve only the appetites of those institutional grant seekers with salaried time exclusively geared to the exploration of these possibilities.

8.1. General Sources of Grants

Annual Register of Grant Support. (1967–). Chicago: Marquis Academic Media. Annual.

Covers both federal and private sources and is not limited by the size or level of activities of donors.

Directory of Research Grants. (1975–). Phoenix, AZ: Oryx. Annual.

Considered by many the most worthwhile of these general guides. Excludes grants awarded for institutional development or other nonresearch purposes. Includes grants from federal sources. Covers about 6,000 organizations.

Foundation Center National Data Book. (1975–). New York. Annual.

Lists smaller donors, defined as those giving less than $10,000 each year.

Foundation Directory. (1960–). New York: Foundation Center. Biennial. Also available online.

Lists the 5,000 or so private, nonprofit foundations that have assets of $1,000,000 or more and that disburse monies in excess of $100,000 each year. Updated by the bimonthly *Foundation News.*

Foundation Grants Index. (1970–). New York: Foundation Center. Annual. Also available online.

Includes smaller foundations, defined as those giving between $10,000 and $100,000 each year.

Haile, Suzanne W. (Ed.). (1991). *Foundation Grants to Individuals* (7th ed.). New York: Foundation Center. 517 p.

Documents grants awarded to individuals for a variety of purposes. The reader should note that very few research grants are awarded to individuals not affiliated with academic institutions. Revised about every two years.

U.S. Office of Management and Budget. (1965–). *Catalog of Domestic Federal Assistance.* Washington, DC: GPO. Annual.

Includes federal grants of all kinds, including those to organizations and state and local governments. Not recommended for the academic researcher, who is better advised to use one of the more selective guides to federal money cited here. Updated by the *Federal Register.*

8.2. Selective Guides to Grant Sources

The guides listed below should be considered as informed products of their respective disciplines. Their authors can be supposed to have a clear idea of the foundations and public agencies that have traditionally supported their disciplines and of the nature of the research that has been so funded.

Blum, Laurie. (1987). *Free Money for Humanities and Social Sciences* (2nd ed.). New York: Paragon. 194 p.

Cantrell, Karen, & Wallen, Denise (Eds.). (1986). *Funding for Anthropological Research.* Phoenix, AZ: Oryx. 308 p.

Cantrell, Karen, & Wallen, Denise (Eds.). (1991). *Funding for Law: Legal Education, Research, and Study*. Phoenix, AZ: Oryx. 184 p.

Cantrell, Karen, & Wallen, Denise (Eds.). (1987). *Funding for Research, Study, and Travel: Latin America and the Caribbean.* Phoenix, AZ: Oryx. 301 p.

City University of New York. Graduate School and University Center. (1987–). *Calendar of Deadline Dates.* Quarterly.

An example of the kind of selective guide produced by academic institutions. Usually more useful than the comprehensive guides discussed here because it includes only those sources that are sympathetic to applications from individuals (as opposed to institutions). The arrangement by deadline date is also of great value. Intended for both established researchers and graduate students.

Coleman, William E. (1984). *Grants in the Humanities: A Scholar's Guide to Funding Sources* (2nd ed.). New York: Neal-Schuman. 175 p.

Directory of Grants in the Humanities. (1986–). Phoenix, AZ: Oryx. Annual.

Grants, Fellowships and Prizes of Interest to Historians. (1987–). Washington, DC: American Historical Association. Annual.

Herring, Kenneth L. (Ed.). (1987). *The American Psychological Association's Guide to Research Support* (3rd ed.). Washington, DC. 276 p.

Lauffer, Armand. (1984). *Grantsmanship and Fund Raising.* Beverly Hills, CA: Sage. 320 p.

Looff, Carolyn. (1987). *Business and Economics Funding Guide*. Washington, DC: American Association of State Colleges and Universities. 122 p.

Mantegna, Anne G. (Ed.). (1990). *Guide to Federal Funding for Social Scientists* (2nd ed.). Washington, DC: American Political Science Association. 368 p.

Policy Grants Directory. (1977–). Urbana, IL: Policy Studies Organization. Irregular.

"A directory describing governmental and private funding sources for policy studies research."

Rubin, Mary. (1983). *How to Get Money for Research*. Old Westbury, NY: Feminist Press. 78 p.

8.3. Proposal Writing

Works listed in this section address the preparation of proposals for either a dissertation committee or a funding body. The demands of the two are remarkably similar. Both seek to approve projects that are meaningful in their general significance, clear in their focus and purpose, and manageable in terms of the researcher's time and the scope of primary resources that must be accommodated. It would be nice to think that a proposal that entranced a dissertation committee would be assured of a grant. This is impossible due to the limited money available to those who do not yet have a doctorate and the restrictions that surround its use. It is the lucky dissertation student who gets support from both the academics who approve projects and the functionaries who may fund them.

Behling, John H. (1984). *Guidelines for Preparing the Research Proposal* (2nd ed.). Lanham, MD: University Press of America. 88 p.

Coley, Soraya M., & Scheinberg, Cynthia A. (1990). *Proposal Writing*. Newbury Park, CA: Sage. 130 p.

Francis, J. Bruce. (1988). *The Proposal Cookbook: A Step by Step Guide to Proposal Design and Writing* (5th ed.). Minneapolis: Microfutures. 104 p.

Hall, Mary S. (1988). *Getting Funded: A Complete Guide to Proposal Writing* (3rd ed.). Portland, OR: Portland State University. Continuing Education Publications. 206 p.

Kalish, Susan E., et al. (Eds.). (1984). *The Proposal Writer's Swipe File: 15 Winning Fund Raising Proposals—Prototypes of Approaches, Styles, and Structures* (3rd ed.). Washington, DC: Taft. 162 p.

Krathwohl, David R. (1988). *How to Prepare a Research Proposal: Guidelines for Funding and Dissertations in the Social and Behavioral Sciences* (3rd ed.). Syracuse, NY: Syracuse University Press. 302 p.

Lefferts, Robert. (1990). *Getting a Grant in the 1990s: How to Write Successful Grant Proposals.* New York: Prentice Hall. 239 p.

Locke, Lawrence F., Spirduso, Waneen W., & Silverman, Stephen J. (1987). *Proposals That Work: A Guide for Planning Dissertations and Grant Proposals* (2nd ed.). Newbury Park, CA: Sage. 271 p.

Reif-Lehrer, Liane. (1989). *Writing a Successful Grant Application* (2nd ed.). Boston: Jones & Bartlett. 282 p.

White, Virginia P. (1983). *Grant Proposals That Succeeded.* New York: Plenum. 240 p.

8.4. Scholarship Grants

Grants, fellowships, and other awards are available to support graduate students in their course work or research activities. Competition for them in this day and age is quite fierce. Those with an interest in them are best advised to consult the financial aid offices of their own institutions, as external funds are much more difficult to obtain, and certainly more onerous to apply for, than are those closest to home.

The concern of this book is not for the undoubted needs of the graduate student seeking financial support to complete predissertation requirements. This having been said, the three outstanding directories that address only students in this situation are considered below. There are a number of others that focus more comprehensively on the needs of students in general. These are not mentioned here.

Cassidy, Daniel J. (1990). *The Graduate Scholarship Book: The Complete Guide to Scholarships, Fellowships, Grants, and Loans for Graduate and Professional Study* (2nd ed.). Englewood Cliffs, NJ: Prentice-Hall. 441 p.

College Blue Book. (1923–). New York: Macmillan Information. Annual.

One volume of this is entitled *Scholarships, Fellowships, Grants, and Loans.*

Wells, John H., and Goldstein, Amy J. (Eds.). (1989). *Peterson's Grants for Graduate Students, 1989–90* (2nd ed.). Princeton, NJ: Peterson's Guides. 291 p.

9. ELECTRONIC BULLETIN BOARDS AND OTHER COMPUTER NETWORKS

One truly revolutionary development of the 1990s and beyond is the further extension of the computer into our personal and academic lives. The already-vast and expanding scope of the electronic bulletin board (EBB) promises to have tremendous implications for scholarly communication. EBBs are computer systems through which subscribers can communicate instantly. Interactions can be between two individuals (one-on-one), from one to many (as in mailing systems), or conferencing systems allowing for all members of a specified group of users to send data to all others. Communications can be as extensive as one wishes—students can, for example, transmit parts of their dissertations to their mentors immediately and for relatively little cost. Unbelievable as it sounds, EBB technology has actually outmaneuvered the various telephone companies to permit international communication for the price of a local call.

Apart from this important aspect of EBBs, there are others to be considered: In these days when every academic person owns a computer, numbers of subscribers to EBBs are immense. Some networks have tens of thousands of subscribers and are expanding rapidly. In the United States alone there are at least 30,000 EBBs, many of which are subdivided into hundreds of separate files. Not all users beam into the same grand network. Large systems such as INTERNET, TELNET, and BITNET (Because It's Time NETwork) are subdivided into an apparently infinite number of subnetworks. The "invisible college," discussed in chapter 1, has achieved a new dimension. Scholars working in the same field do not now have to communicate by reputation or telephone or enjoy the occasional pleasure of encounters at academic meetings. They can do so by identifying or establishing an appropriate user subgroup. For those who are even marginally computer-literate, the EBB is moving toward replacing traditional means of communication within groups that have similar academic concerns. Scholars with important thoughts or findings can present them at academic conferences and meetings. Now they can also communicate through their specialized networks on EBBs. Bulletin boards supplement and in some cases replace the kinds of scholarly communication traditionally allowed by journals and conferences.[6]

Publishing patterns have also been influenced by this development. Recent and recessionary pressures are putting many scholarly journals out of business. Those that remain may take a year or more to publish accepted articles. As an alternative to conventional publishing, a number of journals are now published in electronic form only on EBBs. The companies that produce them gain the advantages of lower production costs; their subscribers gain access to their contents more quickly. A time may come when access to EBB systems may be essential for access to important journal literature.[7]

The most revolutionary aspects of EBBs go even beyond this. Most of the computerized library catalogs and networks discussed earlier (section 6 of chapter 6) are now accessible through bulletin boards. Virtually all of the 400 or so networks presently available online can now be searched by this means. EBBs are not the only way of gaining access to them, but they are already the most convenient way. Searches of library catalogs (and of other bibliographic databases) are rapidly shifting from the library to the home- or office-based PC.

The standard EBB networks noted earlier are used heavily by academics, but are not for their exclusive use. Scholars are, however, now about to acquire an electronic resource of their very own. Federal legislation enacted in 1991 authorized support for the creation of the National Research and Education Network, an EBB devoted entirely to communication between scholars and between educational institutions.[8] In 1996, when it is scheduled to be fully operational, this network will undoubtedly include many more bibliographic resources than are now available.

This movement has yet greater significance. Electronic communication also encompasses greater access to *primary* data. Many of the directories of EBB resources and guides to network searching already refer to the many collections of archival data now available in this way. These data can now be *transmitted* electronically and in a variety of formats. In this important way EBBs are coming to represent a means for obtaining primary data as well as sources for their identification. It is difficult to overemphasize the importance of this development to scholars in almost every field of endeavor.

Access to networks is simpler than one might suppose. Most colleges and universities support many kinds of computer networking and generally offer workshops in their use. Every campus seems to have a coterie of knowledgeable EBB users who proselytize enthusiastically. The several sources discussed here provide current overviews of the almost bewildering range of networks now in existence. These sources will be valuable for those who wish to gain a clearer idea of the present state of development and future potential of computer networking. For others, including those primarily interested in searching library systems, a knowledge of major networks used by academics will suffice. This can usually be acquired at one's home campus or research institution. Most of the sources noted are serials or are revised regularly. This circumstance reflects the dynamic changes now occurring in this area. Current information on implications for the academic world can be obtained through the weekly *Chronicle of Higher Education* (in its regular "Information Technology" feature), the *Annual Review of Information Science and Technology*, and, of course, from news information provided by the bulletin boards themselves.

Barron, Billy. (1991–). *UNT's Accessing On-Line Bibliographic Databases.* Denton, TX: University of North Texas. 1 vol., loose-leaf.

Lists over 350 library networks (including BLAISE, OCLC, and RLIN) and describes procedures for entrance and exit.

Boardwatch Magazine. (1987–). Littleton, CO: Boardwatch. Monthly.

The standard current source documenting new developments in electronic conferencing. Also accessible online.

Information Industry Directory. (1971–). Detroit: Gale. Annual.

Formerly entitled the *Encyclopedia of Information Systems and Services.*

Kehoe, Brendan P. (1993). *Zen and the Art of the INTERNET: A Beginner's Guide to the INTERNET* (2nd ed.). Englewood Cliffs, NJ: PTR Prentice Hall. 112 p.

Also has chapters on USENET and TELNET. Discusses newsgroups and conferences within seven broad categories.

Kovacs, Diane K. (1991–). *Directory of Scholarly Electronic Conferences.* Washington, DC: Association of Research Libraries. 1 vol., loose-leaf.

Includes "descriptions of computer-mediated discussions on topics of interest to social sciences and humanities scholars." Entries are arranged within over 30 subject categories (for example, "Urban Planning"). Particular attention is given to accessing BITNET and INTERNET.

Krol, Ed. (1992). *The Whole Internet: User's Guide and Catalog*. Sebastopol, CA: O'Reilly. 376 p.

The most comprehensive guide to the network that is emerging as the principal one used by scholars.

LaQuey, Tracy, & Ryer, Jeanne C. (1992). *The Internet Companion: A Beginner's Guide to Global Networking.* Reading, MA: Addison-Wesley. 196 p.

Lynch, Clifford A., & Preston, Cecilia M. (1990). Internet Access to Information Resources. *Annual Review of Information Science and Technology (ARIST), 25*, 263-312.

Provides a useful background account of the development of electronic networks and patterns in their structure and use.

NSF Network Service Center. (1989–). *Internet Resource Guide.* Cambridge, MA: BBN Systems and Technologies. 1 vol., loose-leaf.

Lists resources by type: library catalogs, bibliographic databases, archives, and so on. Excludes discussion groups.

Quarterman, John S. (1990). *The Matrix: Computer Networks and Conferencing Systems Worldwide.* Bedford, MA: Digital Press. 719 p.

St. George, Art, & Larsen, Ron. (1991–). *Internet-Accessible Catalogs and Databases.* College Park: University of Maryland. 1 vol., loose-leaf.

Primarily a list of library catalogs in the United States and elsewhere. Provides instructions on both access and use. Also lists and describes some campus-based bulletin boards and information systems.

Williams, Brian. (1992). *Directory of Computer Conferencing in Libraries.* Westport, CT: Meckler. 429 p.

Includes discussion of major networks, conferences, and bulletin boards. Notable for discussion of the mechanics of access and search procedures.

NOTES

1. By academic convention the product of research undertaken for a master's degree is a thesis; that for a doctoral degree is a dissertation. Research of an original nature is sometimes required in an acceptable thesis. It is always required in a dissertation.

2. Including anthropology, business and economics, education, linguistics, mass media and communications, political science, psychology, sociology, and social work. Entries do not include abstracts, but indicate the location of these in *DAI.*

3. The British Library is developing a computerized union list of newspaper indexes that presently includes almost 1,000 titles.

4. Blau, Peter M. (1963). *The Dynamics of Bureaucracy: A Study of Interpersonal Relations in Two Government Agencies*. Chicago: University of Chicago Press.

5. The author obtained a grant for his own dissertation research, which necessitated the use of old court records as the major primary resource. At the interview with the foundation, he was somewhat unnerved by the first question: "On the morning of your first day in the legal archives, you will take off your jacket and get your notebook and pencil out. What will you do next?." Questions can be as focused as this.

6. It was reported early in 1992 that 350 electronic conference groups in the social sciences and humanities had been created within the previous 18 months.

7. In 1992 an important publisher of journals in the policy sciences decided to restrict its entire range of journals to this medium: Wilson, David L. (1992). Major Scholarly Publisher to Test Electronic Transmission of Journals. *Chronicle of Higher Education, 38* (3 June), A17, A20.

8. McClure, Charles R., et al. (1991). *The National Research and Education Network (NREN): Research and Policy Perspectives.* Norwood, NJ: Ablex.

16

ARCHIVES AND OTHER PRIMARY SOURCES

The distinction between primary and secondary sources is of paramount importance. Primary sources are those that document an event (or an institution, an individual, or some other routinely occurring phenomenon) naturally and in the normal course of business. Secondary sources are those that are commentaries or analyses *based* on some set of primary data or some perception of it. A scholar investigating the early development of the law in the state of Nuevo Albion would undoubtedly analyze court records as *primary* materials for a study. The individual's successful dissertation might be an important resource for later scholars interested in legal changes in this sovereign state. This dissertation would, however, be a *secondary* source, as it is an interpretation of the records and all they represent. It adds nothing to the original documentation of legal events in this jurisdiction.

Social research in one sense is always a group activity; no scholar works in a vacuum. Scholars always build on (or correct, or modify, or supplement) research that has gone before. For this reason alone, a thorough knowledge of the secondary literature is a necessary precursor to the process of original research with primary materials.[1] It is, however, the primary sources that are the meat of research and whose use, incidentally, provides the unique excitement of exploring new ground.

The distinction between primary and secondary sources has nothing to do with the *forms* in which they are available. Both primary and secondary materials may be published or unpublished. If unpublished, they can be in manuscript or some other form. (The machine-readable data archives discussed in chapter 12 are a variety of primary material which could scarcely have been imagined earlier in this century. The same thing goes for the full-text numeric databases mentioned in the same chapter.) Primary sources are essentially defined by how they are *used.* In this sense the category can incorporate a wide variety of materials. Newspapers have already been mentioned as primary sources when they are used for purposes such as the evaluation of popular perceptions of a specific historical event or circumstance (see also the discussion in section 5 of this chapter). Interviews with survivors of an event provide information of a primary nature that may be used to supplement the written record. Scholars have, and to great effect, used contemporary paintings to evaluate historical perceptions of family life, novels to examine how those in the early 19th century related concepts of liberty to the power of emerging agencies of control, and the rules of hospitals and armies to illuminate the origins of the prison as a metaphor for the modern bureaucratic state[2] The materials that can be considered as primary sources are, it seems, only limited by the knowledge and imagination of the researcher.

Archives are the kind of primary material most used by social and policy researchers. For historians, archival research has been the traditional route to scholarship. (This continues to be so. However, the range of materials considered by those of a historical bent to be appropriate has expanded in recent decades to accommodate a parallel diversion of interest from diplomatic to social and public history.) In the narrowest sense of the term (and that commonly used by archivists and historians), an archival collection includes those surviving records that document the routine business of a public or private organization, or perhaps of a family or individual. These records may be in printed or manuscript form. For our legal historian from Nuevo Albion, they would include any published records of the courts studied (calendars, appellate decisions, and annual, statistical, and other reports). They would also include any surviving manuscript records generated by the courts, including trial transcripts of cases on appeal, indictments, grand jury minutes, briefs of counsel, and any other documents likely to shed light on the courts' functioning, particularly its decision-making processes.

Rarely do archival researchers limit their attentions to a single collection. Research is driven by a desire for answers to important questions and is not necessarily restricted by the limitations of any single body of data. The legal historian should also examine published statutes, decisions of superior courts, common-law sources, and legislative histories (which are frequently unpublished). Someone interested in the development and operations of an administrative agency would use the various records of that agency and materials generated by bodies affecting its functioning. These could include legislative and regulatory records documenting external changes modifying the powers and responsibilities of the agency and even materials such as the private papers of individuals influential in the agency's origin or development.[3] A researcher's choice of which sets of archives to use is personal and driven by perspective and focus. It is only restrained by the availability of material and, of course, by the fact that research time and resources are of finite quantity.

Distinctions between published and unpublished archives are artificial in this context. Agency decisions on whether or not to publish records (for example, statistical series or internal reports) are frequently situational. Distinctions are further complicated by the fact that manuscripts later considered important have often been published a century or more after their creation. This is especially true for archives generated in the colonial period. The later activities of local history societies in collecting and publishing such records have been invaluable in making them accessible to scholars. A researcher's question in using archives published in this way is whether they have been edited or otherwise altered in content. Once this issue has been resolved, such records are for many purposes as valuable, and as stimulating, as the original records.[4]

Historians' long and intimate acquaintance with the world of archives has produced definitions and terminology that should be understood by all archival users. To qualify as true archives, collections must be *cohesive* and *primary*, produced as by-products of the routine activity of an organization or body. They must be *natural* or *organic*, created for institutional purposes and not for any other reason. Collections constructed artificially, perhaps by persons interested in reconstructing the historical record of any agency or individual, are traditionally referred to as "manuscript collections," not archives. Such terms are descriptive and are not value-laden. However, someone using a collection of primary records that has been put together at some time after the events documented should certainly inquire as to any bias resulting from the purposes of those responsible for this reconstruction, and the extant sources from which the materials were drawn.[5]

Terms such as "historical records" or "historical manuscripts" are used broadly to refer to collections of primary material that can include archives as well as those created artificially. These definitions are important because many of the major archival finding tools do not refer to archives in their titles (for example, the *National Union Catalog of Manuscript Collections*, popularly referred to as *NUCMC*, cited in section 1).

Although most of the terminology and reference works were produced by historians, the traditional users of archival material, archives are the province of those working in any academic discipline. Historical research is defined by most as that which examines *change over time*. Social scientists who seek to explore this usually do so for pragmatic reasons. It is difficult to analyze and explain a social institution in its entirety and in absolute terms. Often a more productive approach is to examine it during a volatile period of its history. By looking at its structure and operation at two extreme moments in this period, and at the processes that appear to link these moments, one can perhaps achieve a better and more functional understanding of it. For example, someone studying formal structures for maintaining racial segregation in the United States would undoubtedly seek to relate these to the underlying social fabric. Studies of these structures as dynamic (that is, historical and changing) entities add a great deal to our understanding of this fabric because they have shown how and why these structures have been artifacts of political conflicts within white society, as well as means of limiting the aspirations of non-whites.[6]

Historical research therefore reflects a unique analytical perspective rather than any exclusionary concern for structures and mentalities of the past. Someone who studies changes in the structure and functioning of an administrative agency between 1980 and 1990 is as much a historical researcher as someone who studies the emergence of the same agency as an early 19th-century exemplar of the modern bureaucratic form. Both examine change over time. Both presumably relate the changes they analyze to other interesting movements in the public sector and on the overall social front. Each is an archival researcher and applies the historical method.

There are, however, differences between the circumstances of these two researchers. These are not necessarily differences of theoretical orientation or approach. Rather, they concern the practical matter of availability of sources. Studies of modern bureaucracies (and almost all other modern social phenomena) have the advantage of extensive primary support. Modern institutions generate a great deal of documentation. When this is publicly available, it can be analyzed. When it is not, accessible records can be supplemented by interviews with present and former functionaries, ethnographic research, the findings of investigative journalists, and any other of the many sources of our information-oriented world. Students of earlier times are more limited in this regard. They must deal with a world that did not feel the modern compulsion to lay such a trail of paper documenting (and justifying) its actions and thoughts. For them, the written record (published or manuscript) is usually sparse. It is also a *fait accompli* in that it cannot be supplemented by the recollections of those of its constituents who are both knowledgeable and in the land of the living.

Historians (defined here to include those whose interests reflect a historical perspective) are at a decided disadvantage when they choose research settings far removed from the present moment. They usually compensate for the lack of records dealing with their immediate object of choice with creative approaches. Students of the impact of bureaucratic structure on 18th- and 19th-century life, for example, have used novels and plays as evidence of contemporary perspectives, whether of the object or its social context. Published memoirs and private papers of individuals illuminate conceptions of bureaucracy and of its functioning. Immersion in related primary sources is regarded by most working on topics set in the distant past as necessary, both to supplement primary sources that are immediately related to the topic in point and to help understand the social context in which this topic is embedded. Supplementary sources are important to students of the distant past. However, they are generally used to extend or reinforce analysis of the major body of sources documenting the institution (or event or circumstance) of interest. They constitute evidence of an important but persuasive nature. They are not substitutes for the immediate situation under study. Scholars use them because they are imprisoned by the availability and limitations of the official record.

These brief observations on the problems of those who deal with a historical past that excludes modern memory are not intended to discourage anyone from historical research of this nature. Its rewards can be tremendous; nonetheless, its limitations must be recognized. Researchers who choose to go far back in time for their inspiration must recognize the peculiar nature of their quests at an early stage in the process. Dissertation proposals that are historical should be based on a very good knowledge of the available data sources. The biggest danger in this kind of research is to commit oneself to a research inquiry that turns out to be insupportable by the data available. Any dissertation committee will give greater than usual leeway to a candidate who proposes to investigate the very distant past. It will do so because it recognizes that the historical record is fixed and cannot be massaged by later recourse to survey research or other forms of data extension.

Every historical piece of research is constrained by available resources. "Pretesting" is a feature of most kinds of research and is familiar as a concept to all researchers.[7] Research using the records of long-gone societies requires the kind of detailed knowledge that should be obtained before rather than after the fact. Historical researchers cannot usually command other databases if their records of choice prove unfruitful. Those who are wise only present dissertation proposals, or otherwise conjure their forms of research design, when they have thoroughly investigated possible sources. Such action may delay the project, but it undoubtedly increases the freedom of the researcher and improves the quality of the final product.

1. LOCATING ARCHIVAL COLLECTIONS

Tracking down interesting collections of archives or other primary sources is much more difficult than locating relevant books and articles. These collections have historically been cut off from the library world of system-wide cataloging. There is no central source that automatically indexes them as they are acquired by repositories or otherwise makes knowledge of them accessible to the scholarly community. There are no indexes, abstracts, or databases that have comprehensive policies of identifying these collections. Fortunately, things are changing somewhat in this area. Current bibliographic tools in this area are becoming more extensive in their coverage (see below). Databases that represent the holdings of networks of research libraries are now beginning to include archives as well as monographs; OCLC and RLIN (see chapter 6) both now catalog recent acquisitions of archives in this way. The growing commercial publication of groups of primary sources in microform means that at least a small proportion of these sources are accessible and well publicized (see section 2 below). Electronic bulletin boards have a staggering potential for easing the access, as well as the identification, of primary data collections of all kinds (see section 9 of chapter 15). This chapter should be read with these changes in mind.

These developments aside, the fact is that the hunting down of promising archival collections will probably always be a time-consuming business. By their nature archives are unique resources. Most are used by very few scholars. Repositories holding them can put limited effort into creating indexes and finding aids to them. Preparation of collection descriptions is complicated and time-consuming; many collections are voluminous and include items of a very disparate nature. Typically, neither archivists nor researchers appreciate the characteristics, strengths, and weaknesses of a collection until they have used it in depth. Added to this is the reality that many resources are held by local historical societies, records offices, labor unions, libraries, and other organizations that have limited funds with which to catalog and preserve those records over which they have custody.

Searching for a data set (whether in conventional archival form or otherwise) suitable as the mainstay of a research project is obviously an extremely important matter. The researcher must expect to devote a good amount of time and effort to it. Informal means of searching can often ease the process. Fellow members of an "invisible college" (or its electronic equivalent) can usually provide valuable advice. Books and articles in an area will undoubtedly discuss the collections used and will often refer to the existence of others. Dissertations are particularly important in this respect, as they often include lengthy appendixes providing critical discussions of archival collections used or referred to. Computerized databases can be used to determine who has used (or cited) promising collections that have been identified, as discussed in section 5 of chapter 14. (This section also discusses the methodology of historical research and the major published guides to it.)

Moreover, printed access tools are extremely helpful. Federal government archives are very accessible. The National Archives and Records Administration (NARA) is well organized and makes great efforts to encourage use of its collections. NARA is unusual (if not unique) among governmental agencies in responding with intelligent detail to written, or even telephone, inquiries. Many individual archival repositories do publish guides to their resources. Although these can be difficult to obtain outside of their geographical localities, the NARA Reference Room in Washington, DC, has an extensive collection of them. Visitors can be assured of knowledgeable help in using them to find collections relevant to particular scholarly concerns. Such help is even provided long-distance and through the mails. In addition, many published finding aids are available in the *National Inventory of Documentary Sources in the United States* (below).

Those seeking access to formerly classified or otherwise sensitive archival material from government sources are assisted by the provisions of the Freedom of Information Act. Guides to the rights of citizens under this act and to strategies for their enjoyment are discussed in section 6 of chapter 13. This section also pays some attention to sources and strategies used to locate promising bodies of governmental information.

One can anticipate a world in which bibliographic control of archival collections is better and more centralized than it is now. However, finding suitable archival collections will always involve its own unique difficulties. Archival guides and finding aids rarely provide detailed access to the contents of collections. Archival researchers must go through the process of first identifying collections of promise and then locating and examining them physically to determine which are the most suitable for the project at hand. There are few shortcuts to the second part of this process; use of the sources noted below eases the first. In identifying records recently made accessible, particular attention should be paid to *NUCMC* and to the *American Archivist*'s annual listing of published "Descriptions of Archival Holdings."

Anuario Interamericano de Archivos. (1974–). Cordoba, Argentina: Centro Interamericano de Desarrollo de Archivos.
Formerly *Boletín Interamericano de Archivos.*

Archives Accessions Annual. (1988–). Westport, CT: Meckler.
Intended to provide more timely documentation of new collections than *NUCMC* (below). Also includes new collections documented in databases such as RLIN and OCLC. It ceased after one year. The only volume published was criticized for inadequate coverage.

Burger, Barbara L. (Comp.). (1990). *Guide to the Holdings of the Still Picture Branch of the National Archives.* Washington, DC: U.S. National Archives and Records Administration. 166 p.
One of several guides produced by NARA to specialized groups of holdings.

Campbell-Kease, John. (1989). *A Companion to Local History Research.* Sherborne, UK: Alphabooks. 384 p.
Addresses British sources only.

Carnegie Institution. (1906–1943). *Guides to Manuscript Materials for the History of the United States.* Washington, DC. 23 vols.

A tremendous resource particularly valuable for its coverage of collections located outside of the United States. Only limited by its age.

Directory of Canadian Archives. Annuaire des Dépôts d'Archives Canadiens. (1981-). Ottawa: Bureau of Canadian Archivists. Annual.

A Directory of State Archives in the United States. (1980–). Chicago: Society of American Archivists. Irregular.

A valuable supplement to Posner (below). Does not include archives of county or other local governments.

Foster, Janet, & Sheppard, Julia. (1989). *British Archives* (2nd ed.). New York: Stockton Press. 834 p.

The best and most up-to-date general guide to British repositories and collections. Well indexed and includes a bibliographic guide to the more specialized archives of this country.

Freidel, Frank B. (Ed.). (1974). *Harvard Guide to American History* (rev. ed.). Cambridge, MA: Belknap Press. 2 vols.

Designed primarily as a selective guide to the major works in this general area. Includes several chapters dealing with the identification and use of archival and other primary sources. (These sections are more extensive in the 1954 edition of this work, edited by Oscar Handlin.) Updated by reviews appearing in the *Journal of American History*.

Fritze, Ronald H., Coutts, Brian E., & Vyhnanek, Louis A. (1990). *Reference Sources in History: An Introductory Guide.* Santa Barbara, CA: ABC-Clio. 322 p.

Like other bibliographic guides in its field (see chapter 4, section 4.9), pays considerable attention to sources of primary data and their use.

Galbraith, V. H. (1934). *An Introduction to the Use of the Public Records.* Oxford, UK: Clarendon Press. 112 p.

Despite its title, essentially a guide to using the contents of the British Public Record Office (see below).

Gersack, Dorothy H. (1973). Colonial, State, and Federal Court Records: A Survey. *American Archivist, 36*, 33–42.

Discusses the availability and usefulness of court records as sources for original research. Principal guides, finding tools, and indexes are discussed in the text.

Great Britain. Public Record Office. (1963–68). *Guide to the Contents of the Public Record Office.* London: HMSO. 3 vols.

Discusses the structure and holdings of the British equivalent of the U.S. National Archives and Records Service. Updated by the periodical *Guide to the Public Records.*

Great Britain. Royal Commission on Historical Manuscripts. (1991). *Record Repositories in Great Britain: A Geographical Directory* (9th ed.). London: HMSO. 46 p.

Covers the United Kingdom as a whole. Revised every year or two and therefore useful for its currency, but no substitute for Foster and Sheppard (above).

Hamer, Philip M. (Comp.). (1961). *A Guide to Archives and Manuscripts in the United States.* New Haven, CT: Yale University Press. 775 p.

A selective guide to the holdings of about 1,300 public institutions in the United States and its dependencies. Includes descriptions of collections and references to any published documentation. Should be supplemented by the latest edition of the *Directory of Archives and Manuscript Repositories in the United States* by the U.S. National Historical Publications and Records Commission (below).

International Directory of Archives. Annuaire International des Archives. (1988). Munich: K. G. Saur. 351 p.

Of greatest consequence for its coverage of countries in Western Europe. (For Latin America, see Nauman below.)

Leab, Daniel J., & Mason, Philip P. (Eds.). (1992). *Labor History Archives in the United States: A Guide for Research and Teaching.* Detroit: Wayne State University Press. 286 p.

A guide to the holdings of about 40 specialized archives in the United States. An expansion of information published in the quarterly journal *Labor History.*

National Inventory of Documentary Sources in the United States. (1983–). Teaneck, NJ: Chadwyck-Healey. Microfiche collection; updated regularly.

"Consists of published and unpublished finding aids to archives and manuscript collections . . . [accompanied by] indexes."

Nauman, Ann K. (1983). A Handbook of Latin American and Caribbean National Archives. Guía de los Archivos Nacionales de América Latina y el Caribe. Detroit: Blaine Ethridge. 127 p.

Text is in English and Spanish.

New York State Archives. (1981). *Guide to Records in the New York State Archives*. Albany, NY. 165 p.

Cited here as an example of a finding tool for the records of a particular state.

Posner, Ernst. (1964). *American State Archives*. Chicago: University of Chicago Press. 397 p.

One of the outstanding guides in the field and essential reading for researchers concerned with public records of agencies below the federal level. Archival agencies and arrangements are considered state by state, and the major repositories and published guides are discussed in the text. Archives of local agencies are also discussed. Update using the *Directory of State Archives in the United States* (above).

Primary Sources and Original Works. (1981–). Binghamton, NY: Haworth. Quarterly.

"Devoted entirely to research, documentation, and curatorship of primary sources and original works in archives, museums, and special library collection." Individual issues foucs on particular areas and discuss sources, methods for their location and use, and secondary bibliography. One recent issue, for example, is entitled "Bibliographic Foundations of French Historical Studies." Formerly entitled *Special Collections*.

Raimo, John W. (Ed.). (1979). *A Guide to Manuscripts Relating to America in Great Britain: A Revision of the Guide Edited in 1961 by B. R. Crick and Miriam Alman*. Westport, CT: Meckler. 467 p.

One of a number of guides updating the work of the Carnegie Institution (above).

Riden, Philip. (1987). *Record Sources for Local History*. London: Batsford. 253 p.

The most comprehensive source of its kind. Only concerned with the United Kingdom.

Schick, Frank L., Schick, Renee, & Carroll, Mark. (1989). *Records of the Presidency: Presidential Papers and Libraries from Washington to Reagan*. Phoenix, AZ: Oryx. 309 p.

A thorough guide to these resources that has the practical value of describing the physical range as well as the nature of the materials. Cited here in part as an example of the excellent documentation available for many collections generated at the federal level of government.

Smithsonian Institution. (1975). *Catalog to Manuscripts at the National Anthropological Archives*. Boston: G. K. Hall. 4 vols.

Reproduces catalog cards documenting a collection developed by the Bureau of American Ethnology between 1879 and 1965.

Sokal, Michael M., & Rafail, Patrice A. (1982). *A Guide to Manuscript Collections in the History of Psychology and Related Areas*. New York: Kraus International. 212 p.

A guide to about 500 major collections and one of the few sources addressing the social and behavioral sciences.

Stephens, W. B. (1981). *Sources for English Local History* (rev. ed.). Cambridge, UK: Cambridge University Press. 342 p.

Provides thorough coverage of sources at the county and parish levels.

Stephens, W. B. (1991). *Sources for U.S. History: Nineteenth-Century Communities*. Cambridge, UK: Cambridge University Press. 558 p.

Narrative chapters address primary and secondary sources documenting regional, state, and local history.

Szucs, Loretto D., & Leubking, Sandra H. (1988). *The Archives: A Guide to the National Archives Field Branches*. Salt Lake City, UT: Ancestry Publishing. 340 p.

The major guide to NARA records held outside of Washington. Provides brief descriptions of contents and citations to finding aids.

UNESCO. (1984). *Guide to the Archives of International Organizations*. Paris. 279 p.

This volume covers only collections documenting the United Nations, but is projected as the first of a series addressing a broad range of international organizations.

U.S. Library of Congress. (1959–). *National Union Catalog of Manuscript Collections*. Ann Arbor, MI: Edwards. Annual, with regular cumulations.

The major source for identifying archival collections of all kinds, other than those emanating from the federal government. Provides access by subject. Annotations indicate the characteristics and size of collections, the holding repository, and the existence of any finding aids. So far, documents almost 30,000 collections, and its scope has been redefined to include oral histories, sound and film archives, and other nonconventional sources. In spite of this, *NUCMC* is still far from being a comprehensive source.

U.S. National Archives and Records Service. (1974). *Guide to the National Archives of the United States.* Washington, DC. 884 p.

Documents the vast collections of NARA (excluding records held in presidential libraries) and discusses finding aids and other means of access to them. This general guide is supplemented by many specialized guides addressing particular groups of collections. Updated by the quarterly *Prologue: The Journal of the National Archives.*

U.S. National Historical Publications and Records Commission. (1988). *Directory of Archives and Manuscript Repositories in the United States* (2nd ed.). Phoenix, AZ: Oryx. 853 p.

Similar in form to Hamer (which it supplements but does not replace). Describes over 4,000 collections.

Vasquez de Parga, Margarita, & et al. (1991). *International Bibliography of Directories and Guides to Archival Repositories. Bibliographie Internationale des Guides et Annuaires Relatifs aux Dépôts d'Archives.* Munich: K. G. Saur. 195 p.

Perhaps useful for many of the 75 countries addressed, but not adequate for the United States.

Wasserman, Paul, & Herman, Esther (Eds.). (1980). *Catalog of Museum Publications and Media: A Directory and Index of Publications and Audiovisuals Available from United States and Canadian Institutions* (2nd ed.). Detroit: Gale. 1,044 p.

Useful for locating documentation and finding guides to museum-based archives, which are not covered well elsewhere. Will be of much greater value when revised.

Whalen, Lucille (Ed.). (1986). *Reference Services in Archives.* New York: Haworth. 210 p.

A collection of essays intended for reference librarians, but valuable to the researcher because of its discussions of the nature and availability of archival finding tools.

In addition, there are many specialized guides to groups of collections, especially those relating to the various branches of the federal government. These are cited in the various publications of NARA and in some of the guides to the use and location of archives noted here. Several sources identify collections as they are released, cataloged, or otherwise made available to interested parties. In addition to *NUCMC*, there are several journals that include such listings as a regular feature. Included among these are the *American*

Archivist (1938–), the *Journal of American History* (1914–), *Manuscripts* (1948–), *Prologue* (1969–), and the annual *Writings on American History* (1902–).

2. ARCHIVAL COLLECTIONS IN MICROFORM

In a previous section reference was made to the fact that the increasing involvement of commercial publishers in the world of primary sources has made at least a small proportion of these much more accessible. This involvement has primarily been in the direction of publication in microform (film or fiche). Collections accessible in this way are, naturally enough, those likely to be attractive to a large number of researchers (and therefore likely to be purchased by research libraries). However, the numbers of collections published in this way now number in the many thousands, and their range is constantly expanding. Moreover, many are published by public and other non-profit organizations that are concerned with encouraging the use, rather than simply the purchase, of these resources and make their publishing decisions accordingly.

Microform collections are readily identifiable through the sources noted below. They can also be tracked down easily enough. Most research and academic libraries now invest in such collections as members of consortia and allow access by all individuals associated with their consortium. Once a promising collection has been identified, it only remains to locate a copy of it in your locality. The way to determine the most convenient location of a desired collection is to search it as a title on one of the large library databases, such as OCLC or RLIN (see chapter 6 and section 9 of chapter 15).

One further important characteristic of microform collections should be stressed. Many libraries allow them to be borrowed. If your collection of choice is on microfilm, this may not be a great advantage, as microfilm readers, and especially reader-printers, are notoriously expensive. Many collections, however, are on microfiche. Fiche readers are quite cheap. Fortunate researchers may find that much of their use of primary sources can actually be done in their own homes or offices.

For these reasons, the potential archival researcher should determine whether an appropriate collection is available in microform. This can be done quickly and painlessly using the finding tools mentioned here. The rewards of a successful search can be out of all proportion to the effort.

Dodson, Suzanne C. (Ed.). (1984). *Microform Research Collections: A Guide* (2nd ed.). Westport, CT: Meckler. 670 p.

Includes good descriptions of a limited number of collections. Use to obtain information on collections identified through the *Guide to Microforms in Print.*

Guide to Microforms in Print. (1961–). Weston, CT: Microform Review. Annual.
The major guide to collections of this kind. Entries are usually included in two volumes: author/title and subject. Subject headings used are those of the Library of Congress. Includes only collections published in the United States. Older editions of this work are valuable, as they often include important sets that are no longer being marketed. Formerly *International Microforms in Print.* Sources generated outside North America are now covered by a supplement.

Microform Market Place: An International Directory of Micropublishing. (1974–). Weston, CT: Microform Review. Annual.
Best for its coverage of European sources.

Microform Review. (1972–). Westport, CT: Microform Review. Quarterly.
Includes critical reviews of recently filmed collections and identifies documentation associated with them. These cumulate every five years in *Cumulative Microform Reviews* (1976–). Use to supplement Dodson and *Guide to Microforms in Print.*

New York Metropolitan Reference and Research Library Agency. (1980). *A Union List of Selected Microforms in Libraries in the New York Metropolitan Area, 1979.* New York. 181 p.

New York State Library. (1983–). *A Guide to Microform Collections in the New York State Library.* Albany, NY. Loose-leaf; updated by supplements.
The two New York sources are examples of the many directories covering holdings in a particular institution or geographical area.

Niles, Ann (Ed.). (1984). *An Index to Microform Collections.* Westport, CT: Meckler. 891 p.
Largely an index to the contents of collections of books and therefore of limited value to the seeker of primary sources. Indexes those collections included in Dodson (above).

U.S. National Archives and Records Service. (1947–). *Catalog of National Archives Microfilm Publications.* Washington, DC. Irregular.
"Lists and describes briefly the many series of records of high research value in the National Archives that are now available as microfilm publications."

3. ARCHIVAL COLLECTIONS IN LIBRARIES

The distinction between libraries and archival repositories is by no means absolute. Many libraries house archives of their home institutions and other bodies, as well as collections of rare books and other printed primary sources. As academic and research libraries are now becoming more willing to include these holdings in the database networks in which most now participate (see section 1), electronic access to them is constantly improving. However, it will be many years before most significant collections are accessible in this way. In the meantime, the directories described below are invaluable for this purpose. Regardless of their titles, all provide significant help in locating collections of primary sources.

Ash, Lee, Miller, William G., & McQuitty, Barbara J. (Comps.). (1985). *Subject Collections: A Guide to Special Book Collections and Subject Emphases as Reported by University, College, Public, and Special Libraries and Museums in the United States and Canada* (6th ed.). New York: Bowker. 2 vols.

Bartz, Bettina, Lochar, Ruth, & Opitz, Helmut (Eds.). (1990). *World Guide to Special Libraries* (2nd ed.). Munich: K. G. Saur. 2 vols.

Documents holdings of over 30,000 libraries. Collections of primary materials are noted, but these are difficult to locate through the indexes.

Billington, Ray A. (Comp.). (1952). *Guides to American History Manuscript Collections in Libraries of the United States*. New York: P. Smith. 496 p.

Attempts to list published guides to archival collections held in federal and some other libraries. Useful as a starting-point, but should be updated using more recent works cited here.

The Center for Research Libraries. *Handbook*. (1990). Chicago. 161 p.

Provides an overview of the resources of the 150 or so member institutions of the Research Libraries Information Network (RLIN).

Filby, P. William (Comp.). (1988). *Directory of American Libraries with Genealogy or Local History Collections*. Wilmington, DE: Scholarly Resources. 319 p.

Useful for its documentation of collections in public libraries and others not in the academic circuit.

Makower, Joel (Ed.). (1988). *The American History Sourcebook*. New York: Prentice-Hall. 548 p.

Rostenberg, Leona, & Stern, Madeleine B. (Eds.). (1989). *Special Collections in College and University Libraries.* New York: Macmillan. 639 p.

Schieber, Philip, Voedisch, Virginia G., & Wright, Becky A. (Comps.). (1988). *A Guide to Special Collections in the OCLC Database.* Dublin, OH: OCLC Online Computer Library Center. 120 p.

Schreyer, Alice D. (Ed.). (1984). *Rare Books, 1983–84: Trends, Collections, Sources.* New York: Bowker. 581 p.

Williams, Moelwyn I. (Ed.). (1985). *A Directory of Rare Book and Special Collections in the United Kingdom and the Republic of Ireland.* London: Library Association. 664 p.

4. LEGAL MATERIALS

Sources documenting the substance of the law and of legal change are primary in their nature and purpose. They are in fact often the first body of primary data encountered by the beginning social researcher. As earlier discussion has suggested, analysis of legal materials can profitably be undertaken for purposes other than strict legal interpretation. Change in the law is usually functional and purposive and related in some way to broader social movement. Legal codes and the ways these are applied can be important indicators of social (or at least governmental) concerns. Their power as social indicators is buttressed by the important fact that the ways the law functions documents what society does in given circumstances and not just what it thinks or feels.

Guides to legal research and the legislative process (see sections 2 and 3 of chapter 13) are therefore also guides to primary sources and the appropriate methods for their analysis. Reference works cited below are those of particular interest to scholars with historical concerns for several reasons. A definitive characteristic of Anglo-American legal systems has been their reliance on common law principles and case- ("judge-made") law. Common law systems rely on precedent and legal tradition. In theory, this will be followed by the courts regardless of the antiquity of the source (sometimes because of its antiquity) unless there is compelling reason to do otherwise. In practice, courts in these systems have at certain times in their histories had considerable discretion in interpreting and even changing the body of operational law. At these times, judges frequently went beyond the slim corpus of official legal documentation for guidance in their decisions. Because of this, *unofficial* sources (encyclopedias, treatises and other commentaries, privately-compiled reports of cases) have in past times been of tremendous importance to jurists, and consequently to present-day legal historians. The sources noted here are intended to document these influences on the development of legal thought.

Social scientists using legal primary sources are usually very much interested in how the law was or is applied as well as in the nature of its content. A law whose violations are prosecuted vigorously and successfully is clearly a stronger statement of policy than one which is not. It is therefore common in sociolegal research to examine court records to identify prosecution patterns. For someone working with modern sources, relevant court records, whether published or in manuscript, can be identified using the guides to federal, state, and local documents discussed in chapter 13. Those addressing historical settings may find these guides to be inadequate. Collections of old court records may not have been preserved. On the other hand, they may subsequently have been published by local historical societies, microform publishers, or others. If official records have not survived in any form, contemporary newspaper reports may be concerned detailed and accurate enough to be acceptable substitutes (see Lawson, below).

A further characteristic of a common law system is its recognition of decisions and opinions from other common law jurisdictions. Currently, such decisions would be accepted as of persuasive (secondary) authority only. However, in the past, they were accorded something approaching primary (binding) authority. It is for this reason that the student of American legal history should at least be aware of the structure and bibliography of relevant foreign legal systems. Guides to legal research in some common law jurisdictions outside of the United States are cited in section 3 of chapter 13. Other related material is noted below.

Information included in the sources documented here can be used to supplement that given in the guides to archival collections mentioned elsewhere in this chapter. Also of interest here is the *Legal Bibliography Index* (cited elsewhere). This serves the function of indexing bibliographies of both primary and secondary materials. The reader should also be aware that legal histories published as monographs or dissertations commonly include detailed discussion of the primary materials on which analysis was based.

Baker, John H. (1985). *English Legal Manuscripts in the United States of America: A Descriptive List.* London: The Selden Society. 2 vols.

Cites and describes over 1,500 manuscripts and collections of manuscripts held in 50 or so major repositories in the United States. A high proportion of the sources listed are available in microform.

Breem, Wallace, & Phillips, Sally (Eds.). (1991). *Bibliography of Commonwealth Law Reports.* Rutherford, NJ: Publishers Distribution Center. 332 p.

Best used to update the massive *Legal Bibliography of the British Commonwealth.* Entries are arranged by jurisdiction and some historical sources are included.

Dobbs, Kimberly W. (Comp.). (1980). *Law Volumes Microfilmed by the Library of Congress*. Washington, DC: The Library. 280 p.
Primarily an unannotated list of legal treatises published in the United States in the 19th and 20th centuries. Some Latin American publications are included. Unindexed and difficult to use.

Hall, Kermit. (1984). *A Comprehensive Bibliography of American Constitutional and Legal History, 1896–1979.* Millwood, NY: Kraus International. 5 vols.
"A comprehensive bibliography of the writings of American legal culture." Updated by a 2-volume supplement covering 1980–87.

Hicks, Frederick C. (1942). *Materials and Methods of Legal Research* (3rd ed.). Rochester, NY: Lawyers Cooperative. 659 p.
This edition is valuable for its exhaustive listings of official and unofficial law reports for the United States, Britain, and its colonies.

Hines, W.D. (1990). *English Legal History: A Bibliography and Guide to the Literature.* New York: Garland. 201 p.
A thorough survey of the methods and sources of this area which also presents a selective review of major findings and approaches.

Law Books, 1876–1981: Books and Serials on Law and Its Related Subjects. (1981). New York: Bowker. 4 vols.
Includes primary and secondary works published in this period.

Lawson, John D. (Ed.). (1914–36). *American State Trials: A Collection of the Important and Interesting Criminal Trials Which Have Taken Place in the United States, from the Beginning of Our Government to the Present Day.* St. Louis, MO: F.H. Thomas. 17 vols.
A valuable collection even though "Important and Interesting" are defined as those cases which attracted the most detailed press coverage in the 19th and early 20th centuries. See the comments on this source cited in footnote 5.

Maxwell, W. H., Maxwell, L. F., & James, J. S. (Eds.). (1955–64). *A Legal Bibliography of the British Commonwealth of Nations* (2nd ed.). London: Sweet & Maxwell. 7 vols.
The first two volumes are particularly valuable because they address primary sources published before the mid-19th century, a period that includes the colonial

United States and also a later period when British legal sources were widely used and cited. Volume 3 covers Canadian and British American colonial law.

Nelson, William E., & Reid, John P. (1985). *The Literature of American Legal History.* New York: Oceana. 356p.
A collection of essays which includes the "Legal History" review articles appearing regularly in the *Annual Survey of American Law* between 1962 and 1985. Many present discussion of primary sources as well as secondary analysis.

Ritz, Wilfred J. (Comp.). (1984). *American Judicial Proceedings First Printed before 1801: An Analytical Bibliography.* Westport, CT: Greenwood. 364 p.
Although this work is primarily devoted to published accounts of trials, coverage also includes court rules, grand jury records, criminal biographies and other forms of "gallows literature." No sources in manuscript are cited and no encyclopedias or other published sources now considered as persuasive authority.

Taylor, Betty W., & Munro, Robert J. (1984). *American Law Publishing, 1860–1900: Historical Readings.* Dobbs Ferry, NY: Glanville. 4 vols.
Volumes 3 and 4 include author and subject listings of legal works (mainly encyclopedias and treatises) published in the period.

Winfield, Percy H. (1925). *The Chief Sources of English Legal History.* Cambridge, MA: Harvard University Press. 374 p.
Covers unofficial as well as official sources, including the encyclopedias and collections of privately reported leading cases so important until the middle of the 19th century. Also a guide to the early secondary literature.

5. NEWSPAPERS AND POPULAR MAGAZINES

In section 2 of chapter 15 it was shown how newspapers (and popular magazines—the two are for this purpose the same) are considered primary sources if they document an event, or at least contemporary perceptions of it. Newspapers, among other materials, can be used as primary sources for this purpose in one very structured way. The technique of *content analysis* seeks to use the text of contemporary writing as the basis for constructing indicators of popular values, beliefs, and perceptions associated with given social settings. Content analysis can take many forms. One of its simplest recent applications has been in the several scholarly examinations of crime waves. By the straightforward process of categorizing and counting news reports of crime, scholars have been able to compare the actual incidence and nature of crime (as reflected by victim surveys or police records) to public perceptions of it, which are largely generated by the media, including the press. Common findings of analyses of this kind reveal the extent to which crime reporting distorts readers' ideas of the extent and characteristics of the phenomenon studied.[8]

Content analysis can involve more than the counting of newspaper reports. Typically, content analysts select a series of indicators (words or phrases) associated with a social or personal value and assess the relative incidence of these in reports published over time. They do so in the hope of identifying changing patterns of popular perception and belief. As in most areas of social research, the crucial aspect of this analysis is the extent to which the chosen indicator can be presumed to measure the belief or value under consideration. Most criticism of content analyses (assuming, of course, that their sampling and other methodological techniques are sound) concerns their choices of indicators. As these are often based on the opinions of "panels of experts," or on other less-than-absolute criteria, indicators used can clearly be obvious subjects of debate.

Early uses of content analysis (in the late 1930s and 1940s) were moved by the belief that public opinion (Nazi and otherwise) could somehow be specified and mobilized. Later applications of this method have been used in more interesting ways. One of the simplest of these later applications is also one of the most frequently cited. In 1965 R. L. Merritt used content analysis to address the interesting question of when residents of colonial America first began to think of themselves as Americans, and not as British expatriates. By analyzing the relative use of terms of self-identification appearing in colonial newspapers, he felt able to pinpoint this date fairly accurately.[9] Newspapers and periodicals are not the only printed forms to have been used in this way. One author has applied the technique to a group of magazines and to discussions in published reports of law-enforcement agencies in the early decades of the 20th century. His objectives were, first, to document contemporary perceptions of drug users, and second, to suggest the influences that produced these perceptions. His findings were that demonic characterizations (the "dope fiend" mythology) became predominant, and that these were largely achieved by the filtering down of characterizations from official reports to the popular press. The strength of his findings is supported by his contention (based on secondary sources) that the mythology had little basis in actual behavior.[10]

Many different kinds of material, printed and otherwise, have been subjected to content analysis. Magazines and newspapers, however, are typical raw data for this kind of study, and primary data to support such studies are readily available. Sources noted in the previous chapter and in section 2 of this chapter suggest the great range of periodicals available in microform or in the original hard copy. This alone often makes content analysis a technique attractive to the researcher.

As with all kinds of research, the best content analyses are those that reflect thoughtfulness and imagination on the part of the researcher. Nonetheless, any exercise of this nature must also be designed and carried out with a concern for rigor and form. Some of the many guides to this are cited below.

Sources of newspapers and magazines, and indexes to them, are discussed in the previous chapter.

Berger, Charles R., & Chaffee, Steven H. (Eds.). (1987). *Handbook of Communication Science*. Beverly Hills, CA: Sage. 946 p.

Discusses content analysis and its applications as part of a broad range of approaches used to analyze the mass media and their products.

Block, Eleanor S., & Bracken, James K. (1991). *Communication and Mass Media: A Guide the Reference Literature*. Englewood, CO: Libraries Unlimited. 198 p.

Cited here for its inclusion of references to content analysis and other techniques using media products as the material of original research.

Krippendorff, Klaus. (1980). *Content Analysis: An Introduction to Its Methodology*. Beverly Hills, CA: Sage. 191 p.

Perhaps the clearest and most useful of the current guides. Other works cited in this section are included because of the variety of their illustrative examples.

Pool de Sola, Ithiel (Ed.). (1959). *Trends in Content Analysis*. Urbana: University of Illinois Press. 244 p.

An older work whose contents locate the technique in its original setting of political science, in particular the study of propaganda.

Rosengren, Karl E. (Ed.). (1981). *Advances in Content Analysis*. Beverly Hills, CA: Sage. 283 p.

Essays include extensive reviews of recent trends.

Weber, Robert P. (1990). *Basic Content Analysis* (2nd ed.). Newbury Park, CA: Sage. 96 p.

Valuable as a concise introduction. Also important for its inclusion of citations to recent illustrative studies.

A number of journals in the broad areas of communication and journalism regularly note recent books and articles that have applied the technique. *Communication Abstracts*, published bimonthly since 1978, is the major printed abstracting service covering the area. *Communications Information (Comm)* is a database produced by the University of Guelph in Ontario. Its holdings cover the literature back to 1960.

6. DIARIES AS PRIMARY SOURCES

Personal papers of individuals are as acceptable as primary sources as records of organizations. Diaries usually provide the most sustained documentation of a person's life, particularly if they have been maintained in consistent detail and over a long period of time. They are valuable to the social scientist as well as to the historian or literary scholar, as they present the very personal observations of those who may have been intimately involved in the events or institutional developments that are the broader object of study. Rarely do social researchers rely on diaries as their major source of data, but they can often be important as supporting evidence. It does not matter in principle whether a diary is in manuscript or published form. In practice, users of a published diary must have some basis for determining the extent to which the original manuscript was edited, or otherwise altered in its transformation into the printed form. This point was brought into prominence by the well-known controversy concerning the veracity of the published diaries of Mary Chesnut, survivor of the Civil War siege of Atlanta.[11]

There is an important distinction between diaries and autobiographies. The latter, which are almost invariably published, are also products of an individual's quite personal experiences in life. However, an autobiography is by definition a work at least designed for publication. It may therefore be assumed to represent views or perceptions designed to sway or impress a readership. Diaries are presumed to be private records, intended for individual expression rather than public consumption. This distinction between the diary and the autobiography is, of course, to some extent artificial. Diaries are published that were undoubtedly intended for the eyes of the world.[12]

The major sources for identifying diaries in published and manuscript form are noted below. Two biographical sources, the *Dictionary of American Biography* and the *Dictionary of National Biography*, are of great importance since they usually include discussion of diaries, collections of papers, and other sources relating to the individuals or families they discuss. Of particular interest are the several works by Matthews. These are the standard bibliographies of diaries published (or written) in English and are updated or supplemented by more recent works, including those by Arksey, Pries, and Reed, and Havlice. The *Biography Index* covers diaries, as well as other biographical materials, published in essays, articles, or books and is the major current source. In keeping with comments made earlier, bibliographies and other sources documenting autobiographies are only cited here if they give significant coverage of diaries. Those interested in other forms of biographical material should consult Cimbala, Cargill, and Alley (below).

There do not appear to be any adequate guides to the use of this material, although some attention to this subject is included in several of the guides to archival research methods discussed in chapter 14. Appreciation of the value of diaries to the social researcher is best achieved by examination of their use for a particular purpose[13] or their place in a particular social context.[14]

Arksey, Laura, Pries, Nancy, & Reed, Marcia. (1983–87). *American Diaries: An Annotated Bibliography of Published American Diaries and Journals.* Detroit: Gale. 2 vols.

Biography and Genealogy Master Index: A Consolidated Index to More than 3,200,000 Biographical Sketches in over 350 Current and Retrospective Biographical Dictionaries (2nd ed.). (1980). Detroit: Gale. 8 vols. Kept up-to-date by annual supplements which cumulate quinquennially.

Surveys articles appearing in biographical directories, encyclopedias, and works of literary criticism, as well as in books and articles. Its main purpose is to index secondary sources, but it is also valuable for its consideration of primary materials.

Biography Index. (1946–). New York: H. W. Wilson. Quarterly, with biennial cumulations.

Mainly indexes works about individuals appearing in articles and books, but also covers autobiographies and diaries published in journal-article or monograph form.

Briscoe, Mary L., Tobias, Barbara, & Bloom, Lynn Z. (Eds.). (1982). *American Autobiography, 1945-1980: A Bibliography.* Madison: University of Wisconsin Press. 365 p.

Cites about 5,000 autobiographies, the genre being defined broadly to include journals, diaries, collections of letter. A supplement to Kaplan.

Burnett, John, Vincent, David, & Mayall, David (Eds.). (1984–89). *The Autobiography of the Working Class: An Annotated, Critical Bibliography.* New York: New York University Press. 3 vols.

Cimbala, Diane J., Cargill, Jennifer, & Alley, Brian. (1986). *Biographical Sources: A Guide to Dictionaries and Reference Works.* Phoenix, AZ: Oryx. 146 p.

Cline, Cheryl. (1989). *Women's Diaries, Journals, and Letters: An Annotated Bibliography.* New York: Garland. 716 p.

Dictionary of American Biography. (1928–37). New York: Scribner's. 21 vols. Updated by supplements.

The Dictionary of National Biography. (1885–1902). London: Oxford University Press. 66 vols. Reissued in 22 vols.
A British source that overlaps with the *DAB* in that both include Americans from the colonial period. Updated by decennial supplements.

Forbes, Harriette (Comp.). (1967). *New England Diaries, 1602–1800: A Descriptive Catalogue of Diaries, Orderly Books, and Sea Journals.* New York: Russell & Russell. 439 p.

Havlice, Patricia P. (1987). *And So to Bed: A Bibliography of Diaries Published in English.* Metuchen, NJ: Scarecrow. 698 p.
Includes a short "Bibliography of Bibliographies."

Huff, Cynthia. (1985). *British Women's Diaries: A Descriptive Bibliography of Selected Nineteenth-Century Women's Manuscript Diaries.* New York: AMS Press. 139 p.

Kaplan, Louise (Ed). (1962). *A Bibliography of American Autobiographies.* Madison: University of Wisconsin Press. 372 p.
The major source for materials written before 1945. Supplemented by Briscoe et al.

Matthews, William. (1959). *American Diaries: An Annotated Bibliography of American Diaries Written prior to the Year 1861.* Boston: J.S. Canner. 383 p.

Matthews, William. (1974). *American Diaries in Manuscript, 1580–1954: A Descriptive Bibliography.* Athens: University of Georgia Press. 176 p.

Matthews, William. (1950). *British Diaries: An Annotated Bibliography of British Diaries Written between 1442 and 1942.* Berkeley, CA: University of California Press. 339 p.

Matthews, William. (1950). *Canadian Diaries and Autobiographies.* Berkeley, CA: University of California Press. 130 p.

Muccigrosso, Robert (Ed). (1988–90). *Research Guide to American Historical Biography.* Washington, DC: Beacham. 5 vols.
Biographical sketches include evaluative discussion of primary and secondary sources (including diaries). Valuable for its coverage of minorities, women, and others not well represented in traditional sources.

Ponsonby, Arthur P. (1923). *English Diaries: A Review of English Diaries from the Sixteenth to the Twentieth Century with an Introduction on Diary Writing.* London: Methuen. 447 p.

Ponsonby, Arthur P. (1927). *More English Diaries; Further Reviews of Diaries from the Sixteenth to the Nineteenth Century with an Introduction on Diary Reading.* London: Methuen. 250 p.

Ponsonby, Arthur P. (1927). *Scottish and Irish Diaries: From the Sixteenth to the Nineteenth Century.* London: Methuen. 192 p.

Reference Sources for the Library of Congress Index to Biographies in State and Local Histories. Baltimore, MD: Magna Carta. 31 p.
Lists those biographies analyzed in this LC collection, accessible through "a card index of approximately 170,000 cards housed in the Local History and Genealogy Room of the Library."

Use of diaries, letters, and reminiscences as supporting primary material frequently brings unanticipated bonuses. Anyone who doubts the considerable personal pleasure that reading these documents can bring has never read any of the personal testaments of people like Horace Walpole (18th-century man-about-town), Mary Wortley Montagu (acerbic critic of polite society), Henry Kyd Douglas (sometime aide to Stonewall Jackson), or the historians Edward Gibbon and Thomas Babington Macaulay.

7. ORAL HISTORY

The concept of using living memories to flesh out knowledge of a past event or circumstance is, of course, timeless. Uses of it in some formal sense have characterized social research for well over a century. Henry Mayhew, the mid-19th-century journalist and social reformer, collected extensive verbatim accounts of the lives of the London underclass.[15] Use of ethnographic research to record the speech and thoughts of classes of people who do not usually write their memoirs characterized the work of Charles Dickens.[16]

In the last 50 years, however, with the development of sophisticated means of recording and analyzing verbal information, this concept has become the basis of its own branch of historiography. Oral history is much more than the simple recording and collation of reminiscences to provide the substance of an explanatory narrative. It has its own rules establishing how attempts must be made to verify the data so collected and to test its internal consistency.

There are several excellent guides to the craft of this kind of research (see, for example, the works by Frisch and Grele, below). All emphasize that a respondent's recollections must be checked by questions from an interviewer familiar with the topics of discussion. "Free-association" narratives are discouraged, and the interviewer constantly seeks details in the narrative that are verifiable and can therefore indicate the veracity of the account in its entirety. Accounts of the same event are checked against one another. They are also checked against the substance of the documented record.

Social researchers rarely use oral histories to provide their primary body of data. Oral histories, like diaries, are generally used to provide a critical examination of the data available in written form. In this sense these histories usually serve the larger purpose of enabling researchers to examine a chosen circumstance from a different, though related, perspective. Someone concerned, for example, with the historical efficacy of narcotics-control policies might seek information from those who have been their traditional objects.[17]

A number of extensive collections of groups of interviews now exist (see Mason and Starr, Meckler and McMullin, and Smith, below, for sources of them). Some have been transcribed; others are accessible only in their original recorded form. There are no indexes or abstracts exclusively devoted to this area, although those in the discipline of history do report a good number of relevant studies. This field is, however, fairly self-contained. The Oral History Association publishes the two major current sources in the area, as well as a membership directory. These serial works are generally sufficient for the informed practitioner to keep abreast of developments in this field.

Allen, Barbara, & Montell, William L. (1981). *From Memory to History: Using Oral Sources in Local Historical Research.* Nashville, TN: American Association for State and Local History. 172 p.

Frisch, Michael. (1990). *A Shared Authority: Essays on the Craft and Meaning of Oral and Public History.* Albany, NY: State University of New York Press. 273 p.

Grele, Ronald J. (1985). *Envelopes of Sound: The Art of Oral History* (2nd ed.). Chicago: Precedent. 283 p.

Havlice, Patricia P. (1985). *Oral History: A Reference Guide and Annotated Bibliography.* Jefferson, NC: McFarland. 140 p.

International Annual of Oral History. (1980–). Westport, CT: Greenwood.

The only current source of scholarly material in this area (see the *Oral History Review* below). Before 1990 published three times a year as the *International Journal of Oral History.*

Mason, Elizabeth B., & Starr, Louis M. (Eds.). (1979). *The Oral History Collection of Columbia University.* New York: Columbia University. Oral History Research Office. 306 p.
The catalog of one of the major collections in this area. (Others are cited in other reference works noted here.)

Meckler, Alan M., & McMullin, Ruth (Comps.). (1975). *Oral History Collections.* New York: Bowker. 344 p.
Supplement with Smith (below).

Oral History Association. (1978–). *Annual Report and Membership Directory.* Denton, TX: North Texas State University. Annual.

Oral History Association. (1967–). *Newsletter.* Denton, TX: North Texas State University. Quarterly.

Oral History Index: An International Directory of Oral History Interviews. (1990). Westport, CT: Meckler. 434 p.
International coverage is limited to Canada, Great Britain, Israel, and the United States. Not as reliable as a starting point as the guides to collections by Meckler and McMullin and by Smith.

The Oral History Review. (1973–). Denton, TX: North Texas State University.

Smith, Allen. (1988). *Directory of Oral History Collections.* Phoenix, AZ: Oryx. 141 p.
A supplement to Meckler and McMullin (above).

8. PSYCHOHISTORY

Most, if not all, social explorations make implicit assumptions about the motivations of individuals or groups. It is hard to imagine how this could not be so. Adam Smith's "economic man" was assumed to base his life decisions on perceptions that were rational, self-serving, and consciously appreciated by the individual. Jeremy Bentham's juggler of pain and pleasure was similarly conceived of as one who could both understand and act upon objective concepts of his own self-interest. These caricatures of human rationality have long since been shot down, but their shadows persist. If social scientists cannot assume some consistency in human behavior, then they can do very little.

Psychohistory is a rather controversial endeavor that recognizes this dependence in an explicit fashion by encouraging the direct application of behavioral theory to the nonretrievable past. By its very nature, this approach is difficult to subject to the test of falsification (how could one attempt to disprove it?). Because of this, psychohistory causes some unease among many social scientists. At its best, however, this perspective is used to examine important situations that are simply unapproachable through conventional means.

Gordon Rattray Taylor's *The Angel Makers*, for example, addresses the interesting and generally accepted finding that gender relations took a definite turn for the worse from the late 18th century on.[18] Taylor's explanation for this concerns supposed influences on the development of the male psyche occasioned by documented changes in child-rearing practices among the upper classes shortly before this time. He suggests that these practices induced certain later and persistent insecurities among males in this social stratum. The point here is not whether Taylor's inferences are right (although the data on which they are based probably are). Rather, it is that he presents a persuasive psychological explanation for a major social shift that has been recognized by social researchers, but has never properly been explained by them.

This approach assumes that psychological influences of the present can be projected with full force to the past. As many of these conditions are undoubtedly the consequences of interactions between culture and individual psyche, such projection may be hard to swallow. Nonetheless, analyses such as those of Taylor serve to provide explanations of situations that conventional social science approaches have so far been unable to address. They may not be right, they may not be provable, but they are the best we have in the circumstances. With these reservations in mind (and they are serious reservations for most social scientists), psychohistory should be considered for the undeniable attraction of its ability to offer irrefutable persuasion when explanation cannot be had.

The problems of finding suitable models through library catalogs and other standard sources will be familiar to readers of chapter 6. "Psychohistory" is a standard Library of Congress subject heading and also one of its standard subdivisions. Life and the Library of Congress being what they are, many important exemplars of this genre are not so cataloged. Taylor's work certainly is not.[19] Gilmore's bibliography is therefore of particular importance in locating this kind of material, as are the two major journals in the area. Anyone interested in this approach should also look for illustrative examples by referring to the bibliographies in the works cited below, as well as applying standard library techniques.

Conventions of the field are well covered by the three monographs noted here. Above all, these works provide valuable discussions of the knotty problems of using the historical record as a basis for application of modern psychological theories.

Gilmore, William J. (1984). *Psychohistorical Inquiry: A Comprehensive Research Bibliography.* New York: Garland. 317 p.

The Journal of Psychohistory. (1973–). New York: Atcom. Quarterly. Formerly entitled *History of Childhood Quarterly.*

Lawton, Henry. (1988). *The Psychohistorian's Handbook.* New York: Psychohistory Press. 241 p.

Psychohistory Review. (1972–). Springfield, IL: Group for the Use of Psychology in History. Quarterly.

Runyan, William McK. (1984). *Life Histories and Psychobiography: Explorations in Theory and Method.* New York: Oxford University Press. 288 p.

Runyan, William McK. (Ed.). (1988). *Psychology and Historical Interpretation.* New York: Oxford University Press. 306 p.

9. OTHER APPROACHES

It should be clear by now that the kinds of methods and sources discussed in this and earlier chapters by no means exhaust the options available to researchers who approach their topics with imagination. The notion of using a broad range of nontraditional materials as primary sources for social research was pioneered many years ago. Thomas and Znaniecki's classic study of working-class Poles at home and abroad was published betweem 1918 and 1920 and is still widely cited for, among other things, its ambitious use of diaries, letters, and other personal documents.[20] More recently, Fogel and Engerman's massive and number-driven study of slavery in the American South has provoked considerable discussion because of the great scope of types of data source used and the methods employed to analyze them.[21]

Techniques such as content analysis are not limited to the printed word. Pictures, paintings, sound, film, and video broadcasts—are all raw material for those who wish to study patterns over time. The analyst's only concern, shared by all social researchers, is to ensure that the symbols used are fair reflections of the values they are taken to indicate. Film is particularly interesting in this respect, as the Western world now has filmed records of most of the last century of its history. Differences in mores, speech patterns, and styles of living are readily discernible over time through this medium.[22] The significance of records such as film is now widely appreciated by those interested in studying social change, and this is reflected in the diverse kinds of uses now being made of them.[23]

The outstanding guides to research using archives of various of the non-print media are cited below. Their scope and range is sufficient indicator of increasing scholarly interest in the artifacts of popular culture.

Armour, Robert A. (1980). *Film, A Reference Guide*. Westport, CT: Greenwood. 251 p.

Discusses reference works, archival collections, research methods, and secondary sources. Less comprehensive than Manchel.

Fisher, Kim N. (1986). *On the Screen: A Film, Television, and Video Research Guide*. Littleton, CO: Libraries Unlimited. 209 p.

A braod guide to primary sources and some of the noteworthy secondary works that have resulted from their analysis.

Godfrey, Donald G. (Comp.). (1992). *Reruns on File: A Guide to Electronic Media Archives*. Hillsdale, NJ: Erlbaum. 322 p.

A guide to radio and television archives in Canada, the United Kingdom, and the United States. Short annotations give some indication of their holdings.

Manchel, Frank (Ed.). (1990). *Film Study: An Analytical Bibliography*. Rutherford, NJ: Fairleigh Dickinson University Press. 4 vols.

A comprehensive and thorough guide to this rapidly-growing field. Six different methodological approaches to it are considered in great detail. The last volume includes lists of bibliographies, directories, archival sources, and other reference sources.

Pruett, Barbara J. (1992). *Popular Entertainment Research: How to Do It and How to Use It*. Metuchen, NJ: Scarecrow. 581 p.

The bulk of the text constitutes a guide to the primary and secondary materials documenting the broadcast media, film, theater, and popular music. A lengthy introduction is devoted to consideration of various of the research methodologies that have been applied in the analysis of these kinds of data.

Smith, Myron J. (1984). *U.S. Television Network News: A Guide to Sources in English*. Jefferson, NC: McFarland. 233 p.

Substantially an annotated bibliography of secondary sources. The first chapter is entitled "Reference Works" and discusses access to primary sources.

Television News Index and Abstracts. (1972–). Nashville, TN: Vanderbilt Television News Archive. Monthly.

Covers the daily programming of the three major news networks: ABC, CBS, and NBC. Archives of the programs themselves are maintained by Vanderbilt.

Transcript/Video Index: A Comprehensive Guide to Television News and Public Affairs Programming. (1990–). New York: Journal Graphics. Annual, with quarterly updates.

Indexes the contents of over 60 televivion news programs all of which are accessible in their original form. A retrospective set brings coverage back to 1968. Also available online and on CD-ROM.

The Video Annual. (1991–). Santa Barbara, CA: ABC-Clio.

Includes listings of producers, distributors, library collections, bibliography, and resource materials.

Wilmeth, Don B. (1980). *American and English Popular Entertainment: A Guide to Information Sources.* Detroit: Gale. 465 p.

A bibliography covering both primary and secondary sources.

Study of other cultural artifacts of modern life has also attracted the social researcher. Anthropologists in particular have contributed greatly to our knowledge of cultural adaptation to modern city living. Analyses in areas such as urban folklore offer insights into the dynamics of social life and the interaction between these and the various cultural systems within which they occur.[24] Given all these developments, no one contemplating the design of an original research project can complain with justice that all possible approaches are limiting or uninspiring.

NOTES

1. There are, of course, other reasons that are implicit in earlier discussion: Secondary works usually stimulate the imagination by showing how others have approached similar research environments. They indicate gaps in the literature and issues that have been inadequately addressed. They suggest new methods of attack. Above all, they help the worker determine how a broad theoretical concern can be explored in a limited research setting.

2. See Ariès, Philippe. (1962). *Centuries of Childhood: A Social History of Family Life.* New York: Knopf; Ousby, Ian. (1976). *Bloodhounds of Heaven: The Detective in English*

Fiction from Godwin to Doyle. Cambridge, MA: Harvard University Press; and Foucault, Michel. (1977). *Discipline and Punish: The Birth of the Prison*. New York: Pantheon.

3. For example, Pinkett, Harold T. (1970). *Gifford Pinchot, Private and Public Forester*. Urbana, IL: University of Illinois Press. This work addresses the considerable influence of Pinchot on the creation and early development of the National Parks Service.

4. Probably the outstanding examination of Durkheim's theories on the social function of crime and the criminal law is based on analysis of records published two centuries after they were created: Erikson, Kai T. (1966). *Wayward Puritans: A Study in the Sociology of Deviance*. New York: Wiley.

5. For example, the series *American State Trials* purports to include verbatim accounts of criminal trials from the 19th and early 20th centuries. However, as these accounts are largely drawn from contemporary newspapers, it seems doubtful if they can be relied upon to include the numerous legal minutiae characteristic of trial proceedings. Moreover, as it has always been only sensational trials that stimulate detailed reporting, one cannot regard the cases in this set as typical of patterns of criminal prosecution. The contents of this set certainly qualify as primary sources, but must be handled with care. A full citation to this source is given in section 4.

6. The classic work documenting this finding is Woodward, C. Vann. (1974). *The Strange Career of Jim Crow* (3rd ed.). New York: Oxford University Press.

7. Pretesting involves applying one's research instrument to a small, not necessarily representative, portion of the research sample. Analysis of the outcome of this helps the researcher determine whether the variables used are productive, and how they might be modified to exploit the fecundity of the overall research situation.

8. For a review of content analysis and the study of "crime waves," see Marsh, Harry L. (1991). A Comparative Analysis of Crime Coverage in Newspapers in the United States and Other Countries from 1960–1989: A Review of the Literature. *Journal of Criminal Justice, 19*, 67–79.

9. Merritt, Richard L. (1965). The Emergence of American Nationalism: A Quantitative Approach. *American Quarterly, 17* (Summer), 319–35.

10. Reasons, Charles E. (1976). Images of Crime and the Criminal: The Dope Fiend Mythology. *Journal of Research in Crime and Delinquency, 13*, 133–144.

11. Williams, Ben A. (Ed.). (1949). *A Diary from Dixie*. Boston: Houghton Mifflin; Woodward, C. Vann, & Muhlenfeld, Elisabeth (Eds.). (1984). *The Private Mary Chesnut: The Unpublished Civil War Diaries*. New York: Oxford University Press. The editors' introduction to the later work includes reference to this controversy.

12. The editor's introduction to one of the diaries most often quoted by 19th-century social historians suggests that the author's purpose in writing it was to emphasize and publicize the extent of the progress of society in his lifetime: Thale, Mary (Ed.). (1972). *The Autobiography of Francis Place (1771–1854)*. Cambridge, UK: Cambridge University Press.

13. For example, Rosenblatt, Paul C. (1983). *Bitter, Bitter Tears: Nineteenth-Century Diarists and Twentieth-Century Grief Theories*. Minneapolis: University of Minnesota Press.

14. D. A. Stauffer's (1930) work is both an examination of the purposes and conventions of biographies (including diaries) in one historical setting and a guide to sources: *English Biography before 1700*. Cambridge, MA: Harvard University Press.

15. *London Labour and the London Poor* was serialized in the *Morning Post* in 1861 and 1862 and later published in a four-volume set.

16. For a discussion of Dickens's interest in underclass living and his informed forays into the haunts of this class, see Philip Collins's 1962 book *Dickens and Crime*. London: Macmillan. Peter Ackroyd, in his 1990 biography, presents compelling arguments to suggest that Dickens recorded his observations faithfully and in detail in all his novels: *Dickens*. New York: Harper Collins.

17. See Courtwright, David, Joseph, Herman, & Des Jarlais, Don. (1989). *Addicts Who Survived: An Oral History of Narcotic Use in America, 1923–1965*. Knoxville: University of Tennessee Press.

18. Taylor, Gordon Rattray. (1974). *The Angel Makers: A Study in the Psychological Origins of Historical Change, 1750–1850*. New York: Dutton.

19. Its assigned subject headings include the subdivisions "Social Life and Customs" and "Moral Conditions."

20. Thomas, William I., & Znaniecki, Florian. (1927). *The Polish Peasant in Europe and America*. New York: Knopf.

21. Fogel, Robert W., & Engerman, Stanley L. (1974). *Time on the Cross: The Economics of American Negro Slavery*. Boston: Little, Brown. Following criticism of their work, the authors felt compelled to issue a supplement, also published in 1974, explaining their sources and techniques: *Time on the Cross: Evidence and Methods, a Supplement*.

22. Anyone who doubts this has only to observe the differences between, for example, Alfred Hitchcock's early and later films. These differences are clearly attributable to a great deal more than improved technology and changing style in direction. They reflect massive changes in social structure and perceptions of it.

23. For example, May, Lary. (1980). *Screening Out the Past: The Birth of Mass Culture and the Motion Picture Industry*. New York: Oxford University Press; MacCabe, Colin (Ed.). (1986). *High Theory/Low Culture: Analysing Popular Television and Film*. New York: St. Martin's; Crawford, Peter I., & Turton, David (Eds.). (1992). *Film as Ethnography*. Manchester, UK: Manchester University Press.

24. See, for example, Schecter, Harold. (1988). *The Bosom Serpent: Folklore and Popular Art*. Iowa City: University of Iowa Press. For discussion of approaches in this area, see Brunvand, Jan H. (1986). *The Study of American Folklore: An Introduction* (3rd ed.). New York: Norton; Dorson, Richard M. (Ed.). (1983). *Handbook of American Folklore*. Bloomington: Indiana University Press.

POSTSCRIPT

The objectives of this book should by now be clear enough. If they are not, then further invocation of them is superfluous. Nonetheless, a few principles should be emphasized, because these are vital to the successful completion of the research enterprise. The reader should be aware that these observations are offered by one whose professional experiences have incorporated the worlds of social research and of library practice.

1. The research process is a dynamic one. One cannot approach it step by step, with the traditional notion of envisioning a topic, developing a methodology, finding or creating a suitable data set, and then searching out a related bibliography. These steps go hand in hand. Each one of them influences the others. Each stage in the activity is part of a continuum, with the information gained in one stage influencing the decisions of the next.

2. Researchers should never feel bound by the strictures of their own discipline. Disciplinary structure is informative, indeed comforting, but it should not be a straitjacket. Dipping into the methods and styles of other social scientists is a right and a privilege of any social researcher. Horses for courses is the motto here. Ways have been suggested to support such a perspective.

3. The literature search is but a part of a much larger enterprise and not an end in itself. Researchers can greatly ease their overall task if they constantly think about the primary phase of the project while investigating secondary sources. Someone conducting an intensive search on a narrow topic would do well to keep an eye out for references to promising methods, theories, models, instruments, and primary sources.

4. Initial conceptualization of the scope and nature of the project is not fixed in stone. It is subject to constant modification and even redefinition as the expanding knowledge of the researcher compels a deeper understanding of its nature and ramifications. The normal direction of this process of topic modification is to whittle down the scope of the project to make it tighter and more manageable. This process is continuous and lasts for most of the life of the project. Dissertation committees are typically sympathetic to this, although they do, of course, like to be kept informed of any substantial changes in the research focus.

5. It is easy to become compulsive in engaging the literature searching process. Unfortunately, this rarely helps. One does not have to find every published work of relevance, especially in ancillary areas such as methodology. Casting one's net as broadly as possible has obvious advantages, but the catch must be manageable as well as relevant. There is no virtue in spending excessive time on literature-searching. It is a means and not an end. Time spent working through indexes and other bibliographic tools is not a substitute for the reading and analysis of the material found. Activity should not be mistaken for accomplishment.

6. Information-finding is most effective when designed as a structured process. This does not, however, deny the value of informal methods. Talking to colleagues and browsing in the library stacks very often produce worthwhile results, especially as these relate to sources outside of one's discipline. Serendipity has its place and can, moreover, leaven an otherwise boring activity.

7. Most people have a great deal of difficulty extricating themselves from their research enterprise. Those who do not tend to have embarked on projects that were inconsequential in the first place. Every interesting research situation has many implications that warrant further investigation. Researchers must decide which of them they can afford to explore, and which they must leave for another time (or another researcher). Those who are unable to resolve this issue run a serious risk of never completing the project. It is a fact that most graduate students in the social sciences who achieve ABD status never actually complete the degree. Inability to exercise proper judgment in drawing lines to define the realistic limits of the project probably characterizes a good many of these permanent ABD.[1]

8. Engaging in original research of one's choice can provide tremendous personal satisfaction unrelated to the production of a worthwhile article, book, or dissertation. This level of satisfaction is unique and qualitatively

different from any personal reward from academic work based only on secondary sources. Not everyone enjoys it to the same extent, but the unsurprising trend seems to be that those who do it best are also those who get the most enjoyment from it. The presumption of this book is that it is this enjoyment that is the ultimate reward of those acquiring the skills discussed here.

Throughout this discussion, the importance of electronic means of access to information, primary and secondary, has been emphasized. As noted, the likelihood is that these means will be greatly expanded in the near future. At the time of writing, a topic of considerable interest is planning for the transformation of America's telephone system into a "data superhighway" which will permit the transfer of vast amounts of information (including visual images as well as text) almost instantaneously. When achieved through the installation of new telecommunications systems, the new arrangement will offer universal and improved access to some expanded version of the bulletin board networks. There is little doubt that out telephone systems will be transformed in this way. The term "superhighway" is a loaded one. It is used to invoke the image of the interstate highway system established in the 1950s and which is generally credited with stimulating new industries and accelerating job creation over the following three decades. In this context telecommunications are widely viewed as an ally in the economic transformation of America. This is why the federal government is so committed to this improved means of access to information.

These and other developments will not, however, come in the form of a free lunch. Access to electronic networks is now achieved at the cost to the consumer of a local telephone call. The major factor presently inhibiting the development of the "superhighway" is the question of how the immense costs of retooling the national telecommunications system can be recouped. Related developments also have profound cost implications for the user. In section 6 of chapter 9, attention is given to the current movement to provide speedy access to the full texts of journal articles through library catalogs. This is generally achieved at some cost to the researcher. As noted there, this development may well encourage libraries to cancel journal subscriptions and divert the costs of accessing them to the individual user. Most of the extraordinary developments outlined in the preceding pages have similar cost implications. Computerized information systems of the future will undoubtedly improve information access, but will probably do so by increasing the costs of the research enterprise.

These same developments have a further aspect to their distaff side which must once again be emphasized. Vast amounts of information imply the existence of more items of information important to the individual researcher or, rather, more gems in a greatly expanded heap of debris. This means that sifting techniques must be increasingly sophisticated. In a world of almost infinite information resources, the acquisition of the kinds of skills of information selection discussed in this book are more important than they have ever been.

NOTE

1. Simpson, Antony E. (1986). Hurdling the Dissertation Barrier: The Library and the Needs of the ABD. *Behavioral and Social Sciences Librarian, 6* (Fall/Winter), 111–29.

Appendix 1

ANNUAL REVIEWS

All of the reviews cited in this appendix are currently being published, in most cases annually. All survey recent developments in the fields they cover. Such developments are usually interpreted to include findings, methodologies, data sources, recent trends, and bibliography. The best annuals only include articles written specifically for them reviewing the area addressed. Others include articles published elsewhere during the year covered.

The lists provided here are necessarily selective. Additional titles are provided in the subject-oriented bibliographic guides discussed in chapter 4 and in the guides to serials in individual disciplines noted in chapter 7. Most standard indexing and abstracting services cover the contents of relevant annual reviews. These are generally listed in cumulations of the services. Reviews themselves usually provide information on which services they are covered by. Many are also covered by one or more of the computerized bibliographic databases discussed in Chapter 9.

1. GENERAL

The only general annual reviews of value in the social sciences are those concerned with methodological issues. These are listed in section 11.

2. PUBLIC ADMINISTRATION

Annuaire Européen d'Administration Publique. (1978–). Paris: Centre de Recherches Administratives.

Institut International d'Administration Publique. *Année Administrative*. (1979–). Paris.

The Municipal Year Book. (1934–). Washington, DC: International City Management Association.

New Directions in Public Administration Research. (1986–). Boca Raton: Florida Atlantic University. College of Public and Urban Affairs. Semiannual.

Policy Studies Review Annual. (1977–82, 1985–). Newbury Park, CA: Sage.

Progress in Rural Policy and Planning. (1980–). Norwich, UK: Geo Books. Earlier titles are *Countryside Planning Yearbook* and *International Yearbook of Rural Planning*.

Research in Law and Policy Studies. (1987–). Greenwich, CT: JAI Press.

Research in Public Policy Analysis and Management. (1981–). Greenwich, CT: JAI Press.

Research in Social Policy: Historical and Contemporary Perspectives. (1987–). Greenwich, CT: JAI Press.

Research in Social Problems and Public Policy. (1979–87). Greenwich, CT: JAI Press.

Research in Urban Policy. (1985–). Greenwich, CT: JAI Press.

Sage Yearbooks in Politics and Public Policy. (1975–). Newbury Park, CA: Sage.

Urban Affairs Annual Reviews. (1967–). Newbury Park, CA: Sage.

Urban History Yearbook. (1974–). Leicester, UK: Leicester University Press.

Urban Studies Yearbook. (1983–). Sydney: Allen & Unwin.

Yearbook of Social Policy in Britain. (1971–). London: Routledge & Kegan Paul. Formerly entitled *Yearbook of Social Studies.*

3. MANAGEMENT AND ORGANIZATIONAL THEORY

Advances in Applied Business Strategy. (1984–). Greenwich, CT: JAI Press.

Advances in International Comparative Management. (1984–). Greenwich, CT: JAI Press.

Advances in Organization Development. (1989–). Norwood, NJ: Ablex Publishing.

Advances in Strategic Management. (1983–). Greenwich, CT: JAI Press.

Research in Organizational Behavior: An Annual Series of Analytical Essays and Critical Reviews. (1979–). Greenwich, CT: JAI Press.

Research in Organizational Change and Development. (1987–). Greenwich, CT: JAI Press.

Research in the Sociology of Organizations. (1982–). Greenwich, CT: JAI Press.

4. POLITICAL SCIENCE

Advances in Political Science. (1982–). Newbury Park, CA: Sage.

Année Politique, Economique et Sociale. (1874–). Paris: Editions du Moniteur.

Annual Review of European Community Affairs. (1991–). London: Centre for Europoean Policy Studies.

Annual Review of Political Science. (1986–). Norwood, NJ: Ablex.

Political Power and Social Theory: A Research Annual. (1980–). Greenwich, CT: JAI Press.

Research in Political Economy: An Annual Compilation of Research. (1977–). Greenwich, CT: JAI Press.

Research in Political Sociology. (1985–). Greenwich, CT: JAI Press.

Research in Politics and Society. (1985–). Greenwich, CT: JAI Press.

Studies in American Political Development. (1986–). New Haven: Yale University Press.

5. SOCIOLOGY

Advances in Experimental Social Psychology. (1964–). New York: Academic Press.

Advances in Group Processes. (1984–). Greenwich, CT: JAI Press.

Année Sociologique. 3ième serie. (1940/48–). Paris: Presses Universitaires de France.

More comprehensive than its English-language counterparts. Continues earlier series that began in 1896.

Annual Review of Sociology. (1975–). Palo Alto, CA: Annual Reviews.

Comparative Social Research. (1978–). Greenwich, CT: JAI Press.
Formerly entitled *Comparative Studies in Sociology.*

Current Perspectives in Social Theory: A Research Annual. (1980–). Greenwich, CT: JAI Press.

Current Research on Occupations and Professions. (1980–). Greenwich, CT: JAI Press.
Formerly *Research in the Interweave of Social Roles.*

Knowledge and Society: Studies in the Sociology of Culture Past and Present. (1978–). Greenwich, CT: JAI Press.
Formerly entitled *Research in Sociology of Knowledge, Sciences, and Art.*

Research in Rural Sociology and Development. (1984–). Greenwich, CT: JAI Press.

Research in Social Movements, Conflicts, and Change. (1978–). Greenwich, CT: JAI Press.

Research in Social Stratification and Mobility: A Research Annual. (1981–). Greenwich, CT: JAI Press.

Research in Sociology of Education and Socialization: A Research Annual. (1980–). Greenwich, CT: JAI Press.

Research in the Interweave of Social Roles: A Research Annual. (1980–). Greenwich, CT: JAI Press.

Research in the Sociology of Health Care. (1980–). Greenwich, CT: JAI Press.

Research in the Sociology of Work. (1981–). Greenwich, CT: JAI Press.

Research in Urban Sociology. (1989–). Greenwich, CT: JAI Press.

Sociological Practice. (1976–). Chicago: Progresiv Publishr.

6. ECONOMICS

Advances in Econometrics. (1982–). Greenwich, CT: JAI Press.

Advances in the Economic Analysis of Participatory and Labor-Managed Firms. (1985–). Greenwich, CT: JAI Press.

Advances in the Economics of Energy and Resources. (1979–). Greenwich, CT: JAI Press.

Advances in the Study of Entrepreneurship, Innovation, and Economic Growth: A Research Annual. (1986–). Greenwich, CT: JAI Press.

Research in Economic History: An Annual Compilation of Research. (1976–). Greenwich, CT: JAI Press.

Research in Experimental Economics: A Research Annual. (1979–). Greenwich, CT: JAI Press.
Despite its subtitle, it appears at irregular intervals.

Research in Finance. (1979–). Greenwich, CT: JAI Press.

Research in Human Capital and Development. (1979–). Greenwich, CT: JAI Press.

Research in Labor Economics. (1977–). Greenwich, CT: JAI Press.

Research in Law and Economics: A Research Annual. (1979–). Greenwich, CT: JAI Press.

Research in Population Economics. (1978–). Greenwich, CT: JAI Press.

Research in the History of Economic Thought and Methodology. (1983–). Greenwich, CT: JAI Press.

Research in Urban Economics. (1981–). Greenwich, CT: JAI Press.

7. PSYCHOLOGY

Advances in Behavioral Economics. (1987–). Norwood, NJ: Ablex.

Advances in Descriptive Psychology. (1981–). Greenwich, CT: JAI Press.

Advances in Developmental Psychology. (1981–). Hillsdale, NJ: Lawrence Erlbaum Associates.

Advances in Environmental Psychology. (1978–). Hillsdale, NJ: Lawrence Erlbaum Associates.

Advances in Motivation and Achievement. (1984–). Greenwich, CT: JAI Press.

Advances in Personality Assessment. (1982–). Hillsdale, NJ: Lawrence Erlbaum Associates.

Advances in Test Anxiety Research. (1982–). Heereweg, Netherlands: Swets.

Advances in the Psychology of Human Intelligence. (1982–). Hillsdale, NJ: Lawrence Erlbaum Associates.

Advances in the Study of Behavior. (1965–). New York: Academic Press.
Addresses research in human and animal behavior.

L'Année Psychologique. (1894–). Paris: Presses Universitaires de France. Semiannual.
Includes summaries in English. Use in preference to its English-language equivalent, when possible, as it is more extensive.

Annual Advances in Applied Developmental Psychology. (1981–). Norwood, NJ: Ablex.
Earlier title was *Advances in Applied Developmental Psychology.*

Annual Review of Psychology. (1950–). Palo Alto, CA: Annual Reviews.
The major English-language source.

Human Stress: Current Selected Research. (1986–). New York: AMS Press.

Perspectives in Law and Psychology. (1977–). New York: Plenum.

Progress in Behavior Modification. (1975–). New York: Academic Press. Irregular.

Psychology of Learning and Motivation: Advances in Research and Theory. (1967–). New York: Academic Press.

Research in Community and Mental Health: An Annual Compilation of Research. (1979–). Greenwich, CT: JAI Press.

Review of Behavior Therapy: Theory and Practice. (1973–). New York: Guilford.
Formerly *Annual Review of Behavior Therapy: Theory and Practice.*

Review of Personality and Social Psychology. (1980–). Newbury Park, CA: Sage.

Stress and Emotion. (1975–). Washington, DC: Hemisphere.
Formerly *Stress and Anxiety.*

8. ANTHROPOLOGY

Annual Review of Anthropology. (1972–). Palo Alto, CA: Annual Reviews.
Continues the *Biennial Review of Anthropology.*

Biennial Review of Anthropology. (1959–71). Stanford, CA: Stanford University Press.

Folklife Annual. (1985–). Washington, DC: U.S. Library of Congress, American Folklife Center.

Law and Anthropology. (1986–). Vienna: Verband der Wissenschaftlichen Gesellschaften Oesterreichs.

Political and Legal Anthropology. (1980–). New Brunswick, NJ: Transaction. Formerly *Political Anthropology.*

Research in Economic Anthropology: An Annual Compilation of Research. (1978–). Greenwich, CT: JAI Press.

9. HISTORY

A number of specialized annuals covering particular time periods or geographic areas do exist. For general and theoretical approaches, see the few reviews with a specifically historical orientation included in the other subject specialties included here.

10. PHILOSOPHY

The contents of annuals in many disciplines considered here have come to include articles on ethical issues. This reflects a perspective that regards such issues as of importance for theory as well as practice.

American Philosophical Society. *Yearbook.* (1937–). Philadelphia.

Annuario Filosofico. (1985–). Milan: Mursia Editore.

Danish Yearbook of Philosophy. (1964–). Copenhagen: Museum Tusculanum Press.

Philosophisches Jahrbuch. (1888–). Freiburg: Karl Alber.

Research in Phenomenology. (1971–). Atlantic Highlands, NJ: Humanities Press.

Research in Philosophy and Technology. (1978–). Greenwich, CT: JAI Press.

Studies in Christian Ethics. (1988–). Edinburgh: T. & T. Clark.

11. METHODOLOGY

Advances in Social Science Methodology. (1989–). Greenwich, CT: JAI Press.

Advances in Statistical Analysis and Statistical Computing. (1986–). Greenwich, CT: JAI Press.

Progress in Experimental Personality and Psychopathology Research. (1964–). New York: Springer.
Covers experimentation on both normal and abnormal behavior. Formerly *Progress in Experimental Personality Research.*

Sociological Methodology. (1969–). Washington, DC: American Sociological Association.

Studies in Qualitative Methodology. (1988–). Greenwich, CT: JAI Press.

Studying Organizations: Innovations in Methodology. (1982–). Newbury Park, CA: Sage.

12. HUMAN RESOURCES

Advances in Industrial and Labor Relations. (1983–). Greenwich, CT: JAI Press.

Human Resource Management Yearbook. (1969–). London: Kogan Page.
Several earlier titles, the last being *Personnel Yearbook.*

Human Resources Yearbook. (1986–). Englewood Cliffs, NJ: Prentice-Hall.

Research in Personnel and Human Resources Management. (1983–). Greenwich, CT: JAI Press.

Research on Negotiation in Organizations. (1986–). Greenwich, CT: JAI Press.

13. EDUCATION

Advances in Educational Administration. (1990–). Greenwich, CT: JAI Press.

Review of Research in Education. (1973–). Washington, DC: American Educational Research Association.
Usually includes research related to educational administration.

14. CRIMINAL JUSTICE AND LAW

Advances in Criminological Theory. (1989–). New Brunswick, NJ: Transaction.

Crime and Justice: An Annual Review of Research. (1979–). Chicago: University of Chicago Press.

Criminal Justice History: An International Annual. (1980–). Westport, CT: Meckler.

Issues in Crime and Justice. (1986–). Monsey, NY: Criminal Justice Press.

Police and Law Enforcement. (1972–). New York: AMS Press.
Articles not original.

Studies in Law, Politics, and Society. (1978-). Greenwich, CT: JAI Press.
Formerly entitled *Research in Law and Sociology* and *Research in Law, Deviance and Social Control.*

Annual Review of Criminal Law. (1982–). Agincourt, Ont.: Carswell.
Addresses Canadian developments only.

Annual Survey of American Law. (1942–). New York: New York University.

Criminal Law Review. (1979–). New York: Clark Boardman.

Supreme Court Review. (1960–). Chicago: University of Chicago Press.

Windsor Yearbook of Access to Justice/Recueil Annuel de Windsor d'Accès à la Justice. (1981–). Windsor, Ont.: University of Windsor. Faculty of Law.
Text in English and French.

15. OTHER AREAS

Advances in Computers. (1960–). San Diego, CA: Academic Press.

Advances in Computing Research. (1983–). Greenwich, CT: JAI Press.

Advances in Health Economics and Health Services Research. (1979–). Greenwich, CT: JAI Press.
Formerly entitled *Research in Health Economics.*

Advances in Human-Computer Interaction. (1985–). Norwood, NJ: Ablex.

Advances in Information Processing in Organizations. (1984–). Greenwich, CT: JAI Press.

Advances in Library Administration and Organization. (1982–). Greenwich, CT: JAI Press.

Advances in Man-Machine Systems Research. (1984–). Greenwich, CT: JAI Press.

Advances in the Study of Communication and Affect. (1974–). New York: Plenum.

Annual Review of Computer Science. (1986–). Palo Alto, CA: Annual Reviews.

Annual Review of Information Science and Technology. (1966–). Norwood, NJ: Ablex.

Annual Review of Public Health. (1980–). Palo Alto, CA: Annual Reviews.
Worldwide coverage.

Annual Review of United Nations Affairs. (1949–). Dobbs Ferry, NY: Oceana.

Communication Yearbook. (1977–). New Brunswick, NJ: Transaction Books.
Sponsored by the International Communication Association.

Creativity and Innovation Yearbook. (1974–). Manchester, UK: University of Manchester Business School.

Information Management Year Book. (1980–). London: Institute of Data Processing Management.

Progress in Communication Sciences. (1979–). Norwood, NJ: Ablex.

Progress in Cybernetics and Systems Research. (1975–). New York: Hemisphere.

Recreation: Current Selected Research. (1989–). New York: AMS Press.

Research in Contemporary and Applied Geography: A Discussions Series. (1977–). Binghamton: State University of New York at Binghamton.

Research in Corporate Social Performance and Policy. (1978–). Greenwich, CT: JAI Press.

Research in Governmental and Non-Profit Accounting. (1985–). Greenwich, CT: JAI Press.

Research in International Business and Finance. (1979–). Greenwich, CT: JAI Press.

Research in Race and Ethnic Relations: A Research Annual. (1979–). Greenwich, CT: JAI Press.

Research in the Sociology of Health Care: A Research Annual. (1980–). Greenwich, CT: JAI Press.

Research in Transportation Economics. (1983–). Greenwich, CT: JAI Press.

Research on Technological Innovation, Management, and Policy. (1983–). Greenwich, CT: JAI Press.

Research on Transport Economics/Recherche en Matière d'Economie des Transports. (1968–). Paris: European Conference of Ministers of Transport.

Sage Yearbooks in Women's Policy Studies. (1976–). Newbury Park, CA: Sage.

Studies in Communications. (1980–). Greenwich, CT: JAI Press.

Women and Work. (1985–). Newbury Park, CA: Sage.

The Women's Annual: The Year in Review. (1981–). Boston: G. K. Hall.

Yearbook of Law, Computers, and Technology. (1984–). London: Butterworth.

Appendix 2

LIBRARY OF CONGRESS "H" AND "J" SCHEDULES

H SOCIAL SCIENCES

H	1	- 99	**Social sciences (General)**
HA	1	-4737	**Statistics** Including collections of general and census statistics of special countries. For mathematical statistics, *see* QA
			Economics
HB	1	-3840	**Economic theory. Demography**
	1	- 846.8	Economic theory Including value, price, wealth, capital, interest, profit, consumption
	848	-3697	Demography. Vital events
	3711	-3840	Business cycles. Economic fluctuations
HC	10	-1085	**Economic history and conditions**
	94	-1085	By region or country
HD	28	-9999	**Economic history and conditions**
	28	- 88	Production Including industrial management
	101	-1395	Land use Including public lands, real estate, land tenure
	1401	-2210	Agriculture Including agricultural laborers
	2321	-4730.9	Industry
	2709	-2932	Corporations. Cartels. Trusts
	2951	-3575	Industrial cooperation
	3611	-4730.9	The state and industrial organization
	4801	-8943	Labor Including wages, strikes, unemployment, labor unions, industrial relations, social security, professions, state labor. For civil service, *see* J
	9000	-9999	Special industries and trades
HE	1	-9900	**Transportation and communications**
	331	- 380	Traffic engineering. Roads and highways. Streets
	380.8	- 971	Water transportation
	1001	-5600	Railways
	5601	-5725	Automotive transportation
	5746	-5990	State lines. Ferries. Express service
	6000	-7496	Postal service. Stamp collecting
	7601	-8700.9	Telecommunication industry. Telegraph
	8689	-8700.9	Radio and television broadcasting
	8701	-9715	Telephone
	9719	-9721	Artificial satellite telecommunications
	9761	-9900	Air transportation

HF	1	-6182	Commerce
	294	- 343	Boards of trade. Chambers of commerce
	1701	-2701	Tariff policy
	5001	-6182	Business. Business administration
	5549	-5549.5	Personnel management
	5601	-5689	Accounting
	5801	-6182	Advertising
HG	1	-9999	**Finance**
	201	-1496	Money
	1501	-3550	Banking
	3691	-3769	Credit
	3810	-4000	Foreign exchange
	4001	-4280.7	Financial management. Business finance. Corporation finance
	4301	-4480.9	Trust services
	4501	-6051	Stocks, investment, speculation
	6105	-6270.9	Lotteries
	8011	-9999	Insurance
HJ	9	-9995	**Public finance**
	2005	-2216	Income and expenditure. The budget
	2240	-5957	Revenue. Taxation
	6603	-7390	Customs
	7451	-7977	Expenditure
	8003	-8963	Public credit. Debts. Loans. Claims
	9011	-9695	Local finance
	9701	-9995	Public accounting
			Sociology
HM	1	- 299	**Sociology (General and theoretical)**
	251	- 291	Social psychology
HN	1	- 981	**Social history. Social problems. Social reform**
	30	- 39	The church and social problems
	50	- 981	By region or country
HQ	1	-2039	**The family. Marriage. Woman**
	12	- 449	Sexual life
	450	- 471	Erotica
	503	-1064	The family. Marriage. Home Including child study, eugenics, desertion, adultery, divorce, polygamy, the aged
	1101	-2030.7	Women. Feminism. Women's clubs
	2035	-2039	Life skills. Coping skills. Everyday living skills

			Sociology - Continued
HS	1	-3369	**Societies: Secret, benevolent, etc. Clubs**
			Including Freemasons, religious societies, ethnic societies, political societies, Boy Scouts
HT	51	-1595	**Communities. Classes. Races**
	51	- 65	Human settlements
	101	- 395	Urban sociology. The city
	390	- 395	Regional planning
	401	- 485	Rural sociology
	601	-1445	Social classes
			Including middle class, serfdom, slavery
	1501	-1595	Races
			Here are classed works on the race as a social group and race relations in general
HV	1	-9960	**Social pathology. Social and public welfare. Criminology**
	40	- 696	Social service. Charities
	697	-4959	Protection, assistance, and relief
			Arranged by special classes of persons, as determined by age, defects, occupation, race, economic status, etc.
			Including protection of animals
	4961	-4995	Degeneration
	4997	-5000	Substance abuse
	5001	-5720.5	Alcoholism. Intemperance. Temperance reform
	5725	-5770	Tobacco habit
	5800	-5840	Drug habits. Drug abuse
	6001	-7220.5	Criminology
	6251	-6773.3	Crimes and offenses
	7231	-9960	Criminal justice administration
	8301	-9920.5	Penology
			Including police, prisons, punishment and reform, juvenile delinquency
HX	1	- 970.7	**Socialism. Communism. Anarchism**
	806	- 811	Utopias
	821	- 970.7	Anarchism

POLITICAL SCIENCE J

J	1	- 981	**General legislative and executive papers**
	(1	- 9)	Official gazettes
			The Library of Congress now classes this material in Class K
	10	- 87	United States documents
			For congressional hearings, reports, etc., *see* KF
	80	- 85	Presidents' messages and other executive documents
	86	- 87	State documents
	100	- 981	Other documents
			For documents issued by local governments, *see* JS
JA	1	- 98	**Collections and general works**
JC	11	- 628	**Political theory. Theory of the state**
	311	- 323	Nationalism
	325	- 341	Nature, entity, concept of the state
	345	- 347	Symbolism, emblems of the state: Arms, flag, seal, etc.
	348	- 497	Forms of the state
			Including imperialism, the world state, monarchy, aristocracy, democracy, fascism, dictatorships
	501	- 628	Purpose, functions, and relations of the state
	571	- 628	The state and individual. Individual rights. Liberty
			Constitutional history and administration
JF	8	- 2112	**General works. Comparative works**
	201	- 723	Organs and functions of government
			Including executive branch, cabinet and ministerial government, legislative bodies
	751	- 786	Federal and state relations
	800	- 1191	Political rights and guaranties
			Including citizenship, suffrage, electoral systems, representation, the ballot
	1321	- 2112	Government. Administration
	2011	- 2112	Political parties
			Special countries
JK	1	- 9993	**United States**
	2403	- 9501	State government
	9661	- 9993	Confederate States of America
JL	1	- 3899	**British America. Latin America**
JN	1	- 9689	**Europe**
JQ	1	- 6651	**Asia. Africa. Australia. Oceania**
JS	3	- 8399	**Local government**
	141	- 231	Municipal government
	241	- 285	Local government other than municipal
	301	- 1583	United States

JV	1	-5810	**Colonies and colonization. Emigration and immigration**
JX	1	-5810	**International law. International relations**
	63	-1195	Collections. Documents. Cases
	101	- 115	Diplomatic relations (Universal collections)
	120	- 191	Treaties (Universal collections)
	1305	-1598	International relations. Foreign relations Here are classed international questions treated as sources of or contributions to the theory of international law. For histories of events, diplomatic histories, etc., *see* D-F
	1625	-1896	Diplomacy. The diplomatic service
	1901	-1995	International arbitration. World peace. International organization Including peace movements, League of Nations, United Nations, arbitration treaties, international courts
	2001	-5810	International law (Treatises and monographs)

Source: US Library of Congress. Office for Subject Cataloging Policy. (1990). LC Classification Outline (6th ed.). Washington, DC. Pages 16-20.

NAME INDEX

SUBJECT INDEX

About the Author

ANTONY E. SIMPSON, Executive Officer, Ph.D. Program in Criminal Justice, The City University of New York, has long specialized in archival research and in guiding doctoral candidates in original research projects. His previous publications include, among others, *The Literature of Police Corruption: A Guide to Bibliography and Theory* (1977) and *Guide to Library Research in Public Administration* (1977). Simpson also holds an appointment as Adjunct Professor at the Queens College Graduate School of Library and Information Studies.